# Whose Votes Count?

# Whose Votes Count?

Affirmative Action
and Minority Voting Rights

Abigail M. Thernstrom

*A Twentieth Century Fund Study*

Harvard University Press
Cambridge, Massachusetts
and London, England
1987

Copyright © 1987 by the Twentieth Century Fund, Inc.
All rights reserved
Printed in the United States of America
10 9 8 7 6 5 4 3 2 1

This book is printed on acid-free paper, and its binding
materials have been chosen for strength and durability.

*Library of Congress Cataloging-in-Publication Data*
Thernstrom, Abigail M., 1936–
    Whose votes count?

    (Twentieth Century Fund study)
    Includes index.
    1. Afro-Americans—Suffrage.   2. Hispanic
Americans—Suffrage.    3. Minorities—United
States—Political activity.    4. Intervention (Federal
government)—United States.    I. Title.    II. Series.
KF4893.T46    1987        323.1′196073        87-7406
ISBN 0-674-95195-6 (alk. paper)

*To Stephan Thernstrom*

# Contents

*[Handwritten annotations:]* 1970 am — So Strat, only effort & limit, · literacy test banned nationwide, incl 50% bigger → NY · 75 am · Court Cases · preclearance + bailout. · arguments re section 2. · Courts, Confusing · Justice Dept. · } 1982 amend.

# Foreword

Many Americans are so casual about the right to vote that they frequently fail to exercise it. But most southern black Americans, until a little over twenty years ago, did not even have that right. The Voting Rights Act of 1965—often called the most important of the civil rights statutes—gave meaning to the Fifteenth Amendment to the Constitution, ratified almost a hundred years earlier. It took a long, bitter, and frequently bloody struggle to remove state restrictions, some blatant, others devious, that disfranchised blacks. But when the barriers came tumbling down, as a result of political action at the federal level motivated by guilt and compassion and outrage, it was the beginning of the end of disfranchisement.

In the past two decades, the original act has been broadened far beyond its original focus on voter registration. Through administrative and judicial interpretation, as well as by congressional amendment, the Voting Rights Act has become an instrument for assuring not only that blacks and Hispanics can exercise their right to vote, but that minority officeholders are elected, often in proportion to the minority population.

This expansion of the purposes of the act has encountered relatively little opposition. The Reagan administration, which has frowned upon affirmative action and is not known for advancing minority rights, has gone along, so that affirmative action has been brought into the voting booth. Yet the Voting Rights Act, as amended and enforced, raises fundamental questions about the meaning of "one man, one vote," and the place of race in our society. Many Americans like to think that we have become increasingly color-blind. Yet it can legitimately be asked whether we have become so conscious of our differences that we no longer assume, for instance, that whites can represent blacks and that electoral procedures are equally fair to all citizens regardless of race or ethnic origin.

The Fund, which has long been interested in assuring electoral rights for all Americans, saw in Abigail Thernstrom's proposal an opportunity to examine the changes that have been transforming the Voting Rights Act into something very different from what it was at the outset. Her book has been a long time in the writing, not least because shortly after we agreed to sponsor it, the debate over the 1982 amendments resulted in many new developments requiring careful and detailed study. A conscientious scholar, Abby Thernstrom did not allow the burden of increased research to weaken her commitment. Indeed, as anyone who reads her book will quickly realize, it was time well spent.

Thernstrom's book will, I believe, provoke controversy. That is because she asked tough and embarrassing questions—and fearlessly pursued the answers. It is also because she is something of a possessed scholar, not taking anything for granted. The result is a bold, absorbing, and sobering history and analysis of our changing perspective on perhaps the most fundamental right of citizens—the right to vote.

M. J. Rossant, Director
The Twentieth Century Fund
January 1987

# Acknowledgments

The initial research for this book was made possible by a one-year grant from the Institute for Educational Affairs. Subsequent funding was provided by the Twentieth Century Fund. In supporting a woman who for many years devoted more attention to child rearing than to scholarship, the Fund took a risk, and I am grateful for its willingness to do so. I am particularly indebted to Murray J. Rossant, director of the Fund, for his commitment, encouragement, and consistently excellent advice, and to Beverly Goldberg, assistant director, who, in supervising the editorial process, took special care of me and my prose. I benefited, too, from the counsel of many members of the staff—from that of Carol Barker and Marc F. Plattner, who guided the application process; James A. Smith and Katherine Yatrakis, who briefly served as "program officers" overseeing my work; and Diane Englander, who read the manuscript with great care and whose strong disagreement with many of its conclusions prompted me to rethink and rewrite. The Fund assigned the manuscript to a superb editor, Michael Massing, who tolerated neither needless words nor incoherent ideas. The commitment and attentiveness of the Fund were matched by those of Harvard University Press. Aida Donald, executive editor, handled the manuscript with unerring skill. My editor, Mary Ellen Geer, had a light and precise touch for which I am grateful.

Others contributed substantially to the book. When I was still almost wholly preoccupied with domestic concerns, Nathan Glazer took me out to lunch and encouraged me to get to work. My preliminary conclusions about minority voting rights were published in *The Public Interest,* the journal he co-edits. In the course of working on that piece, I met David Hunter, an attorney in the voting section of the Department of Justice. I must have run every argument in the book past Dave at least three times, and although we did not always agree on substantive points, his intellectual rigor and integrity set the standard I tried to meet. I made other friends in the course of working on the book, among them Katharine Butler, Timothy O'Rourke, and Mark Stern, all of whom have written important articles on voting rights. Matthew Cooper brought keen political insights to many conversations on civil rights and black politics. An old friend and a distinguished scholar of ethnic politics, Donald Horowitz, was an invaluable resource. Another long-standing friend, Diane Ravitch, kept my spirits up and sharpened many an idea. I also learned much from conversation and debate with William D. Barnard, Randall T. Bell, James U. Blacksher, Thomas Boyd, Armand Derfner, Joseph Logsdon, Stephen J. Markman, and Alan Parker, among others. William C. Velasquez brought his wide knowledge of Hispanic politics and his subtle views to a study group at Harvard's Institute of Politics that I was fortunate to attend. Bill McKibben, then a Harvard undergraduate, did research for me in Texas that greatly enriched my understanding of rural politics. Many of my arguments took shape in the course of my own research trips to the South and Southwest. I am extremely grateful for the generosity and candor of those whom I interviewed, most of whom were assured anonymity, as my footnotes will indicate. Mayors, community organizers, and reporters alike stopped their own work to attend to mine; I could not have written the book without their help.

A number of people looked at earlier versions of the manuscript. For their close readings and excellent suggestions, I am indebted to Edward C. Banfield, Martha Derthick, Lance Liebman, Charles Silberman, Michael Walzer, and, again, both Nathan Glazer and David Hunter. Emily MacFarquhar came up with a title when everyone else was stumped.

I spent a number of happy years working alone at home on this project. Toward the end, however, I moved to the Gordon Public Policy Center at Brandeis University, a place of camaraderie and intellectual vitality. I am grateful to the director, Martin Levin, for the invitation to join the Center, and to my colleagues for the stimulation and good company they provide.

Throughout the long process of writing and revision, my husband, Stephan Thernstrom, was a critic and steadfast colleague. I drew extensively on his expertise as a historian of American ethnic groups, but relied above all on his unwavering friendship.

Abigail Thernstrom
Lexington, Massachusetts

# Whose Votes Count?

# Introduction

But under all our talk floated a latent sense of violence;
the whites had drawn a line over which we dared not
step and we accepted that line because our bread was
at stake.

Richard Wright, *Black Boy* (1937)

The South that Richard Wright so graphically described has all but disappeared, and perhaps most striking is the change in politics. Maynard Jackson's mother (in her middle age) was the first black in Atlanta to obtain a library card; in 1973 her son was elected mayor. In Selma, Alabama, in 1965, Andrew Young placed his life in jeopardy on behalf of black voting rights; only seven years later he was the first black congressman elected from the Deep South since Reconstruction. When the southern journalist Marshall Frady was asked what kind of documentary he would like to do on the South, he replied, "I would like to go to Tuskegee and do a story on the black mayor, Johnny Ford." And what would the message be? "That it ain't perfect, but centuries have passed since Johnny was a small boy."[1]

The breathtaking changes in southern politics, unfolding over the last two decades, had a clear starting point: the 1965 Voting Rights Act. Passed in the wake of the bloody civil rights march in Selma, it enfranchised the southern black, thereby fulfilling the promise of the Fifteenth Amendment ninety-five years late. "The right of citizens of the United States to vote shall not be denied or abridged . . . on account of race, color, or previous condition of servitude," that amendment had promised. But when the last federal troops abandoned the South in 1877, blacks were left to fend for themselves in a society dominated by white supremacists. For a time white Redeemers, fearful of another northern crusade, reconciled themselves to seeing blacks at the polls; by the 1890s, however, the way had been cleared for massive disfranchisement. (Literacy and "understanding" tests, poll taxes, the white primary, intimidation, violence—these and other techniques were used to deprive most blacks of the right to vote.)

By 1965 blacks had made some progress. In 1940 an appalling 3 percent of the 5 million southern blacks of voting age were registered to vote; by 1964 the figure for Georgia was 27.4 percent and for South Carolina, 37.3 percent.[2] In fact, in every state except Mississippi, white supremacists were losing ground. But they were far from beaten. In 1964, ten years after the Supreme Court exposed the fiction of separate but equal schools and signaled the end of Jim Crow, Florida and Tennessee were the only southern states in which as many as half of all voting-age blacks were registered. And in many places resistance to black enfranchisement seemed to be hardening.

Overt, violent resistance, though, was the white South's fatal error. In March 1965, an outraged nation watched Selma police assault blacks and whites marching to secure the right of citizens to vote. Eight days later President Johnson went on national television to urge new legislation, and on August 6 he signed the Voting Rights Act into law. The core of the act was simple. State and counties that met two criteria—the use of a literacy test and a voter turnout below 50 percent in the 1964 presidential election—were "covered." And "coverage" meant the immediate suspension of all such tests, the assignment (when necessary) of federal registrars to replace local authorities, and other stringent measures to ensure access to the ballot. It was a formula designed to target the South, and its impact was immediate. In 1964 heroic Student Nonviolent Coordinating Committee volunteers working in Le Flore County, Mississippi, had enlarged the ranks of black voters by 300; within two months of the arrival of federal registrars, the number had swelled by 5,000.[3] By 1967, in Mississippi as a whole, the percentage of voting-age blacks registered had jumped from 6.7 to approximately 60 percent.[4] Elsewhere the change was less dramatic but still impressive.

With black enfranchisement, of course, came a radical shift in the rules of the political game. Racist politicians either changed their tactics or bowed out, and in many places the new voters swept new faces (both black and white) into office. There has never been even an approximate count of the number of white elected officials in the covered states of the South who owe their position to black support, but the number of elected blacks rose from less than 100 in 1965 to more than 1,800 by 1980.[5]

"Before we had the right to vote, politicians publicly called us niggers," stated a 1981 political advertisement aimed at black voters in an Alabama city. "After we received the right to vote, but our numbers were few, they called us Nigras. When we reached 5,000, they called us colored. 10,000, they called us black people. Now that we have reached 50,000, they call us Commissioner Wicks, Judge Cain Kennedy, Representative Yvonne Kennedy, and Senator Figures. If you don't want to go back to square one, vote for Mims and Greenough."[6] In almost every southern community with a substantial black population, the new black vote has had an unmistakable impact.

Almost nowhere, in fact, is explicit racism still politically advantageous. The career of South Carolina's Senator Strom Thurmond exemplifies the change. Leader of the Dixiecrat rebellion from the Democratic Party in 1948, he proudly refused to clap when President Johnson addressed the Senate on the subject of civil rights. But in 1970 he added a black to his own staff. Earlier that year he had thrown his support to a gubernatorial candidate who had made his racial views clear by wearing a white tie, only to see that candidate lose to a moderate who had the votes of blacks, and he drew the obvious lesson. He quickly secured federal funds for South Carolina's black mayors and black colleges and extended his famed constituent services to black voters. "When I want something done, I call Strom Thurmond," a prominent black Charleston businessman remarked in 1982. "Fritz Hollings . . . the liberal . . . would take a month to get back to me." In his reelection campaign in 1978 Thurmond actively solicited black votes, with considerable success.[7]

When Mississippi Governor Ross Barnet stood in the University of Mississippi doorway to block integration in 1962, he had nothing to fear from the inconsequential black vote; in 1982 the governor of that same state urged voters to elect the first black congressman from the rural South since Reconstruction.[8] That change is a result of the sheer number of black registrants. But numbers alone have not been responsible for the number of blacks now holding office; the impact of those numbers has been significantly heightened by new, federally mandated methods of voting.

The aim of the Voting Rights Act—the *single* aim—was black enfranchisement in the South. Obstacles to registration and voting, that is, were the sole concern of those who framed the statute. Four years later the focus began to shift, when a minor provision, designed to guard against inventive new barriers to political participation by mandating federal approval of all changes in voting procedure in covered jurisdictions, acquired an unexpected purpose. By 1969 public officials in Mississippi and elsewhere had made all too plain their readiness to alter the electoral environment by instituting, for instance, county-wide voting, eliminating the single-member districts from which some blacks were likely to get elected. The Supreme Court, in response, sanctioned federal objections not simply to discriminatory innovations involving registration and the mechanics of voting, but to gerrymandered districts, the introduction of at-large voting, and other such changes. The Court thus turned a minor provision of the act—section 5—into a major tool with which to combat white resistance to black power.[9] *allen*

The decision was the opening wedge in a profound transformation of the act. Clearly, the Court could not stand by while southern whites in covered states—states with dirty hands on questions of race—altered electoral rules to buttress white hegemony. Yet a right to protection from action intended to minimize black power, once established, could not be easily contained. By acting to avert such rearguard measures, by prohibiting the adoption of county-wide voting and other electoral procedures that threatened to rob black ballots of their expected worth, the Court had implicitly enlarged the definition of enfranchisement. Now there were "meaningful" and "meaningless" votes—votes that "counted" and those that did not. And once that distinction had been made, a meaningful vote was almost bound to become an entitlement. It was a subtle but important change: the shift from black ballots safe from deliberate efforts to dilute their impact, on the one hand, to a right to a vote that fully counted, on the other.

A provision initially inserted to guard against the manipulation of an electoral system for racist ends has thus evolved as a means to ensure that black votes have value—have the power, that is, to elect blacks. For that is the meaning of ballots that carry their proper weight. The initial protection against white resistance to simple black enfranchisement has become a means to stop the use of electoral rules that lessen the likelihood that blacks will gain the legislative seats to which they appear entitled. When a city chooses for economic reasons to expand its municipal boundaries, when population changes force a political jurisdiction to redistrict, when a county abandons the gubernatorial appointment of county commissioners in favor of at-large elections, black candidates acquire a level of protection that politics as usual would not provide. The substantial number of blacks in office in the South today is attributable, in part, to massive black enfranchisement, but it is also the result of a powerful, continuing federal presence. Since 1975 (when the act was amended) the impact of Hispanic ballots, too, has been heightened by electoral arrangements introduced to enhance their political effectiveness. Moreover, statutory amendments in 1982 gave blacks and Hispanics nationwide dramatic new power to challenge methods of election on grounds of discriminatory result.

We have arrived at a point no one envisioned in 1965. The right to vote no longer means simply the right to enter a polling booth and pull the lever. Yet the issue retains a simple Fifteenth Amendment aura—an aura that is pure camouflage. An alleged voting rights violation today is a districting plan that contains nine majority-black districts when a tenth could be drawn.* The question is: how much special protection from white competition are black candidates entitled to? For instance, when a different plan might give a seat to another black, should the interests of white incumbents give way to the goal of minority officeholding? The temptation to provide maximum protection (a maximum number of seats) is strong and has been only intermittently resisted. The Court, in labeling annexations and redistricting "voting" matters, imposed upon federal authorities the task of fashioning acceptable electoral arrangements. These are boundary alterations that cannot simply be reversed. If an annexation—usually undertaken for sound economic reasons— reduces the black proportion of the population and thus its voting strength, a remedy short of deannexation must be found. Districting plans are torn up following every decennial census. Again, there is no going back; revised lines that meet the equal population standard must be drawn. There is thus a need to devise new plans, to determine when black ballots "fully count." The phrase itself invites a definition that gives those ballots maximum weight, defined as officeholding; anything less suggests a compromised right. Yet maximum weight implies an entitlement to proportionate ethnic and racial representation—a concept that is no less controversial with respect to legislative bodies than with

---

*Or, after 1975, nine majority-black and Hispanic districts. Throughout the book, points that are made with reference to blacks often apply equally well to Hispanics.

reference to schools and places of employment. Voting rights has become another immensely complex affirmative action issue, distinctive only in not being acknowledged as such.

The myth of moral simplicity has largely insulated the voting rights issue from debate, yet perhaps no other affirmative action question is more significant. "Political power . . . is probably the most important . . . good in human history," Michael Walzer has written. It is "the regulative agency for social goods generally. It is used to defend the boundaries of all the distributive spheres, including its own, and to enforce the common understandings of what goods are and what they are for."[10] Disputes over voting rights have become a familiar feature of American politics, and their outcome redistributes political power among blacks, whites, and (since 1975) Hispanics. In the covered jurisdictions (mainly in the South and Southwest), every districting plan drawn after every census for every city council, county commission, state legislature, and other legislative body must be submitted for federal review either to the District Court for the District of Columbia or the Department of Justice. In noncovered counties and states, districting is often challenged in a local court.

Thus in Los Angeles and Chicago blacks and Hispanics have used federal judicial power to overturn redistricting plans. A redistricting suit in Chicago altered the balance of power between Mayor Harold Washington and his opponents within the city council, breaking a political stalemate. A plethora of suits or threatened suits (settled out of court) are succeeding in replacing at-large methods of voting with single-member districts, which again must meet federal standards with respect to racial "fairness." Annexations are frequent occurrences in the South and Southwest, and municipalities that add more whites than blacks to their populations are rarely permitted to retain city-wide elections. Courts and the Department of Justice are altering the American electoral landscape in ways that will affect not only the racial and ethnic makeup of governing councils but their partisan composition as well, for changes in the former also affect the latter. If the number of safe black districts is increased, the number that are overwhelmingly white—and often overwhelmingly Republican—will likewise go up.

In this book I address the questions raised by this "landscaping." When are citizens who are free to register and vote nevertheless "disfranchised"? When is federal intervention to facilitate minority officeholding appropriate? Are blacks and Hispanics entitled to "safe" minority seats reflecting their proportion of the population? Are minorities sometimes better off with fewer seats but more diffused influence—a smaller number of blacks in office, but a greater number of representatives who owe their election to black constituents?

Congress and the courts have declared that members of minority groups are entitled to "an equal opportunity to elect representatives of their choice." What does that high-sounding phrase really mean? Who counts as a "representative of their choice," and when are opportunities truly equal? If the ballots of white Democrats in an overwhelmingly Republican county "count," if Democrats who are never able to elect "candidates of their choice" are nevertheless fully enfranchised, what about black Democrats when no black ever wins? Are blacks and Hispanics ever properly represented by whites? Are black candidates who run as part of a white-dominated ticket consequently "white" candidates? Do socioeconomic disparities between whites and blacks mean that members of the two groups stand on unequal political footing, and that compensation in the form of special protection in the electoral process is appropriate? Is at-large voting, which favors white candidates in majority-white jurisdictions, inherently discriminatory? If black turnout is now higher than white, does that long history of political exclusion still have political relevance?

As these questions suggest, this book attempts to define the right to vote and the conditions under which the federal redistribution of power among ethnic and racial groups is appropriate. In the American constitutional tradition, it is often said, there are no group rights to representation. Farmers, for example, have no special claim to political representation; like other citizens, they can organize for common ends, cast their ballots, and hope their effort will pay off. We do not question the system when that effort has failed. If an election yields a new Congress with no physicians, trade unionists, Baptists, or Polish-Americans, no one concludes that those groups have been denied proper political access. This model of individual representation, though, seems less clearly appropriate when applied to southern blacks, so recently barred from the polls and subordinated as a *group*. A county commission in a southern black-belt county on which no white Methodist sits is hardly cause for alarm; few would argue that southern Methodists are outside the political system, mere second-class citizens. But we are rightly less complacent when that commission remains all white.

I am suggesting that concern over the continuing paucity of black officeholders, repeatedly voiced by civil rights groups, members of Congress, and others, cannot be lightly dismissed—at least with respect to the South. The conservative attack on such race-conscious counting ignores too much history. But is equal concern justified with respect to other minorities? The 1965 act named no group, instead protecting all citizens denied the right to vote on account of race or color; the 1975 amendments extended protection to four specifically designated "language" minorities: "American Indians, Asian Americans, Alaskan Natives, [and persons] of Spanish heritage." Is this a defensible list? The courts and the Justice Department have primarily focused on voting rights violations involving blacks and Mexican-Americans. Should these two minorities be grouped together in creating safe districts, on the assumption that their shared minority status unites them politically? Are the differences between them less important than their similarities? A review of the legislative history of the 1975 amendments and the record of their enforcement will suggest an answer.

This book, then, addresses issues basic to contemporary public policy: how to identify electoral inequality and the conditions that warrant federal intervention in state and local electoral affairs. It is, as well, a history of the Voting Rights Act. I am interested, that is, both in where we have been and where we should go. We have arrived at an unexpected destination. The historical tale I tell here reveals much: how small statutory changes had large and unanticipated results; the difficulty of arresting that process; the significance of the structure and procedures of Congress in understanding the passage of extensions and amendments to the act; the insignificant difference between Republican and Democratic administrations with respect to this legislation; the distinctiveness of voting rights politics.

The original act was amended by judicial and administrative interpretation as well as by congressional action. The judicial decisions illuminate the limited capacity of the bench to sort out complex issues of democratic representation. In an early reapportionment case Justice Felix Frankfurter called questions of representation a "political thicket."[11] These are decisions that contain a story of vain thrashing through that thicket, of attempts to cut paths that resulted in still deeper entanglement. The problems were compounded by numerous constitutional and statutory decisions, with solutions propounded in one sphere often repudiated in the other. Equally important, the judicial decisions were shaped less by the statute than the statute by the decisions. The expected pattern has been reversed in this and other respects. One assumes that the decisions of the Supreme Court govern those of the lower courts—but not always, as it turns out. In the enforcement of voting rights the D.C. district court, on a course of its own, appears to have had the last word, for reasons I attempt to explain.

Few voting cases actually reach the courts; most conflicts are either settled without litigation or resolved by the Department of Justice acting as a surrogate court. The department's role in administering the 1965 act, originally quite limited, quickly grew. Are Justice Department attorneys in fact satisfactory surrogate judges? Is the administrative process sufficiently judicious? The record shows that the department has been both enforcing and inventing law. Why this should be so, and why both Republicans and Democrats have permitted this enormous administrative latitude, is an important part of the story. The Reagan administration has been a frequent foe of civil rights groups on busing and employment quota questions, yet in the enforcement of minority voting rights its record has differed little from that of its predecessors. This too calls for examination and explanation.

Minority voting rights is perhaps the most debatable, yet least debated, of all affirmative action issues. Scholars, journalists, and public figures alike have been almost silent on the question. A 1982 congressional hearing made some attempt to define the right to vote in an ethnically and racially complex environment, but discussion was late and limited, and the audience small. Ironically, more questions were raised about voting rights in 1965—when the issue was morally clear-cut—than in later years, when amendments and patterns of enforcement should have stirred more controversy. Access to the ballot without respect to race was not a complex public policy question; gerrymandering to maximize minority officeholding is.

I attempt in this book not only to tell a story but also to suggest a way of thinking about the meaning of the right to vote that remains true to generally shared values with respect to race, politics, and local autonomy. In the end, however, views on this issue turn on a much more intractable question: the continuing pervasiveness of American racism. In a caste society, where horizons of trust do not extend beyond race and ethnicity, justice may demand a system of reserved seats for separate castes. Is the American city, county, or state that fits this model the rule or the exception? Where one stands on this fundamental question determines one's judgment on every concrete issue involving minority voting rights.

No one today suggests that the latent sense of violence described so vividly by Richard Wright is still pervasive. Yet some argue that racism has just become more subtle, the lines between races simply less visible, that white domination is still vulnerable only to federal force. My own view is one not of complacency but of considerable optimism. And this optimism informs the ensuing discussion of where we have been and where we might now go.

# The First Five Years

The Voting Rights Act of 1965 had a simple aim: providing ballots for southern blacks. Within five years, in suits based on the statute, complex questions of electoral equality would arise, but certainly at the outset no one envisioned that turn of events. The extraordinary power that the legislation conferred on both courts and the Department of Justice, permitting an unprecedented intrusion of federal authority into local electoral affairs, was meant to deal with an extraordinary problem: continued black disfranchisement ninety-five years after the passage of the Fifteenth Amendment.

Judicial power would quickly come to be seen as a powerful tool to heighten the impact of the black vote. Yet ironically, it was precisely the failure of courts to protect basic Fifteenth Amendment rights that prompted the passage of the Voting Rights Act. The 1957 Civil Rights Act had created a Civil Rights Division within the Department of Justice and had given federal authorities new power to sue recalcitrant registrars and other local officials determined to keep blacks from the polls. Both the 1960 and 1964 Civil Rights acts had further enhanced that power. But such case-by-case adjudication had proved arduous, expensive, and limited in impact. Preparation for a trial often required examining hundreds of witnesses and scouring thousands of pages of registration records. In one case involving Montgomery, Alabama, for instance, the government introduced sixty-nine exhibits, one of which consisted of 10,000 documents filling five filing cabinets.[1]

The government was invariably rewarded in its efforts, winning every suit it brought. But only those counties most vulnerable to attack were sued, and victory was often neither swift nor complete. As John Doar, in charge of voting rights litigation under John F. Kennedy, later put it, the Justice Department "faced tough judges"[2] (some of whom Kennedy had himself appointed)—tough not in the sense of rigorous or exacting, he meant, but eager to find for the defendants. Too often, access to public records was reluctantly conceded, trials were delayed, cases improperly dismissed, rulings inadequate, and enforcement half-hearted. Kennedy's Justice Department initiated fifty-seven suits.[3] The result, as Doar described it in 1963, was to move "from no registration to token registration."[4] He referred to areas targeted by federal attorneys. The primary concern was with the rural and small-town South—with, for instance, the twenty-two Alabama counties in which fewer than 10 percent of voting-age blacks were registered, the four heavily black Louisiana parishes with not a single black on the voter lists, the sixty-nine Mississippi counties with abysmal records of receptivity to black political participation.[5]

In such strongholds of white supremacy, the Justice Department did not battle alone. As government attorneys prepared their lengthy and elaborate legal briefs—combing voter rolls, compiling the demographic statistics, interviewing registrars and registrants—valiant civil rights volunteers simply tried to register blacks to vote. As attorneys got ready to take legal action, workers went door to door urging blacks to exercise their Fifteenth Amendment rights.

The strength of these volunteers' effort was unprecedented, yet it largely failed. Or rather it failed to enlarge substantially the ranks of black registrants, but succeeded, by the violence of the resistance that it provoked, in finally convincing the nation that radical new legislation was needed. Certainly as important to the enactment of the Voting Rights Act as the frustrating experience of federal litigators were the murders of three civil rights workers in Mississippi in the summer of 1964, the eruptions of violence in response to voter registration drives elsewhere, and the brutal assault by the police on the peaceful marchers from Selma to Montgomery, Alabama, in the spring of 1965.

In the view of many blacks today, the Voting Rights Act is the crowning achievement of the civil rights movement. Yet in the early 1960s, voter registration was not the highest priority for civil rights groups. The revolution instead got its start in the 1956 Montgomery bus boycott and the 1960 lunch counter sit-ins in Greensboro, North Carolina. The massive demonstration in Birmingham in 1963 was in response to discrimination in the downtown department stores and, again, at the lunch counters. Not until the march at Selma did voting rights become the movement's focus.

In fact, the energy devoted to voter registration drives after 1962 was due, in great part, to pressure from the Kennedy administration and interest by philanthropic foundations. Following the Freedom Rides in the spring of 1961, which had attempted to force the desegregation of interstate transportation facilities, Attorney General Robert Kennedy had met with representatives from several civil rights groups to urge greater involvement on their part in voter registration work. Holding out the prospect of money from private sources, Kennedy argued that agitation for the vote was likely both to encounter less immediate white resistance and to promise greater long-run social change. It was the key to every other right, he contended: "From participation in elections [would] flow . . . all of what they wanted to accomplish in education, housing, jobs, and public accommodation."[6] *Schlesinger*

Nevertheless, not everyone in the movement was convinced that the Kennedys meant well. Many members of the Student Nonviolent Coordinating Committee (SNCC) were skeptical. "I felt that what they were trying to do was to kill the Movement, but to kill it by rechanneling its energies," one SNCC worker reported.[7] These warriors in the racial backwaters of the South wanted to revolutionize the social order, and voter registration seemed unequal to the task. As historian Clayborne Carson has written, an important faction within SNCC hoped to "free people's minds from the restraints of established order," and to create a world in which people would "not even have to do such things as vote or have leaders or officers."[8] Others, less ambitious in their goals, viewed the concentration on voter registration as a concession to the forces for law and order in the lawless Jim Crow South.[9]

In the end, a majority in the movement was persuaded to follow the electoral politics strategy, and under the umbrella of a new organization, the Voter Education Project, a massive registration drive was launched. Even the most militant quickly agreed that such work was not a retreat—that it offered plenty of opportunity to confront southern racists directly. Soon after the June 1961 meeting at which Robert Kennedy had pressed civil rights organizers to place greater emphasis on enfranchisement, SNCC began a voter registration drive in McComb, Mississippi, and surrounding counties.[10] Led by Robert Moses, a black field secretary who had quit his job as a private-school mathematics teacher in New York to work full time on voter registration in the South, the registration effort proved enlightening. Between the middle of August and the end of October, Moses was attacked and beaten by a cousin of the sheriff; a co-worker was ordered out of a registrar's office at gunpoint and then hit with a pistol; a black sympathizer was murdered by a state representative; another black who asked for Justice Department protection to testify at the inquest was beaten (and three years later killed); a white activist's eye was gouged; and, finally, twelve SNCC workers and local supporters were fined and sentenced to substantial terms in jail. Those in McComb that summer discovered that voter registration work certainly signified no surrender, and gave those eager to display their courage ample opportunity. As one participant answered those still agitating for direct action such as sit-ins, "If you went into Mississippi and talked about voter registration they're going to hit you on the side of the head and that's about as direct as you can get."[11]

Of course the walls of segregation and discrimination were not going to come tumbling down simply because blacks could vote, as Kennedy had hoped. But enfranchisement did portend massive change; southern whites who had so carefully erected and guarded the barriers to suffrage had always understood that. "Right or wrong, we don't aim to let them vote. We just don't aim to let 'em vote," a Mississippi Democrat told V. O. Key in the mid-1940s.[12] It was a matter not of principle but of power. As Maynard Jackson, Atlanta's first black mayor, recently remarked, the Talmadges, Stennises, the Bilbos, and the Thurmonds all knew that once blacks got their Fifteenth Amendment rights no white supremacist would hold office securely.[13]

This, then, was the context in which the march at Selma took place and the Voting Rights Act soon thereafter was passed. The civil rights community had become more or less united in making black enfranchisement its highest priority, and that determination could only have been strengthened by the passage of the Civil Rights Act of 1964. That measure provided extensive protection against discrimination in the areas of public accommodation, employment, and education, but it left basic voting rights—elementary access to the ballot—at the mercy of local courts. The limited receptivity of many southern judges to voting rights suits was clear, yet civil rights activists could do little on their own; voter registration drives had had no more impact than litigation. Progress had been meager; change, incremental. Federal help was obviously needed, but in a new form. And that is precisely what the Voting Rights Act provided.

Lyndon Johnson, in 1965, called for the "goddamnedest, toughest, voting rights bill" that his staff could devise.[14] And he got it. Critics and supporters alike agreed that it was "radical."[15] A 1972 report calling for more rigorous voting rights enforcement described the act's provisions as "harsh," but necessarily so.[16] Its remedies were characterized as "stringent" by the Supreme Court,[17] and the assistant attorney general for civil rights readily acknowledged in 1975 that it was "unusual" legislation.[18]

The "usual" legislation, however, had failed to break the usual pattern of black disfranchisement. Voting rights litigators working in the South in the early 1960s had learned several lessons. The first concerned the literacy test. "No matter from what direction one looks at it," V. O. Key had written in 1949, "the Southern literacy test is a fraud and nothing more."[19] It was no less a fraud in 1965. In the 1960s southern registrars were observed testing black applicants on such matters as the number of bubbles in a soap bar, the news contained in a copy of the *Peking Daily*, the meaning of obscure passages in state constitutions, and the definition of terms such as *habeas corpus*. By contrast, even illiterate whites were being registered. Booker T. Washington had believed that "brains, property, and character" would "settle the question of civil rights," but eighty years after the founding of Tuskegee Institute, blacks with brains, property, and character in the city of Tuskegee still found themselves unable to establish their literacy. "If a fella makes a mistake on his questionnaire, I'm not gonna discriminate in his favor just because he's got a Ph.D.," the chairman of the Board of Registrars righteously maintained.[20]

Government attorneys trying voting rights cases in federal district courts had struggled with the question of a proper remedy for the discriminatory use of literacy tests. One option was to insist upon the fair administration of such tests: *all* illiterate applicants—black and white—would fail, and all those who could read and write would pass. Yet often these tests could not be objectively scored. For example, potential registrants would be asked to interpret a provision in the state constitution to the satisfaction of the registrar, when no definition of "satisfactory" had been—or could be—provided. In any case, the consequence of suddenly administering a test to blacks that whites had never been asked to take was unacceptable. While illiterate blacks would be barred from voting, whites who were already registered would remain so, and thus white illiterates who had never been "fairly" tested would be left permanently on the rolls.

The alternative to permitting a color-blind literacy and understanding test was what attorneys called a true "freeze" order: do not freeze the announced registration test, they said, but the one to which whites had been actually subjected. That is, no change should be allowed in the real test that whites took. Since no literacy test had, in fact, been used to screen whites, none should be used for blacks. This, then, was the first conclusion dictated by trial experience in the early 1960s: to eliminate the literacy test entirely was the only proper remedy for its misuse.

Federal attorneys drew three further lessons. First, southern judges could not be trusted; federal district courts in the immediate locality were not the appropriate agency to enforce voting rights. Second, questions of disfranchisement should not, in fact, be litigated at all. To prove the obvious was both expensive and time-consuming, and victories were too often transient or incomplete. Finally, banishing literacy tests might not be enough. Unless preventive steps were taken, old methods of disfranchisement might simply be replaced by new ones, and the tedious and prolonged legal process would begin again.

These were the lessons that shaped the Voting Rights Act—that made it the "tough" legislation President Johnson wanted. What the litigators learned in the field, the framers of the act wrote into law. In place of the extended and complex judicial process traditionally used to establish voting rights violations, the architects of the statute substituted a simple statistical rule of thumb. They required no judicial findings. Instead, knowing literacy tests to be the chief means of disfranchising southern blacks, and using voter registration and turnout figures, they devised a statistical test to identify the discriminatory use of such tests. They took a well-established relationship between the impact of black disfranchisement on the general level of political participation in the heavily black southern states, on the one hand, and the fraudulent use of literacy tests, on the other, and used the first to identify the second. The statistical test permitted the finding of vote denial by a simple formula, eliminating the need to ferret out Fifteenth Amendment violations in an unmanageably large number of counties in states with abominable records with respect to black voting rights.

The statute thus identified a voting rights violation wherever total voter registration or turnout in the presidential election of 1964 fell below 50 percent and a literacy test was used to screen potential registrants. A state or county which had employed such a test in November 1964, and in which less than half the voting-age population (black *and* white) had cast ballots, was assumed to have engaged in electoral discrimination, with the burden on the jurisdiction to prove otherwise.

From the inferred presence of constitutional violations, several consequences followed. In "covered" jurisdictions, literacy tests were suspended, initially for five years. Federal registrars ("examiners") and election observers could be dispatched to those areas whenever necessary. Moreover, those states and counties could institute no new "voting qualification or prerequisite to voting, or standard, practice or procedure with respect to voting" without "preclearance" (approval) by the Attorney General or the District Court for the District of Columbia. No southern court was given jurisdiction. As the chairman of the House Judiciary Committee later put it, the law provided "an arsenal of readily available and highly effective remedies."[21]

Why the figure of 50 percent? Because those who wrote the legislation knew the states they wanted to "cover" and, by a process of trial and error, determined the participation level that would single them out. Those central, temporary provisions of the 1965 act—suspension of the literacy test chief among them—applied to six southern states in their entirety, a seventh in substantial part, and only scattered counties elsewhere. And why not an outright ban on all literacy tests, without the intervening, indirect test for Fifteenth Amendment violations? Because it was assumed that such a ban would not survive a constitutional challenge. As recently as 1959, the right of states to screen potential registrants for their ability to read and write had, in principle, been upheld.[22]

The impact of the act's passage was almost instantaneous. The history of Dallas County, Alabama, of which Selma is the seat, is illustrative. Prior to the bloody days of early 1965, when blacks and whites risked their lives marching for voting rights, the Justice Department had engaged in four years of litigation. Twice a federal court had found widespread Fifteenth Amendment violations, and at first glance it might seem that unmistakable progress had resulted: black registration had increased more than twentyfold, from 16 to 383. But there were approximately *fifteen thousand* blacks of voting age in that majority-black county.[23] On August 6 the Voting Rights Act became law, and by August 14 a federal examiner (registrar) had listed another 381 blacks. The effort of four years had been duplicated in a single week. By November nearly 8,000 black applicants had been enrolled.[24] In Alabama as a whole an estimated 19.3 percent of all blacks were registered as of March 1965; the figure rose to 51.6 percent by September 1967. Impressive changes also took place in Georgia, Louisiana, South Carolina, and Virginia. North Carolina, which began with relatively high black registration (46.8 percent), naturally experienced fewer gains. At the other extreme, Mississippi took off from a low point of 6.7 percent, but two years later it had the highest percentage of black registered voters (59.8 percent) anywhere in the South.[25]

What the Voting Rights Act accomplished—black enfranchisement—was precisely what it aimed to do. Every section of the statute must be viewed in light of that purpose. Attorney General Katzenbach made that goal very clear on the opening day of the congressional hearings held prior to the passage of the legislation. "Our concern today is to enlarge representative government," he said. "It is to increase the number of citizens who can vote."[26] The point was reiterated throughout his testimony: "The whole bill is really aimed at getting people registered," he explained.[27] Other witnesses did not even mention the purpose of the bill, viewing it as obvious and beyond discussion. Instead, they poured forth in detail the continuing obstacles to rudimentary electoral participation. Every advocate had the same thing in mind—realizing the promise of the Fifteenth Amendment almost one hundred years after its passage.

Although the Voting Rights Act was permanent legislation, its central provisions were temporary. For instance, the statute permanently protected all citizens from procedures denying the right to vote on account of race or color (the Fifteenth Amendment guarantee). On the other hand, those sections that banned literacy tests, required the "preclearance" of every new "voting qualification or prerequisite to voting," and made available federal examiners and observers were enacted as short-term "emergency" measures. Assuming powers traditionally left in local hands, these provisions consequently had an expected life of only five years. Indeed, had the "special" provisions also been proposed on a permanent basis, the law would not have passed. As it was, the sponsors of the bill had wanted a full decade and had had to settle for half.

In 1965, that is, ten years seemed an unacceptably long time to permit such extraordinary federal control in much of the South over matters of suffrage. The powers given to the Justice Department—which later became much greater than anyone originally contemplated—have become so much a part of our political and legal landscape that it is now hard to recognize how remarkable they are. It was clear enough at the time, however. In a 1966 decision upholding the law, Supreme Court Chief Justice Earl Warren acknowledged that its "constitutional propriety" had to be understood in context, "with reference to the historical experience which it reflect[ed] . . . [the] insidious and pervasive evil which had been perpetuated in certain parts of our country through unremitting and ingenious defiance of the Constitution."[28] As it was, the doubts of the great liberal justice, Hugo Black, were not assuaged. "Section 5 [the preclearance provision]," he said, "by providing that some of the States cannot pass State laws or adopt State constitutional amendments without first being compelled to beg federal authorities to approve their policies, so distorts our constitutional structure of government as to render any distinction drawn in the Constitution between State and Federal power almost meaningless."[29]

Justice Black was not alone, of course, in finding portions of the act objectionable. In fact, most Republican members of the House Judiciary Committee had preferred an alternative bill. They complained that "fair and effective enforcement of the 15th amendment call[ed] for precise identification of offenders, not the indiscriminate scatter-gun technique evidenced in the 50 percent test." That test, they said, "would engulf whole States in a tidal wave of Federal control of the election process, even though many of the counties or parishes within that State may be acknowledged by all to be absolutely free of racial discrimination in voting."[30] These Republican views were shared by the *Wall Street Journal*. "To play with complicated formulas, to measure justice by percentages, and to aim punitive laws at some States," it said, "not only violates both the spirit and letter of the Constitution, but buries the real moral question in sophistry."[31]

Southerners, of course, saw the ghost of Reconstruction. They, too, labeled the act punitive legislation aimed at the South, without regard for the guilt or innocence of particular localities. Representative William M. Tuck from Virginia argued that not even the U.S. Commission on Civil Rights had found discrimination in his state. Yet Virginia, along with Mississippi, was required "to prostrate itself before a three-judge Federal court in a foreign jurisdiction and establish its innocence."[32] The reference was to the "bailout" provision, whereby jurisdictions could escape coverage by obtaining from the D.C. district court a declaratory judgment that in the previous five years the literacy test they had used had not actually been employed to deny or abridge the right to vote on account of race. "Do you think it is a fair system of justice which compels people to travel 250 or 1,000 or 3,000 miles in order to gain access to a court of justice?" Senator Sam Ervin asked in the Senate hearings prior to the passage of the act.[33] It was a "studied insult" to the people and the "honorable judges" of the South, Tuck agreed, made even worse by the permission given to "Federal personnel to overrun areas of a State or subdivision as intimidating symbols of Federal power."[34]

The charges were not persuasive. The act was a blunt and harsh instrument, but in 1965 the South was in no position to protest its passage. It came to the argument with exceedingly dirty hands. And all attempts to secure Fifteenth Amendment rights by more orthodox means had failed. In retrospect, the most notable aspect of the debate is not the South's predicament—having the weight of constitutional tradition on its side, yet being so clearly in the wrong. Most striking is the fact that critics ignored the one provision that should have caused alarm and focused entirely on those that would soon gain wide acceptance. The elimination of the literacy test throughout most of the South, the provision for federal examiners and observers, and, to a lesser extent, the exclusive reliance on the D.C. district court—these provisions, so controversial in 1965, were hardly matters of discussion five years later. Only a few southerners (Senators Ervin and Thurmond, most notably) continued to resent their applicability to the South alone. But the "preclearance" requirement that quickly came to occupy center stage—the demand that covered jurisdictions check with federal authorities before altering any voting procedures—was hardly noticed in the initial debate.

The reason is clear. In 1965, the preclearance provision (section 5) was seen as nothing more than a corollary of section 4—the latter banning literacy tests, the former making sure that the effect of that ban stuck. The demand that federal authorities preclear any new voting procedure in counties and states in which literacy tests had been suspended had an unambiguous and limited aim: guarding against renewed disfranchisement, the use of the back door once the front one was blocked.

The ingenuity of racists had kept litigators attempting to secure the basic franchise always running and always behind, and those who shaped the Voting Rights Act could not be sure that eliminating the literacy test would do the trick. Although federal examiners could be assigned to register blacks where local officials were recalcitrant, it was hoped that the use of such registrars could be kept to a minimum. In any case, new regulations could keep blacks from actually voting. Of course, such regulations could be overturned judicially, but the whole purpose of the act was to eliminate the need for an army of federal litigators doing battle in every southern district court.

References to section 5, the preclearance provision, were sparse in the 1965 congressional hearings, but Attorney General Katzenbach did briefly explain it. "Our experience in the areas that would be covered by this bill," he said, "has been such as to indicate frequently on the part of state legislatures a desire in a sense to outguess the courts of the United States or even to outguess the Congress of the United States." That is, the courts and Congress could ban familiar disfranchising devices only to confront novel ones devised by southern states bent on evading the law. But for such changes in voting procedure to be rejected, Katzenbach went on, they would have to have the effect of denying the rights guaranteed by the Fifteenth Amendment.[35] And numerous witnesses at the hearings reassured their audience that those rights, which it was the entire purpose of the act to secure, were expected to be narrowly defined.

Thus Roy Wilkins, executive director of the NAACP, spoke of the need to protect the citizen "from the beginning of the registration process until his vote has been cast and counted."[36] New York Representative William F. Ryan referred to the act as eliminating discrimination at the ballot box.[37] Another New York congressman, Jonathan Bingham, urged legislation that would reach "every essential activity affecting the vote"—political party meetings, councils, conventions, and referenda as well as primaries and general elections.[38] Never during the hearings was "every essential activity affecting the vote" defined to include redistricting, annexations, or changes to at-large voting. No one could imagine the future scrutiny to which such changes would be subjected under section 5.

Two points, then, emerged from the House and Senate Judiciary Committee hearings on the original Voting Rights Act. First, preclearance was just one of several measures intended to reinforce the ban on literacy tests contained in section 4; second, as such it was seen as relatively unimportant, drawing little attention. The Senate Committee report, in fact, fails even to mention section 5 in its summary of the bill's key provisions, and the House report gives it only a cursory and unilluminating glance.[39] As the distinguished civil rights attorney Joseph Rauh put it, the provision was included in the statute "to stop ways around voting legislation . . . simply [as] self-defense."[40] Congress was well aware that southern states were adept at the fine art of circumvention. Banishing literacy tests, it was feared, might not be sufficient; new devices could be created with the same impact as old ones, and the vote could be blocked anew.

The initial understanding of section 5 thus envisioned objections only to innovations involving registration and the mechanics of voting. Quite suddenly, however, a much broader view emerged—one that allowed the Department of Justice to review annexations, new district lines, and other changes affecting minority voting strength. The turning point can be precisely dated—March 3, 1969, when the Supreme Court handed down its decision in *Allen v. State Board of Elections*.[41] Before *Allen* one district court opinion had suggested that, under section 5, extending the terms of office for white incumbents was a change that required federal approval.[42] And South Carolina, most consistently, did submit some preclearance requests for newly drawn district and municipal boundaries, as well as for newly instituted at-large and other methods of voting. But these legislative initiatives had never met with any objection from the Department of Justice.[43] *source of preclearance subm.*

The picture changed overnight. Within three months of the decision in *Allen*—by the time Congress began hearings on the first extension of the act's temporary provisions—the central importance of section 5 was well established. Preclearance protected blacks not only against obvious disfranchising devices, but also against those which in more subtle ways "diluted" the impact of their vote.

*Allen* was actually a consolidation of four cases. The most important involved a 1966 amendment to Mississippi law that allowed counties to replace district with at-large voting in the election of local supervisors (commissioners). Were such amendments changes in voting "practice" or "procedure" and, as such, subject to the preclearance requirement of section 5?

Given the magnitude of the question, Chief Justice Warren disposed of it with striking ease. "The Voting Rights Act was aimed," he wrote, "at the subtle, as well as the obvious, state regulations which would have the effect of denying citizens their right to vote because of race."[44] In the 1965 hearings the assistant attorney general for civil rights had flatly stated that "the problem that the bill was aimed at was the problem of registration."[45] In Chief Justice Warren's view, however, more important were statements such as, "There are an awful lot of things that could be started for purposes of evading the 15th amendment if there is a desire to do so."[46] The reference to an "awful lot of things," the Chief Justice argued, was incompatible with a narrow definition of voting practices and procedures. And it was clear, he went on, that "the right to vote can be affected by a *dilution* of voting power as well as by an absolute prohibition on casting a ballot. Voters who are members of a racial minority might well be in the majority in one district, but in a decided minority in the county as a whole. This type of change could therefore nullify their ability to elect the candidate of their choice just as would prohibiting some of them from voting."[47]

*dilution*

Chief Justice Warren's reading of legislative history showed considerable ingenuity; the hearings nowhere betray any concern with changes affecting not access to the ballot but the weight of ballots cast. Nonetheless his central point, though considerably overstated, did have merit. The adoption of at-large voting did not necessarily "nullify" the ability of black voters "to elect the candidate of their choice"; rarely would county-wide or city-wide elections have the *same* impact as a fraudulent literacy test—leaving blacks disfranchised despite their access to the polling booth. But they might. The setting would have to be one in which white voters consistently voted as a bloc against candidates (white or black) preferred by blacks. Elections would then amount to a racial census, with the result that blacks in a majority-white jurisdiction would have nothing to lose by remaining home on election day. The breakdown of registrants by race would determine the outcome. But such white solidarity in the face of black enfranchisement is seldom permanent; blacks become a powerful swing vote when white candidates begin to compete. A substantial black electorate in an at-large setting is unlikely to remain indefinitely without influence—truly without reason to register and vote.

Yet the indefinite future was clearly not of immediate concern to Mississippi legislators in 1966. As the number of registered blacks climbed sharply, state representatives had acted swiftly to amend state law to reduce the impact of the new voters. According to the U.S. Commission on Civil Rights, in 1966 at least thirty bills were introduced in regular and special legislative sessions, and twelve were passed introducing substantial alterations in the state's election laws.[48] Among them was the bill at the heart of *Allen*, giving county boards of supervisors the option of providing for the at-large election of their members. The bill had been sponsored almost entirely by representatives who came from counties with either potential black majorities or at least one majority-black district. In theory, of course, in counties where blacks were a majority, county-wide voting could enable them to make a sweep of legislative seats. But the whites who initiated the legislative move were counting on poor black turnout (and thus a white majority) and bloc voting along racial lines to ensure white control for some time to come.

In an eloquent dissent in *Allen*, Justice Harlan argued that section 5 could only be interpreted to reach such ill-disguised, racially biased actions as had occurred in Mississippi if sections 4 and 5 were viewed as independent provisions. Enfranchisement, the majority opinion implied, had one meaning in one section, another in the other. Section 4 did not ban procedures that "diluted" the black vote, only those that kept blacks from the polls. Yet after *Allen* federal authorities under section 5 could prohibit the *introduction* of new methods of voting (such as at-large elections), although those same methods were not considered disfranchising by the definition contained in section 4.

The two provisions, Justice Harlan wrote, were "clearly designed to march in lock-step." The purpose of preclearance (section 5) was not "to implement new substantive policies but . . . to assure the effectiveness of the dramatic step that Congress had taken in §4."[49] Enforcement and reinforcement—these were the inseparable goals of the two interlocked provisions. Thus, when the need for section 4 expired, when the ban on literacy tests terminated, the protection provided by section 5 should also end. "As soon as a State regains the right to apply a literacy test or similar 'device' under §4, it also escapes the commands of §5."[50]

Justice Harlan's point is incontrovertible: as a result of *Allen* these two provisions, envisioned as inseparable, were now separated by distinct definitions of enfranchisement. Yet Mississippi had unmistakably attempted to avert a likely consequence of black enfranchisement in existing majority-black single-member districts: the transfer of some public offices from white hands to black. Basic enfranchisement had been the sole goal of the statute, but confronted with such a bald maneuver, the Court could hardly refuse to act. Section 5, the preclearance provision, had been envisioned as a prophylactic device to prevent backsliding, and Mississippi had clearly tried to pull blacks from the gains they had made.

Nevertheless, *Allen* marked a radical change in the meaning of the act: the majority opinion had found a Fourteenth Amendment right to protection from vote dilution in a statute that rested unequivocally on the Fifteenth Amendment. As Justice Harlan pointed out, and Chief Justice Warren acknowledged, the decision in *Allen* adopted "the reapportionment cases' expansive concept of voting."[51] It adopted, that is, that concern with the *weight* of the ballots cast that was at the heart of the one-person, one-vote (Fourteenth Amendment) decisions. Thus the door was opened to unprecedented federal involvement in local electoral matters. The reach of federal authority had been quite restricted as long as its limit was set by the boundaries of section 4. New election procedures not already prohibited by section 4, but nevertheless violating basic Fifteenth Amendment rights, could not be instituted. This had initially been the power of federal authorities under section 5 in its entirety: to block the introduction of new devices that kept blacks from the polls, and to require continued adherence to preexisting rules—in other words, to force a return to abandoned procedures.

That power was greatly expanded by *Allen*. As I suggested in the Introduction, if there were now votes that "counted" and those that did not, then a vote that counted had obviously become a right; blacks casting "meaningless" ballots were certainly entitled to relief. But when were ballots meaningful? *Allen* forced an answer. For instance, proposed districting plans and annexations—both "voting" procedures and, as such, subject to preclearance—cannot simply be vetoed by federal authorities. If the D.C. court (or the Department of Justice as its surrogate) objects to redistricting in the wake of a decennial census, the jurisdiction cannot in response simply reinstate the earlier, now malapportioned plan. New districts that conform to the one-person, one-vote standard must be devised. And federal authorities must define racial equity—the point at which black ballots "fully" count.

Likewise, an annexation may be judged discriminatory in impact if more white voters than black have been added to a city's rolls. Yet neither the D.C. court nor the Supreme Court on appeal has sanctioned forcing financially squeezed cities to return to their circumscribed, preannexation boundaries. An alternative remedy must be formulated—one that meets federal standards of racial fairness. The Justice Department must thus both identify the objectionable and specify the acceptable. In a suggested districting scheme, are black ballots "fully meaningful" if there are only six majority-black districts when a seventh can be drawn? The purpose of preclearance, Justice Harlan had argued, was not "to implement new substantive policies."[52] But nothing short of substantive policy would answer the questions that redistricting and other proposals submitted for federal review posed after *Allen*. It was, as Harlan put it, "a revolutionary innovation in American government that [went] far beyond that which was accomplished by §4."[53]

The Department of Justice and the D.C. district court alone have the authority to "preclear" proposed changes in electoral procedure, but their freedom to restructure local arrangements is not absolute. To begin with, federal action depends on local action. Thus, an at-large method of voting is invulnerable to attack unless it is either newly proposed or has acquired new meaning as a result of a change in the racial balance of a city following an annexation. And an at-large system in place prior to November 1964 cannot be dislodged unless the city employing it chooses to incorporate surrounding territory. Districting plans, however, can never be frozen; they must be revised after every census. At a minimum, there is thus local initiative every ten years, and every such initiative in a jurisdiction covered by section 5 triggers federal scrutiny.

The second constraint upon federal authority is less restrictive: there must be some evidence that the proposed change could be interpreted to "deny or abridge the right to vote on account of race or color." Not all annexations, all new district lines, or all newly instituted at-large systems of voting qualify as potentially discriminatory. But the burden is on the covered jurisdiction to prove an absence of wrongdoing; if the D.C. court or the Attorney General *suspects* the presence of discrimination, an objection will be lodged.[54]

When is the introduction of an at-large or other method of election a violation of black voting rights? The freedom of federal authorities to define the condition of vote "dilution" was greatly enhanced by the wording of section 5, which permits preclearance of those electoral practices and procedures that "do not have the purpose and will not have the effect" of denying or abridging the right to vote on account of race. In 1965 the reference to discriminatory effect was innocuous and thus unnoticed. The framers and sponsors of the act hoped to eliminate every device whose impact was to keep southern blacks from the polls— whatever its stated purpose. And, in the context, "effect" and "purpose" were close to interchangeable terms; the former was simply circumstantial evidence of the latter. That is, when the question was the legality of a recent alteration in voting procedure in a jurisdiction known to have had a long history of Fifteenth Amendment violations, the effect of the alteration was assumed to suggest strongly its purpose. The adverse impact of a sudden change in rules involving the franchise was viewed as a signal of improper motive when that change took place in the South and affected newly enfranchised blacks.

Once changes such as annexations and redistrictings were covered by the preclearance provision, however, "effect" was released from its intimate connection with "purpose." When a municipality annexes a suburban area, it may add more white voters than black to the city's voting rolls, but such an effect is not necessarily a clue to its purpose. The Court's decision in *Allen* suddenly applied the prohibition of section 5 to all changes that might have a disparate racial impact, whether intended or not. A districting plan that was racially neutral in intent could nevertheless be found discriminatory in effect.

*Allen* was crucial in the evolution of the Voting Rights Act from the first truly effective vehicle for southern black enfranchisement to a means by which political power is redistributed among blacks, whites, and (since 1975) Hispanics. Ostensibly, the decision involved only the question of coverage—what sorts of changes qualify as alterations in voting "practice" or "procedure." But questions of coverage, disfranchisement (or "dilution"), and federal power are inseparable. Once the area of scrutiny is expanded, both the definition of enfranchisement and the power of the federal government to insist on methods of voting allegedly in the interest of minority voters become enlarged.

*Allen v. Board of Elections* began the process by which the Voting Rights Act was reshaped into an instrument for affirmative action in the electoral sphere. But the impact of the decision would have been limited without two other developments: repeated extensions of the "special" (temporary) provisions of the act by Congress, and a key judicial ruling. *Gaston County, North Carolina v. United States*, which was decided (like *Allen*) in 1969, closed the door to escape from the act for southern states and counties. [55]

Section 4 had suspended literacy tests wherever turnout in the presidential election of 1964 was under 50 percent, but jurisdictions could sue for release from coverage on the ground that no test had been employed for discriminatory ends in the preceding five years. In 1968 Gaston

County, North Carolina, went to court. Six years earlier the county had replaced its traditional oral test with a written one, and had begun a well-publicized process of reregistering all voters. The D.C. district court (with sole authority to hear "bailout" suits) did not question either the new test's impartiality or the sincerity of the county's effort to reach black voters.

The southern setting, of course, made the test suspect, but although the Voting Rights Act was clearly aimed at the South, it did permit particular localities to prove themselves exceptions to the general rule of southern racism, and Gaston County believed that it qualified. The court, however, turned the county's petition down, finding the test to be discriminatory not in purpose but in effect. Until 1965 the local schools had been segregated, creating the unequal educational opportunity that, according to Judge Skelly Wright, left blacks less prepared than whites to pass a literacy test. In other words, such a test penalized blacks for an inadequacy imposed by the state.[56] The opinion was a variation on a familiar theme: when opportunities have not been equal, meritocratic systems do not work. Gaston County had been attempting to administer a test of merit in a context of unequal educational opportunity.

Did inequality of educational opportunity in fact account for black illiteracy? A concurring opinion argued that blacks were disproportionately unable to read and write because they went to work rather than staying in school; even the education provided by segregated schools would have enabled blacks to pass Gaston County's very simple test.[57] That argument failed to persuade the Supreme Court, to which the county subsequently appealed. The burden was on the county to prove an absence of discriminatory effect, and that burden had not been met, Justice Harlan wrote for the majority. Judged by such measures as teacher training, facilities, and resources, black schools in the county prior to 1965 had clearly been inferior. And, in Harlan's words, those "inferior Negro schools provided many of [the county's] Negro residents with a subliterate education, and gave many others little inducement to enter or remain in school."[58]

*Gaston* labeled the literacy test—however fairly administered—a disfranchising device for southern blacks. The Voting Rights Act, as initially conceived, had maintained the traditional distinction between practices used to abridge Fifteenth Amendment rights and the normal exercise of a community's constitutionally sanctioned authority to set standards for voting. The statute assumed that potential registrants could still be screened for literacy, if not race. The North Carolina decision, however, collapsed that distinction. No amount of evidence presented by a covered jurisdiction could prove that voter turnout levels were unconnected to the use of a literacy test. No county could demonstrate that the statistical rule of thumb at the heart of the act had been inappropriately applied in its case—that although total voter turnout had been below 50 percent, blacks had had free access to the polls. *Gaston* thus heightened the significance of *Allen*. A jurisdiction, once covered, remained so. And coverage meant close federal scrutiny of every change in election procedures, from the relocation of a polling place to a districting or annexation decision.

In part this chapter has attempted to describe the central features of the Voting Rights Act, to convey a sense of the setting in which it grew and thus to explain its distinctive design. In part, however, it has introduced an argument that I will develop at length as the book continues. The statute was, by all accounts, radical. The architects of the Constitution had left matters of suffrage almost entirely in state hands, although subsequent amendments had prohibited a poll tax and denial or abridgment of the right to vote on account of race, gender, or age (after eighteen). In enforcing the Fifteenth Amendment, the Voting Rights Act broke with constitutional tradition. It established the presence of constitutional violations not on the basis of comprehensive judicial findings but by the use of a statistical rule of thumb, and to an unprecedented degree it placed local electoral affairs in federal hands. Covered jurisdictions were subject to a stringent set of remedies, often enforced by the Department of Justice, to which broad administrative discretion had been granted. This was emergency legislation, necessitated by the persistent and egregious infringement of basic rights. Its sole concern was simple enfranchisement—ballots for southern blacks. And that limited aim, to which the Constitution was unequivocally committed, legitimized the drastic nature of its central provisions.

The act was structured to deal with one kind of question, but after 1969 quite another kind was raised. Preclearance, a barely noticed provision in 1965, permitted the Department of Justice to halt renewed efforts to proscribe the exercise of basic Fifteenth Amendment rights; it allowed swift administrative relief for obvious constitutional violations. Attorneys in the Civil Rights Division were expected to confront a straightforward question: will the proposed change in voting procedure keep blacks from the polls? But after the decision in *Allen*, the questions were no longer so simple. The decision was correct, but, as I will subsequently argue, the consequences troubling. The statute was not designed for the purpose to which it would be put—resolving through administrative channels basic matters of electoral equality, determining when ballots "fully" count. A statute is not carved in stone, and old tools can be used for new purposes. But the revised aim must be legitimate, and the tools appropriate to the task at hand.

The decision in *Allen* was both correct and inevitable. Mississippi, while providing the immediate catalyst, was not alone in attempting to soften the impact of the law. In addition, the meaning of enfranchisement was changing in constitutional cases and was likely to change in statutory ones as well. In the 1965 statute, the right to vote meant the right to register and cast a ballot, but already by that year a Fourteenth Amendment case had raised the issue of protecting minority citizens from electoral arrangements that diluted the impact of their votes. The question, I will argue in Chapter 4, logically followed from the one-person, one-vote decisions, with their guarantee of "fair and effective participation." By 1969, in fact, the notion that ballots should fully count, that participation should be "fair and effective," was permeating other institutions, too. For instance, the Democratic Party had altered its rules for delegate selection following its 1968 convention. A commission chaired by George McGovern called upon party officials to take "affirmative steps to encourage minority group participation, including representation of minority groups on the national convention delegation in reasonable relationship to the group's presence in the population of the State."[59] That recommendation became party policy.

One further point needs to be made here. While southern whites had feared that their world would crumble once blacks could freely go to the polls, many civil rights activists were skeptical that votes alone could shake the pillars of the racist status quo. Their laudable goal had been the radical transformation of relations between the races—true equality—and although the movement subsequently changed, that commitment remained. In most places black enfranchisement would, by itself, bring black power—black political influence—but not necessarily blacks *in* power. Yet holding public office came to be viewed as critical to the larger civil rights goal. Thus the statute was altered not only by judicial decisions and changing views on democratic participation; pressure from the civil rights community, too, helped transform the Voting Rights Act into an instrument for affirmative action, a means to ensure ballots that promoted "full" and "effective" representation.

# Inadvertent Gains

In reshaping the Voting Rights Act, the Supreme Court did not work alone. Congress, too, played an important role—by extending the extraordinary protection of sections 4 and 5 to groups without the extraordinary history of southern blacks; by covering places outside the South that had no comparable history of racism; and by easing the burden on minority plaintiffs seeking to overturn allegedly discriminatory electoral systems.

There is, in fact, a paradoxical element in the history of the act. By 1969 black registration in the South was dramatically on the rise; to a remarkable degree, the problem the statute had been designed to solve had been successfully attacked. Whereas ten years after *Brown v. Board of Education* signs of school integration in the South were few and far between, four years after the passage of the Voting Rights Act the hopes and dreams of its framers appeared close to realization. Yet 1969 was the year in which *Allen* had been decided, and the process of both extending and strengthening the act's special provisions—by the courts and Congress in turn—had begun. With black enfranchisement came new efforts to protect against disfranchisement. As the emergency subsided, the emergency powers expanded.

The temporary provisions of the act—those designed to right a historic wrong swiftly by the use of extraordinary federal power—were first extended in 1970. By now, the act has become so firmly fixed in our legislative firmament that it seems unthinkable that Congress would have let sections 4 and 5 expire just five years after the enactment of the statute. Yet 1970 was the only year in which the preclearance provision was in serious trouble. When the sense of national shame aroused in 1965 by Selma and the ugliness of southern resistance to basic Fifteenth Amendment rights should have been most fresh, Congress came closest to cutting back on the protection contained in the act. In 1975 and 1982 the choice would be between straight extension or expanded enforcement; only in 1970 were conservatives able to make the reduction of federal power over state and local electoral affairs a serious issue.

"The right to vote is one civil right that Southern Senators are prepared to concede," the *New York Times* explained in March 1970.[1] If so, this had certainly not been apparent to the White House nine months earlier. After numerous delays and amid much speculation, the Nixon administration in June 1969 attempted to ally itself with the South by advocating a revision of the act that, as one southerner put it, would "spread the misery" but also alleviate it.[2] The proposal involved banning literacy tests nationwide and eliminating the preclearance requirement of section 5, with the result that the South would no longer carry a special burden. Wherever discrimination was suspected—whether in the moving of a polling place in Chicago or the redrawing of district lines in a Louisiana parish—the Attorney General could enjoin the changes in a federal district court pending a full-scale trial. Under existing law, every alteration in the electoral practices of a covered jurisdiction (one which had used a literacy test and in which voter turnout had been low) was suspect, and thus subject to federal scrutiny prior to final enactment. Moreover, the burden was on the local authorities to prove that the change was racially neutral. The Nixon administration wanted only those changes arousing suspicion to be subject to review. It advocated, as well, removing the power of review from the Department of Justice, terminating the D.C. court's exclusive jurisdiction, and shifting the burden of proof to federal authorities.

The House Judiciary Committee, before whom the proposal was presented, was unenthusiastic. For one thing, as every litigator knows, judgments in court are often determined by who carries the burden of proof. Furthermore, the suggested amendment would force the Justice Department to bring suits against southern lawmakers in southern courts, and to monitor every change in voting procedure in both North and South. That is, it would now be up to federal authorities themselves to keep track of new polling sites and altered district lines; not even in the hitherto suspect covered states would local officials be obligated to bring revised procedures to federal attention. The old game of "chase the legislature" would be revived, one Democratic congressman complained;[3] federal attorneys would return to the pursuit of racist legislatures whose ingenuity kept them one step ahead of the law. The ranking Republican on the House Judiciary Committee, William M. McCulloch of Ohio, refused to go along. "The administration creates a remedy for which there is no wrong and leaves general wrongs without adequate remedy," he said.[4] He anticipated little danger of electoral "wrongs" in the North, but feared that continuing and massive discrimination in the South would no longer be adequately addressed. McCulloch was not alone: not a single northern Republican on the committee was willing to sponsor the bill in floor debate, and both Democrats and Republicans expressed some doubts as to the administration's real aim.[5]

The prospects for passage looked dim. Yet clearly the administration had something to gain from a gesture of sympathy to southern conservatives: it would help to pay off a political debt incurred in the 1968 election—eighty-six electoral votes from the South. And it was money in the bank for the future. George Wallace had won five southern states in the last election, and Nixon surely saw the Wallace vote as potentially Republican.

The widely held view that the administration bill would get nowhere proved correct, but only initially. The Judiciary Committee backed a straight five-year extension of the statute. Undoubtedly the House as a whole would have followed suit had not the Rules Committee (with its chairman from Mississippi) intervened to give the Nixon proposal new life. The decision of that committee to clear the bill for floor action was the turning point: under heavy pressure from the White House, Republicans joined southern Democrats to pass the measure with a five-vote margin.

It was a "major defeat" for civil rights forces, the *New York Times* commented; the House had voted to "terminate" the Voting Rights Act.[6] In fact, the central provision of the legislation—the suspension of literacy tests where voter turnout was low—remained safe. And although the action of the House could not be ignored, the Senate was highly unlikely to approve the bill. Liberal Republicans, led by Hugh Scott from Pennsylvania, were committed to extending the preclearance provision, and not even the South had its heart in Nixon's cause. Southern senators were faced with an unpleasant choice: allowing a quick resolution of the voting rights issue or risking delay and growing opposition to the confirmation of Florida's G. Harrold Carswell (whom they strongly supported) as Supreme Court Justice. The vote on Carswell was scheduled to follow that on the voting rights bill; action on the former awaited decision on the latter. Scott fashioned an acceptable compromise: extending the special provisions for another five years; banning literacy tests nationwide during that period; and, finally, expanding coverage to include states and counties that employed such tests and had had a voter turnout in 1968 of less than 50 percent. Thus, jurisdictions covered in 1965 (on the basis of the 1964 voter participation figures) would remain covered, but they would now be joined by those counties in which turnout had dropped below 50 percent in the 1968 election. Moreover, not even states lacking a history of discrimination or a significant minority population would be allowed to screen voters for literacy.[7]

It now seems anomalous to call the final bill a "compromise." Not only the South, with its history of Fifteenth Amendment violations, but the entire nation would henceforth be forbidden to exercise its traditional freedom to set literacy qualifications for voting. The change in the "trigger" for coverage also gave the act a more national cast. Preclearance and other stringent remedies had been imposed upon all counties which used a literacy test in 1968 and in which fewer than half the eligible voters cast ballots in that same year. In three New York City boroughs (counties) voter turnout dropped a few percentage points between 1964 and 1968, and that drop in turnout suddenly made them subject to section 5—this despite the fact that blacks had been freely voting in New York since the enactment of the Fifteenth Amendment in 1870 and for fifty years had held public office in the city. Likewise, counties in such disparate states as Wyoming, Arizona, California, and Massachusetts unexpectedly found themselves subject to a level of federal scrutiny initially permitted as an emergency measure to deal with black disfranchisement in ex-Confederate states.[8]

A more encompassing act was a stronger act, and it might be assumed that civil rights groups would welcome the changes—notwithstanding their Republican inspiration. The proposed amendment of section 5 having been defeated, black voters in the South remained as protected as before against the dilution of their voting strength by the adoption of at-large voting, the relocation of a polling place to an inconvenient site, and other changes in the electoral environment. The geographic reach of existing federal authority had simply been lengthened; blacks in addi-

1970
amend.

1970 –
literacy ban
nationwide

tional jurisdictions outside the South were newly covered. Nevertheless, from beginning to end, both civil rights spokesmen and the
liberal press were almost unanimously opposed to the compromise bill.
Their opposition suggests that civil rights questions are often more
complex than civil rights advocates like to admit, and that yesterday's
truth may look different tomorrow.

It is the liberal objection to the five-year nationwide suspension of
literacy tests that now seems most odd. It was the Republican Attorney
General, John Mitchell, who argued that "the undereducated ghetto Negro [is] . . . today's forgotten man in voting rights legislation." The
literacy test "unfairly denies the franchise to those who have been denied educational opportunity because of inferior schooling in the North
and the South," he said. "Perhaps more importantly, it is a psychological
obstruction in the minds of many of our minority citizens."[9] And it was
John J. Conyers, Jr., a black congressman from Michigan, who responded: "Black people in the North are not being prevented from
voting because of their education."[10]

"A higher percentage of Negroes voted in South Carolina and Mississippi, where literacy tests are suspended, than in Watts or Harlem,
where literacy tests are enforced," the Attorney General pointed out.[11]
But California Representative Don Edwards, known for his unfailing
support of civil rights causes, was unmoved. Referring to Watts, the
black ghetto of Los Angeles, he said: "There are no voting problems.
The only reason for the low voting records of the residents of Watts has
to do with other elements in their background, their education, their
motivation."[12] Representative Emanuel Celler, a staunch liberal from
New York, compared the attack on literacy tests in his and other northern states to "trying to stem a flood in Mississippi by building a dam in
Idaho or Wyoming."[13] New York City's commissioner of elections said
he doubted that the literacy test had held down voting in that city,[14] and
the *New York Times* called the "flat ban on literacy tests . . . a form
of unacceptably rough justice—that because some men steal, all men
must have their hands cut off."[15] In a subsequent editorial it had this to
say: "Decidedly dubious is the inclusion in the Senate bill of a nationwide
requirement for suspension of literacy tests even where there is no
suggestion that they are applied on a discriminatory basis. Even the
original law's provision prohibiting the state to require voters to prove
literacy in English impressed us as a mistake, one that would delay

integration rather than foster it. We see even less justification for compelling the states to drop all literacy requirements."[16]

Liberal spokesmen were no more enthusiastic about bringing more northern jurisdictions under section 5 coverage. Thus, New York Mayor Lindsay's office objected strongly to having to preclear all changes in voting procedure in the Bronx, Brooklyn, and Manhattan. "The need in New York is for educative and organizational efforts to enfranchise, in fact, the hundreds of thousands of people who have the legal right to vote but do not use it," a spokesman for the mayor said. "Here in New York the problem is not one of discrimination, nor is there anything but a desire to have as many people vote as possible," he went on.[17] And the *Times*, which some years later would condemn as discriminatory the city's councilmanic district lines, unequivocally stated that "systematic discrimination against potential voters of the sort sometimes encountered in sections of the South does not exist in New York City."[18]

Even the *New York Times*, of course, is entitled to change its mind. But in the world of politics changes of the heart are hard to distinguish from accommodations to necessity. In 1970 northern liberals could still question the wisdom and justice of making northern cities the target of an act designed to deal with a southern injustice. Within five years, however, that question could not be so freely raised. Blacks had discovered the usefulness of section 5 in promoting black officeholding, and support for extending (or strengthening) the act had become a civil rights litmus test. In 1970 the *Times* could say that "systematic discrimination . . . simply does not exist in New York City," but by 1975, when the special provisions were once again due to expire and the process of renewal and revision was replayed, these had become fighting words in the community of organizations for black advancement. By then, the finding of electoral (and other) discrimination was understood to have tangible benefits—such as districts drawn to protect black candidates—and neither such newspapers as the *New York Times* nor individuals of liberal persuasion were willing to risk their liberal standing by opposing legislative initiatives supported by blacks.

Moreover, in 1970 it was still possible to support literacy tests by arguing that illiterates were ill-prepared to make informed political choices. It was argued, as well, that a national ban on literacy tests was unnecessary because the number of illiterate blacks outside the South was so small as to make the impact of such tests negligible. Thus Representative Edwards could contend that "motivation" and "other elements" in the background of ghetto blacks—not inability to pass a literacy test—were responsible for the low level of minority participation. But five years later, mention of motivation in explaining low black registration and turnout had become taboo.

Thus a mere five years after the enactment of the Voting Rights Act, when near unanimity on the need for renewal might have been expected, the White House sided with the South in making what would be the only serious effort to reduce the extraordinary federal power conferred by section 5. Moreover, when that effort failed and Senate Republicans offered a compromise, supporting arguments that soon became liberal orthodoxy fell on deaf liberal ears. It was Attorney General John Mitchell who insisted that unequal educational opportunities made literacy tests discriminatory; those who fancied themselves staunch supporters of civil rights stood firm in their conviction that "there [were] no voting problems" in the North that warranted either the nationwide ban on such tests or broader section 5 coverage. Finally, both the prohibition on literacy tests and the supplemental use of the 1968 turnout figures, offered as efforts to reduce the stigma attached to the South, in the long run strengthened the act. The amendments were thus directly contrary to the interests of the southern whites whom the Republicans had sought to placate. The white South had hoped that the preclearance requirement would in fact prove temporary, as initially promised, but that prospect became even more unlikely as the act gathered strength.

The 1970 amendments reinforced the act in two respects. Use of the 1968 figures brought scattered counties from New York to California under coverage, many of which had substantial minority populations. The more counties covered, the greater was the number of congressmen under pressure from minority constituents to oppose any attempt to weaken the statute or let the temporary provisions expire. Blacks in newly covered jurisdictions took new interest in how their congressmen voted on questions involving the act. A more national act, in short, was more entrenched. A process that the further amendments of 1975 and 1982 would greatly accelerate had begun.

The second respect in which the act was strengthened was more subtle. The fraudulent manipulation of literacy tests was known to be the chief means of black disfranchisement in the South, and at the heart of the 1965 statute was a statistical test for their misuse: turnout under 50 percent. That misuse was reliably remedied by simply eliminating the test. States and counties found by statistical inference to be using literacy tests to disfranchise blacks thus lost their traditional and constitutionally enshrined prerogative to bar illiterates from the polls. Moreover, to prevent the substitution of any new method of disfranchisement, in those same jurisdictions federal approval was required for all proposed changes in electoral procedure.

With literacy tests banned *everywhere*, however, clearly the statistical formula no longer served to target that minority of states and counties in which the tests were used for discriminatory ends. Yet the statistical trigger had a continuing purpose: selecting additional jurisdictions that would henceforth be required to preclear all proposed changes in their method of voting, as well as those to which federal examiners and observers could be sent.

Literacy tests were thus everywhere suspended, but the preclearance provision (which had been included only to reinforce the initially selective suspension of the tests) was not likewise everywhere made applicable. The consequence of this use of the statistical trigger *solely* to establish section 5 coverage was to sever irrevocably the originally intimate connection between suspension and preclearance—to further that separation between two inseparable provisions that the 1969 *Allen* decision had already begun. Thus not only the Court but Congress as well remade section 5, giving the provision an independent validity that permitted its emergence as an instrument to promote the election of blacks to public office. This new use of section 5 both increased the usefulness of the act to blacks in already covered jurisdictions and alerted other groups in other states to its benefits. And the additional protection these groups were to win in 1975 again broadened the geographic scope of the legislation, further decreasing the likelihood that the preclearance and other temporary provisions would soon be allowed to expire. In 1970 the nationwide ban on literacy tests had been a concession to the wounded sensibilities of the white South; within a few years it was plain that southern whites, who had hoped to see a quick end to preclearance, had lost more than they gained.

The 1970 amendments, then, reinforced the act in unintended and unforeseen ways. Yet what the statute gained in strength, it lost in coherence. In 1965 the act had had one aim—enfranchisement of southern blacks—and every part fit the overall design. No provisions were extraneous; none were superfluous. But after 1970 the aim was confused and the construction no longer clean. And once the outlines of the original act had been partially obscured, further distortions were less apparent.[19]

In 1965 those who wrote the Voting Rights Act knew which states they wanted to cover and designed a test to single them out. Few jurisdictions outside the South were caught in the federal net, and few offenders in the South eluded it. True, some southern counties that were in fact registering blacks were caught, while those in eastern Texas with poor records of black enfranchisement were not. But if the fit was not perfect, it was extraordinarily close.

Applying the benchmark of 50-percent turnout to the 1968 figures, however, had a very different result: an assorted collection of counties with no history of black disfranchisement were brought under coverage. None of these counties were in the South, and no other evidence suggested that these were jurisdictions in which minority voters were at a distinctive disadvantage. The evidence, in fact, pointed in quite another direction. For example, under the revised act, three counties in New York City were covered. But turnout for the 1968 presidential election had been low across the nation, and participation in New York, reflecting the national trend, had dropped slightly to just under the determining 50-percent mark. This did not mean that the city had changed; the doors of political opportunity had not suddenly been closed to blacks and Puerto Ricans. Rather, faced with a choice between Nixon and Humphrey, a few more New Yorkers than before had stayed home.

The ban on literacy tests was not likely to change the level of minority electoral opportunity in New York and other such counties. In 1965 those who wrote the legislation designed the statistical trigger to bring under coverage states known to have *intentionally* barred blacks from the polls. It was reasonable to assume that those states, deprived of the opportunity to use literacy tests for purposes of disfranchisement, would deliberately search for other means to accomplish that same end. But there was no cause to suspect similarly those places that had been brought under coverage in 1970, all of which were outside the South and none of which had a record of official hostility to black political participation.

If, indeed, there were northern counties in which the extraordinary requirement of preclearance was required, some new test was needed to identify them. The discovery that a jurisdiction used a literacy test and that voter participation had dropped a few points in the last presidential election was not revealing. And if a new trigger were to be devised, those at the drawing boards would have to proceed as the framers of the original legislation had: by first selecting those counties likely to adjust electoral procedure to keep black officeholding down, and then ascertaining the characteristics they had in common. Perhaps a statistical measure would again allow a shortcut to avoid the laborious judicial process that the identification of discriminatory communities otherwise required, but the level of voter registration and turnout was not likely to be that measure.

As a consequence of the use of the 1968 figures, without evidence of distinctive need, the most stringent remedies contained in the act thus came into play in counties scattered across the nation but outside the South. These were, in general, extraordinary remedies, it will be recalled, designed to meet an extraordinary need. The act was originally intended to deal with the distinctive and shocking problem of black disfranchisement in the South; the contrast implicitly made was precisely between places like New York and Neshoba County, Mississippi, where in the summer of 1964 three civil rights workers were murdered for their participation in a black voter registration drive. Yet in 1970 three New York City boroughs and Neshoba County came to be equally restricted in their freedom to structure their own electoral arrangements. The preclearance provision had come to have a validity independent of the proven presence of wrongs requiring it. And the consequence was, in ways unrecognized at the time, to undermine the legitimacy of the act itself. In 1966, well before the provision acquired its subsequently greatly enlarged meaning, the Supreme Court had made very clear the constitutional irregularity of the remedies, justified by the magnitude of the need. Had the original act in 1965 been less precise in its aim, had it upset the normal balance in federal-state relations in both North and South, it would not have stood up to constitutional scrutiny.

It can be argued that the statutory net continued to catch only culpable jurisdictions because the law allowed those counties that had not actually used literacy tests for discriminatory ends to "bail out." Indeed, New York did briefly extricate itself from coverage by establishing its racial neutrality before a three-judge panel of the D.C. district court. But coverage was reinstated on the basis of another lawsuit arguing that the use of English ballots in a city with a large Puerto Rican population constituted, in effect, a discriminatory literacy test. Had the city's failure to provide election materials in Spanish truly disfranchised minority voters?[20]

Ironically, it was probably the political strength of New York's minority community that prevented the city from permanently bailing out of the act. Both blacks and Hispanics had long participated in the city's political process, and numerous minority organizations were ready and able to fight for the benefits that the Voting Rights Act conferred. Hispanics succeeded in reinstating coverage by equating a fraudulent literacy test that acted as an outright bar to black suffrage in the Jim Crow South with ballots printed in English in a city with a large Hispanic population. That Congress was later to accept this equation illustrates the basic point: the amendments of 1970 furthered the process of change that slowly but effectively obscured the original purpose of the act. Alterations made to serve the political ends of Republicans pursuing a southern strategy left the act vulnerable to civil rights groups and their Department of Justice allies with an agenda of their own.

I have focused on three New York counties as the most blatant example of jurisdictions that came under coverage in 1970 but were clearly outside the sphere of congressional concern five years earlier. New York had originally been the implicit standard against which the racism of southern politics was judged. It was with *distinctive* regional problems, not nationwide ones, that the act was designed to deal; hence its (never explicitly acknowledged) southern focus.

During congressional hearings in 1969, Senator Sam Ervin had complained that 1.3 percentage points in voter turnout had saved New York County (Manhattan) from coverage in 1965, while, for want of three-tenths of 1 percent, Hyde County, North Carolina, had been "condemned."[21] (In Hyde County 49.7 percent of the voting-age population had turned out to vote in 1964; the figure for Manhattan was 51.3 percent.) Yet the percentage mark was not arbitrary: those who wrote the legislation knew the places they wanted covered, and New York was not among them. The statistical test was carefully designed to meet their ends. But the coverage of New York and other exclusively non-southern jurisdictions in 1970 injected precisely that element of arbitrariness into the act that Senator Ervin had erroneously found before. To blur the difference between protection for minorities in localities with well-documented histories of blatant Fifteenth Amendment violations, on the one hand, and protection where the barriers to political equality were either linguistic or socioeconomic, on the other, was to destroy the clean lines and logical construction of the act. Thus the propriety of further change—whether by Congress, the courts, or the Department of Justice—became increasingly hard to judge; the acquired legitimacy of one change obscured the questionable legitimacy of another. Once minorities in New York qualified for the extraordinary benefits of the Voting Rights Act, there was no logical place to stop—if it applied to New York, then why not Chicago? The 1970 amendments pointed toward the changes of 1975 and 1982, when the act was revised, first, to extend even further the geographic reach of section 5 protection, and then to give black and Hispanic voters more leverage in challenging at-large and other methods of voting across the nation.

When the national ban on literacy tests and the use of 1968 turnout figures were first proposed, many liberals objected. It was not that they failed to appreciate better Fifteenth Amendment protection, nor that they automatically rejected amendments sponsored by nonliberal forces. Rather, they viewed the act as solely concerned with southern black enfranchisement, and believed that states without a record of electoral discrimination should be allowed to insist on a literate electorate and to govern their own electoral affairs. Nineteen hundred and seventy, however, was the last year in which anyone argued that Fifteenth Amendment violations in the South were the sole problem that the Voting Rights Act should attack.

# THREE

# The Mexican-American Connection

Congressional extensions and revisions of the Voting Rights Act reversed the old adage: the more things appeared to stay the same, the more they changed. This was true not just for the seemingly minor amendments of 1970. The special provisions were once again due to expire in 1975, and a superficial reading of that year's deliberations would find little that was new. Every witness at the congressional hearings, for instance, spoke of continuing minority disfranchisement, and of the consequent need for further protection. The rhetoric was deceptive, however; the facade of continuity masked new meanings, new commitments, and new demands.

The framers of the Voting Rights Act in 1965 saw section 4 as the pivotal provision, with section 5 as mere reinforcement. It was a view with a short life. The Supreme Court's 1969 decision in *Allen v. Board of Elections* gave preclearance unanticipated importance. Yet if section 5 had emerged as a "revolutionary innovation in American government," as Justice Harlan charged, it was not depicted as such by witnesses urging its renewal in congressional hearings later that same year. In 1969 even southern critics kept to the old terrain, seemingly unaware that they had new ground on which to stand.

By 1975, however, the importance of section 5 was evident. Arthur Flemming, the chairman of the United States Commission on Civil Rights, described the preclearance provision as the "centerpiece of the statute."[1] Likewise, civil rights attorney Frank Parker referred to section 5 as "possibly . . . the most effective provision ever enacted by

Congress for blocking and deterring racial discrimination affecting the right to vote."[2]

Parker's statement was an eloquent tribute to the success of the act. Ten years earlier most southern blacks could not even register to vote, and it was section 4, banning literacy tests where their use was suspect, that had solved the primary problem. By 1971–1972 the spread between black and white registration was down to 2.8 percent in Georgia, 9.4 percent in Mississippi, 3.2 percent in South Carolina, and 7.2 percent in Virginia.[3] These were extraordinary figures, given not only the recent and prolonged history of black disfranchisement but the disparity between black and white income and educational levels. By 1975 J. Stanley Pottinger, assistant attorney general for civil rights in the Department of Justice, could assure the House Subcommittee on Civil and Constitutional Rights that "enforcement of §5 is the highest priority of the Voting Section."[4] Pottinger's staff could concentrate on reviewing submissions for preclearance only because rudimentary access was largely a problem of the past.

The switch in focus from section 4 to section 5 was perhaps encouraged as well by a shift in perspective. By 1975 most civil rights advocates, both in and out of government, were dismissing traditional liberal goals as inadequate, regarding opportunity without results as an empty promise. The freedom to enter any restaurant or to register and vote, in their view, secured formal—but not substantive—equality. In the view of these civil rights spokesmen, section 4 was thus to voting what *Brown v. Board of Education* had been to schooling. Both had sought to increase access, yet access per se had assured neither the racially balanced classroom nor an "effective" vote—one that brought minorities into office. And an effective vote was what section 5, as it had evolved, seemed to promise.

The new and now obvious importance of section 5 was officially acknowledged by the Justice Department two years after the *Allen* decision. In September 1971 the department issued regulations to guide jurisdictions in submitting changes in electoral procedure for federal approval.[5] The Supreme Court's 1969 decision—reinforced by others that made clear the long reach of section 5—had laid the groundwork.[6] The success of section 4 in spurring black registration, and the shift in perspective among liberals on civil rights questions in general, had heightened the importance of those judicial rulings. But only with the announcement of the "Procedures for the Administration of Section 5" did the process of enforcing the preclearance provision truly begin. In 1970 only 255 voting changes were submitted to the Attorney General; by 1975 the figure had risen to 2,078.[7]

This was the setting in which the 1975 renewal and revision of the Voting Rights Act took place. The 1970 amendments had strengthened and expanded the original law, but the discovery and maturation of section 5 shaped the immediate politics of extension. What minorities demanded in the way of change, and the response of Congress, can only be understood within the context of an already altered act.

Though the act had been altered, the rhetoric remained unchanged, I have suggested. In the congressional hearings that began in February 1975, both witnesses and members of Congress spoke of persistent disfranchisement. They offered, however, few examples of hostile registrars and purged voting rolls, but referred instead to the "disfranchising" effect of at-large voting and districting plans that fragmented minority voting strength.

"Beatings and gerrymanderings," Senator Tunney said, both "keep people from registering and voting."[8] Clearly, the right to vote had been redefined. Tunney had drawn a parallel between blacks denied access to the polls by the use of violence and blacks voting in districts that fragmented black voting strength—blacks without a majority-black district in which to cast their ballots. The equation was not his alone; nor was it applied solely to redistricting. Civil rights attorney Frank Parker likened the results of election-related violence in Mississippi in 1964 to those that flowed from the retention of an at-large electoral system in the state capital ten years later. "Where newly enfranchised black voters *may* be continually outvoted by white voting majorities in at-large districts, the effect . . . is the *same* as continuing to prevent blacks from voting at all," he said.[9] Arthur Flemming of the U.S. Commission on Civil Rights agreed: "A jurisdiction may seem to conform to the letter of the law by permitting minority registration and voting but *rob* that participation of its meaning by structuring the system against minority political victories." And looking back to the bloody days of Selma, Alabama, he saw disfranchisement then as only more "spectacular" than that which still occurred in 1975.[10]

The goal of the act, in the view of such spokesmen, had not altered; the demand was simply for its more complete attainment. Not enfranchisement, but "full" enfranchisement. Not participation, but "meaningful" participation.[11] In claiming that the aim of the statute remained unchanged, these advocates were doing more than expressing their commitment to Fifteenth Amendment rights; they were also building the case for renewing the special provisions and further strengthening the act by extending its geographic reach.

Few barriers to registration and voting remained. Traditional arguments for renewing the special provisions, arguments that focused on basic questions of access, would thus have carried little weight. But if the right to vote was nevertheless still the issue, if there was no distinction between votes and votes that "counted" (basic enfranchisement encompassing both), then those who advocated continuing action to ensure the former logically had to press for measures to secure the latter. And on that basis the case for renewal could be built.

There was a further point. Without the conflation of opportunity and result, the fact of massive black enfranchisement posed an awkward problem. The goal of opportunity, as initially conceived, had clearly been met. But the continued references to disfranchisement, to blacks without a vote, to the allegedly indistinguishable effects of beatings and gerrymanderings, allowed civil rights advocates to ignore the fact that recent progress had been dramatic. Clarence Mitchell, director of the Washington Bureau of the NAACP, argued that progress should never be grounds for letting protective legislation die. Criminal statutes, he noted, are not repealed when the murder rate goes down.[12] The analogy was poor. The Voting Rights Act could have been better compared to a curfew imposed in the wake òf a riot—an emergency measure taken with the expectation that it would be lifted as soon as conditions allowed. Criminal statutes, on the other hand, are permanent, but affect only those who commit a crime. They impose no burden on the innocent, and thus improved conditions (a lower murder rate, for instance) offer no argument for their repeal.

Most spokesmen for civil rights groups argued not that the progress made was irrelevant, but that it was negligible. And if at-large voting is taken to be tantamount to disfranchisement, then a record of success can indeed be read as one of failure. That is, progress as initially conceived might be unmistakable, but redefined to mean representation by black officeholders, it disappears. Opening the Senate hearings, Birch Bayh referred to the gains as "more apparent than real." Of the 191 elected blacks in Mississippi, he pointed out, most resided in heavily black counties or districts. Moreover, throughout the South there remained a "wide discrepancy between the number of blacks of voting age and their representation as officeholders."[13] The same notes were struck in both House and Senate by almost every witness allied with the civil rights cause; the hearings were filled with statistics attesting to the slim success of blacks at the polls. Only "the beginning of significant changes in political life in the covered Southern jurisdictions" had been made, the House Judiciary Committee concluded in its final report; progress had been "spotty and modest."[14] "Now the blacks register and vote, even in great numbers, *but it doesn't make any difference,*" one civil rights attorney argued before the subcommittee.[15] Clearly, if things were no better, then the need for protection was no less.

Indeed, the widespread problem of disfranchisement through "dilution" suggested both the inadequacy of existing relief and the necessity of even greater federal protection. That is, the new definition of disfranchisement not only committed Congress to renewing the special provisions, but invited the extension of protection to new groups in new jurisdictions—jurisdictions without a history of Fifteenth Amendment violations comparable to that of Mississippi, Alabama, and other initially covered states. The argument that blacks remained without a meaningful vote as long as their numbers in office were disproportionately low clearly applied to Hispanic and perhaps other groups as well. A right to representation was one that other minorities with free access to the polls but relatively few members in office could likewise claim.

In 1970 the act was expanded as an inadvertent result of efforts by northern Republicans to woo the South by making the legislation less regional in its application. But both the judicial decisions (beginning with *Allen*) and the later statutory revisions, I am suggesting, contain a different tale: the reinforcement and geographic extension of federal power advocated by civil rights groups and justified by the alleged appearance of new problems of disfranchisement that required both old and new solutions. The acquisition of the ballot, it was said, had exposed the inadequacy of the ballot alone. Registration sites and polling places might be open to all, but the impact of that access could be deliberately limited by new districting plans and other changes in the method of voting. The obvious sign of progress, black registration, was thus deceptive, and the need for further protection manifest. Moreover, the protection of blacks exposed the special needs of other groups as well. From this perspective, the extensions and alterations in the act—in the hands of Congress and the courts—were simply a response to the new, but no less meritorious, demands.

The argument was compelling in part because it was partly true: without continuing protection against actions such as that taken by Mississippi in 1966, the value of the vote for blacks would unquestionably have been severely diminished. Moreover, the disproportionately low number of southern blacks in office was a legitimate source of concern. Against a backdrop of historic disfranchisement, access to the polling booth alone did not everywhere open the doors to black political opportunity. Finally, although blacks had suffered a distinctive kind of oppression, other groups, most notably Mexican-Americans, had arguably shared aspects of that same experience. But the case, as framed, obscured the real demand: that the courts and Congress be willing to attack at-large voting, districting plans, and other aspects of the electoral environment with the same extraordinary force that they had used against outright denials of the right to vote, whenever their use might adversely affect the electoral prospects of minority candidates.

Unquestionably, multimember districts, at-large voting, and districting plans that fragment minority voting strength decrease the likelihood of minority officeholding. Divide a majority-white city into wards, create some heavily black or Hispanic districts, and the election of minorities to office will usually be assured. In such districts, black and Hispanic candidates will have been largely protected from white competition; often, in fact, no white will even bother to run. But if all candidates must campaign at large, every minority contestant will face white opposition; there will be no "safe" minority seats. Thus, provided the lines are drawn to create black and Hispanic wards, single-member districts promote minority officeholding.

Does ward voting thereby enhance minority representation? Officeholding and representation are different questions. Where white candidates (as well as black and Hispanic) actively seek minority votes and those votes often influence the outcome of every electoral contest, at-large elections may provide fewer seats but more influence—and by that token more representation.[16]

The advocates of renewal and amendment in 1975, however, had a simpler view. These civil rights spokesmen believed that the right to vote included the right to representation; that minority representation could be measured by the number of minority officeholders; that justice demanded a national commitment to protecting black candidates from white competition; and that black ballots were meaningless in the absence of black electoral success. Moreover, they applied these principles to Hispanics and certain other groups as well. And with a minimum of debate and little understanding, Congress was persuaded to go along.

I argued in Chapter 2 that, as the emergency subsided, emergency powers paradoxically expanded. Congressional receptivity in 1975 suggests a further paradox: the more potent the legislation became, the fewer were the objections raised. As the scope of the act was enlarged, the ranks of its opponents thinned. The meaning of section 5 had been radically transformed, yet, in the 1975 congressional debate on renewal, the voice of critics could scarcely be heard. No proposals to stop the encroachment of federal power over local electoral affairs were seriously entertained. Almost no one opposed extending the preclearance and other special provisions, witnesses at the hearings could happily claim. Addition, not subtraction, was the question: how much additional protection should Congress provide?

The argument that disfranchisement remained a serious and persistent problem was pertinent primarily to the question of renewal. Witnesses at the 1975 hearings meticulously built the case for further section 5 coverage. In fact, however, renewal was a foregone conclusion; the only contentious issue was the extension of coverage to new groups in new areas. Gerald Ford, who assumed the presidency following Nixon's resignation in August 1974, was eager to avoid a replay of the conflicts of 1969–1970 and met with the Congressional Black Caucus within a month of taking office. In November the Attorney General announced his support for a five-year renewal of the act without major revisions. On January 14, 1975, Martin Luther King's birthday, Ford publicly embraced this same position.[17] Congress, of course, would have the final say, but in the absence of signals from the President, Republican resistance to extension was not likely to be strong. Civil rights groups apparently were content with a straight renewal of the act.

Except, that is, for groups representing Mexican-Americans. The growing importance of section 5 had mobilized the Mexican-American Legal Defense and Education Fund (MALDEF) to demand for its constituency the same extraordinary protection accorded blacks. Cities in Mississippi could initiate no district plan, annex no territory, move no polling place without federal approval. San Antonio, Texas, however, could freely alter its municipal boundaries (with a consequent change in the city's ethnic balance) without abandoning its at-large method of voting. Most important, the redistricting that occurred in Texas following each decennial census was not subject to federal scrutiny.

Yet providing protection for southwest Hispanics posed a number of problems. Black and other non-Hispanic groups belonging to the Leadership Conference on Civil Rights (an umbrella lobbying organization that included many largely white groups) were initially far from enthusiastic, fearing that new demands would jeopardize old protection.[18] Statutory amendments might ignite the flame of congressional opposition, and a fire, once begun, might consume the entire act.

The tension between blacks and Mexican-Americans over coverage in the Southwest erupted into "an awful political fight," one participant recalls. "I remember Clarence Mitchell [director of the Washington Bureau of the NAACP] pointing his finger [at representatives for MALDEF] and saying, you want to take us back to the dark days of 1963, with lynchings in Mississippi."[19] Mitchell and others feared both adverse congressional response and second thoughts on the part of the administration. Trying to expand the protection might serve only to remind conservatives of how much they already disliked the legislation. Why open a Pandora's box?

Yet persuading the Leadership Conference on Civil Rights was essential. If Mexican-Americans could not even convince hard-core civil rights enthusiasts of the merits of their case, they had no hope. Salvation came through the intervention of Joseph L. Rauh, Jr., counsel for the Leadership Conference, vice-president of Americans for Democratic Action, and a long-time civil rights warrior. "He gave us credibility with the rest of the civil rights lobby in Washington," one member of MALDEF's team later recalled. "He was the first one to breach that wall of consensus, and say, 'Look, I'm sorry, these people have got problems too, and we've got to do the right thing, and I'm going to put my credibility on the line for the Mexican-Americans' . . . He just bull-dogged it, and didn't let go, until he had broken down that wall of resistance."[20] By March 1975, when hearings began in the House, black organizations had agreed to lobby for the Hispanic cause.

Black opposition, however, was only one of several problems that MALDEF faced in bringing California, Texas, and other southwestern states under the aegis of the act's special provisions. Mexican-Americans were most anxious to have Texas covered, yet the state had never had a literacy test. In other words, the chief means used to disfranchise blacks in the South had never been employed in Texas. The presence of a literacy test had been an essential component in the trigger for coverage designed in 1965; turnout figures were included only as a means of identifying the fraudulent use of such a test. The link between Fifteenth Amendment violations, low turnout, and a literacy test was viewed as well established, while that between low turnout and disfranchisement alone was seen as speculative. The framers of the Voting Rights Act understood that a depressed level of political partici- pation could have many causes; some segments of the white population, after all, rarely voted. In the absence of a literacy test, a device that was unquestionably manipulated to screen registrants by race, black or His- panic disfranchisement could not be inferred. To extend coverage to Mexican-Americans in Texas thus required different assumptions and different statutory language.

There was the additional problem of whether Mexican-Americans were in fact a racial group. The Fifteenth Amendment rights secured by the statute protected against denial or abridgment of the right to vote only on account of "race or color." If Mexican-Americans were white, they were ineligible for special protection. In the congressional hearings in the spring of 1975, the Justice Department brushed the problem aside. In implementing the act in already covered jurisdictions, its memorandum stated, "the practice . . . has been to treat Indians, Puerto Ricans, and Mexican-Americans as racial groups." In 1921 the popula- tion of Mexico had been 10.3 percent white, 29.2 percent Indian, and 60.5 percent Mestizo. Since the present breakdown was roughly the same, and since the vast majority of Mexican-Americans were either part Indian or part black, the memorandum maintained that it could justly be said that they were racially distinct.[21] These arguments hardly settled the issue. With the single exception of 1930, the Census Bureau had historically classified Mexican-Americans as white, and substantial num- bers of Hispanics continued to think of themselves as white.

In solving this cluster of difficulties, Congress again substantially al- tered the act. It simply skirted the problem of having to agree officially to designate Mexican-Americans members of a "race." A new term was found: "language minority." And because the Fifteenth Amendment could not be stretched to protect against disfranchisement on account of language, the base of the act was broadened to include the Fourteenth as well.

But how would states that did not use a "test or device" to screen potential registrants come under coverage? That problem was solved by redefining such a test—by equating the provision of ballots or other voting materials in English alone with the fraudulent southern literacy test used to bar blacks from the polls.[22] Thus the act was amended to apply to states or counties that met the traditional low turnout test, and in which, in addition, elections were conducted only in English and more than 5 percent of the voting-age citizenry were members of a single "language minority" group. The entire states of Texas, Arizona, and Alaska, as well as scattered counties in California, Colorado, Florida, New Mexico, Oklahoma, and South Dakota, among others, were henceforth required to submit for federal review annexations, redistricting, and all other changes in electoral procedure.

The list of covered jurisdictions would have been considerably longer had not the term "language minority" been carefully defined. The 1965 statute had mentioned no group explicitly, although the disfranchisement of blacks was the obvious concern. The act gave life to the clear constitutional command that the franchise was not to be restricted by virtue of the irrelevant, ascribed characteristic of race. In 1975 an attempt was made to state an analogous principle: there must be no denial or abridgement of the right to vote on account of language. But lest that principle be interpreted too literally—lest anyone think that Italians or French, in sufficient concentrations, were "language minorities" and eligible for protection—four groups were specifically named: Asian Americans, Alaskan Natives, American Indians, and persons of Spanish heritage. Why these four groups and no others? Or why not just Mexican-Americans? The amended act provided extensive federal protection for certain designated groups whose distinctive characteristics were never explained.

Other important changes were made in 1975: the national ban on literacy tests was made permanent, and the trigger was once again updated to include the turnout figures for November 1972. The only uncovered states and counties affected by this reliance on 1972 participation figures, however, were those that provided no bilingual ballots for a designated minority language group with the requisite population concentration. There were no jurisdictions employing traditional literacy tests, since they had been banned nationwide in 1970.

Finally, an altogether new form of protection was provided. Bilingual election materials were required in every state or county that met the criteria of the new trigger: English-only ballots and a language minority concentration in the context of low voter turnout. Bilingual ballots and other material were also obligatory in every county (whatever the level of electoral participation) where the minority-language citizens had an illiteracy rate higher than the national average. Illiteracy was defined as "failure to complete the fifth primary grade."

The Voting Rights Act was universally acknowledged to be, as black congresswoman Barbara Jordan put it, "very, very strong medicine."[23] As one assistant attorney general remarked, it entailed "a substantial departure from ordinary concepts of our federal system."[24] In once again extending the act in 1975, Congress sanctioned that "substantial departure" on an ongoing basis, stamping with approval actions such as that taken against Charleston, South Carolina, in 1974. Over the previous decade the city had annexed twenty-five outlying areas, reducing the black population by 2 percent. When submitted to the Justice Department for preclearance, these annexations were found to be discriminatory in impact, and the city was forced to replace its at-large method of voting with single-member districts. The drop in black population from 47 to 45 percent thus removed the traditional prerogative of the local community to structure elections to meet local demands.[25]

By 1975 in Charleston four out of every ten voters were black. In the covered jurisdictions of the South as a whole, the figure was one out of four.[26] In this context of growing black political power, was an extension of the preclearance provision—permitting the Justice Department and the D.C. district court to continue to take such aggressive action to facilitate black officeholding—really warranted? And were revisions of the act that imposed federal power upon new areas, gave protection to new groups without the same experience of disfranchisement, and even further reduced the rights of states and their political subdivisions to choose their method of voting also appropriate?

Congress paid only perfunctory attention to the question of renewal, I have already suggested. In part, its willingness to extend and strengthen section 5 and other special provisions reflected a legitimate concern with the level of black political integration, and a heightened awareness of the illegitimate uses to which a state's power to redistrict and institute other electoral changes could be put. But other factors played a role, I have argued. Civil rights spokesmen skillfully minimized the revolution in southern black politics, conflated the concepts of dilution and disfranchisement, and convinced Congress that the right to vote remained massively denied.

The question of revision was a somewhat separate one. Was the extension of coverage to Texas and elsewhere justified? Mexican-Americans were the central concern of those who pushed for the 1975 amendments, and the search for evidence of Mexican-American disfranchisement began well before the start of the congressional hearings on the proposed amendments. One member of the MALDEF team remembers "being on the phone to Texas with members of the Chicano community, saying, find . . . a Fannie Lou Hamer, find . . . a really bad little county with ten little stories, find . . . someone who's convincing to come up here and testify before Congress . . . to convince the Congress and the administration . . . to . . . change the rules of the game so that Texas will get covered."[27]

Both the administration and a majority in Congress did need to be convinced, but the Democrats controlling the committee that held the hearings were early converts to MALDEF's cause. Representatives of Hispanic and black organizations thus worked hand in hand with the committee staff to establish a persuasive record. Witnesses were carefully selected on the basis of their established views. And when, in spite of careful selection and preparation, they failed to cover the proper points, the committee chairman was quick to step in as guide.

"I am anxious to get a bill through the Senate," Senator Tunney told Vilma S. Martinez, president and general counsel of MALDEF. "I am going to be quoting from your testimony and others' testimony on the Senate floor, so that is why I am giving you the opportunity to make the kind of statements that you feel ought to be used."[28] The statements that Martinez thought ought to be used, however, differed from those Tunney had in mind. But the Senator was not easily defeated. "We had to file a lawsuit in Texas challenging the statute . . . which prohibited giving assistance to a non-English-speaking voter," Martinez testified. To which Tunney replied, "As I understand the testimony that we have had today, the main areas of discrimination have *not* been the fact of the elections being held in English, but the fact that you have had the multimember districts, the . . . gerrymandering." And Martinez responded, "As I was trying to say earlier, language is evidence of discrimination."[29] If witnesses wandered—if they focused on a state's resistance to providing assistance for the non-English-speaking voter rather than on such obstacles as at-large voting—Tunney made the necessary points himself. The congressional record was not left to chance.

If the hearings were a staged event, the performance was less than perfect. "We were able to produce those [needed] horror stories," a MALDEF representative would later say. "But not many of them . . . We did it really by the skin of our teeth."[30] Those who wrote the original legislation in 1965 had had a rich source upon which to draw—the extensive litigation experience of the Justice Department. But there were no equivalent suits against Texas registrars and other officials. As Joseph Rauh, counsel for the Leadership Council on Civil Rights, bluntly put it, "You do not have the same situation . . . the murders, the awful things that happened to blacks."[31] A U.S. Civil Rights Commission staff memorandum made the same point: "Statistics on minority registration and voting and the election of minorities to office do not paint the shocking picture that, for example, 1965 statistics on Mississippi did."[32]

In the congressional hearings, advocates of an amended act thus had little to rely on beyond those phone calls to Texas that the MALDEF spokesman had recalled and statements from ethnic activists such as Martinez. Assistant Attorney General J. Stanley Pottinger justifiably voiced skepticism in testifying before the House subcommittee: "If we are put to the task of supporting with the same degree of statistical and anecdotal information as was existing in the past two enactments of the Civil Rights Act, the same kind of support here . . . we do not yet have that," he said.[33] Speaking before the Senate subcommittee six weeks later, he declared:

> In my testimony before the House Subcommittee, I suggested that if a strong case were made of widespread deprivations of the right to vote of non-English-speaking persons . . . expansion of the special provisions of the act might be warranted . . . Since that time, considerable testimony had been presented to this subcommittee and to the House subcommittee . . . In light of the other remedies available and in light of the stringent nature of the special provisions, the Department of Justice has concluded that the evidence does not require expansion based on the record currently before us. *In other words, that record is not compelling.*[34]

Of what did that allegedly inadequate record consist? By the traditional measures of restricted access to the ballot, the evidence of Mexican-American disfranchisement was certainly thin. No registrars asked potential Mexican-American registrants to interpret obscure passages from the state constitution. No legacy of disfranchisement comparable to that experienced by southern blacks inhibited political participation. Unlike blacks, Mexican-Americans had never been barred from casting their ballots in Democratic primaries; in fact, at least in southern Texas, their votes had become an important source of Democratic power by the late nineteenth century.[35]

Witnesses at the 1975 hearings argued, however, that economic pressure often kept Mexican-Americans from becoming politically active.[36] Thus it was reported that in Frio County, Texas, a Mexican-American who engaged in political organizing had lost his regular job; whites had boycotted the business of a Mexican-American candidate; a white loan officer at a local bank had visited Mexican-American clients to solicit support for his candidacy, and so forth. One witness described an instance of paper ballots being filled out at open tables, but did not specify whether that had been an isolated event. Another witness told of a challenge (again in Frio County) by whites to Mexican-American election victories, whereupon ballot boxes were opened, signed stubs matched with ballots, and voters for Mexican-American candidates identified, thus facilitating economic reprisals against them.

In addition, Mexican-Americans were said to have been discouraged from voting by actions such as a reluctance to hand out registration cards to volunteers assisting others to register; a refusal to appoint deputy registrars; the demand that Mexican-American registrants furnish street addresses; the location of the town's sole polling place in a white neighborhood; the relocation of polling places with little notice; the harassment of campaign workers for La Raza Unida (a militant party); and the visible display of guns by law-enforcement officers at several predominantly Mexican-American polling places.

This roster, which might seem convincing, is somewhat deceptive. Many of the charges came from a handful of witnesses reporting on very few Texas counties: Frio, Uvalde, and La Salle, most notably. These counties were just to the south and west of San Antonio; others referred to were also mostly in the middle of the state, where the Mexican-American population was substantial but whites were still a majority. "What we found," one lobbyist later frankly admitted, "we portrayed . . . as a giant, state-wide pattern, which it really wasn't."[37] The pattern was not characteristic, in fact, of those counties along the Mexican border with the greatest Hispanic concentration; there, Hispanics held a substantial proportion of all public offices. In fact, in the thirteen counties in Texas with the largest Mexican-American concentrations, with one exception either three or all four county commissioners were Hispanic.[38]

This situation was in glaring contrast with the Deep South prior to the Voting Rights Act, where the existence of large black populations had not forced white racists to share power with blacks. In fact, it was precisely in the areas of greatest black concentration that white supremacy thrived most.

Another set of charges clearly pertained to the whole state. The provision of English-only election materials, it was said, inhibited the political participation of a language minority group whose educational opportunities had been inferior to those of whites. In other ways, as well, Texas failed to encourage registration and voting on the part of Mexican-Americans. But the state had already taken steps to remedy a number of the problems identified: for instance, bills had been introduced in the legislature to provide bilingual election materials, to protect registered voters from the removal of their names from the rolls, and to increase the number of hours in which to vote.[39] More important, neither these state-wide problems nor those confined to scattered counties actually kept Hispanics from the polls. The inconvenient location of a polling place, the presence on election day of armed police, the demand for more evidence of residence from Hispanics than from whites, even the provision of English-only ballots—none of these barred Mexican-Americans from political participation. Only economic harassment was sufficient to keep Mexican-Americans home on election day, and the evidence of such harassment was from only one county. In any case, the Voting Rights Act could neither stop white boycotts nor secure jobs for Mexican-Americans laid off because of their political activity.

The hearings thus produced little evidence of basic disfranchisement. A number of problems involving access were apparently being resolved; most forms of harassment (while serious) did not actually stop Mexican-Americans from voting; and those that did were beyond the reach of the Voting Rights Act. Moreover, there was almost no discussion of discrimination involving any group other than the Mexican-Americans. Nevertheless, a majority on the House Judiciary Committee found the case for extending protection to "language" minorities "overwhelming," a judgment in which their Senate colleagues concurred.[40] "Weighing the evidence before it on the voting problems encountered by language minority citizens, the Committee acted to expand the protections of the Voting Rights Act to insure their free access to the franchise," the Senate report announced. "In 7 days of hearings and testimony from 29 witnesses, the Subcommittee [had] documented a systematic pattern of voting discrimination and exclusion against minority group citizens who are from environments in which the dominant language is other than English."[41] Buried in the House report, however, was the real point. The "central problem documented," it said, "is that of dilution of the vote—arrangements by which the votes of minority electors are made to count less than the votes of the majority."[42]

This, then, was the main concern: electoral arrangements that gave minority voters "unequal" electoral power. At-large voting, annexations, districting plans that fragmented Hispanic voting strength, majority-vote requirements, numbered posts, and other procedural rules that were said to lessen the likelihood that Mexican-Americans would gain office—these were the true grievance. In stating this, however, witnesses at the hearings, together with their congressional friends, confused two issues: on the one hand, the widespread, well-established use of at-large elections in Texas, and, on the other, annexations, redistricting, and newly introduced at-large voting. "The at-large structure, with accompanying variations of the majority run-off, numbered place system, is used extensively among the 40 largest cities in Texas. And under state statute, the countless school districts in Texas elect at-large," the House Judiciary Committee reported in May 1975.[43] As those in Congress should have known, however, such voting would rarely be vulnerable to attack under the preclearance provision; longstanding at-large systems are subject to federal review only if a city chooses to annex a suburban area. When an annexation adds more whites than minorities to a city, and consequently reduces minority voting strength, single-member districts must be drawn to "fairly reflect" the minority population. The city must compensate minorities for their loss in electoral power by abandoning its at-large elections.[44] A municipality that does not alter its boundaries remains free to run all candidates city-wide—unless that system is successfully challenged on constitutional grounds.[45] The extension of section 5 coverage to Texas would thus affect the use of at-large voting only marginally; only annexations would trigger federal review of at-large schemes established prior to November 1964. But the mandatory preclearance of all districting plans—whether for local, state, or national office—would undoubtedly alter the level of Hispanic officeholding. The number of Mexican-Americans in office was disproportionately low in relation to the Mexican-American population (just how low is a difficult question to answer, and one to which I shall return). With districting plans drawn under the watchful eye of the Justice Department, the number of "safe" minority seats was bound to rise.

That the real concern of civil rights advocates and their congressional allies was the electoral map (primarily districting plans and annexations) becomes clear with a close look at the trigger itself. In theory, providing protection against disfranchisement as a result of a language barrier was the point of extending coverage. But even with respect to Mexican-Americans (upon whose experience almost the entire case rested), it was far from clear that language difficulties explained their failure to vote. The 1965 act had permitted an inference of discrimination from the joint presence of literacy tests and low levels of voter participation. Now, however, the act permitted a similar inference where voting fell short of the 50 percent mark and where no bilingual ballots were provided for Filipinos, Japanese, and other designated language minorities.

The original act had used an impact test (low turnout) to identify the intentionally fraudulent use of literacy tests. Such tests were assumed to have been *purposefully* manipulated to disfranchise blacks. But that crucial element of implicit intention was entirely absent from the trigger for coverage as amended in 1975; there was no suggestion that election materials had been printed exclusively in English for the purpose of keeping otherwise qualified voters from the polls.

Of course, a national interest in maximizing minority political participation might suggest a need for bilingual election materials. But if language were truly the barrier, then the provision of such materials would appear sufficient to rectify the problem. Again, the contrast with conditions in the South prior to 1965 is striking. The framers of the original statute feared that merely suspending literacy tests might not be enough, since southern states had a long record of evading federal antidiscrimination laws with ingenious ploys. Hence the preclearance requirement, as a prophylactic measure—a means to stop mischief before it started. But it was precisely the historical commitment of these states to keeping blacks from the polls that made section 5 necessary, and no equivalent discriminatory commitment had been shown to lie behind the absence of bilingual election materials in the Southwest and elsewhere. In other words, there was no reason to assume that new mischief—new disfranchising efforts—would follow from eliminating the barrier of ballots in English alone. Thus, unlike the traditional literacy test, the use of single-language ballots alone could hardly be cited to justify the imposition of the preclearance requirement.

The equation with the southern literacy test was thus technically satisfying but not otherwise convincing. No one actually believed that the primary problem in the Southwest was the disfranchising effect of English-language election materials. Rather, the new formula was devised as a means of combating districting plans and other aspects of the electoral environment that the Mexican-American groups believed to be discriminatory. The point of the 1975 amendments—unlike that of the 1965 act—was not access to the polls for citizens disfranchised in clear violation of the Fifteenth Amendment, but increased protection for minority candidates through the advantageous drawing of single-member districts. In 1965 the preclearance provision was a means of reinforcing the suspension of literacy tests; in 1975 the definition of literacy tests was expanded to secure the benefits that preclearance brought.

If the extension of section 5 coverage to southwest jurisdictions without a traditional literacy test could not be justified by the logic that sustained preclearance in 1965, was it nevertheless defensible? Were state officials engaging in such widespread manipulation of districting lines and municipal boundaries as to suggest the inadequacy of the traditional judicial route as a remedy? Did the level of Mexican-American officeholding in Texas and elsewhere signify Hispanic exclusion from the electoral process? Texas contained about two-thirds as many blacks as Mexican-Americans, yet one study calculated that in 1971 no more than 50 blacks held public office in that state, while more than 700 Mexican-Americans had been elected to a variety of posts.[46] How impressive, however, was that figure of 700? Mexican-Americans constituted 18.4 percent of the state's population yet held only 6.7 percent of the elected and appointed posts, one witness testified at the 1975 congressional hearings.[47] But the gross population figure was not the relevant standard: a substantial proportion of that 18.4 percent were either still Mexican citizens or under the voting age. Among American immigrant groups, Mexican-Americans have had the lowest naturalization rate, and in 1974 approximately 25 percent were aliens. In addition, the high fertility rate of the group has resulted in a skewed age structure. In 1980 nearly 40 percent of the Mexican-American community was below voting age. Close to 50 percent of Mexican-Americans were below 24 years of age—a pertinent figure because the 18-to-24 age group has a poor record of political participation. With age and citizenship factored in, the figure of 6.7 percent assumes quite a different meaning.[48]

Moreover, to the extent that Mexican-American officeholding was disproportionately low in proportion to the voting-age citizen population, discrimination was clearly not the only cause. Grebler, Moore, and Guzman, in their classic 1970 work, attributed the electoral ineffectiveness of Mexican-Americans not only to gerrymandering and other voting procedures, but to internal disunity and a culture of political passivity as well. "Many urban Mexican-Americans are relatively recent migrants from rural areas," they wrote, "and have probably maintained the limited view of their own potential role in political life that was derived from their experience in small towns and in the countryside."[49] Opportunities for assimilation may also have detracted from Mexican-American political solidarity and success. "The fact that some Mexican-Americans can 'pass' or 'escape' from Anglo-American color consciousness has affected the development of political solidarity," one scholar has noted. "Mexican-Americans are not inextricably bound to being Mexican-American."[50] The consequence of assimilation has been residential dispersion, making "safe" Hispanic districts harder to draw. And the fact that Mexican-Americans have generally had greater economic opportunities than those available to blacks has meant relatively less dependence on politics as an avenue of social mobility. Finally, the cultural assimilation of well-off Mexican-Americans has perhaps reduced the pool of eager and available spokesmen with the middle-class skills that political success demands.[51]

To argue that discrimination has played a comparatively smaller role in affecting Mexican-American electoral success is to question the analogy between blacks and Hispanics—on which the case for extending the special provisions of the Voting Rights Act to language minorities had substantially to rest. If factors other than racism played a significant part in keeping Mexican-American officeholding disproportionately low, then protection from racism—the promise of section 5—is correspondingly less necessary. Preclearance indirectly protects minority candidates from white competition and thus facilitates the election of spokesmen for the group; but the job of electing spokesmen can be entirely left to the resources of the group itself unless group membership disqualifies potential candidates for public office. How good, in fact, was the analogy between blacks and Hispanics? Unquestionably, Donald Horowitz has argued, Mexican-Americans suffered from a "spillover from anti-black racism." Yet he concludes that "in terms of social mobility, group boundaries and identity, political culture and behavior, and the relation of groups to territory, once controls are instituted for continuing migratory influx, Mexican-American patterns are not replicas of black American patterns so much as they are consistent with the general fluidity of the American ethnic system."[52]

The Horowitz view was not shared by advocates of language-minority coverage in 1975. They saw the similarities between the black and the Hispanic experience as more important than the differences, and advocated "affirmative action . . . the frank use of racial and ethnic considerations" to "undo the effects of past discrimination."[53] Was their more pessimistic picture correct? The question demands a subtle judgment call, an assessment of inconclusive facts. But congressional hearings are poor fact-finding instruments, and lawmakers have little use for inconclusive data. In any case, in 1975 the Democrats on the congressional committees handling the bill to extend and revise the Voting Rights Act were committed to passing the legislation well before the actual hearings began. And to that end civil rights spokesmen and their congressional allies speciously equated an English-only ballot with a fraudulent literacy test and audaciously maintained that the issue had not changed—that minority citizens were equally disfranchised by gerrymandered districts in Texas in 1975 and the demand in 1965 that Mississippi blacks interpret obscure passages for the state constitution to the satisfaction of redneck registrars. In short, they skillfully created a facade of continuity that masked new meanings, new commitments, and thus new demands.

## · FOUR ·

# Travels in a Political Thicket

---

This chapter examines a series of constitutional rulings that, beginning in 1965, explored the meaning of the right to vote as guaranteed by the Fourteenth and Fifteenth Amendments. These decisions—running parallel to those interpreting the Voting Rights Act—are important for two reasons. The act was amended again in 1982, and the most significant of the revisions of that year cannot be understood without a grasp of the constitutional cases. In addition, these decisions have played a role in the enforcement of the preclearance provision—although of a rather mysterious sort. Their story with respect to section 5, it might be said, forms a play within a play, with a vital, though somewhat elusive, relation to the main drama.

The distinction made in *Allen* between "meaningful" and "meaningless" votes committed the courts and the Department of Justice to defining precisely when votes "fully" counted. The question was implicitly raised again by the renewal of the act in 1975; if ballots "diluted" by districting and other electoral arrangements had become the primary problem, then there was an unspecified point at which the minority vote would acquire its "proper" weight. Yet the issue of electoral equality was directly addressed only in the constitutional cases. Prior to 1982, claims based on the Voting Rights Act involved whites in covered jurisdictions suspected of manipulating electoral arrangements to pull blacks and Hispanics back from gains they would otherwise have made. The question in statutory cases (at least in theory) was backsliding or relative deprivation. In those resting on the Constitution, however, minority plaintiffs challenged procedures by which elections had been run in both North and South, often since early in the century; they charged that blacks and whites were on unequal electoral footing in some absolute sense. In the constitutional suits the question of when minority and white votes equally count was thus posed with unparalleled clarity.

The problem of defining electoral equality did not appear unannounced in minority vote dilution claims. It had been fully apparent in the reapportionment decisions—those involving legislative districts unequal in population, yet electing equal numbers of legislators. Its presence in that line of cases, in fact, had led Justice Frankfurter to wage a prolonged battle against deciding them. It was a "political thicket," he warned as early as 1946.[1] But in 1962, in *Baker v. Carr*, the Supreme Court threw caution aside and plunged ahead. It was not that Frankfurter's doubts had been assuaged. What had actually been asked of this Court, he said, was nothing less than "to choose among competing bases of representation—ultimately, really, among competing theories of political philosophy."[2]

Justice Frankfurter was convinced that courts and politics did not mix, and that political choices (beyond the competence of judges) were an inevitable component of every apportionment decision. That is, the *means* by which political influence was distributed inescapably suggested an *end*. To choose a particular distributive principle was to adopt a particular definition of democratic government. In every apportionment rule there lurked an implicit theory of representation, and no case of alleged malapportionment could be judged without such a theoretical framework. That is, the means not only suggested an end, but without a carefully delineated end, appropriate means remained uncertain. Lacking clearly articulated political values, Frankfurter asked, how could courts judge the equity of particular contested district lines? Without settled standards, how could judges weigh such competing considerations as the desirability of population equality, the value of an experienced incumbent, the need to honor community integrity or to provide a strong rural voice (despite a sparse rural population)?

Justice Frankfurter's justly celebrated dissent in *Baker v. Carr*, the first of the reapportionment decisions, was eloquent, but the force of the argument faded fast. Frankfurter had not misjudged the degree to which the Court had penetrated a "political thicket," but he had underestimated the ease with which the judges would find a means of retreat. From the outset, the reapportionment decisions had clearly involved more than the individual's right to vote. The legislatures, plaintiffs had argued, did not truly express the popular will. As Frankfurter correctly perceived, such suits were an invitation to define the meaning of representative democracy, but one that the Court quickly found a means of substantially declining. By 1964, it had embraced the principle of equal representation for equal numbers of people: one person, one vote. And it had turned its back on the more complicated questions that that simple quantitative rule did not dispose of.[3] The plaintiffs had gone to court to protest the underrepresentation of urban dwellers; with the growth of cities, the number of representatives apportioned to urban areas had not proportionately grown. Yet the decisions themselves upheld not the right of urban (or other) interests to their equitable share of legislative seats, but only the right of the individual, autonomous voter to cast a ballot of no less weight than that of his neighbor—as measured by the standard of a uniform ratio between residents and representatives throughout the jurisdiction. Having entered the "political thicket," the Court took the first exit out, leaving considerable territory unexplored.

This was instantly recognized by Justice Harlan. The majority in *Reynolds v. Sims* (1964), the most important of the Supreme Court's reapportionment decisions, argued that "legislators represent people, not trees or acres."[4] In apportioning representatives, legislatures should count residents, not territory or foliage. But as Justice Harlan pointed out, in dissent, "people are not ciphers . . . and legislators can represent their electors only by speaking for their *interests*—economic, social, political." In Harlan's view the Court had not established, or even attempted to establish, that "conflicting interests within a State can only be adjusted by disregarding them."[5] The Court had averted its gaze, but the problem of diverse and often unrepresented group interests had not disappeared.

Creating equally populated districts —mathematical parity—did not necessarily result in equal representation, Harlan had suggested. Such a stripped-down version of the American system of representation was clearly open to challenge. There were bound to be questions about the representational rights of groups left by the wayside—interest groups that found themselves without a voice. A system of apportionment that neglected the vitality of group life, the importance of rural, ethnic, and other such ties, could be as inequitable as one that ignored the distribution of the population. Multimember districts and at-large voting, for instance, raised precisely this question of the right of interest groups to representation, and as Harlan presciently predicted, questions about the constitutionality of such electoral schemes were soon raised. The power to elect representatives, the Court had said, must be evenly distributed among voters. What, beyond equal population districts, did that mean? "The right to suffrage," the majority opinion had contended, "can be denied by a debasement or dilution of the weight of a citizen's vote just as effectively as by wholly prohibiting the free exercise of the franchise."[6] But when were votes debased or diluted? "Each and every citizen has an inalienable right to full and effective participation . . . an equally effective voice."[7] But when was the exercise of the franchise "full and effective"?

*Reynolds v. Sims* promised more than it delivered, and the promises were bound to whet the appetite of voters whom the mathematical formula (one person, one vote) did not entirely satisfy. One year later— the year the Voting Rights Act was passed and four years before that act was interpreted to protect against the dilution or debasement of the minority vote—plaintiffs in a Georgia suit began to pick up where the reapportionment decisions left off.

That Georgia case was *Fortson v. Dorsey,* and the complaint was the inequity of Georgia's mixed use of multimember and single-member districts in the state's senate reapportionment plan. Plaintiffs sought exclusive use of single-member districts, each with its own senator, elected by the residents of that district alone.[8] Residents of a county represented by a single senator, they argued, elected that senator; residents of a county electing several representatives at-large, however, often had their senator chosen (in effect) for them. Fulton County (Atlanta) was a district from which seven senators were elected; those senators resided in and represented seven "subdistricts" within the county. But because all seven were elected at-large, the residents of any one subdistrict might vote overwhelmingly for a particular candidate, only to find that candidate defeated by voters elsewhere in the county. The subdistrict would then be "represented" by a senator rejected by those whom he or she was elected to represent.

Those who brought suit were white, not black, and the issue was proper representation, not racial exclusion. Nevertheless, the Supreme Court's response betrayed an awareness of the lurking problem of black electoral inequality. The year 1965 was a time of stiffening national resolve on civil rights questions, and although the Court denied relief to the Georgia plaintiffs, it nevertheless acknowledged that "it might well be that, designedly or otherwise, a multi-member constituency apportionment would operate to minimize or cancel out the voting strength of racial or political elements."[9]

One year later, in 1966, the issue was back before the Court in *Burns v. Richardson,* a case involving reapportionment in Hawaii. The Court's decision reiterated the *Fortson* dictum.[10] The announced principle—the potentially discriminatory impact of multimember districts—clearly extended to other forms of election as well. At-large voting was an obvious target; it, too, had the potential to "minimize or cancel out the voting strength of racial or political elements." At-large elections for city and county councils, as well as school boards, are particularly common in the South and, as I argued in the previous chapter, affect the level of black officeholding (although not necessarily the level of black representation, since whites can represent black constituents). Cities with a maximum number of "safe" minority single-member districts will most likely have more minority officeholders than majority-white jurisdictions in which blacks, as well as whites, must run at-large. When blacks are a numerical minority in a municipality, black candidates cannot win running city-wide without white support. How substantial that white support must be is determined in part by the presence or absence of other devices. A majority vote requirement, for instance, forces black candidates with a plurality of the vote to enter a runoff, often against a white. A full-slate rule prevents blacks from voting for only the two black candidates when there are five open seats; they must cast five ballots and vote for the "full slate," thereby increasing the tally for three whites and reducing the relative weight of support for those who are black. In their dicta hinting at future judicial receptivity, *Fortson* and *Burns* virtually invited civil rights groups to initiate further litigation challenging electoral arrangements with a discriminatory impact on the "voting strength" of racial and other interest groups.

The invitation was readily accepted. But plaintiffs faced an immediate problem. *Burns* had made it clear that neither apportionment plans for state legislative bodies containing multimember districts nor at-large voting for city or county council seats was unconstitutional per se; plaintiffs would have to prove actual dilution of their voting strength. Two years later, in 1968, unexpected aid came in the form of the Kerner Report (the Report of the National Advisory Commission on Civil Disorders).[11] Chaired by Otto Kerner, governor of Illinois, and convened in the wake of urban riots in the summer of 1967, the commission had conducted an inquiry into the history of racial conflict, black unemployment and family structure, the formation of ghettos, the causes and effects of ghetto crime, relations between the police and community, and the sources of black alienation. "Our Nation," the report concluded, "is moving toward two societies, one black, one white—separate and unequal." Frustrated by their continuing powerlessness, politically excluded blacks had turned to violence. In the riot-torn cities, the commission found, blacks were substantially underrepresented in politics, and in two-thirds of those cities either all or some legislators were elected at large.[12] The report left no doubt that it regarded the racial turmoil as directly tied to blacks' inadequate say in the policies that shaped their lives.

Within a year of the Kerner Report's publication, plaintiffs (in *Chavis v. Whitcomb*) made the first serious effort to demonstrate that a method of election did, indeed, deprive blacks of their fair voice in the political process.[13] The suit attacked Indiana's state legislative apportionment—specifically, the creation of one multimember district for all of Marion County, from which eight state senators and fifteen assemblymen would be elected. The plan, it was charged, unconstitutionally minimized the voting power of the county's blacks, who were largely concentrated in Indianapolis's "Center Township Ghetto."

The district court was convinced. Although Indianapolis had not experienced any riots, the court drew a picture of two separate societies—one with power, the other without—that closely resembled the description of American society contained in the Kerner Report. This was perhaps not surprising, since the *Chavis* decision had been written by Otto Kerner himself, who had become a judge on the Seventh Circuit and, in this capacity, had been appointed to a special three-judge panel to try the case.

Judge Kerner looked at the distinctiveness of Indianapolis ghetto life, at the degree of residential concentration and the relative poverty of the black population—as well as at the lack of legislators elected from the "Center Township Ghetto"—and concluded that the multimember district impermissibly diluted the voting strength of inner-city blacks. Even though ghetto residents had a special interest in such public policy matters as housing and welfare, he argued, the number of black legislators was disproportionately low. Moreover, said Kerner, the tight control exercised by the political parties over their officeholders prevented representatives with county-wide constituencies from giving more than perfunctory attention to the special needs of such unique neighborhoods.[14]

The reapportionment decisions had left unanswered the question of what electoral equality—beyond one person, one vote—meant. In *Chavis v. Whitcomb*, Judge Kerner picked up where those decisions left off. Building on *Burns*, he suggested that residentially clustered groups with distinctive interests were without the political influence to which they were entitled as long as their votes were submerged in a multimember district.

*Fortson, Burns, and Chavis* implicitly equated electoral exclusion with a disproportionately low number of minority officeholders. Electoral defeat, Judge Kerner clearly assumed, invariably had a different meaning for blacks and whites; whites lose for a variety of reasons, blacks for only one—race. But the actual level of black political opportunity in Indianapolis made clear just how misleading that assumption was. Black residents of the "Center Township Ghetto" certainly had special, identifiable concerns, but there was no evidence that they lacked an opportunity to voice them in the political process. Although few state senators and assemblymen actually came from the ghetto, the blacks of Marion County were active participants in Indianapolis political life. In fact, the Democratic Party routinely slated black candidates chosen by black districts, and in general elections those candidates fared no worse (and no better) than those who were white. The stumbling block was the repeated defeat of the entire Democratic slate.[15] This was a Republican county, and Democrats (whether white or black) seldom won.

Reviewing the district court's decision, the Supreme Court (in *Whitcomb v. Chavis*) took a second look at the status of Indianapolis blacks and found nothing abnormal in the way of political isolation or unequal access. It was not exclusion, but the process of party competition and the principle of majority rule that denied blacks the representation they sought. Since blacks were Democrats in a largely Republican county, the dilution of their voting strength was, in the Court's words, a "mere euphemism for political defeat."[16] It was not race but party that had determined electoral outcome. In fact, faced with a choice between white Democrats and black Republicans, voters in the ghetto chose whites. Disproportionately low black officeholding, the Court concluded, was not evidence of invidious discrimination "absent findings that ghetto residents had less opportunity than did other Marion County residents to participate in the political processes and to elect legislators of their choice."[17]

The task that Judge Kerner imposed upon the courts had been relatively straightforward: identifying groups with distinct, compelling, and inadequately represented interests. That of gauging the electoral environment was much more difficult. The Supreme Court's decision in *Whitcomb* asked courts to judge the setting in which the voting took place and to distinguish those situations in which minority candidates lost as a result of unequal opportunity from those in which blacks either did not run or went down to defeat for reasons *other than race*. Subsequent decisions would make clear how large that assignment was.

*Whitcomb* had raised doubt that minority plaintiffs in a northern jurisdiction could successfully challenge a method of election. Political opportunities open to blacks in Philadelphia, Boston, and Chicago, for example, appeared as great as those enjoyed by blacks in Indianapolis. More than ten years would pass, in fact, before another attempt was made to persuade a court that minorities in a northern city met the *Whitcomb* standard, that their "opportunity . . . to participate in the political process and to elect legislators of their choice" was less than that of other residents. And that attempt was prompted not by a new reading of the Indiana case but by a revision of the Voting Rights Act that signaled renewed receptivity to such suits.[18]

Texas was the setting for the next case. Even though the state was neither in the Deep South nor considered a candidate for coverage by the Voting Rights Act in 1965, the Supreme Court sharply distinguished it from Indiana. In *White v. Regester*, decided in 1973, black and Mexican-American plaintiffs prevailed in a suit that challenged a portion of the 1970 reapportionment plan for the Texas House of Representatives.[19] The Court held that multimember districts, used in two counties, violated the Fourteenth Amendment guarantee of equal protection.

The Court viewed the electoral problems of the two minority groups as distinct, and it dealt with each separately. Upholding the claim of black plaintiffs in Dallas County, Justice White cited a history of official discrimination and black underrepresentation, the continuing control of Democratic Party nominations by a white-dominated slating organization, the use of racist campaign tactics, and the presence of majority vote and other rules that "enhanced the opportunity for racial discrimination."[20]

The barriers to Mexican-American participation in Bexar County (which included San Antonio) were somewhat different. Mexican-Americans had also suffered from a history of "discrimination and treatment in the fields of education, employment, economics, health, politics, and others." In addition, Mexican-American officeholding was disproportionately low in relation to the minority population. But, equally important, the Court found that "the typical Mexican-American suffer[ed] from a cultural and language barrier that [made] his participation in the community processes extremely difficult." Combined with a poll tax and "the most restrictive voter registration procedures in the nation," this "cultural incompatibility" had denied Mexican-Americans political access "even longer than the Blacks were formally denied access by the white primary."[21]

Two leading civil rights attorneys have described these findings as "difficult to catalogue"[22]—or to put it less politely, they lacked coherence. What made the case of Texas so different from that of Indiana? The Court pointed to a history of discrimination. Was it stating only that these are groups that warrant special concern—that the history of blacks and Mexican-Americans is not to be confused with that of Poles?

Discrimination has affected blacks in every community. That history may set the context in voting rights cases, but it does not help to pinpoint those communities in which minority voters need extraordinary protection. Perhaps the additional criterion of low minority voter registration serves to isolate areas requiring special attention. It can be argued that because the links between discrimination, depressed socio-economic status, and political passivity are well documented, and because the state is at least partially to blame for persistent discrimination, the state should act to remedy the resultant political passivity. Yet the Supreme Court mentioned the low registration rate only in Bexar County, not in Dallas; was this an oversight? In fact, it referred to the history of discrimination in Dallas County as having only "*at times touched* the right of Negroes to register and vote and to participate in the democratic processes."[23] Obviously its impact was less than crippling. And wasn't that "touch" becoming ever lighter, as discrimination in the nation waned? Finally, and most important, if past discrimination depressed current registration, then the obvious solution would be to attack the registration problem head on. Instead of revising the entire electoral system, the Court could have required the counties to provide mobile registrars and extend registration hours. That approach, however, would be inadequate if it were determined that members of groups suffering past discrimination had distinctive needs and were entitled to representation by one of their own. In that case, the protection of minority candidates in advantageously drawn single-member districts would be considered a right. But it was precisely the theory of entitlement to minority officeholding that the Supreme Court had rejected in its *Whitcomb* decision on black electoral opportunity in Indiana.

Only in Dallas County, not in Bexar, did a white-dominated organization control the process of candidate selection. If such control was present in one place, absent in the other, how significant was it in the Court's ultimate judgment? And how was such slating defined? Perhaps white power (however slight) over the process of candidate selection is discriminatory. Was it slating per se or white racism—bloc voting against black and Hispanic candidates—that accounted for the disproportionately low number of minority officeholders? The decision did not even discuss racial polarization—voting patterns among whites, blacks, and Hispanics—although such patterns have subsequently been labeled the linchpin of vote dilution cases. Racist campaign tactics were allegedly used in Dallas County to defeat candidates supported by the black community. But "racist tactics" are not as easily identified as it might seem. Overt racism having become largely a phenomenon of the past, the question has now become the use of such code words as the "bloc" or "special interest" vote, with clear reference to blacks. What code words, employed by whom, are beyond the bounds of acceptable rhetoric?

In the case of Bexar County, the Court pointed to the existence of highly restrictive registration procedures, including an annual registration requirement. That requirement, however, was not an outright bar to voting and, moreover, could have been readily rectified. There was, in addition, the Court's reference to "cultural incompatibility"—barriers of language and culture—as an apparent element in the discriminatory picture. When two ethnic groups inhabit the same political space, are they necessarily "incompatible"? Was the Court suggesting that the distinctiveness of Mexican-American culture entitled the group to its own representatives? Were the Mexican-American candidates who had won election not "representative"—brown on the outside, white inside, the equivalent of Uncle Toms? Perhaps their numbers were insufficient—if so, by what measure? Finally, why did the Court fail to mention a seemingly crucial fact—that since 1961, the county had been represented in Congress by Henry B. Gonzalez, a Mexican-American? *White v. Regester,* it should be clear, does not withstand close scrutiny. The opinion rested on "factual findings" that, in reality, were unexplained assertions of indeterminate weight.

The ballot alone does not secure electoral equality—reliable and meaningful electoral access. But such access does not depend on any one method of voting; elections can legitimately be structured in a variety of ways. Multimember districts, used in Texas and elsewhere, are not, per se, discriminatory. Every method, it is true, affects the distribution of seats among partisan, ethnic, and other groups. And none can promise every citizen equal power; inevitably, some individuals, like some groups, will be better positioned and more skillful than others. In any case, as Michael Walzer has put it, it is not power itself but only the *"opportunities* and occasions of power" that must be properly shared. In a true democracy, every citizen is "a *potential* participant, a *potential* politician."[24] But how to recognize those "opportunities and occasions"? How to know when the potential is there? That is the hard but unavoidable question that these constitutional minority vote dilution cases raised.

Three months after *White v. Regester,* the Fifth Circuit in *Zimmer v. McKeithen* attempted to make sense of the Supreme Court's abstruse judgment.[25] *Zimmer* involved the method of voting for the school board and the police jury (the equivalent of a county council) in a rural Louisiana parish that was 58.7 percent black. Traditionally divided into districts, the parish, which was home to fewer than 13,000 people, had adopted an at-large system in 1968 following a successful suit to ensure fidelity to the one-person, one-vote principle.

Black voters at once objected, and their claims were sustained by the Fifth Circuit, which tried to devise a clear-cut test for electoral discrimination. The court had held that the Fourteenth Amendment's guarantee of equal protection was violated whenever minority plaintiffs could show some combination of primary and "enhancing" factors. The primary factors were lack of minority access to the slating of candidates; a "tenuous" state policy (backed by neither tradition nor persuasive reason) underlying the preference for at-large voting; and a history of past discrimination that limited political participation. The significance of any one of these factors was considered "enhanced" when accompanied by any combination of the following elements: large districts, a majority vote requirement, a prohibition against voting for less than a "full slate," and an absence of subdistricts, such that all candidates running at large could reside in one neighborhood—affluent and white, for instance.[26]

*Zimmer* promised to let federal courts off the hook, so to speak. It propounded a simple solution to what seemed an intractable problem: how to detect situations in which inequality between minority and white voters mandated a new method of voting. The constitutional cases, more often than not, took weeks to try. The factual record was voluminous. But courts now had a checklist which they could—and did—use. From 1973 to 1980, vote "dilution" claims were tested by the *Zimmer* criteria.[27]

However, *White* and *Zimmer* solved only the rhetorical, not the substantive, problem. While providing a vocabulary on which courts could draw, these decisions left unsettled the basic question of why the particular facts listed had been selected. The *Zimmer* list looked systematic; in fact, it was no less arbitrary than the one contained in *White*. But criteria that measure an undefined phenomenon are necessarily arbitrary. The primary issues had not been tackled. When is the right to vote assured? When is the election process one in which all citizens can choose to partake? What does a democracy look like in practice? Slating groups, annual registration requirements, linguistic barriers, a history of inequality, a majority-vote requirement, low levels of minority office-holding—the significance of each depends on how they fit in a broader framework, a vision of the political whole.

*White* and *Zimmer* offer "a laundry list of factors, but . . . never [orient] the inquiry," James Blumstein has argued. They demand "a balance" but provide "no scale." Left without a "scale" and deprived of bearings, judges weighed facts and arguments on a purely intuitive basis; the orientation became their own.[28] With the *Zimmer* criteria to guide it, "the judicial investigation into dilution assume[d] an orderliness and rationality that disguise[d] the subjectivity of the enterprise," Timothy O'Rourke has noted.[29] In *Zimmer* the court had found disparities in the electoral opportunities open to whites and blacks in a Louisiana parish. Yet the facts of the case could have supported a contrary finding. For example, there was no indication that single-member districts were especially advantageous to black candidates or constituents; three blacks had been elected when voting was by wards, and three under the new at-large system. In the latter case blacks had won with the help of the white vote, but the court dismissed the white support that blacks had received running at large, suggesting that the *wow!*

right votes had been cast for the wrong reasons.[30] (Did the court really mean to add to the test for equal electoral opportunity a probe for pure motive?) In addition, the parish was a majority-black one; if voting remained at large and blacks registered in proportion to their numbers, black candidates could win every legislative seat. Benjamin Hooks, executive director of the NAACP, was later to say that he could not define electoral discrimination but knew it when he saw it.[31] This was close to the standard at which the courts had arrived in these constitutional cases.

Such subjectivity is doubly dangerous. Unbridled discretion is undesirable in itself; the validity of a voting procedure should not depend on judicial whim. Arbitrary federal interference with local and state electoral arrangements is in clear violation of the Constitution, which leaves most franchise questions in state hands.[32] In fact, interference on any ground (arbitrary or not) has been consistently assumed to lie outside the scope of federal power, unless an adopted procedure violates either the right to vote irrespective of race, sex, or age (after eighteen), or the guarantee of an equal protection of the laws. There are lines that states cannot cross, in other words, but these prohibitions are exceptions to the general presumption in favor of local freedom to design electoral arrangements to meet local needs. Disrespect for that presumption is obviously particularly egregious when the infringement on state prerogative is a consequence of apparent judicial whim—when the decision appears more random than reasoned.

Highly subjective judicial judgments are dangerous for a second reason. As Blumstein has noted, the presence of intricacy combined with ambiguity "is an invitation . . . to give great weight to numerical outcomes," that is, to the number of minority officeholders. Reliance on a statistical standard for electoral fairness "reduces the complexity of cases, adds uniformity and narrows the range of discretion for court."[33]

A Supreme Court decision in April 1980 abruptly ended the reign of *Zimmer. City of Mobile v. Bolden* wiped the slate clean and replaced the Fifth Circuit Court's test with one that seemed principled, simple, and tight.[34] The issue was the long-standing form of government in Mobile, Alabama: three commissioners elected at large, with the office of mayor rotating among them. Elections were nonpartisan; candidates ran for specific seats; and a majority vote was required for election. Although more than one-third of the city's population was black, no black had ever

*Mobile,*

won. The district court held for the black plaintiffs, and the Fifth Circuit affirmed that decision. The Supreme Court, however, reversed the decision, concluding that a successful attack on an at-large or other method of voting would have to demonstrate invidious *intent* in the adoption or maintenance of the electoral procedure in use. That is, as long as the method of voting had not been designed or perpetuated to keep minorities from public office, blacks and whites would be considered to be on equal political footing. The right to vote meant the entitlement of citizens to cast their ballots in an electoral system uncontaminated by racial purpose.

The Supreme Court had laid down a seemingly simple rule that it could not, in fact, follow. In 1982 the Court, in *Rogers v. Lodge*, overturned at-large voting in Burke County, Georgia, even though the evidence of discriminatory intent was no greater than that on which lower courts had erroneously relied in *Mobile*.[35] A new label had rescued a discarded product. Judges could still use the *Zimmer* criteria to assess the "totality of the circumstances," as the Fifth Circuit had directed, provided they simply announced a finding of invidious purpose. They need not mend their ways, only their description of them.

In the difficult terrain which the reapportionment decisions (one person, one vote) left unexplored, the Court had clearly lost its way. It had created and abandoned trails, but could draw no map. Yet, as I have tried to suggest, the inadequacy of the Court's response to the challenge posed by the vote dilution cases only reflected the magnitude of the task before it. That is, the true question it was confronted with was one it was understandably eager to avoid. Of what does political justice consist? these cases asked. What is the "normal" relation between racial and ethnic groups in the political sphere? When are "opportunities and occasions of power" improperly shared? When is a member of a particular group neither a "potential participant" nor a "potential politician"? Identifying inadequate electoral opportunity demands a definition of democratic representation. The Court had attempted to provide such a definition in *Mobile*, with its discriminatory intent standard. As *Rogers v. Lodge* made clear, however, it was a standard to which the Court itself could not adhere.

As I suggested at the outset, the constitutional decisions involving minority voting rights are important for two reasons. First, they are crucial to understanding the most significant of the 1982 amendments to the Voting Rights Act. In 1982 Congress became persuaded by civil rights spokesmen that plaintiffs seeking to overturn at-large and other methods of voting on equal-protection grounds could not prevail if forced to prove intent as required by *Mobile*. It thus amended the act so that all suits challenging electoral procedures could rest on statutory grounds, and, by writing into the statute a "results" test for electoral discrimination, it obviated the need for plaintiffs ever to prove discriminatory purpose. Demonstration that a method of voting had an invidious result henceforth sufficed to condemn it. The "new" results test, however, was simply that which had been previously but inadequately developed in *White v. Regester*. Even before *Rogers* implicitly resurrected the old criteria, the test for discrimination contained in *White* had been endowed with a second (but now statutory) life. Thus the standard set by *Mobile* for judging electoral discrimination continued to govern the outcome of constitutional suits, but plaintiffs could choose to rest their claim, instead, on the Voting Rights Act, and that statutory claim would be judged by the criteria developed in *White* and *Zimmer*. This story is developed in full in the next two chapters.

Second, the constitutional decisions have played a role in the enforcement of the preclearance provision—although one that has never been fully defined. In 1965 the statutory meaning of the right to vote (that implicitly contained in the Voting Rights Act) was access to the ballot. The point of the statute had originally been, of course, to make good on the constitutional promise contained in the Fourteenth and Fifteenth Amendments. But, in fact, the definition of that promise underwent substantial change. Thus by 1975 the equal protection clause had been interpreted to ensure the equal opportunity of minority voters to elect candidates of their choice—equality of quite a different sort from that secured initially by the Voting Rights Act. What was the impact of that revised meaning of the right to vote on the statute, the chief mechanism for enforcing the constitutional guarantee? The answer was unclear, and has, in important respects, remained so. At the heart of the act there is thus an unresolved but central question, to which I return in Chapter 8.

The reapportionment decisions—those dealing with population inequality between legislative districts—opened a Pandora's box. One person, one vote barely began to fulfill the promise of protection against "debasement" or "dilution." Yet the commitment to true electoral equality, once made, could not easily be curtailed. Beyond the individual voter—counted but otherwise unidentified—there were interest groups, the building blocks of political life. Equality clearly had a dimension that the focus on numbers alone overlooked. At a time of rising civil rights consciousness, the question of proper representation for at least certain groups—those defined by race, ethnicity, and political marginality—was bound to arise. Yet the trail that the courts blazed into the "political thicket" created by the question of group representation had no clear destination and permitted no retreat. Lower court judges were left to bushwhack their way out—a solution the Supreme Court had, to a limited degree, implicitly sanctioned. Assessments of electoral exclusion, the Court had said in *White v. Regester*, require an "intensely local appraisal."[36] It was a directive to courts of appeals: lower court findings should not be lightly overturned. The close observation of trial judges was usually accurate. But the Supreme Court's directive contained a larger message—that fumbling toward a goal was not a bad way to get there.

The message was relevant not only to the constitutional cases but to enforcement of the Voting Rights Act as well. Statutory controversies are handled either by the Department of Justice or the D.C. district court, and although broad questions of electoral equality are, in theory, outside the scope of the act, they have, in fact, become a primary concern of these federal authorities. By the Supreme Court's own admission, such questions are best left to those most familiar with local nuances involving race and politics—those able to appraise a local situation "intensely," as the Court put it. Local trial judges, the Court had declared, occupy a "special vantage point";[37] their position permits a perspective available to neither the D.C. court nor the career attorneys who roam the halls of the Department of Justice, but seldom the streets of a southern town.

If accurate judgment depends on close proximity, it depends, as well, on a sense of what to look for. I will argue in subsequent chapters that the problem of vague and subjective standards has become increasingly serious. The large questions concerning "fair and effective participation," settled on an ad hoc basis in the occasional constitutional cases, now regularly surface in the course of Voting Rights Act enforcement. These questions go to the heart of the democratic process and the American tradition of federalism. Minority voters seek to overturn decisions that affect only the residents of the jurisdiction in which they reside and to which a majority within it have subscribed. In so doing, they attempt to undo the work of a democratic process. When plaintiffs win and secure external intervention, the judgment should rest on clearly articulated and generally accepted principles.

· FIVE ·

# The Politics of Passage in the House

"If I know anything about Congress," Benjamin Hooks, executive director of the NAACP, said in 1981, "once they start tinkering with something, we do not know how far it will go."[1] Hooks was urging restraint in
the face of proposals to reduce voting rights protection after seventeen
years of change in the South. In fact, he had little to fear. It is true that
once amendments are offered, the outcome is never entirely certain.
Important changes can slip through unnoticed; the imperative of political
compromise can bring about unforeseen consequences; one change can
lend legitimacy to another. But the picture Hooks drew of unlimited
potential for congressional mischief was far from accurate. Legislators
could tinker with the act, but not in ways that would reduce the protection it afforded minorities; appearing to oppose minority aspirations was
politically risky. That lesson, learned by Republicans in 1970, was almost forgotten by 1982.

On the face of it, those who hoped to weaken the act when the special
provisions were up for renewal in 1982 seemed to be dealing from
strength. The election of Ronald Reagan had raised expectations of an
across-the-board change in civil rights policy, and the President's stance
was likely to carry great political weight. In addition, with fifty-three
seats in the Senate, the Republicans had their largest margin since the
election of 1946, and the sixteen new Republicans tilted decidedly to the
right. Moreover, Strom Thurmond had assumed the chairmanship of
the Judiciary Committee. To civil rights spokesmen and the national
media, the picture seemed bleak. *Time*, for instance, suggested that the
administration might "attempt to undo the civil rights gains."[2] A prominent civil rights attorney, articulating a widely held belief, wrote, "It is

not an exaggeration to say that minorities stand perilously close to where they were in 1877, when the nation, grown weary of the race issue, agreed to let local officials deal with voting rights as they saw fit."[3] In the end, however, civil rights groups, seeking to strengthen the act, easily carried the day, winning by margins of 389 to 24 in the House and 86 to 8 in the Senate. What was the secret of their continuing strength? This chapter on the House debate on the 1982 amendments and the following one on the subsequent Senate deliberations attempt to answer that question.

The August 1982 expiration date of the act's "special" (temporary) provisions might seem odd. Why a seven-year extension, rather than five or ten? The date had been a compromise. Ten years seemed unnecessarily long; these were emergency provisions intended to have a limited life. A mere five years, however, would have meant that redistricting in the covered jurisdictions following the 1980 census would not have been subject to federal review.

Early in 1981, long before the expiration date, civil rights groups, working with key liberals in both the Senate and House, began to draft legislation and sketch strategy. On April 7 Representative Peter Rodino (D-N.J.) and Senator Charles Mathias (R-Md.), among others, introduced bills to extend the life of the temporary provisions and alter a minor but permanent provision. The proposed amendment would permit minority plaintiffs in voting rights suits to ignore the Supreme Court's 1980 decision in *City of Mobile v. Bolden.* Suspected discriminatory "effect," it should be clear, sufficed to overturn districting and other methods of voting instituted in covered states and counties since November 1964. But those who sought to attack either electoral systems in jurisdictions beyond the reach of section 5, or those put in place before that date, had to rest their claim on the Constitution. After *Mobile* they would prevail only if they demonstrated discriminatory "intent." This was the requirement that advocates of an amended act sought to circumvent.

It is important to understand that the intent test did not apply to questions of electoral discrimination alone. In a 1976 employment case the Court had declared that, as a general principle, "the invidious quality of a law claimed to be racially discriminatory must ultimately be traced to a racially discriminatory purpose."[4] The burden imposed by *Mobile* was thus not novel, yet civil rights spokesmen found it intolerable in the voting rights context. The Court had demanded, they said, the display of a still-smoking gun: overtly racist statements by often long-dead public officials whose work a particular electoral system of voting had been.[5]

It was a rhetorically powerful argument of questionable validity. The Court had not demanded the display of a smoking gun in other equal protection cases. In fact, in a housing discrimination case three years before the *Mobile* decision, it had explicitly endorsed the use of circumstantial evidence to prove invidious intent.[6] But civil rights spokesmen were not wrong in suggesting that *Mobile* had made cases harder to win; discriminatory purpose was unquestionably more difficult to prove than racially disparate effect. And, clearly, the decision had ruled out disparate impact as sufficient to condemn an at-large or other electoral scheme.

Yet impact, civil rights advocates believed, was the right question. And even though Congress could not revise the constitutional standard, it could neutralize it by amending the act. Section 2, a seemingly insignificant preamble to the statute, presented a clear opening. As originally written, the section banned qualifications and procedures "imposed or applied . . . to deny or abridge the right . . . to vote on account of race or color." That is, it introduced a statute resting on the Fifteenth Amendment by simply restating the core of that amendment. With its clear link to the Constitution, it also implicitly contained an intent test. A minor alteration in wording, however, would sever the Fifteenth Amendment connection and eliminate the intent requirement. Congress could replace "to deny or abridge" with "in a manner which *results* in a denial or abridgment of." The provision would thus read: "No voting qualification or prerequisite to voting or standard, practice, or procedure shall be imposed or applied by any State or political subdivision in a manner which results in a denial or abridgment of the right of any citizen of the United States to vote on account of race or color." It was a change that would leave the constitutional test standing, but idle; suits that once rested on the Fourteenth and Fifteenth Amendments could henceforth be based on section 2. That is, the provision was permanent and nationwide in scope, and could thus substitute for those constitutional amendments. The change would greatly ease the burden on plaintiffs challenging not only long-established at-large voting in cities such as Mobile, but also recently drawn districting plans and other electoral arrangements in southern jurisdictions and others not subject to automatic review under section 5.

The proposed change in section 2—the institution of a nationwide "results" test for electoral discrimination—was at least as significant as any previous amendment. Section 5 directed federal authorities to look at the "effect" of electoral changes on the weight of black ballots, but only in jurisdictions already known to have been engaged in systematic violations of the Fifteenth Amendment. In such communities—historically committed to disfranchisement—the discriminatory impact of a redistricting scheme was likely to indicate invidious purpose. In jurisdictions where it seemed probable that the number of minorities in office would drop as a consequence of a new districting plan, it seemed safe to say that the proposed scheme was tainted by racism. But section 2 applied, as well, to jurisdictions in which minorities had never been disfranchised and had long held public office. The greatly heightened power that it promised to give minority plaintiffs in voting rights suits would thus be used to challenge methods of election in jurisdictions that could not be regarded as suspect in the sense that Alabama was in 1965.

Moreover, "effect" had been defined as backsliding for section 5 purposes. A proposed districting plan or other scheme was objectionable only if it left minority voters with less power to elect minority officeholders than they had previously had. The relative standing of minority voters—before and after the proposed electoral change—was thus the focus of a section 5 inquiry. The question was therefore limited and manageable. But the amended section 2 would direct courts to ask whether a method of election had a discriminatory result in some absolute sense. As critics of the amendment were quick to point out, the change carried the obvious danger that the courts, in searching for an absolute standard against which to measure the impact of an electoral system, would adopt the obvious numerical one: proportionate racial and ethnic representation. True, *Whitcomb, White,* and other decisions that predated *Bolden* (with its intent test) had not equated racial equity with proportionality; but the constitutional amendments on which those decisions rested had not explicitly directed the courts to look at impact. Moreover, if those decisions had rejected the standard of proportionality, they had provided no well-worked-out alternative, as I argued in the previous chapter.

For all its potentially radical implications, the proposed amendment drew remarkably little attention either at the press conference held on April 7, 1981, following introduction of the bills in the House and Senate, or in the House subcommittee hearings that began a month later. The reason is clear: potential opponents were asleep at the switch, and enthusiasts had nothing to gain from rousing them. Civil rights supporters, in fact, downplayed the magnitude of the suggested amendment. The altered wording was described as a "clarification"; they argued that, in viewing section 2 as merely a restatement of the Fifteenth Amendment, the Court had misconstrued the intentions of the statute's framers.[7] Civil rights spokesmen claimed that, since the preclearance provision prohibited electoral changes that were discriminatory in effect as well as purpose, the failure of section 2 to make a similar reference to invidious impact was merely an oversight.

The agenda for hearings conducted by the House Subcommittee on Civil and Constitutional Rights was set by its chairman, Don Edwards (D-Ca.), and the civil rights groups, with whom he worked closely. But in their effort to deflect scrutiny of the proposed amendment to section 2, Edwards and his allies received an unexpected boost from Henry Hyde, the ranking Republican from Illinois. Hyde too readily accepted the change, and, for the sake of harmony, chose not to call witnesses himself. More important, he had a bill of his own to offer, and, once proferred, it became the focus of debate, distracting those who might otherwise have questioned the proposed revision of section 2.

The bills that Rodino, Mathias, and other key liberals had submitted to the House and Senate had extended the special provisions, but otherwise left the statute intact—except, of course, for section 2. Hyde both accepted the section 2 amendment and proposed an additional change: a substantial modification of section 5. His bill permitted an aggrieved party in any jurisdiction to bring suit in a local district court to institute preclearance for a four-year period. No states would automatically be subject to section 5; thus the South would no longer be the special target of the legislation. And the district courts in the South (and elsewhere) would regain their power to judge the need for federal intervention in electoral matters. The proposal strongly resembled the one supported by Nixon in 1970. But whereas Nixon's bill had required a trial on the merits for every allegation of discrimination, Hyde's allowed entire states or counties to be brought under preclearance—to be placed in what he called a "penalty box."[8]

There was another contrast. The Nixon bill was designed to solicit southern conservative support; Hyde's sought to protect the core of the act against an expected assault from that same quarter. The Rodino-Mathias bill, he warned, was unlikely to survive its journey through the

Senate. As he delicately put it: "I believe there are some individuals in the other body who would like to see the preclearance provisions expire altogether."[9] That he had Strom Thurmond, chairman of the Judiciary Committee, particularly in mind was evident.

Hyde viewed his proposal as a strategic "third choice," rejecting a ten-year renewal, at one extreme, and expiration, at the other.[10] But in the view of Vernon Jordan, president of the National Urban League, there was no "midground when it comes to . . . voting rights."[11] As Jesse Jackson put it: "Members of Congress may compromise on budgets . . . But the right to vote is too precious and fundamental to be compromised."[12] From Hyde's perspective, such principled stands, for all their appeal, neglected the reality of politics: "All or nothing might end up with nothing at all."[13] The momentum of a moderate bill, he reasoned, would be harder to stop.

Hyde's proposal was part political calculation, part principle. The act should be changed to respond to change in the South, he believed, contending that the preclearance provision—the substitution of administrative for judicial procedure—was a "drastic" remedy.[14] "If you were injured and struck by a car," he said, "you [couldn't] get relief through the mail."[15] Moreover, he argued, the act continued to stigmatize the South, even though the region had become "vastly different" from what it once was.[16] Indeed, "voting rights abuses in those previously selected jurisdictions [were now] no better or worse than [in] the rest of the country."[17] Hyde's views obviously set him poles apart from the civil rights community, which regarded the statute as so "moderate and mild"[18] (in the words of the mayor of Richmond) that only someone bent on mischief would tamper with it. Yet seventeen years after the passage of the Voting Rights Act, it was surely legitimate to point to progress in the South and to suggest ways in which the statute might be altered to reflect it.

Hyde's proposal was a gift to his opponents. It diverted attention from section 2—from the effort to strengthen the act radically—and focused all eyes on a proposed *reduction* in protection, thus allowing the civil rights groups to turn debate on the Rodino-Mathias bill into an occasion on which to count the friends and enemies of existing minority voting rights. Hyde's alleged political calculation was in fact a miscalculation; he worried about the Senate when he should have been tending his own backyard. By inviting civil rights advocates to argue that the core of the act was under attack, Hyde's maneuver enabled them to raise the specter of renewed disfranchisement. Those who urged a revision of section 5, they said, "simply [did not] want minorities to be part of the political process."[19] "Without . . . the preclearance provision," they maintained, the South would "surely slip back into that post-Reconstruction period" when northern troops were withdrawn and blacks denied the right to vote.[20] The House hearings, the press releases, and the news coverage were full of such ominous images—clocks being turned back, South African apartheid come to America, betrayed Freedom Riders, resurgent Klan-style racism, America's sullied reputation abroad, and blacks deprived of hope.

Yet no one had suggested repealing the permanent sections of the act. Hyde, in fact, had accepted an amendment that would greatly strengthen one of those provisions—section 2. Nevertheless, the Joint Center for Political Studies, a respected black research organization, warned that "if the protections of the Act are terminated there will be virtually no remedy for voting discrimination."[21] "If we lose this law," commented John Lewis, head of the Voter Education Project, "we stand to lose nearly all that we've gained."[22] Ralph Abernathy alluded to the plight of "20 million Black South Africans," and a witness from Mississippi foresaw "widespread corruption, intimidation, and political slavery."[23] Jesse Jackson and many other witnesses pointed to increased Klan activity, and Representatives Don Edwards, Harold Washington, and Robert Drinan all viewed Hyde's proposal as a potentially tragic signal to Africa and "the rest of the world."[24] These spokesmen skillfully played the old tunes; they mobilized support by bringing the sixties back again, denying the fact of change, and rekindling the old moral outrage.

This morality play would have been harder to stage had there been no one to play the villain. But Strom Thurmond, spokesman for the segregationist South in the 1960s and opponent of preclearance, fit the part perfectly, and the Reagan administration appeared to be waiting in the wings to join him if called upon. The warnings from Hyde's opponents thus had a measure of credibility. The presence of genuine opposition—or threatened opposition—allowed civil rights spokesmen to place all those outside the camp of true believers in the enemy ranks.

The witnesses who testified at the House hearings in May, June, and July of 1981 delivered an unvarying message. "Every one of the witnesses has unreservedly supported extension of the act, and has specifically endorsed the Rodino bill," the Joint Center for Political Studies reported in mid-May.[25] This was true, but not (as the Center implied) because the issue was so morally clear that no critics could be found. The effort to pass the Rodino bill (straight extension except for modification of section 2) was spearheaded by a steering committee of the Leadership Conference on Civil Rights, an umbrella group with close ties to Don Edwards, and in putting together the list of witnesses, Edwards followed its advice. As Michael Pertschuk reports in his book on lobbying, the "almost 120 witnesses testifying in support [of the bill] were orchestrated by the steering committee." He also notes that "Edwards had instructed the subcommittee staff to work closely with the conference in developing a set of hearings," and that, as a consequence of that collaboration, the staff gained access to a diverse and effective group: "The major membership organizations [in the Leadership Conference] could draw upon their roster of 'stars,' prominent civil rights spokespersons such as Benjamin Hooks of the NAACP . . . The community-based litigators on the steering committee were able to identify and prepare local witnesses from the South and Southwest."[26]

By House rules, the Republican minority was entitled to a full day of its own, yet Hyde chose, in effect, not to schedule separate hearings. Nor did he propose more than a few names to Edwards, who had expressed willingness to invite witnesses whom Hyde wanted. The minority counsel, Thomas Boyd, explained: "Don Edwards never invited a critic of the House bill on his own initiative. The only critics were supposed to come from us, and we didn't want to call them because we weren't really critical of the act, only of certain provisions, and didn't want to be perceived as against the act. So when they say they invited everyone we asked them to invite, that was true, but we were reluctant to ask."[27]

Hyde's hesitancy—his reluctance to appear an opponent of civil rights—might seem odd. Having led the congressional effort to ban abortions, he was not known for his sensitivity to liberal causes. Moreover, he represented a district that was Republican by a margin of two to one. But experience with the Democratic machine of Chicago Mayor Daley had alerted him to the problem of vote fraud and other electoral abuses, and as Ralph Neas, executive director of the Leadership Conference, noted, Hyde was no stranger to civil rights causes. As Neas put it: "On certain civil rights issues he prided himself on leaving the fold of the conservative Republican administration; he didn't want to be pigeonholed solely in the extremist camp." Perhaps Hyde had statewide or national ambitions; in any case, by pursuing a moderate course with respect to the Voting Rights Act, he hoped "to compensate for [his] Far Right image," Neas suggested. He aimed to be "the architect of some type of grand compromise . . . [to play] an historic role."[28]

Hyde's hopes and ambitions meant that few witnesses appeared at the hearings whose views did not coincide with those of the Leadership Conference. And those few who did come were treated, as Hyde feared, as "against the act," outside the moral community. Wilbur O. Colom, a black Mississippi attorney, told the House committee he had been pressured not to testify. "It stopped being pressure and started being intimidation at some point," he said. "Apparently, someone called most of my colleagues in Mississippi and I found my friends, my black friends in the Republican Party, calling me up asking if I was coming up here to testify against the Voting Rights Act." He went on: "I do a great deal of civil rights litigation, but it was offensive to me when friends of mine called me and told me such things. It would be like . . . a John Bircher having one of his friends call him up and say I understand you are a Communist." Harassment could take a more direct form. In the course of the hearings, Representative Harold Washington publicly accused the city attorney for Rome, Georgia, of coming with "unclean hands."[29] That the Democrats, on their own, had asked only those whom they totally trusted meant that all others acquired the status of messengers from an enemy camp.

Thus, although the witnesses who appeared at the hearings spoke almost as one, the consensus on display was deceptive. The Democrats had created a setting in which critics felt unwelcome, and Hyde, as the ranking Republican, had been unwilling to act with independence and resolution on his own. That the issues raised by the revision of the act were, in fact, complicated and that there were scholars and attorneys ready and willing to debate the complexities would be demonstrated later in the Senate hearings.

Most of the hearings were held in Washington, but for one day each they moved to Austin, Texas, and to Montgomery, Alabama. The Alabama session, held on June 12, was a turning point for Hyde. Four witnesses came forward to testify that registration hours in Montgomery lasted from only 9:00 A.M. to 4:00 P.M.; that only twelve counties in the state permitted deputy registrars; that white establishments, such as stores and churches, were used as polling places; that almost every polling official was white; and that numerous counties had no voting booths to protect secrecy. The list of ways used to discourage blacks from registering and voting was long.[30] Terming such conditions "absolutely outrageous," Hyde abruptly withdrew his opposition to a straight extension of the preclearance provision.[31]

The Montgomery experience aside, Hyde's original position had become increasingly untenable. "There haven't been a lot of witnesses on the other side of the issue," he noted at the end of May.[32] The problem was not only the lack of critical witnesses; supporters of the Rodino bill made claims that were difficult to evaluate. Was it true, as alleged, that blacks in Alabama stayed away from the polls because they were required to vote in a "white store"?[33] Some testified against the use of paper ballots, while others maintained that the intimidating complexity of voting machines made them discriminatory.[34] Did the police, as claimed, photograph those who assisted black voters, and if so, how often, in how many places, and why?[35] Was the Klan, in fact, thriving? There were no rewards for accuracy and no penalties for rhetorical excess. As a result, the hearings produced little of value.

In principle, statements by witnesses were open to challenge and verification. But the charges were often vague (that racism was on the increase, for instance); Hyde was reluctant to appear in an adversarial role; and verification would have required more extensive research than the size of his staff would allow. Hyde had one attorney to assist him; the subcommittee chairman had a staff of five. In addition, Edwards had the support of all four Democrats on the subcommittee, while Hyde was backed by only Dan Lungren of California. More important, Edwards had the enormous resources of the civil rights community at his disposal. The Leadership Conference on Civil Rights, in effect, functioned as an extension of Edwards's staff. In addition to selecting and guiding witnesses, it conducted a massive lobbying effort and drafted legislation. The crucial role of this sophisticated organization will be explored at some length in the following chapter.

Hyde had an additional problem: not only was he short-handed, but he had little available documentation to support his position. The only available studies on voting conditions in the South were produced by civil rights groups or the like-minded U.S. Commission on Civil Rights. The American Civil Liberties Union, the Leadership Conference on Civil Rights, and the Voter Education Project had all funded studies on the status of blacks and Hispanics in the South and Southwest, but none of them was exactly impartial. The volume produced by the Civil Rights

VRA 46

Commission (*The Voting Rights Act: Unfulfilled Goals*) was little more than a brief for the Democrats' bill.

Thus, with few troops, little ammunition, and some reservations about his own cause, Hyde took on the entire civil rights community. And the issue was one on which his adversaries would not compromise. No provision was more important to civil rights groups than section 5, which put the force of the federal government behind the election of blacks and Hispanics. And it lessened the need for grass-roots organizing, since the existence of "safe" black districts reduced the importance of high black turnout. As one attorney in the Department of Justice put it: "No matter how well blacks can do on their own, section 5 will give them extra bargaining strength."[36] The civil rights groups put up a fight that Hyde should have expected, and against which he was no match.

In addition to standing firm on section 5, civil rights groups resisted Hyde's commitment to restoring states' authority over franchise matters at the earliest possible date. In Jesse Jackson's words, "States' rights [was a] code word, which . . . has always meant states' wrongs."[37] It was not just that "placing our fate in the hands of local governments . . . [was] frightening," as one Mississippi witness reported.[38] Civil rights activists saw no significant cost on the other side. The choice, according to them, was the right of minority citizens to vote versus the "hurt feelings" of a state: "When we weigh the enormous harm that is done to an individual in a democracy who is denied or harassed or has his vote diluted against the hurt feelings, I guess, of a geographic entity, it seems to me that we have not made out much of a case for change," said Representative Barney Frank (D-Ma.) in late July. [39] His colleague, Sam B. Hall, Jr. (D-Tx.), dismissed the possible "inconvenience" that the act might cause.[40]

Hyde had what he called "a little different view of the Federal system";[41] damaged feelings and inconvenience were not the issue. States' rights was, undeniably, a familiar cover for a great deal of wrong. In the past, as Donald Horowitz has written, "Federalism . . . plainly propped up ethnic subordination by making Jim Crow a local or regional problem. When black-white relations became a national policy issue, first during Reconstruction and then after 1954, this was at the expense of the prevailing federal-state balance."[42] In Hyde's view the cost was considerable. As soon as conditions permitted, he believed, the power of local communities to structure electoral systems to meet local needs should be restored.

His plea fell on deaf ears for three reasons. First, civil rights spokesmen launched an aggressive campaign to combat the suggestion that the South could be trusted. "I don't trust white people in the South with my rights," Vernon Jordan proclaimed on the first day of hearings. "I didn't before the act; I don't 17 years later."[43] Hyde was quite helpless against such assertions. Indeed, it is hard to imagine what sort of evidence could have overcome such inbred distrust. "We have yet to have any organization of black citizens of Alabama come forward to say it is time to end the participation of this State in the Voting Rights Act," Don Edwards reminded the mayor of Montgomery.[44] Edwards had a point. The argument that blacks should set the timetable for releasing the South from bondage carried considerable moral force.

Second, states' rights was not a popular cause outside conservative circles. In advancing an argument based on states' rights, Hyde was addressing an audience that simply was not there. Justice Hugo Black had, early on, argued that section 5 entailed a "radical degradation of state power," so distorting "our constitutional structure . . . as to render any distinction drawn in the Constitution between state and federal power almost meaningless." By depriving states of their right to pass laws, he said, it came "dangerously near to wiping the States out as useful and effective units in the government of our country."[45] But Justice Black, though a liberal hero, was from the South, and his arguments on this issue were open to the charge of regional bias.

Finally, Hyde's position on the preclearance question crumbled because he was totally without administration support. He needed friends in high places. Hyde recalls that William Bradford Reynolds, the assistant attorney general for civil rights, once came to Capitol Hill for a "superficial and preliminary" chat, and that he was able on one occasion to catch the President's ear during a flight aboard Air Force One.[46] However, it was not until four months after the close of the House hearings that the administration broke its public silence, and by then it had become an aid to its enemies and a burden to its friends.

Defeated in his attempt to amend section 5, Hyde remained determined to change the statute to allow the restoration of normal federal-state relations wherever possible. He had a fallback proposal—changing the "bailout" criteria by which states and counties were judged to be ready for release from coverage. The *Boston Globe* echoed a common misperception when it argued that "the current act provides no bailout procedure."[47] In fact, the act allowed states or counties to prove that discrimination had been improperly inferred from the existence of low turnout in conjunction with the use of a literacy test. But the Supreme Court's decision in *Gaston* (discussed in Chapter 1) had labeled all southern literacy tests discriminatory, thereby closing the door to escape for southern jurisdictions. Thus, until section 5 expired, no county in the "covered" South would have the same freedom to structure its electoral arrangements that all counties in, say, Kansas enjoyed. And that, in Hyde's view, had become a fundamental flaw that he proposed to correct.

Hyde suggested the following bailout criteria:

1. The absence of a literacy test used to discriminate during the preceding ten years.

2. Over the same period, the lack of substantial objections by the Justice Department to changes in voting methods submitted for preclearance.

3. The submission of all proposals that the jurisdiction was legally obligated to submit.

4. The existence of "constructive efforts to enhance minority participation in the electoral process."[48]

This new proposal had much in common with Hyde's earlier suggestion for modifying section 5. Both were aimed at establishing selective, county-by-county coverage. Yet the two proposals were different enough to make the second one considerably more acceptable to civil rights groups. The key difference was that Hyde's first plan would have wiped the slate clean, releasing all jurisdictions from section 5 coverage but permitting its selective reimposition where necessary. Southern states and counties would have been as free as any in the North to alter their electoral arrangements until a "pattern or practice of voting rights abuses" had been proved in court. The new bill left the slate untouched but permitted some erasing here and there. Jurisdictions would remain covered until they had proved themselves "saintly" (Hyde's word). The first proposal would have made preclearance the exception, even in the South; the second left it the rule.

"Hyde's was a very appealing argument," Ralph Neas later noted. "He was raising some valid points—why couldn't we come up with something to let those counties which either had no minority population or had conscientiously eliminated their discriminatory practices get out from under preclearance?"[49] On its face, it was an attractive proposal, but it "threatened to sunder the Leadership Conference," Pertschuk reports. Moderates believed it could be reshaped to good ends, while those who took a harder line "viewed it with dark suspicion."[50] That suspicion was evident in the hearings themselves. "The time to compromise is not in advance," Edwards announced. "You see," Dr. Aaron Henry explained, "when you go to the negotiating table with your fall-back position as your primary position, you are not likely to get that."[51] Yet from the perspective of Neas and others, the civil rights groups had a great deal to gain from cooperating with Hyde. If Hyde voted for the bill and carried his Republican colleagues on the subcommittee along with him, the legislative proposal would have "irresistible force" on the House floor, Neas reasoned. "If we had, on our side, an ally as vocal as Hyde, especially someone who had been labeled the opposition . . . it would be difficult for our opponents to rebound." As Neas presciently observed, "Hyde was playing into our hands."[52]

Thus the momentum for passage would gather strength with Hyde behind the bill. Critics would be even more isolated than before, even more vulnerable to the charge of extremism. In addition, the civil rights groups would have acquired a conciliatory image. The public view would likely be that voiced by Reginald Stuart in the *New York Times Magazine*: "The bail-out provisions represent a dilution of existing law. The leaders of the voting-rights legislative effort compromised," he reported.[53]

The cooperation that Neas advocated was not simply good politics; to work with Hyde's proposal was not necessarily to settle for second-best. For instance, to make release from coverage conditional upon a showing that "constructive efforts to enhance minority participation" had been made gave the civil rights community new leverage in their campaign to eradicate at-large voting. Civil rights spokesmen viewed such voting as discriminatory per se; drawing an analogy between at-large elections and the poll tax, one advocate had suggested their elimination by constitutional amendment.[54] A document placed in the record by a witness at the hearings labeled the at-large system "probably the single most harmful device used against minorities."[55] It "perpetuate[s] past discrimination," another testified.[56] Asked whether "at-large elections [were] . . . in and of themselves discriminatory," the political scientist

Richard Engstrom replied, "definitely."[57] Hyde's new bill did more than give covered jurisdictions (eager to bail out) an incentive to adopt single-member districts; it suggested that such districts were preferred national policy. Civil rights groups thus had not one but two potential tools for removing what a Fifth Circuit judge had called "the last vestige of racial segregation in voting in the South."[58] Both the new section 2 and the altered conditions for bailout promised more widespread use of single-member districts.

Hyde's proposal was in the interest of civil rights groups for yet another reason: it would logically permit the permanent extension of section 5. Congress could skip its periodic assessments of the need for continuing preclearance if district courts hearing bailout suits were doing the job on a case-by-case basis. The new bailout provisions would release every county that had earned its freedom from federal control. Section 5 could thus remain on the books indefinitely, affecting only those jurisdictions that actually deserved continuing surveillance.

A permanent extension of section 5 had long appealed to many civil rights spokesmen. In 1980 the President's Commission for a National Agenda, chaired by Benjamin Hooks, had termed the temporary status of the special provisions a "built-in defect" of the act.[59] "I would like to see the Voting Rights Act made as permanent as the 13th amendment to the Constitution," Dr. Aaron Henry, president of the Mississippi Conference of the NAACP, testified at the hearings.[60] (He referred, of course, only to the temporary provisions; much of the act was already permanent.) Fred Gray, an Alabama attorney, expressed doubt that the southern states would ever "on their own" protect black rights.[61] A black member of the Mississippi state legislature argued that "the debate should not be over whether to extend, but whether to make permanent" the special provisions.[62] "If I had my druthers," Harold Washington declared, "I would extend it [section 5] in perpetuity."[63]

There was no chance, however, that Representative Washington would have his druthers. In his view, guilt established in 1965 would justify distinctive treatment one hundred years later. Southerners had initially charged that the legislation was punitive, and evidently that was what Washington wanted it to be.

Hyde's proposal was thus less than Harold Washington and others wanted, but more than they had originally hoped for. How close it would come to the desired mark would depend, of course, on how easy it would prove to bail out. From the civil rights perspective, Hyde's bill was only a promising start. The criteria for exemption were too liberal; too many jurisdictions would escape preclearance coverage.

In the hands of Edwards, his staff, the Leadership Conference, and the black and Hispanic congressional caucuses, Hyde's bill was remade. After weeks of negotiation, it emerged from the Judiciary Committee radically altered. The terms of bailout were made much more stringent. Of the original four requirements for exemption, only two had survived more or less intact: those demanding the absence of literacy tests and the existence of a perfect record of section 5 submissions. Hyde's other two criteria were toughened and joined to a host of new conditions, all of which made it harder to escape coverage.

Hyde accepted a number of compromises. Among them were the following:[64]

1. The D.C. district court would retain sole jurisdiction to hear bailout suits. Hyde had proposed using federal courts in the localities bringing suit.

2. *Any* section 5 objection and any final court judgment against a jurisdiction on a question of voting rights abuses would be sufficient to preclude escape from coverage.

3. Bailout would be conditional for ten years following the initial exemption, rather than the five years initially suggested.

4. The term "constructive efforts" would be further defined to "show that any such efforts must be directly aimed at the elimination of all structural or procedural barriers to minority voter participation as well as the eradication of voter harassment and intimidation where it exists."

These were not trivial additions. Hyde and his colleagues had initially opposed granting exclusive jurisdiction to the D.C. court, for instance, believing that propinquity was an advantage in judging the complex question of racial progress in a particular locality. Moreover, if cases had to be tried in Washington, transportation, hotel, and additional legal costs could impose a severe burden on impoverished rural counties and other plaintiffs. But the civil rights groups lacked Hyde's faith in southern courts, at least for purposes of bailout. Section 2 questions were another matter: in section 2 suits neither the plaintiff nor the defendant was located in the nation's capital, whereas the United States was the defendant in a bailout case. In addition, the new section 2 was, in theory, simply the old Fourteenth Amendment in revised packaging, and the constitutional cases had always been tried in the local courts.

The effect of assigning sole jurisdiction to the D.C. court was primarily to discourage suits; the process of escaping coverage had become more difficult and expensive. However, making every section 5 objection an absolute bar to bailout sharply contracted the pool of potentially eligible jurisdictions; the number of counties that would qualify would be much lower than Hyde had originally expected. For instance, almost every city that had unexpectedly been obliged to change the location of a polling place just before an election would now be ineligible for bailout, since such last-minute changes were seldom precleared. Hyde had first hoped that polling place switches and other relatively small adjustments in electoral procedure would not be considered significant in a bailout suit, whether or not federal approval had been obtained. Even a series of substantial changes in voting procedure should not bar escape from coverage, Virginia congressman Caldwell Butler argued; objections to them did not necessarily confirm the presence of racism in the electoral process.[65] For example, Justice Department requirements regarding redistricting had never been made clear; a county could draw commissioner precincts in good faith, only to find that it had not met the federal standard. The proposed plan would not reveal the racism of county officials but only their inability to second-guess the federal government.

A separate issue centered on the definition of "constructive efforts" aimed at enhancing "minority voter participation." Hyde had initially proposed language that permitted the D.C. court, in settling a bailout suit, to note a failure to take "constructive" steps to eliminate at-large voting and other "structural barriers." The revised bill, however, appeared to make city-wide voting, multimember districts, runoff requirements, prohibitions on single-shot voting, and other rules an absolute bar to escaping coverage.[66] Nothing in American law or political tradition suggested that procedures such as multimember districts per se violated democratic principle. On the contrary, democracy and diversity were generally thought to be linked, and such electoral arrangements were common features in democracies throughout the world. Majority-vote rules and other procedures had been found discriminatory in particular contexts, but the amended bill failed to distinguish between procedures that had already been found to violate the law and those that continued to be used without objection.

Hyde had originally thought at-large voting, for instance, pertinent to bailout—one of the facts that the court should *consider*. After all, the use of such voting might be a signal of inadequate commitment to making every vote count. Moreover, the reference in the bill to "constructive efforts," Hyde thought, might act as an incentive, putting jurisdictions on notice that certain procedures might bar escape from coverage and nudging them to scrutinize their electoral systems and voluntarily institute changes likely to promote minority officeholding. But the amended bill obviously departed greatly from that initial conception. It also had the potential of subtly altering section 2, a consequence that Hyde certainly never intended when he proposed a revision of the bailout criteria. Certain procedures (single-member districts among them) had apparently been identified as prerequisites of democracy, since jurisdictions that had failed to adopt them were suspect and thus ineligible for bailout. If the bailout criteria were read to suggest that democratic government demanded single-member districts, then plaintiffs challenging an at-large scheme on grounds of discriminatory "result" would certainly have a *prima facie* case. That is, if at-large voting was considered discriminatory when the question was release from coverage, then it would seem to be equally so when the issue was its validity under section 2. County-wide elections, never considered discriminatory per se in the constitutional cases, would then become so as a consequence of the revision of the bailout criteria. [67]

The amended bill contained two conditions for bailout that Hyde adamantly opposed. They made escape from coverage conditional upon the following:

1. The jurisdiction and all units of government within its territory had to prove they could meet the bailout standards. States could not be released until every county within them qualified.

2. The jurisdiction had to defend itself successfully in every vote discrimination suit brought against it. Both pending actions and consent decrees precluded bailout.

Pending legal action was dropped as a condition of bailout in the course of debate on the House floor. [68] But civil rights groups would not budge on the question of consent decrees, which were equated with final judgments in a suit. That is, the provision made no distinction between a jurisdiction's voluntary agreement to minority demands and a judicial finding of electoral discrimination. Hyde and his colleagues argued that the law normally favored such settlements, and that this stipulation would only encourage litigation. Moreover, consent agreements often represent not an admission of guilt but acknowledgment of the political and financial costs of protracted conflict.[69] Advocates of the provision, however, believing that few frivolous suits would be brought, asserted that legal action reliably signaled persistent voting rights problems.

The two sides were equally far apart on the question of "selective release." Was it proper, Hyde asked, that "one stubbornly racist county, over whom the state government [perhaps had] little or no effective control, [should] indefinitely doom the state legislature to what the Supreme Court [had] termed the 'extraordinary' procedures attendant to administrative preclearance?"[70] But Hyde's opponents maintained that a state was at least partially responsible for the electoral practices of its subunits, and further that covered states, eager to be extricated from the law, would pressure obstreperous counties to reform.

In its final form, the bill was a triumph for the civil rights lobby. Yet the road to victory had been exceedingly rocky. In the final vote by the Judiciary Committee, the lone dissent came from Caldwell Butler. But the seeming unison on the committee was deceptive. "I was deeply saddened," Hyde would later write, "at the manner with which the Committee reported HR 3112 on the afternoon of July 31st. While the lopsided vote of 23 to 1 gives the appearance of virtual unanimity, the reality is quite the opposite. Beneath the surface boil strong currents of mutual distrust and discontent."[71] The amendments to Hyde's initial proposal had been tacked on by breaking through the resistance of not only committee Republicans but also moderates within the Leadership Conference, as well as key members of Edwards's own staff.

The hearings ended in mid-July, and in the two weeks before the Judiciary Committee vote, interested members of the committee and minority and civil rights representatives met around the clock. But agreements that had been painstakingly arrived at soon came unraveled. "The situation kept changing on me," Hyde later said. An accord was like a "squid in water"—it would just "wiggle away."[72]

The instability of the negotiating process was due in part to the considerable turbulence within civil rights ranks. "I suppose we just couldn't get the civil rights community to support something that I put together with help from a lot of people," Hyde stated with undisguised bitterness at the mark-up session on July 31.[73] In fact, the situation was more complicated than he allowed: a few had determined the policy of the many. Most who spoke for civil rights organizations believed in working with Hyde on tactical grounds. In the end, though, they were overwhelmed by a determined minority hewing to a hard line. And that group could generally sway Don Edwards, who always seemed eager to avoid the charge of moral laxity on civil rights.

The final collapse of the moderates occurred on July 30, the evening before the mark-up. The chronicle of events, as reported by *The New Republic*, is worth quoting at length:

> It got so hot in the coalition in the last two days of July 1981 that, by the time the differences were reconciled, a splinter group on the Conference's voting rights steering committee had already prepared an angry press release and begun planning how to fight its former allies. Much of the steering committee, fearing hostile amendments on the House floor, wanted to make concessions while the voting rights bill was still in the Judiciary Committee markup. They favored striking a deal with Illinois Republican Henry Hyde that would have diluted crucial enforcement provisions in exchange for his support. Four dissenters said the deal was outrageous. "There was a whole lot of screaming and name-calling," says Antonia Hernandez. "It was a terrible time." Frank Parker, a red-bearded veteran of death threats and voting rights lawsuits in the South, was the purest of the purists. "Their judgment was totally and completely wrong," says Parker . . . "We would have publicly and openly opposed the bill, and in fact were developing a strategy to do that. It threatened to break up the coalition." The deal with Hyde finally fell apart, and the coalition decided— consensus renewed—to stop negotiating with him. There ensued an incident of extraordinary rarity in Congress: the four principal members of Edwards's subcommittee staff, incensed at the risks of abandoning Hyde, staged an angry walk-out and refused to take part in redrafting the disputed section of the bill.[74]

Those who walked out included a black and a Hispanic. But the threat of sabotage by veteran litigator Frank Parker's troops had the greater effect. Their self-proclaimed moral superiority, together with the prospect of infighting among members of the Leadership Conference, was enough to defeat those with soft hearts and weak stomachs.

Late at night, Edwards, Frank Parker, and others from the Leadership Conference tacked onto the bill the amendments to which Hyde had never agreed. "Late in the evening of July 30 and in the early morning hours of July 31," Hyde wrote, "our draft and the agreements which had been reached up to that point, were stitched together and appended to new language, some previously the subject of heated debate during the negotiations and some merely the inspiration of the moment."[75] At 10:40 A.M. on July 31 the full committee reconvened. The bill was introduced less than an hour before the members were asked to vote on it. "There was no opportunity to examine the provisions of the proposal and therefore no opportunity to object," Butler reported.[76]

It was take-it-or-leave-it, and the committee took it, virtually sight unseen. The mood was far from harmonious. Representative Railsback's remarks at the meeting that morning are revealing: "I think many of us believed that we were going to be able to come in this morning and vote out what we hoped would be a largely agreed-upon bill containing a bailout that would be acceptable to Henry Hyde . . . as well as to our chairman . . . And now instead of having sweetness and light, we find there is outright hostility. I have never seen the committee in the shape it is now in with some of the members at each other's throats."[77] Proponents of the amended bill attempted to camouflage their victory, to depict the changes made as inconsequential, the "outright hostility" as ill-founded. They maintained that the redrafted bill was "95 percent . . . Hyde." But Hyde rejected the accolade. "It is not 95 percent of what I wanted," he retorted. "It's 95 percent of what I acceded to, to get a truly bipartisan doable bailout."[78] But while he could puncture the pretense of "sweetness and light," he had no remaining power. He had seen himself as part of an inner group, fashioning a true compromise, but now found himself on the outside. Edwards obtained the bipartisan support he needed without Hyde. Two other Republicans had jumped on board—Sensenbrenner of Wisconsin and Fish of New York.

In the end Hyde, too, voted for the bill. Only Caldwell Butler (white and southern) held out. The risk taken by the diehards had paid off handsomely: they had their bill and Hyde's blessing, however reluctant. From the start Hyde had wanted to be on the side of "civil rights"; to have joined the ranks of the bill's opponents in the final hour would have been the ultimate defeat.

Hyde's defeat was substantial as it was. In proposing to modify the bailout formula, Hyde initially had a dual aim: to provide incentives for progressive change, and to recognize progress where it had occurred. He had not been opposed to making the special provisions permanent.

The renewal process seemed inevitably to pit Republicans against minorities—a predicament that Hyde and his colleagues hoped to escape by acceding in the effort to make preclearance and other "temporary" provisions permanent. But the Illinois congressman wanted to release "those jurisdictions which [had] tried to improve conditions and which [had] abided by the law for nearly 17 years."[79]

"We want to make [release from coverage] difficult," an ACLU representative readily admitted.[80] In that, civil rights groups succeeded admirably. As a result, Hyde's second aim (recognizing progress where it had occurred) had been almost totally frustrated. The civil rights groups had welcomed Hyde's proposal as a means to retain coverage, not terminate it, and their redrafted bailout criteria deftly accomplished that end. That is, the bailout provisions in their final form did not actually permit bailout. And had Congress enacted the House bill intact, with its permanent extension of section 5, every jurisdiction brought under the special provisions of the act from 1965 to 1975 would have been permanently covered. As it turned out, the Senate rejected the indefinite extension and set 2007 as a date for further renewal, thus limiting the extension to twenty-five years.[81] But the bailout criteria passed unaltered, and their stringency made it highly unlikely that any southern county would be released in the intervening time.

Hyde and his opponents, however, had started from opposing assumptions. "I am afraid that Mr. Hyde is more of an optimist than I am," Edwards said. "Unfortunately I have heard no evidence of a cleaning up of their act . . . by these covered jurisdictions. On the contrary—and I'm sorry to have to say this—the evidence is the opposite and the evidence is that the plight of minorities in the United States is *worsening*, not gaining and not becoming better." Given that the number of elected blacks had risen from fewer than 100 in 1965 to more than 5,000 nationwide, how much progress would Edwards have demanded as a condition of release from coverage?[82] Viewing section 5 as a tool for black and Hispanic political advancement, civil rights spokesmen were ready to exempt jurisdictions from coverage only on that never-never day when minority candidates ceased to benefit from preclearance. They hoped that section 5 would remain in place—and believed that it should—until that unlikely hour when black and Hispanic candidates could routinely expect from the normal political process electoral arrangements as advantageous as those that preclearance offered. This was the unstated condition of bailout.

Hyde could not force debate on such matters all by himself. And from the outset he had a problem that plagued him to the end: most of his colleagues paid no more than cursory attention to the matters at hand. The House hearings and mark-up took place during peak months for Congress, a time when members often face scheduling conflicts among several committees. The record of attendance at these particular subcommittee hearings is revealing. Edwards and Hyde appeared faithfully; Washington and Sensenbrenner about two-thirds of the time; the other three only sporadically. "Committee hopping," one scholar has written, "has become a habit, as has casual or symbolic floor voting . . . Moreover, scanty preparation often leaves members dependent on cues from staff and others; the average representative in 1977 reported spending only 12 minutes a day preparing legislation or speeches and another 11 minutes reading."[83] In the decade after 1971, the number of standing subcommittees in the House had increased by one-third; by 1981 the members' assignments far outweighed their capacity either to attend all scheduled meetings or otherwise to keep abreast of important issues.

The press of work, the prevalence of symbolic voting, and the tendency to take cues from staff members all worked to the advantage of the civil rights groups. Scanty preparation led members to cast symbolic votes, and support for anything short of the most uncompromising bill, congressmen knew, would be read as a less than true commitment to minority rights. If symbolic considerations did not fully sway a Democratic member, that member could turn for help to the subcommittee staff. The staff's views, however, were indistinguishable from those of the Leadership Conference. There was nothing extraordinary in this; Edwards had total confidence in the civil rights lobby, and his hiring practices legitimately reflected that faith.[84]

Other factors worked to advance the cause of the civil rights groups. Many committee members came to the issue predisposed to see the question in the clear moral terms that virulent southern racism had made appropriate in 1965. In fact, most members had undoubtedly requested assignment to the committee precisely because of their belief in civil rights as an ongoing moral crusade. "Congressmen," Arthur Maass has written, "join a committee of one type or the other principally because of their own preference; and having joined one, they become socialized so that their preferences are similar to those of their fellow congressmen."[85]

The committee proceedings, moreover, were never out of the public eye. Since the reforms of the 1970s, which opened the doors of all House committee meetings, it took a majority vote to keep the lobbyists and cameras out. One consequence, according to a 1980 select committee report, was to inhibit the range of discussion and increase the pressure for conformity. Thus the slapdash, inattentive habits of Congress and the unflagging attentiveness of the civil rights groups combined to promote only the most hazy understanding of the amendments on which the members were being asked to vote, and the public nature of the process kept those members politically alert. The blaze of light generated by the omnipresent lobbyists and the media illuminated unmistakably the political message that a given member's position would project. Moderates within the Leadership Conference camp had thought they were placing principle above politics in joining those who refused to compromise in the negotiations with Hyde, but members of Congress understood that it was precisely the aura of uncompromising principle that gave the bill the political force that it had.

The bill that emerged from the Judiciary Committee, with near-unanimous support, radically altered section 2, permanently extended preclearance and other "temporary" provisions, and provided strict new bailout criteria. It was a remarkable victory for Edwards and the Leadership Conference—more remarkable than they publicly claimed. They said that the bailout provisions would free 200 covered counties—a quarter of the total.[86] Widely quoted and never questioned, the assertion was effective public relations, but the calculation was flawed in two obvious ways.[87] To begin with, the figure did not take into account those jurisdictions barred from bailout because they had failed to preclear every change in electoral procedure (some of a last-minute, trivial nature). And, indeed, at the time of the hearings the number of such jurisdictions would have been impossible to count. Compliance with section 5 creates a record; noncompliance does not. Yet once a jurisdiction initiated a bailout suit, any incident of noncompliance would be reported by minority residents to the D.C. court.

Second, the estimate took no account of the demand that jurisdictions seeking release show evidence of "constructive steps" taken to enhance minority political participation. Here the problem was only partly one of available data. Information on the method of electing all town and city councils, county boards and commissions, school boards, and special district commissions would have been extremely hard to collect. But, in addition, the statutory language ("constructive steps") was too vague to permit a count of jurisdictions unable to demonstrate their good will. Could a county claim to have taken "constructive steps" if it still required candidates to win by a majority of the vote? Or was a majority-vote rule (often leading to a runoff between a black and a white contestant) evidence of inadequate dedication to minority political participation? Certainly county-wide voting would fall into the category of inadequate dedication. The figure of 200 was therefore inflated—precisely how seriously no one could estimate.

Thus the victory that the civil rights groups partly disavowed was, in fact, fully theirs. They had accepted Hyde's initial proposal and then drastically reshaped it. The redrafted bill was externally recognizable but internally transformed.

The story of the 1982 House amendments effectively ends here. The floor vote was 385 to 24, with 30 abstentions. Though the result was a foregone conclusion, Edwards left nothing to chance. On the eve of the floor debate he sent a letter to each of the 435 House members. "Dear Colleague," he wrote. "Each amendment to be offered by Republicans would do serious damage to the bill. Please vote them all down."[88] And with one exception, they did.[89] While seeming to convey apprehension, Edwards's letter in fact betrayed his strength. He had not been privy to Republican plans, had not seen the amendments he denounced. Confident of his powers of leadership following the near-unanimous vote on the Judiciary Committee, he was able to launch an effective attack on undisclosed proposals.

The emergency powers bestowed by the original Voting Rights Act had necessarily been temporary; the act would not have passed constitutional muster had the special provisions been permanent. Yet it was the limited life of those powers that made possible the transformation of the statute. The process of renewal was inevitably an occasion for amendment, and the amendment process was one of political opportunity.

In 1982 both Republicans and Democrats seized that opportunity, though not with equal success. A Democratic proposal—the revision of section 2—passed without debate. But a Republican proposal aimed at releasing some southern jurisdictions from coverage emerged as an amendment that provided an unprecedented twenty-five year extension of preclearance, with little likelihood that any covered county would successfully sue for exemption.

This chapter has focused on Henry Hyde's political missteps and the

acumen of his opponents. Hyde hoped to be part of the "right crowd"—
to identify himself with the civil rights cause. Yet he proposed to modify
preclearance, the provision the civil rights community cared most about.
He never gained the acceptance he sought but instead diverted attention
from section 2, in effect killing debate on that crucial issue by allowing
the Leadership Conference to raise the specter of renewed disfranchisement and to discredit all critics of the House bill. He fared little better
with his second proposal. In suggesting a change in the bailout criteria,
Hyde had asked whether (after seventeen years) every covered southern county still belonged in the "penalty box." Preclearance had been a
drastic remedy for a grievous wrong; to an unprecedented degree it
removed from local jurisdictions the power to shape their electoral systems to meet local needs. In Hyde's view, the emergency that had justified such radical action had waned, and the problems southern minorities
faced had become little different from those in the North. But the civil
rights lobby, with a different view and thus a different agenda, reshaped
Hyde's proposal, and his congressional colleagues gave the drastically
revised bill only the most cursory glance. Michael Pertschuk, in his book
on lobbying, calls the House story one of "resistance to untimely compromise."[90] Certainly, those who took a hard line within the Leadership
Conference correctly sensed that compromise was politically unnecessary; the moderates were prematurely ready to negotiate. But
Pertschuk assumes that compromise would have been not only a strategic miscalculation but a substantive error—that the upshot would have
been a bill that failed to give minority voters proper protection. And
on that central question there was never adequate debate. The merits of the bill that the House so overwhelmingly passed were barely
considered.

The bailout provisions were not discussed in the Senate. There, the
question of section 2—ignored by the House—would become the sole
topic. And although the civil rights lobby in the end did prevail in that
Republican-controlled chamber as well, it was not for want of skilled and
sustained opposition at the hearings. The next chapter tells the story of
that impressive victory.

# SIX

# Liberal Power in a Conservative Senate

On December 16, 1981, the House bill was introduced in the Senate. By that date sixty-one senators had already pledged their support—enough to cut off a filibuster, should the occasion arise. Moreover, the sixty-one included eight southern Democrats and twenty-one Republicans, among them three conservatives. It was, as the chief counsel to the Subcommittee on the Constitution put it, a "stunning political achievement."[1]

Had the civil rights groups won the long-expected fight even before it began? Not to judge from the comments at the time. "The greatest peril to minority voters' rights will occur in the Republican-dominated Senate," the *Los Angeles Times* reported in May 1981.[2] "Well, Henry, how are we going to get this thing through the Senate?" Harold Washington is reported to have asked Henry Hyde the night of the House vote.[3] The act still has "a long way to go before clearing the Senate," the *New York Times* noted soon after that vote.[4] Throughout the debate in the House, the civil rights groups had stressed the difficulties expected from the Senate Judiciary Committee and its chairman, Strom Thurmond, the Dixiecrat candidate for president in 1948. Thurmond had opposed the original act in 1965 and every extension; and the amendments Henry Hyde initially proposed, it will be recalled, had been offered as a "strategic third choice"—an effort to protect the measure from Senate emasculation. Although the Leadership Conference and its congressional colleagues could not be displeased with their lopsided win in the House, they had reason to worry that the strength of the new bill made it vulnerable to attack. Neither the administration nor Senate conservatives would have dared to oppose moderate legislation, but this bill might invite and legitimize opposition, they had been warned.[5]

If the immediate support of sixty-one senators seemed to belie the fears of pessimists, if the civil rights groups had displayed surprising initial strength, the road to final passage was still far from unimpeded. The most immediate roadblock was not, as so frequently reported, Senator Thurmond, but Utah Republican Orrin Hatch, the chairman of the Subcommittee on the Constitution. Hatch was as conservative on civil rights questions as his House counterpart, Don Edwards, was liberal. Unlike Thurmond, Hatch had no roots in the Jim Crow South, but he opposed the use of federal power to achieve statistical parity among racial and ethnic groups. Residential patterns characterized by ethnic and racial clustering, schools and places of employment in which blacks and whites were not distributed in proportion to their numbers in the population—these were not, in his view, conditions that required remedial action in the absence of evidence of intentionally blocked opportunity. He believed there had been in recent years an ominous slide toward racial and ethnic quotas, and he saw the upcoming Senate debate on the Voting Rights Act as an opportunity to brake the momentum of this trend.

Hatch's position as subcommittee chairman gave him considerable power over the hearings on the bill, allowing him to frame the debate. "Rodino and Edwards allowed us to control the hearing process—there was day to day coordination between the committee staff and LCCR [the Leadership Conference on Civil Rights] [in selecting] 120–130 witnesses," a civil rights lobbyist explained to the political scientist Diane Pinderhughes. "The Senate was important but Hatch chaired [the subcommittee] and we were on the defensive; it was a much different situation than the House of Representatives."[6] That the situation was going to be different Hatch made clear on the first day of hearings. In his opening remarks, he announced that the list of invitees would be "balanced."[7] This would ensure exposure for a much wider range of views, which in itself could significantly erode the support of the sixty-one senators.

Hatch's power was enhanced by the resoluteness of his convictions. At ease with his conservative image, he felt little political pressure to appease the civil rights community, in contrast to Hyde. Utah was one of the most solidly Republican states in the union, and its electorate included few black and Hispanic voters.

The civil rights groups, then, were partly right: the conservatives were not without leverage. The extraordinary support the House bill had commanded, though impressive, was not decisive. Yet the limits of that leverage were also clear. Hatch worked under enormous constraints. The momentum with which the bill arrived in the Senate was in itself a significant factor. Beginning more or less with a clean slate, Edwards had been free to push for quite radical changes; the overwhelming passage of the House bill, however, circumscribed the room in which Hatch had to maneuver. Moreover, the isolation that had plagued Hyde in the House affected Hatch as well. The administration was no help. And the civil rights community, having come of age politically, was extraordinarily well organized; its lobbying effort was equal to that of any other special-interest group. Furthermore, with few exceptions, the media functioned as part of that lobby.

It was a measure of Hatch's political acumen that he understood the limits of his power, and that he chose, as a consequence, to concentrate on only one issue: the proposed revision of section 2. In other words, he accepted the new bailout criteria as passed by the House; the votes were simply not there to modify them. He believed that any attempt to alter those criteria would only deflect attention from the central issue: the effort to circumvent the need to prove discriminatory intent in suits challenging long-standing election methods or voting procedures in jurisdictions not covered by preclearance. As the lobbyists for the bills acknowledged, the revision was an effort to overturn *Mobile v. Bolden*, a constitutional decision that Hatch believed had been right.[8]

As the previous chapter indicated, the proposed change in section 2 was a bold and radical move, one that would greatly ease the burden on plaintiffs seeking to challenge methods of voting not only in the South, with its history of Fifteenth Amendment violations, but in jurisdictions across the nation. That proponents of the change had managed, in the House, to minimize its radicalism had been an impressive feat. But they would not be able to avoid debate in the Senate. Hatch maintained that a "results" test for methods of election would alter the American electoral landscape, instituting race-based gerrymandering wherever minority officeholding was disproportionately low. Such a standard, he said, raised fundamental questions "involving the nature of American representative democracy, federalism, civil rights, and the separation of powers." No issue before the Congress, he added, was more important in defining us "as a Nation and in expressing the values of our Constitution."[9]

Section 2 was the one issue over which Hatch could disagree with the civil rights groups, yet claim to be opposed to any reduction in the protection provided by the act. "The provisions of the Voting Rights Act ought to be extended," he announced at the outset.[10] It was the only politically viable stance: conservative, yet concerned; for preservation, against revision.

Both sides, in fact, scrambled to stand on that same politically safe ground. Passed for no "compelling and demonstrable reasons," Attorney General William French Smith asserted, the House bill "would dramatically change section 2." Civil rights spokesmen depicted their aim as simply to clarify—not alter—the provision.[11] It was the conservatives, they charged, who were offering a "crippling amendment."[12] "The effort of opponents of the amendments to *substitute* a 'purpose' requirement in Section 2 would be a radical *change* in the law," the executive director of the Leadership Conference argued.[13] "The question before us," Senator Kennedy said, "is whether a strong, effective Voting Rights Act will *continue* to protect millions of our citizens. Or, will the Act be crippled . . . [by] sophisticated efforts to *gut* the most successful civil rights law of our time?"[14] The issue, these proponents suggested, was ominously familiar: critics of the House bill would rob minorities of a right that they had been guaranteed for seventeen years. "Mr. Chairman . . . I have a peculiar feeling that I have been here before," Benjamin Hooks told Hatch.[15] "There are those who would open old wounds . . . refight . . . old battles," Senator Kennedy lamented.[16] It was politically dangerous, proponents of the change knew, to allow Hatch exclusive claim to commitment to the existing act. And it was politically useful to charge that *he*, not they, wanted to alter the act.

Hatch's focus on section 2 had a salutary effect: it sparked debate over the meaning of electoral discrimination, the central issue that previous hearings had only obscured. In the end Hatch won far less than he had hoped for, but more than the civil rights lobby had wished.

In describing the journey of the legislation through the House, I focused on the "internal" story—the extraordinarily close tie between Edwards and the Leadership Conference; the political payoff for those within the conference who refused to compromise; Hyde's odd, symbiotic relationship to the civil rights groups, whose power he inadvertently enhanced; the problems caused by his limited legislative resources; and the ways in which House customs worked to the benefit of civil rights groups. In the Republican-controlled Senate, on the other hand, pressures from outside institutions, organizations, and events were much more important. Don Edwards had made the Leadership Conference an internal group; it had played, at his invitation, an integral part in the proceedings. That the House bill survived the Senate basically intact was testimony to the extraordinary effectiveness of pressures from outside the legislative chamber.

To begin with, there was the pressure from the new black and Hispanic vote, which, already important in 1975, became more so with every passing year. In the aftermath of the House vote, the *New York Times* noted that the surge of minority registration in the previous sixteen years meant that lawmakers could no longer risk alienating blacks and Hispanics by opposing the act. As one southern representative observed, those who had backed the President's budget cuts were eager to support the voting rights bill as a way of rebuilding credibility among minorities back home. "You have to cater to those interests just like you cater to other interests," an aide to a southern senator remarked.[17]

There was perhaps no greater testimony to the potency of the new black vote than the changing response of southern white congressmen to the question of extension. When the act first came up for renewal in 1970, southern opposition to its extension was loud and clear. By 1981, however, even Senator Thurmond—who in 1957 had filibustered for twenty-four hours against a civil rights bill—was close to silent. In the intervening years blacks had become one-third of his constituency; he had put blacks on his Senate staff; and he had worked to secure the appointment of a black federal judge in South Carolina. In the spring of 1981 Thurmond had stated that "after 17 years, the states ought to be given a chance to get out from the act."[18] Yet, in fact, even in the Republican Senate Thurmond was no more free to ignore the black vote than were the seventy-one southern representatives who voted for the House bill.

In the 1981–1982 debates the bill was depicted by both its proponents and the media as "above politics," as characterized by such obvious worth that partisan calculations were simply inappropriate. Yet, in fact, it was precisely the bill's status as special-interest legislation that gave it force. Blacks and Hispanics had become important groups within the Democratic Party. It was not the Democratic Party alone, however, that had a stake in successfully courting minority support. Approximately 20 percent of Hispanics had cast their votes for Ronald Reagan in 1980, and although black Republicans remained a rare species, a number of Republicans in Congress—including some conservatives—depended on some black support. Moreover, while many Republicans privately "made clear their unhappiness with the law," as one reporter noted, "most [did] not want to appear hostile to blacks on perhaps the most politically important civil rights issue of the year."[19] In aspiring to become the nation's majority party, the GOP was eager to avoid a racist image.

Not only were blacks and Hispanics registered to vote in unprecedented numbers, but civil rights groups were organized to an unprecedented degree. As Michael Pertschuk notes in his book on lobbying:

> In mobilizing grass roots; in structuring the media; in formulating and implementing legislative strategy; in substantive expertise and legislative draftsmanship; in building and sustaining a close and trusting relationship with its congressional leaders; in seeking out, packaging, and coaching a knockout array of witnesses at a hearing—the Leadership Conference was unmatched . . . When the arms control community sought to organize to fight the MX missile, they turned to the Leadership Conference on Civil Rights as a model.[20]

With equal admiration *The New Republic* noted: "The Leadership Conference managed as impressive a showing of legislative savoir faire as anything done by the big-time agriculture, defense, or business lobbies"; it "displayed a new maturity, an unprecedented unity, and an impressive political clout."[21]

That clout represented the joint effort of the 165 organizations that made up the Leadership Conference. Founded in 1950, the organization included such stalwarts as the NAACP, the National Urban League, the Mexican-American Legal Defense and Education Fund (MALDEF), the ACLU, and the Anti-Defamation League. They were joined by less obvious groups such as the National Council of Catholic Women, the United Hebrew Trades, Actors' Equity, the YMCA, and the YWCA, as well as predominantly black business groups like the National Funeral Directors and Morticians Association and the National Beauty Culturists' League. Some were considerably more active than others on the issue of voting rights. The groups have routinely engaged in horse trading: for instance, AFL-CIO support for a civil rights issue might be swapped for MALDEF support on a labor matter.

The nerve center of activity was the Voting Rights Act Steering Committee, made up of twenty-five of these groups, which regularly met in Washington to map strategy and formulate policy. For sixteen months meetings were regularly scheduled for Fridays, but during the heat of the campaign the committee convened four or five times a week. At the outset of the effort, in April 1981, the Leadership Conference had hired Ralph Neas as its first full-time executive director, primarily to guide what would quickly become a massive lobbying effort. Neas and his colleagues devoted most of their waking hours to the bill. "Lawyers from the Legal Defense Fund, the Joint Center for Political Studies, the ACLU, and the Lawyers' Committee for Civil Rights literally moved to Washington for the . . . campaign," Diane Pinderhughes reports in her study "Interest Groups and the Extension of the Voting Rights Act."[22] For many, the work seemed to recreate the excitement of the sixties. "Morning, noon and night, we knew each other's habits, like you knew the best time of day to reach [lobbyists A and B] was 6:30 in the morning after they were up, but before they took their shower," one participant recalled. "It was beautiful . . . I'll never forget this in my life, never," said another.[23]

In a letter to the Attorney General, Neas and Benjamin Hooks wrote that the Leadership Conference began discussions with Mathias, Kennedy, Rodino, and Edwards in January 1981, four months before the introduction of the House bill.[24] In fact, the campaign to extend and revise the act had begun quietly eight months earlier. As Richard Margolis describes it in *Foundation News*, the decision in *City of Mobile v. Bolden* acted "like a shot of adrenalin." In fact, the April 1980 decision came to be viewed as a "blessing in disguise"; it mobilized first the Rockefeller Foundation and then others. "After *Bolden* the whole thing sort of came together," a Rockefeller staff member recalled. The Rockefeller Foundation began both to make plans of its own and to think about how it might draw other foundations into a larger campaign. In September the Ford Foundation held a meeting "to get donors together with practitioners . . . to talk about what could be done to save the Voting Rights Act," and with that meeting the campaign was actually under way.[25] The dedication of the foundations made possible the total dedication of Neas and his colleagues. "I tell you, the foundations [were] magnificent," a civil rights activist later said.[26] Ford, Rockefeller, Carnegie, and a host of less well known foundations (including Mott, Norman, Taconic, The Campaign for Human Development, and Southern Education) underwrote the activities of Neas and his associates.

In addition to setting overall strategy, the Washington forces led by Neas maintained constant contact with the press, researched the voting records of members of Congress, mapped the makeup of their districts, communicated with congressional staff, and, when possible, met with both congressmen and members of the administration. In the ten weeks between the vote in the House Judiciary Committee and floor action, Hooks and Neas later wrote, "the member organizations of the Leadership Conference and other civil rights organizations campaigned vigorously across the country" on behalf of the House bill.[27] That campaign continued to mount through the Senate deliberations. "To beef up work in the states, Washington lobbyists flew around the country at various times to appear on television interview shows and to talk with newspaper editorial boards in an effort to put pressure on representatives and senators who were considering swing votes," the *Congressional Quarterly* reports.[28] The peripatetic lobbyists based in the capital were aided by extensive grass-roots work. Barton Gellman, writing in *The New Republic*, describes the activity of one local activist, Mona Martin, the president of the Iowa League of Women Voters. Martin had been instructed to bring pressure to bear on Senator Charles Grassley, an Iowa Republican on the Hatch subcommittee.

> The Leadership Conference in Washington sent Martin a list of local organizers from unions, church groups, black and Hispanic groups, farm and education groups, and Common Cause. Martin then applied the heat where it counted. The Church Forum—representing denominations from Catholic to Episcopal and Baptist to Presbyterian—sent out "minister advisories" suggesting sermon ideas on voting rights. A "media committee" held press conferences, distributed slick p.r. packages, wrote Op-Ed pieces, and took out a quarter page ad in the *Des Moines Register*. Borrowing a WATS line phone bank from a local business, Martin organized "telephone trees," which work like chain letters. Grassley got five hundred calls from constituents in one day alone.[29]

Phone banks, sermon ideas, public-relations packages, and op-ed pieces—this was lobbying at its professional best.

The participation of the League of Women Voters contributed to the "above-politics" aura that surrounded the bill. Indeed, both the foundations and the league had treated the bill as simply legislation ensuring the right to vote, and thus a resolutely nonpartisan cause. The league, Pinderhughes reports, usually selects and evaluates issues "through a meticulous, complex and lengthy process, involving every member." Local units discuss a selected issue over the course of an entire year. As one league member describes the process, the national staff "sends out a questionnaire which everyone fills out; they count up the votes on each question so we can develop a consensus . . . the national staff develops a position statement which is then taken back and ratified at the annual convention."[30] Many proposals fail to survive such intense scrutiny, but the Voting Rights Act was never exposed to it. Local affiliates were never asked to study the question; a specific exemption from customary scrutiny had been granted, presumably on the ground that the matter was beyond debate. Thus an organization that prided itself on its great circumspection came to take on a major lobbying effort without obtaining its members' consent. "The purest brand of motherhood" was how one member of the Senate staff described voting rights, and certainly the civil rights groups and their allies depicted it as such.[31]

The civil rights community was thus organized to an unprecedented degree. Never before, perhaps, had so sophisticated a lobbying effort been set up to peddle a product so consistently presented as above politics. A meticulously organized national effort had been launched to sell that which allegedly should need no selling. It was a powerful political potion, the effects of which it was the unenviable task of critics to dispel.

A substantial minority vote, a high level of organization, a highly appealing issue—as if these were not enough, civil rights groups were blessed with additional advantages. One was the absence of any organized opposition to the legislation—a major source of frustration for Hatch. The act "is not the target of any well-organized, well-financed lobby," one lobbyist observed.[32] ACLU lobbyist Laura Murphy subsequently attributed victory to, among other things, the lack of "funded opposition."[33] Indeed, all political pressure came from one direction. "There was *nobody* on the outside," recalled Stephen J. Markman, chief counsel to the Senate subcommittee. "It was our central problem."[34] Even Hatch, representing a state with a tiny minority population, received a deluge of letters urging support of the House bill, many of them from church organizations. And in South Carolina only a handful of constituents wrote to Thurmond in support of Hatch, while thousands urged that the bill be passed. The imbalance was bound to have an impact. As one conservative put it, "There are few members, whatever their philosophy, who can look at mail running a thousand to one on an issue and not give serious consideration to voting for the side with a thousand."[35]

For those "with apprehension about the House bill," Markman later wrote, the Reagan administration "was virtually their only ally."[36] But the administration proved only a grudging companion. The pressure on conservatives to support civil rights was perhaps nowhere more evident than in the White House's response to the voting rights issue.

The first clear move on the part of the administration came on June 15, 1981, a month and a half into the House hearings and just days before Hyde withdrew his proposal to modify the preclearance provision. On that date the President requested an evaluation of the voting rights question by the Attorney General. "The question before us in the months ahead," he said, "will not be whether the rights which the Act seeks to protect are worthy of protection, but whether the act continues to be the most appropriate means of guaranteeing those rights."[37] Clearly the administration was not ready to support the House bill or even a straight extension, yet more striking was its unmistakable distaste for the entire fray. It sent no one to testify at the House hearings—an unusual decision given the importance of the issue. But Edwards was holding hearings before the Justice Department was ready to appear. "There's just no reason for us to march to Don Edwards' agenda," an administration spokesman stated. "Why should we make somebody mad in June of '81, when we've got another year to act?" he asked.[38] Little was to be gained, in other words, from conformity to the congressional timetable, particularly since every position under consideration by the White House was likely to infuriate the organized civil rights community. The decision to lie low also suited Republican senators from the South, who feared a White House move against preclearance. As the *Washington Post* explained on June 13, "Southern GOP leaders hope their agreement to endorse section 5 will pacify their critics, and at the same time avoid putting the GOP leaders in the position of appearing to be against blacks and other minorities that the party is trying to attract."[39]

The hands-off policy went further. The Justice Department under both Nixon in 1970 and Ford in 1975 had played an important role in supplying information from its own records and research and in drafting amendments to the act; under Reagan, the Attorney General provided no significant aid even to the ranking Republican on the subcommittee.[40] In attempting to shape a legislative alternative to the bill favored by civil rights groups, Hyde was, in effect, doing the administration's work. In the process, though, Hyde became a supplicant of the administration as well. In a July 20 memo, he appealed to the President to urge extension.

"If you move quickly," he wrote, "you may be able to broaden your constituency by eliminating a fear which plagues the black community most: that the time will soon return when they [are] literally unable to vote, or in the alternative, made to feel that they have no meaningful impact whatsoever on their destiny."[41]

The administration's reluctance to become involved in the voting rights question was reinforced by the results of a special election held on July 7 in Mississippi's fourth congressional district. Though 42 percent black, the district had been represented by a white Republican who in 1980 had run against a white Democrat and a black independent. In the first nonpartisan round in the summer of 1981 the Republican candidate, Liles B. Williams, had led the field with 45 percent of the vote; in the subsequent runoff, however, the Democrat, Wayne Dowdy, pulled decisively ahead. Dowdy, but not Williams, had campaigned actively among blacks, pledging to vote for extension of the Voting Rights Act. To Republicans, the results were sobering.[42] In fifty-six southern congressional districts, the black population exceeded 20 percent; no "southern strategy" could afford to neglect the power of that vote.

The administration could not avoid taking a position forever, and on October 2 the Attorney General finally responded to the President's June request for an evaluation of the issue.[43] The response was kept secret, however, reflecting the level of White House anxiety. In fact, the letter contained nothing worth hiding. There was scarcely any allusion to section 2; in a twenty-one-page letter, the question merited two brief paragraphs urging retention of the original wording. Most of the report was devoted to the question of bailout, with three optional sets of criteria outlined. Though no explicit recommendation was made, the first of the options seemed the preferred one. It would have made exemption considerably easier than under the House bill. The letter also discussed—and rejected—both a straight extension and nationwide coverage by section 5. The document was mainly noteworthy for what it did not contain: an evaluation of how much protection was still required, a factual framework within which to address the question of appropriate remedies. What kinds of electoral discrimination still affected minority voters? How open were political processes? Did discrimination in the North merit the extraordinary surveillance provided by section 5? Could discrimination be adequately measured by the impact of a method of voting? Justice Department files were full of information on which an informed policy could be based, but the Attorney General made little use of them. His letter was more evidence of the administration's evasiveness.

On November 6—after the final House vote but before the Senate hearings—Reagan finally announced his position: a ten-year extension, easier bailout, and no change in section 2.[44] It was what the Attorney General—but not the White House staff—had wanted, according to the *Washington Post*. The staff had urged the politically safer course: support for the House bill.[45] Perhaps the infighting accounted for the ambiguity in the President's statement, which called for an extension that was either "direct" or in the form of a "modified version of the new bill recently passed by the House of Representatives." Reagan did not explain how the House bill might be modified, noting only that the bailout criteria should be "reasonable."

Even leaving aside such ambiguity, it was too late for the President to provide effective leadership on the issue. A "tardy performance," the *Boston Globe* called it; a "sham," said Vernon Jordon.[46] Congressional consideration of the matter had already been under way for seven months; by its procrastination, the administration had lost the opportunity not only to apply leverage in the House but to frame the issues. In other words, it had allowed the most strongly committed groups to pose the questions and to define the proper civil rights position. "All we wound up doing was standing for less than they stood for," recalls Michael Horowitz, counsel to the Office of Management and Budget (OMB).[47]

In January, on the eve of the Senate hearings, the administration further undermined its credibility by announcing that it would no longer deny tax-exempt status to private schools, colleges, and other nonprofit institutions that practiced racial discrimination. Bob Jones University in Greenville, South Carolina, which allowed no interracial dating and had had its exemption revoked in 1970, was reinstated as a worthy charity. The decision was disastrous. Democratic Party officials immediately denounced it as part of a pattern of capitulation to segregationists. Senator Daniel Patrick Moynihan called it "tragic," "illegal," and "immoral," a surrender to "the forces in Congress that want to undo the civil rights movement."[48] "The Reagan administration has moved from a lack of interest in fighting racial discrimination to active promotion of it," Tom Wicker wrote in the *New York Times*.[49] The decision was only one of many self-inflicted wounds in the area of civil rights. The administration included no veterans of civil rights battles—men and women who, while perhaps disagreeing with current civil rights orthodoxy, understood both the history of discrimination and the persistent fears of blacks. And it displayed both inexperience and ignorance in handling civil rights issues.

The public outcry over Bob Jones further diminished the administration's already limited enthusiasm for aggressive action on the voting rights front. On March 1, however, William Bradford Reynolds, the assistant attorney general for civil rights, did testify in the Senate. In addition, crucial senators were contacted by both Reynolds and William French Smith. But, as one observer put it, it may have been "a case of too little, too late."[50] Little auxiliary support was provided. Even within the Justice Department, the legislative liaison showed "a distinct lack of enthusiasm for the job."[51] And "recalcitrant elements in the White House . . . preoccupied with the civil rights 'image' of the Administration undercut Brad Reynolds' efforts," one reporter wrote.[52] Reluctant to put the President's prestige on the line, the White House was apparently eager to disassociate itself from Justice Department activity. Yet without backing, the Attorney General and Reynolds could not hope to be effective. It was not just a question of inadequate resources. When the President ran from an issue, it was likely to start a stampede.

Buoyed by the administration's delay in taking a position, the civil rights groups found themselves well positioned to define the issues. Their assertion that simple extension was a code word for repeal became the orthodox view; similarly, the claim that the new section 2 simply "clarified" the old took firmer hold with each passing month. Moreover, the Bob Jones affair had a ripple effect; it undermined the credibility of all arguments against the House bill. "There really is a basis to suspect the motives of William Bradford Reynolds . . . et al. on the Voting Rights Act," *New York Times* columnist Anthony Lewis wrote to a reader. "After all, they are the same fellows who produced the lame legal theory underlying the attempt to give tax exemptions to racist schools."[53] The administration's position on Bob Jones and other civil rights issues made its stand on voting rights automatically suspect.

OMB counsel Michael Horowitz later argued that the White House nevertheless could have won. "The Leadership Conference could not have touched us if we had come out for a fifteen-year extension instead of the ten it wanted," he asserted. He believed the administration had "handed victory" to the civil rights groups.[54] But Horowitz assumed that each civil rights battle was an isolated event, and that intelligent strategy could have undermined the Leadership Conference's claim to moral superiority. In fact, there was little likelihood that the civil rights community would have abandoned its quest to amend section 2. And the reputation of the White House aside, it would have been intrinsically difficult to oppose the position of the NAACP, Urban League, MALDEF, and ACLU without seeming to be an enemy of civil rights. "Can you tell me whether there is any civil rights group that is going to be supporting the administration's position . . . and if so, which one?" Senator Kennedy asked the Attorney General.[55] It was a legitimate question. William French Smith, as well as Hatch, had to argue that those groups defined civil rights narrowly in order to advance the interests of black and Hispanic leaders, not those of their constituents or of the public in general.

It was a difficult job, made even harder by the need to explain why "voting rights" did not really mean voting rights. Few understood how far the issue had strayed from literacy tests, black voter harassment, and other basic Fifteenth Amendment concerns. Certainly the press (for the most part) did not. Its view was that of the League of Women Voters: the cause was too clear-cut to debate. And often it suppressed information rather than providing it—a source of constant frustration for Hatch. "There seems," he said, "to be a preoccupation in parts of the media to define the debate in terms of whether or not the Voting Rights Act will be extended this year or permitted to expire . . . There is nobody that I know of who will not extend the present voting rights law, at the very least."[56]

Other distortions were more subtle. A *New York Times* editorial described the House bill as "well calculated to secure the hard-won rights of blacks and Hispanics."[57] The description gave no indication that the issue before Congress was an expansion of existing protection, not just its retention. Another *Times* editorial implied that the proposal to extend section 2 without modification was a "weakening amendment."[58] And the *Washington Post*, which initially had written an editorial sympathetic to the Supreme Court's opinion in *Mobile*, now adamantly maintained, along with almost every other major daily, that discriminatory intent was impossible to prove.[59] Overall, readers of *Newsweek*, *Time*, the *New York Times*, and the *Washington Post* must have thought that time had stood still in the South. David Broder declared that the gap between black and white registration in the South was just as great in

1981 as it was in 1965—a preposterous assertion.[60] News stories commonly profiled black counties with low levels of black political participation, a phenomenon that was always explained by discrimination and inadequate enforcement of the act. Higher participation rates would depend upon continuing (or greater) federal vigilance, such stories implied.[61] Rarely did reporters discuss the respective responsibilities of the federal government and the local black community—precisely how much the Department of Justice should and could do to get out the vote.

In short, the issues were more complicated than the media let on; further, many assertions by the press were simply false. In part, the inaccuracies were due to haste; for reporters on deadline, the message of the civil rights groups was immediately comprehensible. Such intricate questions as the impact of the new section 2 "results" test—whether the change would entitle minorities to single-member districts facilitating proportional representation—required a patient sorting out of issues that went against the grain of journalistic habit.[62] Few papers even understood that important sections of the act were permanent, that blacks could not once again be truly disfranchised.

Spread thin by the demands of the profession, journalists relied on information released by the parties involved: the civil rights groups and their allies, on the one hand, and Hyde and Hatch, on the other. Here again, the imbalance in resources had a clear impact. Moreover, much of the information that came through pro–civil rights channels appeared nonpartisan; it bore the imprimatur of foundations and organizations such as the League of Women Voters. The Rockefeller Foundation, for example, convened a voting rights conference in April 1981 to which journalists were invited. The attorneys and others who presented papers and provided commentary were all advocates of the initial House bill. Yet the context made the message seem impartial.

The press generally viewed the issue as morally simple. It was easy to see it as such. The civil rights groups, representing the righteous cause of people who had unquestionably suffered centuries of injustice, argued that historically disfranchised groups should be given their "fair" share of power. The concerns of their critics seemed both less urgent and more abstract: they challenged their opponents' definition of "fairness," fretted about federal power, and made speculative arguments about black political isolation as a consequence of segregating minority voters in "safe" black and Hispanic districts. "I'd rather err in the direction of being too strong when it comes to a fair electoral process," Representative Ed Bethune of Arkansas, a leading conservative Republican, said.[63] It was a seductive viewpoint.

The image of righteousness enjoyed by the Leadership Conference and its allies was a legacy of the sixties. The historic immorality of white resistance to black demands made all white resistance to black demands seem suspect. In fact, the good guy/bad guy dichotomy that so dominated media perceptions was rooted in the larger history of both southern racism and the Voting Rights Act. In 1965 the debate over the statute had clearly pitted good against evil; again, in 1970, the Nixon administration's effort—inspired by its southern strategy—to reduce section 5 protection reinforced the view that criticism of the act was morally questionable.

In addition, there was considerable merit to the suspicion that whatever share of political power was "fair," blacks and Hispanics did not have it, particularly in the South. Though increasing rapidly, the levels of black officeholding remained low. To equate this with discrimination was no doubt oversimplified, but the statistics suggested that something was probably awry in the political process. Rather than serving as the end of inquiry, however, the figures should have been only the beginning. The assumptions accepted by the press were not totally without foundation; they were *partial* truths.

Thus, as the Leadership Conference staked out the high moral ground, the press gravitated toward it. As a result, reporters failed to grasp the interesting and complex issues raised by the act. But in the Senate hearings, for the first time in the history of debate on the statute, there emerged some "respectable" critics of expanded protection. Hatch managed to round up a group of distinguished scholars opposed to an amendment of section 2 that would permit electoral systems nationwide to be judged by their "results." In a deck stacked so mightily against him, this was Hatch's strongest card.

It was a balanced and an impressive group of witnesses that Hatch brought before the subcommittee. The central contention of those who advocated amending section 2 was the difficulty on resting cases on the Constitution in the wake of the *Mobile* decision. A basis for suits other than the Fourteenth and Fifteenth Amendments was necessary, proponents of the statutory change argued; proving discriminatory intent was virtually impossible. "This is a requirement of a smoking gun,"

Senator Charles Mathias said.[64] Senator Howard Metzenbaum (D-Oh.) told the Attorney General that proving intent was "so unbelievably difficult . . . I have difficulty understanding why the administration is not on the side of the overwhelming majority of the House."[65] "Impossible," echoed Benjamin Hooks.[66] "Impossible, short of having the smoking pistol, the body buried in the shallow grave," asserted Laughlin McDonald, director of the ACLU Southern Regional Office.[67] It was generally agreed that the decision in *Mobile* was the "first obituary to this country's commitment to meaningful protection of voting rights."[68] Constitutional cases were considered hardly worth initiating anymore.[69]

The demand of proving intent was viewed by civil rights advocates as intrinsically unjust. "There is something inherently unfair about requiring citizens to prove the subjective intent of political officials," Harold Washington declared. "It should not be necessary for me to prove that someone is a racist in order to vindicate my rights."[70] It was felt that the intent test asked the wrong question: "If an electoral system operates today to exclude blacks or Hispanics from a fair chance to participate," the Senate Judiciary Committee report argued, "then the matter of what motives were in an official's mind 100 years ago is of the most limited relevance."[71] Archibald Cox concurred: "The injustice is there, regardless of purpose."[72] A Mississippi state senator asked, "How can anyone claim to support the right of minorities to vote and participate in the democratic process and yet oppose an amendment which makes illegal those laws and practices which result in a denial or abridgment of that right?"[73] It was, moreover, "unseemly to be investigating the motives of legislatures," David Walbert, a civil rights attorney, argued.[74] Inquiries into the motivations of individual officeholders "can only be divisive, threatening to destroy any existing racial progress in a community," Arthur S. Flemming, former chairman of the U.S. Commission on Civil Rights, testified. The intent test "would make it necessary to brand individuals as racist in order to obtain judicial relief."[75]

When Senator Hatch and witnesses allied with him countered that no "smoking gun" need be displayed—that circumstantial evidence of discriminatory purpose sufficed to condemn a method of voting—civil rights spokesmen argued that such a standard was intolerably subjective. "In the absence of a smoking gun, victims of discriminatory laws must resort to evidence producing what courts and legal scholars have called 'inferences,' 'suspicions,' and 'likelihoods' of discriminatory intent," attorney Frank Parker testified. "This introduces a wholly subjective and arbitrary factor into judicial decision-making."[76] The Senate Judiciary Committee Report contended, moreover, that defendants could attempt to rebut circumstantial evidence "by planting a false trail of direct evidence in the form of official resolutions, sponsorship statements and other legislative history eschewing any racial motive, and advancing other governmental objectives."[77]

The final argument advanced in support of the amendment was that it would boost plaintiffs' chances of prevailing. At-large systems would become more vulnerable to attack, and single-member districts, which protected minority candidates from white competition, would become easier to institute. "In San Antonio the fact that we now have more minorities in the city government has created a very positive attitude and increased political participation by the community as a whole," Rolando Rios, the legal director of the Southwest Voter Registration Education Project, told the committee. When Hispanic candidates do not get elected, he said, they cease to run, and without minority candidates, Hispanics do not vote. But when suits succeed in getting racially fair single-member districts drawn, minorities get involved and democracy thrives."[78] "Whites aren't hurt when blacks are allowed political access," Laughlin McDonald argued. "The society as a whole is improved."[79]

Those who opposed the amendment readily acknowledged that "political access" did improve "society as a whole." In their view, however, it was precisely the distinction between political access and electoral results that was preserved by the intent standard. To judge electoral systems by their results was implicitly to measure electoral equity by the standard of proportional racial and ethnic officeholding. The number of minorities in office was the obvious objective "result" to look at in judging a question of electoral discrimination. By what other measure "do you evaluate the totality of the circumstances, as the statute would demand?" Hatch asked. "How do you weigh all the factors? What is the question that the court asks?"[80] Or as James F. Blumstein, professor of law at Vanderbilt University, testified: "Under the effects standard . . . [you] aggregate out a series of factors and the problem is, once you have aggregated out those factors, what do you have? Where are you? You know, it is the old thing we do in law school: You balance and you balance but ultimately, how do you balance? What is the core value?" He added: "You are proving deviation from a norm—what can the norm possibly be except racially based entitlements?"[81] The new language of section 2 "does not say what is prohibited and it does not say why it is prohibited. It does not define a violation or an abridgment of voting rights . . . There [will be] an inexorable trend toward using an easy standard, the numbers standard."[82]

Donald Horowitz, professor of law at Duke University, pointed out that although the preclearance provision also contains an effects test for electoral discrimination, the question there is backsliding—whether fewer minorities are likely to gain office as a consequence of the submitted change in the method of voting. The level of minority officeholding can readily be compared to that which existed before. "With section 2, on the other hand, there is no before and after because it applies not merely to changes but to existing electoral law. The only way to judge the effect will be to see whether minority voters have representatives in proportion to their population in that jurisdiction. By what other standard could one possibly judge dilution under section 2?"[83]

Hatch was careful to note that the issue was not "whether or not pure proportional representation will be achieved overnight. It is whether or not future courts and future Justice Departments will look into the proportional representation as the standard against which all electoral and voting practices are assessed. If such a practice does not at least move a jurisdiction in the direction of proportional representation . . . it will be . . . legally suspect."[84]

According to those who opposed the amendment, section 2 would amount to a statistical test because numbers would provide a norm, reduce the complexity of cases, add uniformity, and narrow the range of judicial discretion.[85] In addition, a results test would alter the question asked and thus the expected response. To make the question of discriminatory intent irrelevant to the inquiry would be to shift the focus away from discrimination as well. "No one is entitled to thwart another's choice to vote on account of race. Discrimination is the act of thwarting this and other liberties on the basis of race. Like any act, discrimination requires intent," contended Michael Levin, professor of philosophy at the City University of New York. "Tay-Sachs strikes only Jews, but chromosomes are not anti-Semitic," he said. "To divorce discrimination from intent is to abandon the distinction between human action and blind natural forces."[86] The intent test, Blumstein added, "retains our universalistic notion of what nondiscrimination means."[87] When effect replaces intent, a "fair shake" becomes a "fair share." A racially proper outcome or "result" assumes the existence of a racially based entitlement to a proper share.[88]

Thus, according to this view, the concept of discrimination would crumble once the element of intent was removed, and disparate impact would take its place. Courts would then ask whether a particular method of voting had disadvantaged black candidates relative to white, and to that inquiry a statistical answer would be appropriate—for example, a pattern of one black usually elected to office when three would be likely if voting procedure were changed.

A "fair share" would mean the representation of racial and ethnic groups in proportion to their population. Was this an aim the federal government should embrace? The modification of section 2 would "create racially defined wards" and accentuate "race-based allegiances and divisions," William Van Alstyne, professor of law at Duke University, wrote to Senator Hatch.[89] "Of course, we know that racial and ethnic identity has much to do with voting behavior," Donald Horowitz testified, "but it is wrong to make it have everything to do with voting behavior, so that political ethnicity ultimately smothers democratic choice and threatens democratic institutions."[90] In other words, democratic choice and democratic institutions require a fluidity and freedom that are at odds with the concept of labeling citizens for political purposes on the basis of race or ethnicity. They also require a sense of community. "In a good many countries that have been torn by ethnic and racial conflict," Horowitz argued, "the electoral system has been one of the tools of amelioration. A range of electoral formulae and ballot structures has been employed to achieve a variety of conflict-reducing tools . . . If these conflict-reducing devices had to be tested by a rigid 'effects' standard, they could not be implemented."[91] That is, at-large voting might create bonds across a community and reduce strife, even though its "result" (the statutory question) might be to reduce minority officeholding. "The racial piece-of-the-action approach," Blumstein wrote in his prepared statement, "reflects the path of cynicism . . . [It] encrusts rather than exorcises a previous system of racial politics."[92]

Amending section 2, these opponents argued, was neither in the public interest nor in the more narrowly defined interest of minorities. Horowitz contended that "assured minority representation encourages local white politicans to say to the minority communities: 'You have your own representatives. Don't come to us with your problems; speak to them.' " And "at best, under such circumstances, it can be said that separate representation postpones interethnic and interracial political contact and bargaining until after the election results are in, when polarization may already have occurred and when a minority on a local council may be powerless."[93] In the end, minority influence may thus be reduced. The amendment was "very good . . . for prospective black officeholders but not for their constituents."[94]

Critics of the statutory change warned of single-member districts, instituted by courts, spreading like a blight across the nation. It was clear that at-large voting was "the principal immediate target" of the amendment, the subcommittee report asserted. At the 1975 hearings Armand Derfner, a distinguished voting rights litigator and indefatigable lobbyist for the section 2 change, had flatly announced his hope "that maybe ten years from now we would have learned and progressed enough to say that . . . we might want to put in [the act] permanent bans that bar at-large elections not only in the covered states but perhaps in the rest of the country as well."[95] The change in section 2 would accomplish precisely such a permanent ban, Hatch believed. His subcommittee report stated: "To establish a results test in section 2 would be to place at-large systems in . . . jeopardy throughout the Nation, particularly if jurisdictions with such electoral systems contained significant numbers of minorities and lacked proportional representation on their elected representative councils or legislatures."[96] William Bradford Reynolds noted that, according to the Municipal Yearbook, most municipalities of more than 25,000 people conducted at-large elections of their city commissioners or council members as of 1977. Even in the northeast and north-central regions of the country, where elections were at large, black officeholding on city governing bodies was disproportionately low in relation to the black population. "Would the multimember districts in Pittsburgh or Hartford be vulnerable to a restructuring Federal court suit under section 2?" Also those in Wilmington, Delaware, and Kansas City, Kansas, as well? Reynolds asked.[97] Hatch enlarged the list to include Boston, Cincinnati, and Baltimore.[98] He picked northern cities to make a point, of course: although section 5 had chiefly covered the South, the proposed change in section 2 was one that could affect the constituency of every senator.

These were the opposing arguments. How much force did each carry? Spokesmen for the civil rights groups stoutly denied the charge that, in seeking to amend the act, they hoped that proportionate minority officeholding would be the norm against which challenged electoral systems were judged. What they wanted was nothing new, they said; they simply sought a return to the legal standards that had been set in *White v. Regester,* the most important of the Supreme Court's decisions involving minority voting rights under the Fourteenth Amendment prior to *Mobile.* "We are asking merely a return to the *White v. Regester* standards," Joaqin Avila, associate counsel to MALDEF, told the committee.[99] "Really what we are asking for is simply a return to the large body of case law which existed during the 15 year period prior to the *Mobile* decision," Henry Marsh, the former mayor of Richmond, stated.[100] Similarly, Armand Derfner testified that "the results test of section 2 is supposed to be a return to the standard of *White v. Regester.*"[101] It was a point on which all the advocates of amendment agreed.

Under the *White* standard, evidence of disproportionately low minority officeholding had never sufficed to win a suit, nor had proportional representation ever been provided as a remedy, these spokesmen argued. Moreover, the House bill contained an explicit disclaimer: "Nothing in this section establishes a right to have members of a protected class elected in numbers equal to their proportion in the population." But critics of the bill viewed the disclaimer as meaningless. Only the notion of a right to proportional representation per se had been rejected, they asserted. True, disproportionately low black officeholding could not alone condemn a method of voting, but the statistical evidence along with, say, a history of discrimination in the jurisdiction (which plaintiffs could point to in any community) would suffice. Plaintiffs would thus need to do very little more than count elected minorities. The bill itself made this clear, directing courts to look at "the extent to which members of a protected class have been elected to office."

The proposed amendment would provide protection for minority voters against methods of election with a discriminatory "result," but the result could only be said to be discriminatory if it denied "equal access," proponents claimed. "Equal access" was thus the true test. If so, Hatch argued, courts would be working with a "nebulous and undefined philosophical concept."[102] And, indeed, witnesses pressed to provide a definition found it hard to do so. "What does 'equal access' mean, Senator Mathias?" Hatch asked. Mathias replied, "You are well aware of what it means . . . You look at the totality of circumstances." Hatch: "What precisely does the Court ask itself after it has looked at the totality of circumstances? What is the standard for evaluation?" Mathias: "Look at the results."[103] The scenario was frequently replayed. "What I would like to know . . . is how the court evaluates this evidence. In other words, what is the judicial standard? What is the judicial inquiry?" Hatch asked Steve Suitts, executive director of the Southern Regional Council. Suitts: "I think a judge would be bound, under a results test, to look at whether or not the scheme of circumstances created by the jurisdiction creates a discriminatory scheme."[104] Amid the rampant evasiveness, there was one forthright answer: "I know it when I see it," said Benjamin Hooks.[105] It was as solid a definition as the hearings contained.

The evasiveness did not spring from any Machiavellian impulse. Even with the best of intentions, equal access was hard to define. It was that discovery that had led the Supreme Court in 1980 to *Mobile.* The first decisions involving minority vote dilution had promised relief to groups with distinct, compelling and unrepresented interests. By 1973, however, with *White v. Regester,* the focus had shifted from the status of the group to the electoral environment in which minority citizens tried to organize for political ends. The question before the courts became: how open to minority participation is the electoral process? How racist is the environment in which voting takes place? Yet a context unacceptably inhospitable to black and Hispanic political participation was never rigorously defined, and the courts began to take what one authority has called a "Chinese menu" approach.[106] Items from a list that included white candidate slating, a history of discrimination, and a majority-vote requirement were selected at random, and any combination could be used to prove unequal access or discrimination. The "factual" findings, using what was called "the totality of circumstances test," were "so subjective and so nebulous," Katharine Butler has written, "that any trial court [could] 'select' enough facts from the record to support any decision."[107] A circular definition of equal access thus emerged: a denial of access was evident when elements A, B, and F were present, denial being defined as the presence of elements A, B, and F.

In the interim period of political skirmishing that took place between the House and Senate debates, Vernon Jordan had declared that discriminatory effects are apparent to all.[108] But the record of the judicial decisions that relied on the standard to which the modified section 2 would return suggests otherwise. Moreover, asked by Hatch to provide Justice Department guidelines as to the meaning of "effects," "intent," and "denial or abridgment," William Bradford Reynolds confessed that the "Department [had] not issued any [such] guidelines or regulations."[109] Evidently both the courts and the Justice Department worked with concepts that neither could define with any clarity.

Furthermore, virtually every definition of equal access carried potential risks for civil rights spokesmen. When asked to take a stand, they equivocated, hoping to avoid conceding either too much or too little. If they had agreed that minority voters could be equal participants in an electoral system despite disproportionately low minority officeholding—that such officeholding was not the sole test—they would have conceded more than they wished. Yet to reject firmly the possibility that whites could represent blacks or that black candidates could be defeated for nonracist reasons was implicitly to embrace the notion that minorities were entitled to proportional representation.

Frankly embracing proportional representation as a minority right was politically out of the question. In the Senate, unlike the House, the left as well as the right was under constraint. Yet, while civil rights spokesmen were pulled by politics in one direction, they were enticed by conviction in another. A definition of equal access that included situations in which blacks were often the swing vote in the election of whites, for instance, would sharply reduce black plaintiffs' chances of prevailing in most suits; in fact, it would leave them no better off than with the odious intent test.

Equally important, such a definition went against the grain of the underlying belief of civil rights spokesmen that, in this time and place, blacks best represented blacks. That conviction, though obvious, was, for the most part, kept concealed. Yet it appeared indirectly or off-stage. It was clearly the source of the civil rights groups' determination to turn section 2 into an additional means by which to attack at-large voting. At-large systems often afforded blacks and Hispanics the opportunity to exercise considerable political leverage; candidates running city-wide, for instance, were ill-advised simply to ignore a substantial bloc of black votes. But the leverage exercised by minorites in at-large voting was often in contests in which a white won. A single-member districting plan, on the other hand, containing a maximum number of "safe" minority districts, facilitated proportionate minority officeholding by protecting black candidates from white competition.

In the introduction to a 1984 volume on minority vote dilution sponsored by the Joint Center for Political Studies, Chandler Davidson noted that, although blacks made up 25.8 percent of the population in the seven states entirely covered by the Voting Rights Act, they accounted for only 5.6 percent of all elected officials. He concluded that "about one-fifth as many blacks hold office as would be likely in a nonracist society."[110] When appearing in the limelight of Congress, however, witnesses were much more circumspect. For example, when questioning Benjamin Hooks, Hatch asked him to comment on two statements by spokesmen for the civil rights community. One was from Dr. Willie Gibson, president of the NAACP Conference for South Carolina, who had asserted that "South Carolina's population is approximately 30 percent black, and 30 percent of the senate should be black." The other came from Jesse Jackson, who had observed that "blacks comprise one-third of the State of South Carolina's population and deserve one-third of its representation. We believe that taxation without representation is tyranny." Hook's comment: "I think there is a big difference between proportional representation and representation in proportion to their population." To say that " 'we want something that resembles our population' . . . is a far different cry from a mathematical proportional representation."[111]

Neither Gibson nor Jackson had spelled out that difference, and, as Hatch pointed out, Hooks's own response left the crucial question unanswered. If exact proportionality was not required, how inexact could it be? Actually, exactness was never the issue; single-member districts seldom provide it. They can *approximate* it, provided that residential patterns permit the drawing of district lines to the maximum advantage of minority candidates. And that, in fact, was the issue: whether electoral systems that (more or less) ensure officeholding approximately in proportion to the minority population should be written into law as a right. To that idea Hooks had committed himself.

Civil rights advocates were equally fuzzy in defining what evidence would be necessary to rebut an assumption of discrimination when minority officeholding was found to be disproportionately low. Senator Metzenbaum (who spoke, in effect, for the Leadership Conference) stated that a poor electoral showing by minorities could not be considered proof of a discriminatory result if no minority candidates had run.[112] This seemed to imply that if such candidates had run and had then been defeated, discrimination would have been established. Hooks testified that "the failure of [a] predominantly black district to elect a black candidate, without more, certainly would not lead to a finding of discriminatory result."[113] But this was only to state the obvious: that once an effort had been made to draw a maximum number of minority districts, the election of a white in a "safe" black district would not, in itself, suggest that the plan was discriminatory. Something "more" in the way of evidence would be needed, Hooks stated—some additional facts suggesting unequal electoral access for blacks despite their majority status in the district. Presumably such evidence could consist of a finding, for example, that historic patterns of discrimination had made for low black turnout, and that the elected white was thus not the true black choice, a substantial number of blacks having failed to register their choice. As reassurance that judges would not be expected to count minority heads in office when determining whether a violation of section 2 had occurred, this was certainly inadequate.

Finally, the commitment to proportionality surfaced in the statements of those who either hoped or assumed that the meaning of discriminatory "results" in the amended section 2 would be roughly the same as that of discriminatory "effects" in section 5. As I will argue in subsequent chapters, submitted changes in electoral procedure are seldom precleared (under section 5) unless they facilitate, to the degree possible, proportionate minority officeholding. Among those who conflated the two provisions were Arthur Flemming and Joseph Rauh. Flemming, for instance, described sections 2 and 5 as "both headed in the same direction."[114] True, the confusion that characterized the statements of these two witnesses was not shared by the majority of those who spoke for the House bill. Yet no civil rights spokesman was willing to state explicitly that section 2, in contrast to section 5, would give greater weight to factors other than minority officeholding. And statements such as that made by Steve Suitts were telling. "The plurality opinion [in *Mobile*] is perhaps most egregious in denying any relevance to the numbers of black office holders," he noted. "An understanding of the nature of governmental discrimination in voting gives a keen appreciation of the utility of black office-holding and potential black office-holding in identifying the motivation of whites to dilute black voting strength."[115] To identify electoral discrimination, look at the numbers, Suitts came close to saying. The basic test of an environment free of racial prejudice is the degree of black electoral success. And by implication, disproportionately low minority officeholding is a signal that something is wrong and the law has been violated.

In their assessments of the importance of minority officeholding, the two sides in the dispute over section 2 worked with different sets of facts regarding the status of blacks in America. "The dispute about voting rights is as factual as it is ideological," Suitts pointed out. It was an acute observation. "Even in the presence of solid scholarship tracing the ineradicable nature of segregation and its vestiges, the rooted nature of racial discrimination sustained by governmental action in the South is a matter of dispute," he went on.[116] But this was the question: had "solid" scholarship illuminated the "ineradicable nature of segregation . . . the rooted nature of racial discrimination"? Different perceptions of the facts with respect to this crucial question divided the opposing sides, and their differing ideologies flowed to a considerable degree from their disparate factual conclusions.

Suitts saw North Carolina as an example of the "immovable nature of racial discrimination in government and its enduring formulas amid a changing cast of political characters."[117] A state senator from Mississippi testified that the white world "is a different world altogether, and that is the basic problem we are faced with in Mississippi. There are two worlds. There is the black world and there is the white world."[118] In a paper delivered at an American Bar Association meeting convened to consider the House bill, Armand Derfner argued that for "blacks in most of the South and Chicanos in much of the Southwest, minority influence is little or no influence. In those situations, race is a dominant factor in politics, [and] elections are decided largely by which race has the most voters."[119]

Several contributors to the volume on minority vote dilution sponsored by the Joint Center for Political Studies made the same claim. Although the volume was published later, many of its contributors testified at the hearings, all were part of the effort to get the House bill passed, and the views expressed in it are, in effect, extensions of the arguments made at the time. As previously noted, in the introductory essay Chandler Davidson argued that only one-fifth as many blacks held office in the South "as would be likely in a *nonracist* society." The disproportionately low minority officeholding, he believed, could be directly traced to racism.[120] Davidson continued: "White bloc voting against minority candidates is so intense in the South and Southwest that an extremely large minority population is typically necessary for the minority community to elect candidates of its choice under at-large conditions."[121] Frank Parker likewise asserted that the "combination of political powerlessness and racist victimization has devastated poor black, Hispanic, and other minority communities throughout this country."[122] In the view of Suitts, Derfner, Davidson, Parker, and others, nothing had changed since V. O. Key drew his picture of southern politics thirty years earlier. The analysis reflected a profound distrust on the part of civil rights spokesmen of the American political process left to its own devices. Whites, it was assumed, lose elections for a variety of reasons, blacks and Hispanics almost always for reasons of race or ethnicity.

Senate opponents of the amendment disagreed sharply with this tableau, but in challenging it they, too, had to tread cautiously. Hyde had unwittingly rallied support for the civil rights groups by suggesting that American society had changed radically in the seventeen years since the passage of the Voting Rights Act. Hatch and his colleagues were not eager to repeat that error. They spoke, however, indirectly on the issue. "This is not India," said Henry Abraham, professor of government at the University of Virginia. "There is no right to be represented on the basis of group membership."[123] His point was this: a society deeply divided by lines of race, ethnicity, or religion must be organized as a federation of groups. Separate groups are the equivalent of separate nations. But a society in which the horizons of trust extend beyond the ethnic or racial group can become a community of citizens.[124] And in a community of equal citizens individuals, not groups, are the unit of representation, other witnesses suggested. "The amendment . . . inches us along toward a corporate concept of electoral democracy," Donald Horowitz charged.[125] Walter Berns warned that, with the change in section 2, legislators will "represent not undifferentiated people, people defined only as individuals living in districts of approximately equal size, but defined as groups of people, defined by their race or language preference, and they can be said to represent them only if they are of that race or if they . . . prefer that language."[126] Barry Gross argued that "the Constitution speaks only of individuals . . . Individuals choose by election other individuals to represent them from political subdivisions spread out over regions. There is no provision for group representation no matter how shamefully treated they were, nor how tragic their history."[127] It was a point that Hatch himself often made: "Are individuals elected to office to represent individual citizens or are they elected to office to represent ethnic and racial blocs of voters?" he asked.[128]

These statements reflected precisely that optimism about American society and its political process that supporters of the bill lacked. As Abraham and others acknowledged, the question of individual versus group representation could not be relegated to the realm of the abstract. Different social contexts required different responses. Critics of the bill perceived in America both social fluidity and a potential for creating bonds across racial and ethnic lines. Voter interest does not follow color, Michael Levin asserted.[129] Black citizens "would be better encouraged to get out into the broad mainstream of the electoral process, as Mayor Bradley is going to do [in California], and build coalitions," Senator East argued.[130] Of course such coalitions are not possible in all circumstances. But these critics of the bill believed that proper conditions did prevail in 1981, even in the South. "The political strength of . . . [blacks and Hispanics] can no longer be ignored by serious candidates," William Bradford Reynolds told the committee.[131]

Perhaps no issue more deeply divided the two sides, I have argued, than this question of the persistence of racism. The continuing sense of "two worlds"—one black and one white—informed every argument made by the civil rights community. It lay behind their belief that only minority public officials could represent minority interests, and it posed an insurmountable obstacle to framing a definition of equal electoral access. That is, spokesmen for the civil rights groups consistently denied that a finding of disproportionately low minority officeholding alone would suffice to condemn an at-large or other method of voting under the proposed section 2. Yet Hatch was clearly right in asserting that equal access, defined without reference to proportionality, was a "nebulous and undefined . . . concept." How were courts to identify situations in which black electoral opportunity was equal to that of whites despite a poor record of success on the part of black candidates? Equality beyond statistical parity was exceedingly hard to define.

The civil rights groups had no definition of equal access, I have argued—at least none that did not contain an implicit proportional representation norm. But the charge of extreme vagueness can be leveled as well against those who proposed judging such access by the measure of legislative intent. The intent criteria, as spelled out in *Mobile*, were "clear as crystal," Michael Levin argued.[132] Only to him. Both on and off the Supreme Court there was little agreement as to how to detect such intent. All agreed that a disproportionately low level of minority officeholding was not sufficient, but beyond that core of consensus lay chaos.

A minority of witnesses aligned with Hatch proposed, quite simply, that the right to vote be defined as the right to cast a properly counted ballot. Thus Barry Gross argued that "the value of a vote is full when it is freely cast and accurately counted."[133] And Michael Levin suggested that "all that matters is that the voting is spontaneous. Any result is fair which is the result of free choice."[134] Walter Berns told the committee: "If minority groups have the right to vote—then it seems to me their interests can be protected."[135] Such views expressed admirable faith that, with basic suffrage guaranteed, the American political process would everywhere work for blacks. But most of Hatch's allies understood the naiveté of that view.

However, those among Hatch's colleagues who had abandoned a simple definition of electoral access could not offer a clear standard by which to judge vote denial. The Court (in *Mobile*) had attempted to solve the problem by making legislative intent the essential ingredient. But those who endorsed that test looked far beyond legislative motive for evidence of discriminatory purpose. They acknowledged, that is, that what Alabama had had in mind in 1911 in instituting at-large voting was almost beside the point, and they based their arguments on judicial rulings with which their opponents did not, in fact, disagree. Blumstein pointed, for instance, to *Dayton*, a school desegregation case. However, while decisions such as *Dayton* ostensibly rested on findings of purposeful discrimination, in fact courts relied on evidence of disparate impact to establish discriminatory intent.[136] These decisions, in fact, had precisely the flaw that Blumstein had warned about elsewhere: they swallowed up, "by procedural artifice, the underlying intent principle."[137] On July 1, 1982, two days after the Voting Rights Act amendments were signed into law, the Supreme Court ruled in a case that opponents of the revision in section 2 would later hold up as retrospective proof that an intent test was workable. Against allegedly impossible odds, plaintiffs in *Rogers v. Lodge* had demonstrated that a method of election had been tainted by illicit purpose. No smoking gun had been found and none had been demanded. But the "told-you-so" message on the part of critics of the amended law was less than totally convincing. As one commentator put it, the Court in *Rogers v. Lodge,* while professing to uphold a finding of discriminatory intent, had simply adopted a results test "thinly disguised."[138]

As we have seen, the two sides were, in important respects, far apart. The assumptions they brought to the debate had little in common. Yet for all their differences, they shared a political interest in minimizing that disagreement. Proponents of the results test emphasized the centrality of nonnumerical factors; advocates of an intent test stressed the importance of evidence other than motive. Coming from opposite directions, the two sides edged toward a common solution—a strong intent test or a weak effects test, it might be called.

To put it another way: in the end, providing equal access became the common goal. But if such access was a "nebulous and undefined . . . concept" when used by the Leadership Conference and its allies, it was no less so when implicitly adopted by Hatch and his colleagues. As some of the witnesses in Hatch's camp acknowledged, equal access was the test contained in *White v. Regester,* and the passage of time had solved none of the problems in that decision. The two sides had come jointly to occupy mutually and intrinsically unsatisfactory territory. But neither could find a different but acceptable direction in which to head.

The hearings ended on March 1. On March 24 the subcommittee reconvened for the purpose of reporting a bill. Hatch had the votes, but only on his subcommittee. The immediate question facing the three Republicans was thus a strategic one: what form should the reported bill take? What sort of proposal would most likely bring Hatch and his colleagues further success? They settled for a straight ten-year extension, with no change either in section 2 or in the bailout provisions.

There ensued a month of lobbying prior to consideration by the full committee. "As final Committee action approached, a general feeling seemed to exist among members of the Committee that they wished to remain supportive of the mass of outside organizations lobbying for the House version, while at the same time responding to the potentially explosive issue of proportional representation and electoral quotas," wrote Stephen Markman, chief counsel to the subcommittee.[139] From this sentiment emerged the Dole compromise, which won immediate, overwhelming acceptance. Up to that point the Kansas Republican had shown little interest in the issue, to the extent of not even attending the hearings. But Dole's presidential aspirations were no secret, and, as one observer put it, he had "decided to put more than a pinch of incense on the altar of the civil rights lobby."[140]

The compromise further clarified the amendment to section 2. The revised statutory language stated that a method of election was discriminatory in result "if, based on the totality of circumstances," it was "shown that the political processes leading to nomination or election . . ." were "not equally open to participation" by members of the protected minority groups. "Not equally open" was defined as meaning that minority citizens had "less opportunity than other members of the electorate to participate in the political process and to elect representatives of their choice." While the number of minorities elected to office was "one circumstance" that could be taken into account, nothing in the provision established "a right to have members of the protected class elected in numbers equal to their proportion of the population."

In addition to clarifying section 2, Dole proposed to substitute a twenty-five-year extension of section 5 and other temporary provisions. And, though the bill was further amended in minor ways before its final passage, the bailout criteria approved by the House went through untouched.[141]

With the Dole proposal, the politics of passage in the Senate effectively came to an end. It was unlikely that Dole would have forged ahead without the approval of the civil rights groups, since they had virtual veto power. In fact, though, they could not practically have exercised it. For the Senate bill gave them what they professed to have wanted: the *White v. Regester* standard written into law, and given the right label—a test for discriminatory "result." Hatch was not satisfied, but, lacking significant support, he had little recourse. Even the administration backed the compromise. On May 4 the Judiciary Committee voted 14 to 4 to accept the bill. (Hatch and three southern senators held out.) On June 18 the full Senate gave its approval, 85 to 8. Five days later the House accepted the Senate version by unanimous consent, and on June 29 the President held a signing ceremony.

A formula that had never worked—the *White-Zimmer* test for electoral exclusion—thus became an integral part of the act. But, as I will argue at length in Chapter 9, the old problems remained. As before, discrimination was in the eye of the beholder. In fact, the history of the constitutional cases and the amendment to section 2 can be seen as a succession of failed attempts to escape from Justice Frankfurter's "political thicket," attempts that culminated in the construction by Congress of a permanent but barely habitable dwelling.

# SEVEN

# Amendment by Enforcement

The Voting Rights Act has been amended not only by congressional action but by judicial and administrative interpretation as well. This chapter explores one set of judicial decisions—those interpreting the preclearance provision. The courts began to examine the meaning of section 5 in 1969 in *Allen v. Board of Elections*. But *Allen* had addressed a limited inquiry: what counts as an electoral change for which federal approval must be obtained? Mississippi had amended state law to allow counties to elect their boards of supervisors at large. Were these at-large elections, newly instituted in a covered jurisdiction, a voting procedure that required preclearance? And were annexations and redistrictings, likewise, "practices or procedures" subject to section 5? *Allen* (and its progeny) settled that preliminary question affirmatively, but there remained a more complex one. If annexations were subject to federal approval, what constituted an acceptable boundary change? The act prohibited any new "voting qualification or prerequisite to vote, or standard, practice, or procedure with respect to voting" that had the "purpose" or "effect" of "denying or abridging the right to vote on account of race or color." When was an annexation (or other change in electoral method) discriminatory in either purpose or effect? This is the issue that the decisions reviewed in this chapter wrestled with.

These cases represent the rare instances in which jurisdictions covered by the act actually went to court to obtain preclearance for a proposed change in electoral procedure. As I pointed out earlier, state or local governments can choose between a relatively speedy administrative decision or a full-scale hearing before the District Court for the District of Columbia. Opportunity, in fact, knocks twice. If the Department of Justice objects to a proposed plan, local officials can begin again in the D.C. court. Thus, while in some of the cases discussed here the jurisdiction went directly to the court, in others it did so only after having failed to gain administrative approval.

Most jurisdictions settle for the process of Justice Department review and do not go to court. Administrative preclearance being the norm, the judicial record is relatively thin. And the decisions that do exist are hard to decipher; the Supreme Court, in particular, has had difficulty explaining its own opinions. Moreover, when that Court talks often no one listens. Except with respect to annexations, the D.C. court has paid minimal heed to the high Court, and the Department of Justice almost none at all.

The story begins in 1972 with *City of Petersburg, Virginia v. U.S.*, a decision of the D.C. district court.[1] In 1966 a black member of the city council, convinced that the economic health of the city would benefit from expansion of its boundaries, introduced an annexation ordinance that was subsequently unanimously adopted. Although racial considerations did not prompt the expansion, its impact on the racial balance of Petersburg was marked: the minority population dropped from a majority of 56 percent to 47 percent.

Annexations such as Petersburg's must be precleared. In 1971, in *Perkins v. Matthews*, the Supreme Court had held that municipal boundary changes had the potential to dilute the weight of black votes, and thus constituted changes in "practice or procedure with respect to voting" that covered jurisdictions could not enforce without prior federal approval.[2] Subsequent to *Perkins* the city of Petersburg had submitted its annexation plan to the Attorney General, and in February 1972 the Justice Department had interposed an objection not to the boundary change itself, but, it said, "to the voting changes occasioned by the annexation." With the addition of a large number of white residents, the proportional voting strength of blacks had been reduced, and "in re-adopting the at-large election system in the context of [this] significant change of population . . . the potential for an adverse and discriminatory voting effect [had] been written into the Petersburg election law."[3] The letter of objection was, in an important respect, misleading. Petersburg had not "re-adopted" its at-large system; it had simply retained it. Elections for municipal government within both the old and new boundaries were city-wide.

The city next turned to the D.C. district court *de novo*, seeking a declaratory judgment that the proposed electoral change had neither the purpose nor the effect of denying or abridging the right to vote on account of race or color. It was the first of the annexation suits, and it made clear what *Perkins* had not: that these cases posed an unforeseen problem. Annexations were different from the introduction of at-large voting, for instance. By reducing the proportion of black voters and thus altering the balance between whites and blacks, annexations could affect black electoral opportunity in a city, but boundary changes were not, in and of themselves, changes in the method of voting that a court was free to prohibit or modify. The change itself almost always had a legitimate basis; in Petersburg, in fact, had the D.C. court reversed the annexation, it would have denied blacks the economic benefits that they had hoped for in proposing the boundary change. The court did not do so, but endorsed the reasoning of the Attorney General instead. The annexation was legal, but its effect was not, the court held. Petersburg had had a history of discrimination, and racial bloc voting was the norm. The persistence of at-large elections would further reduce the "weight, strength and power" of black votes in the city. The impact would thus abridge the right of blacks to vote, the court concluded. And it ordered Petersburg to institute single-member districts.[4]

The court assumed both that the proposed change could logically be separated from its impact, and that effect was distinct from purpose. Yet the original act had implicitly equated the two. In 1965 concern had been with deliberate and persistent attempts to deprive blacks of the right to vote—with ingenious new tricks drawn from the old racist hat. At that time, all changes that disfranchised blacks anew almost certainly did so purposefully. In labeling at-large elections a voting change that required federal approval, *Allen* had radically altered section 5, but the institution of county-wide elections in Mississippi clearly fell into that category of actions with a discriminatory effect and, implicitly, a racist purpose— whatever the stated intent. Without doubt, Mississippi had hoped to stop the election of black county commissioners by preventing the emergence of majority-black single-member districts. It acted, that is, to pull blacks back from the gains they otherwise would have made as a consequence of the ban on literacy tests and the provision of federal registrars. The Petersburg case, however, was quite different. No one could label the boundary change a subtle racist move to violate Fifteenth Amendment rights.

I am suggesting that annexations are special and therefore should not have been included on the list of practices requiring preclearance. They are seldom discriminatory in purpose, and those enacted for racist ends could have been challenged in constitutional suits. Changes that simply altered the racial balance in a municipality should have been viewed as no different from a spontaneous influx of whites into the city—a change in racial composition irrelevant to the continued use of an at-large method of election.

*Perkins*, however, sealed the matter. And Petersburg was left with only one argument—that the boundary change had not reduced the worth of black ballots. The city's intentions had not been discriminatory. Nevertheless, had the change adversely affected the level of black political opportunity? The argument of the D.C. court was less than fully persuasive. It depicted a political fortress reinforced by new white troops—a city run by racist whites whose power would be augmented by the annexation. The picture was overdrawn: whites had been a minority of the population, but a majority of the registered voters; they had had the electoral weight to keep blacks out of office. But election returns suggested that a certain percentage of whites supported black candidates. In the mid-1960s, in fact, when the city was still overwhelmingly white, two blacks had been elected at large to the five-member city council, and in 1970 a black candidate in at least one councilmanic ward had received substantial white support. The court itself, in response to an intervenor's argument for deannexation, took note of the "proven defection from absolute bloc voting."[5] Of course, a record of frequent defections would have raised questions about just how "absolute" racial bloc voting was, but the court neglected to examine the extent to which that one ward was representative of the city.

Nor was Petersburg a city in which white neighborhoods thrived and black ones decayed. The court did not claim that white councilmen, elected city-wide, were indifferent to the black vote. The council, it said, had been "unresponsive to *some* of the expressed needs and desires of the black community and [had] *on some occasions* rejected or failed to adopt programs, employment policies and appointments recommended by blacks."[6] Yet surely recommendations from white groups were rejected "on some occasions" as well. In fact, some mix of acceptance and rejection would have been the case whether the city government was controlled by whites or blacks. Maynard Jackson, the first black mayor of Atlanta, broke a strike conducted largely by black sanitation workers. Did that establish him as unresponsive to black needs?

The picture drawn by the court was thus more bleak than the evidence contained in its own opinion warranted. But bleakness was central to the court's case. To remove from a jurisdiction its constitutionally sanctioned prerogative to set its own electoral rules in the wake of a black-initiated, economically desirable annexation would have been hard to justify if blacks appeared to play a significant role in city politics. Even accepting the court's picture, the logic of the decision is not easy to discern. The court cited both political exclusion and a demographic shift. Did it mean to imply a right to single-member districts wherever those two elements were found in conjunction with an annexation? What, then, was the difference between an annexation initiated and supported by blacks and a change in the racial balance of a municipality resulting from migration? If the boundaries of Petersburg had remained unchanged, but the 1970 census had revealed a drop in the city's minority population from 56 to 47 percent, no plaintiff could have persuaded a court (on that basis) to eliminate the at-large voting system.

Perhaps the central point in the case was the transformation of blacks from majority to minority status within the city. It could be argued that at-large voting had taken on new meaning. Without the boundary change, registered blacks would soon have outnumbered whites, and city-wide voting would have benefited black candidates. With annexation, though, the black population had dropped nine percentage points, giving white candidates a clear edge. In the old city, with its 56 percent black population, black candidates had had considerable and growing protection, but the annexation had left them exposed to a substantial white majority. The imposition of single-member districts would thus restore to blacks the protection they once had.

This change from majority to minority status may have been the central point, but it was never stated as such. If the argument had been made explicitly, the impact of the decision would have been far less substantial than actually turned out to be the case. Subsequent objections to annexations—on the part of both the Justice Department and the D.C. court—would have been rare; most boundary changes would have been unconditionally precleared. Ward voting would have become the appropriate remedy only when the at-large scheme already in use assumed new meaning—infrequently, that is, for *Petersburg* was an unusual case. The annexation submitted to the Department of Justice for preclearance by Charleston, South Carolina, was more typical: blacks were a minority both before and after, and the change in the relative numbers was small.[7]

The decision in *Petersburg* included another element with potentially weighty implications. The court found that the annexation impaired the "ability of blacks to elect candidates of their choice and to have their ideas on political matters afforded the recognition to which they [were] entitled on their merits and by virtue of their individual citizenship and their *numerical strength* in the community."[8] Black officeholding in proportion to black population—that was the implied entitlement. Any electoral arrangement providing anything less abridged the right of blacks to vote.

This assertion solved a problem raised by the annexation cases. The Voting Rights Act had explicitly exempted long-standing election methods from section 5 review. Preclearance was an emergency procedure, designed to deal with procedural changes with a disproportionate impact on newly enfranchised blacks in suspect jurisdictions—jurisdictions with proven and extensive records of Fifteenth Amendment violations. At-large voting that was established prior to the act, whether in Petersburg or Detroit, was not inherently suspect and could not be challenged except in a Fourteenth or Fifteenth amendment suit. After *Petersburg*, however, city-wide voting that might have withstood a constitutional challenge could be readily struck down whenever the desire for a broader tax base prompted a municipality to annex a predominantly (or potentially) white suburb. Thus, a task difficult to accomplish under the Fourteenth Amendment became quite easy under the Voting Rights Act. It was an anomalous result which the asserted entitlement to single-member districts in *Petersburg* sanctioned. For once proportional racial and ethnic representation had been made a right, the once-vital distinction between old and new electoral methods instantly dissolved. If blacks had a right to single-member districts promoting proportional officeholding, they had that right regardless of the immediate context. At-large voting that was recently adopted in a southern county with a long history of black disfranchisement was logically indistinguishable from that which had existed in a northern city in which blacks had long held office but not in proportion to their numbers.

I have lingered over a district court decision because it set a way of thinking about annexations as electoral changes. *Petersburg* was an incoherent decision, and its very incoherence released both the Justice Department and the D.C. court from the confines of principled decision making. Once the decision was established as precedent, the logic of its disparate elements was never reexamined. And any one element—that of entitlement to proportionate officeholding, for instance—could then be stressed with impunity. Thus the annexation of an area adjacent to Statesboro, Georgia, that caused a mere 0.9 percent drop in the black proportion of the population triggered an objection by the Attorney General.[9] Did that slight drop in proportionate black population in fact truly limit black political access to the political system? *Petersburg* did not compel, but certainly permitted, perfunctory inquiries into the question of political exclusion as a basis upon which to insist on the institution of ward voting, even when the proposed boundary change had a barely perceptible impact on black voting strength.

As I have argued, annexation decisions initiated by a black councilman and opposed by no black organizations—as in Petersburg—are quite different from those changes in electoral procedure aimed at subverting Fifteenth Amendment rights that section 5 was designed to prevent. In fact, expanding a community's tax base is the purpose of most annexations; rarely are cities enlarged simply to capture additional white votes. Likewise, it might seem that redistricting decisions are not inherently suspect. The constitution requires that malapportioned districts be redrawn following each decennial census; thus the fact of change is not in itself suspicious. Yet new ward lines are different from a change in municipal boundaries. Much more frequently, the occasion of mandatory redistricting is used for racist ends. In the absence of clear proof of invidious intent, by what standards should a districting decision submitted for preclearance be judged? The Department of Justice will object to a plan if the jurisdiction has failed to prove an absence of discriminatory purpose or effect. Thus there need be no conclusive evidence that the districting does dilute the weight of the minority vote; doubt, by itself, is sufficient to condemn it. In a plan drawn up by Bamberg County, South Carolina, four of seven districts had majority-black populations, but in only two did the black *voting-age* population exceed 50 percent.[10] Had the jurisdiction carried its requisite burden of proof? That is, was the plan clearly above suspicion—clearly discriminatory neither in purpose nor effect? And if not, to what principle could the jurisdiction refer in formulating an alternative?

These were the issues that the district court addressed in its 1974 decision, *Beer v. United States.*[11] The case involved the redistricting of the New Orleans city council following the 1970 census. Thirty-five percent of the registered voters in the city were black. Two seats on the city council were elected at large, five from wards. None of the old wards had black majorities; the proposed plan, however, provided for two majority-black districts, although only one would have a black *voter* majority. Submitted for preclearance, the plan was found objectionable. The right of blacks to vote has been abridged, the Attorney General wrote, when, for no compelling reason, district lines are drawn in such a way as to put blacks in the minority in every district except one. An alternative plan, in other words, might have given blacks more seats. And only "compelling governmental need"— compelling reason to adopt the proposed lines—could relieve the city of its obligation to adopt such an alternative plan.[12]

New Orleans then turned to the D.C. court, seeking a declaratory judgment that the proposed plan had neither the purpose nor the effect of denying or abridging the right to vote on account of race or color. But the court was unpersuaded. The "inexorable consequence of the plan," it found, would "be a drastic reduction in the voting strength of the black minority."[13]

Unlike an annexation, the redrawing of ward lines adds no new voters to the city rolls. And it was difficult to see how black voting strength had been reduced, since the existing plan had included no majority-black districts. But the court argued that black voting strength (by which it meant blacks in office) had been reduced from what it would have been if "uninhibited by artificial barriers."[14] *Potential* strength, that is, was the gauge. Under "historically unsuppressed conditions," said the court, registration figures indicated that New Orleans blacks had a "natural potential" of 2.42 seats.[15]

With the inclusion of the element of "historical suppression," the test fell just short of a pure proportional representation formula. "The white and black communities of New Orleans are polarized in political matters," the court concluded.[16] No black had ever been elected to the city council. White support for black candidates, in fact, was "minimal," and blacks who ran for office were "hampered both by their generally more individualistic political philosophy [read black militance] and their more limited financial resources."[17] The court conceded that four blacks had been elected at large to offices other than the city council, but it contended that "their victories" were not "truly significant"; such "triumphs represented no more than nominal success."[18]

Perhaps these victories did not count because the politics of the black candidates were insufficiently "individualistic"; perhaps no "true" black would pick up white votes. But, if this was the view of the court, it was not the judgment of those blacks who actually won. Dr. Mack Spears, for instance, certainly did not regard his success in a 1968 school board race as "nominal." From twelve candidates (eleven of whom were white), the field was eventually whittled down to two, but Spears's opponent was a well-financed white attorney. Spears had run on what he regarded as an uncompromising platform, had been endorsed by the city's leading newspaper, and had swept into office backed by a coalition that included the Teamsters Union, white liberals, and blacks.[19] And in the four years following his election, blacks running at-large won three other city-wide positions. Four years after *Beer* the city would have its first black mayor—elected, of course, city-wide. Blacks had clearly been moving into politics in New Orleans at the time the decision was handed down.

Moreover, at the time of the district court decision in 1974, some New Orleans citizens doubted that a plan that would maximize the number of majority-black districts was actually needed in order to maximize black voting strength. These skeptics foresaw the tremendous increase in black registration that would irrevocably change New Orleans politics, forcing white candidates and white money to address black demands. In fact, black political organizations in New Orleans soon overshadowed white ones. Six years after *Beer* a newspaper editor would remark, "Blacks . . . are the key force in political life." "There are no standing white political organizations worth a damn," a state legislator explained, "and nobody can run for city-wide office or in many legislative and council elections—or in statewide elections—without reaching an accommodation with [black] organizations."[20] The district court, in insisting on all-ward voting, assumed that blacks would lack influence except in districts that they controlled. But the black population and thus black political strength were growing so rapidly that, before long, blacks would permanently control the city's two at-large seats.

The changing world of New Orleans politics, however, went unnoticed by the Justice Department and the D.C. court, located a thousand miles away. They clearly believed that without external assistance, blacks would be permanently excluded from political power. The point of section 5 had been to freeze southern electoral arrangements pending federal approval of any proposed change; the D.C. court and the Justice Department viewed the southern political landscape as still frozen and used section 5 to change it. Assuming that race relations in the South were basically unchanged and unlikely to change, they worked with a simple measure of political inclusion: the number of legislative seats that minorities held. And from that assumption, a belief in the entitlement of blacks to electoral arrangements that promoted proportionate racial and ethnic representation naturally flowed.

In its next relevant decision, in 1975, the D.C. court returned to the question of annexations. Richmond, Virginia, had enlarged its boundaries to include part of an adjacent county, causing the proportion of the black population to drop from 52 percent to 42 percent. Blacks had never constituted a majority of registered voters, but in at-large elections both before and immediately after the annexation, candidates endorsed by Richmond's leading black organization had won three of the nine seats on the city council. Hoping, however, to avoid federal objection to the boundary change, and concerned that such evidence of black electoral participation would not suffice, the city adopted single-member districts following the *Petersburg* decision.[21]

Given the switch to ward voting, the court could not find that the "weight, strength and power" of black votes in the city would be further reduced by the annexation. Yet, ruling in 1974, it denied the city's application for a declaratory judgment that the annexation had neither the purpose nor the effect of denying or abridging the right to vote on account of race or color. Different facts, the court ruled, made this a different case. In Petersburg economic considerations had prompted the annexation, but in Richmond fear of black political control had been the motivating force. In Petersburg the additional white voters had been a welcome by-product; in Richmond the boundaries had been altered in order to obtain them.[22]

The city argued that black voters were clearly better off in the enlarged municipality, with its single-member districts. The court disagreed. Without the annexation, black voters might soon have become the majority, at which point at-large voting would have been to their advantage. In any case, the institution of the ward plan was itself suspect: "Since substantial doubt exists that the dilution of the black vote caused by the annexation was eliminated by the adoption of the ward plan, it appears that the white political leadership presently in control of Richmond adopted the ward system for the purpose of doing what they could to maintain the dilution of the black vote produced by the annexation."[23] It was curious reasoning: A cannot be shown to have eliminated B; therefore A has been adopted to promote B. Thus, not only the annexation but also the single-member districts had been found to have the purpose of abridging the right to vote.

If racism had motivated either the boundary change or the subsequent ward plan, the obvious remedy was deannexation. But since the annexation was already four years old by the time the case reached the court, such a contraction would have expelled residents of several years' standing. Moreover, there was evidence (relegated to a footnote) that the annexation had some black support.[24] The court offered an alternative remedy. "When the purpose of the annexation is specifically to dilute the vote of black citizens, an extra burden rests on that city to *purge* itself of discriminatory taint."[25] It added: "To convince a court that such a city . . . had purged itself of a discriminatory purpose . . . it [had] to be demonstrated by substantial evidence . . . that the ward plan not only reduced, but also effectively *eliminated*, the dilution of black voting power."[26] In *Petersburg* a partial accommodation to the demographic change had been expected: single-member districts drawn to reflect black voting strength in the *new* city. But in that city both blacks and whites had agreed to extend the city limits. In Richmond, the aim of the annexation had been (at least in part) to reduce the weight of the black vote, and the court, in response, ordered an electoral system that would reflect potential black voting strength as it had existed in the *old* city. The court held that when a city's racial balance is changed through conscious public action in which racial considerations appear to have played a part, blacks become entitled to the number of legislative seats that they *might* have had under the old demographic conditions.

The district court thus ordered the expanded city to fashion an electoral system that would give blacks not what they formerly had, or even what they might now expect (given relatively fewer numbers), but what they *could* have had in the old city had elections been structured to maximize black officeholding. The court's claim that it insisted only that the city eliminate "the dilution of black voting power" was thus misleading.

The Supreme Court, on review, overturned the decision. Speaking for a majority of five, Justice White held that the ward plan developed by the city would do.[27] The postannexation population of the city was 42 percent black, and the nine-ward plan that had been submitted included four districts with a black majority greater than 64 percent, and a fifth that was 40.9 percent black. The section 5 standard has been met, the Court said, if the system "fairly reflects the strength of the Negro community as it exists after the annexation."[28] The Court could not approve the "requirement that the city allocate to the Negro community in the larger city the voting power or the seats on the city council in excess of its proportion in the new community and thus permanently to underrepresent other elements in the community."[29] In fact, Justice White said, "it would be only in the most extraordinary circumstances that the annexation should be permitted on condition that the Negro community be permanently overrepresented in the governing councils of the enlarged city."[30]

What these "extraordinary circumstances" might be, the Court did not explicitly state. It did suggest that a situation in which deannexation was not possible might qualify.[31] In principle, Justice White made clear, a return to the old boundaries was the appropriate remedy only for territorial acquisitions that were aimed solely at maintaining white political control: "An official action . . . taken for the purpose of discriminating against Negroes on account of their race has no legitimacy at all."[32] The question was "whether there [were] no objectively verifiable, legitimate reasons for the annexation"—a question that the Court sent back to the lower court.[33] The D.C. court had initially found no such reasons, but Judge Skelly Wright had failed to give "adequate consideration to the evidence," the Supreme Court noted.[34] As Justice White pointed out, both a special three-judge Virginia court and the Court of Appeals for the Fourth Circuit (in earlier constitutional litigation on the validity of the boundary change) had been persuaded that Richmond's territorial expansion had been undertaken for legitimate reasons.

The Supreme Court was clearly reluctant to order deannexation; after all, five years had passed since part of Chesterfield County had been absorbed by the city of Richmond. But could a new defense shed new light on a formerly illegitimate action? As Justice Brennan's dissent noted, the Court had suggested that "post hoc rationalization" could dispel the initial "taint of an illegal purpose."[35]

In suggesting that, five years later, Richmond's annexation might be no more intentionally discriminatory than Petersburg's, the Court had effectively turned *Richmond* into *Petersburg* and reaffirmed the reasoning of that earlier decision. It rejected a remedy by questioning whether the harm had, in fact, occurred. It did not touch the district court's holding that, once an annexation had been found to be intentionally discriminatory, a city could not compensate for the altered racial balance by promoting proportionate minority officeholding through the use of single-member districts. But it found no such intentional discrimination, and indeed, given the new test for invidious purpose, such a finding had become highly unlikely. What annexation could not be justified five years later? At first glance the two courts appear to be far apart; in fact, only on the question of intent had the decision of the D.C. court been overturned.

It was an odd holding: intentionally discriminatory action would be upheld if nonracial reasons could subsequently be found to justify it. Only in the complete absence of a defense—and even a *post hoc* one would do—would purposeful discrimination be found and an action prohibited. The decision was particularly strange in light of subsequent rulings. Both the D.C. court and the Department of Justice (in its letters of objection) would later assert that nonracial reasons could not overcome the presumption of invidious intent if there were evidence that the jurisdiction had rejected an electoral scheme that was more advantageous to black candidates. That is, an alternative plan more likely to promote black officeholding cast an existing one in an intentionally discriminatory light. The difference between the two viewpoints should be clear. *Richmond* suggested that any asserted nonracial considerations would override a finding of discriminatory intent; subsequent decisions and objections rendered such assertions worthless as a defense against allegations of discrimination. But the legal standards in these section 5 decisions are extremely fluid, and the hold of precedent weak. And, as I suggested earlier, the Supreme Court's rulings carried little weight in the long run—not even, as it turned out, with the Court itself.

With *Petersburg* and *Richmond*, the legal standards regarding annexations were set in place. The assumptions contained in *Petersburg* were never reexamined, nor was the relationship among its parts ever clarified. The D.C. court and the Department of Justice were thus left free to pick and choose among its elements as they sought to build arguments toward a desired end.

The Supreme Court in *Richmond* had not basically rejected the D.C. court's reasoning with respect to annexations. Justice White had reaffirmed black entitlement to single-member districts drawn to promote minority officeholding in proportion to the minority population in an enlarged city. Districting questions, however, were another matter. Vacating the lower court's judgment in *Beer,* the high Court in 1976 rejected the standard of a maximum number of safe black wards.[36]

Whether New Orleans could have devised a plan likely to result in more black councilmen was not the question, Justice Stewart contended; it was, instead, whether the "ability of minority groups to participate in the political process and to elect their choices to office [had been] augmented, diminished, or not affected by the change in voting."[37] How could a change that improved the position of minorities be called discriminatory? The purpose of section 5 had been to bar changes that would result in a "retrogression in the position of racial minorities with respect to their effective exercise of the electoral franchise."[38] Since the change at issue—new district lines—had actually increased the likelihood of a victorious black candidate, it could hardly be termed "retrogressive."

Thus, with the exception of annexations, changes in the method of voting had a discriminatory effect only when they left minority voters worse off. Those that actually increased minority electoral power were not to be condemned. Section 5 was thus an antibacksliding provision; it entitled blacks and Hispanics only to what they had had before. The Court's interpretation, I will argue in subsequent chapters, was inherently sensible and squared with the structure of the act. It relegated to agencies remote from the scene—the Department of Justice and the D.C. court—a limited, and thus manageable, task: stopping efforts to pull minority voters back from the gains they would otherwise have made, preventing "retrogression." And it left in local judicial hands the power to settle broad questions of electoral equality requiring an "intensely local appraisal"—specific, detailed, idiosyncratic knowledge such as only a local federal district court can obtain.

*Beer* read section 5 right, but there was an obvious problem. In *Richmond* the Supreme Court had affirmed the *Petersburg* holding; when a city altered its external boundary lines, minorities became entitled to representation in proportion to their current population strength. Given the widespread use of at-large electoral systems in the covered cities of the South and Southwest, that requirement has almost always meant a switch to ward voting and a consequent gain in the number of legislative seats held by blacks and Hispanics. But districting cases were treated differently. Why? When a city changed its internal lines, why were minorities entitled only to the representational strength that they had previously possessed? Petersburg might have had no blacks on its city council prior to the annexation, but the jurisdictional expansion committed the city to an electoral scheme that promoted black councilmen in proportion to the black population. By contrast, in New Orleans, if the old districting plan provided for no "safe" black seats, none would be demanded from the new plan either. Thus, a jurisdiction that had made no particular effort to increase black officeholding could maintain the status quo, unimpeded by section 5. A scheme that provided no safe black districts when none had existed before would presumably be precleared, although one that provided five when there had been six would not.

*Beer* thus committed the Court to a double standard, bound to cause trouble. The result was serious tension within the structure of the Voting Rights Act. Justice White, who had written the *Richmond* decision, could discern no rationale for the implied distinction between annexation and redistricting cases, and, as a result, dissented in *Beer*. In racially polarized jurisdictions, he wrote, section 5 is not satisfied unless, "to the extent practicable, the new electoral districts afford the Negro minority the opportunity to achieve legislative representation roughly proportional to the Negro population."[39] His view eventually won out. Today, Justice Department objections routinely demand that redistricting plans "fairly reflect" minority voting strength. Without explanation, the annexation standard has been lifted out of context and applied to redistricting submissions. The district court, too, has found ways around *Beer*'s retrogression test—ways to ignore the high Court's ruling. And, although the Supreme Court has subsequently reaffirmed the holding in *Beer,* both the prior annexation cases and a subsequent landmark ruling (*Rome v. United States*) allowed—even sanctioned—such administrative and judicial license.

Although overturned, the approach of the district court in *Beer* has thus come to prevail. In fact, the lower court's reasoning in *Richmond* has not been entirely discarded either. The holding had been that blacks were entitled to the number of legislative seats they might have had under a prior single-member districting system—had one been in place. In a 1984 case involving redistricting for the South Carolina state senate (*South Carolina v. U.S.*), the Justice Department argued that blacks were entitled to the number of seats that they might have had if the old county-unit system, now unconstitutional, had been retained.

The victory of the district court was perhaps predictable. Only two courts decide substantive section 5 questions: the D.C. court and the Supreme Court. Although in theory the latter has the final word, in practice that of the former usually stands; few lower court rulings are appealed. And, to a remarkable extent, the district court has stuck to its guns. The three-judge panels that hear section 5 cases change in composition, but the court's view has been inexplicably consistent. The retrogression test spelled out in *Beer* is theoretically applicable to all changes in methods of election, except for annexations; whether blacks have been left worse off is thus the question that the Supreme Court directed the lower court to ask whether the issue was a districting plan or, for instance, the institution of at-large voting. In all such nonannexation cases, the D.C. court has continued to disagree with the Supreme Court. Moreover, in doing so, it has been joined by the Justice Department and the civil rights groups, both of which, disliking the Supreme Court's narrow holding in the New Orleans case, have repeatedly filed briefs intended to chip away at the unpopular standard enunciated in that decision. Finally, the Supreme Court itself has been vulnerable to the pressure from the D.C. court. In its constitutional cases, as well as those resting on the Voting Rights Act, it failed to work out clear principles with respect to minority representation, and has thus been left without theoretical support on exceedingly slippery legal ground.

The eventual triumph of the district court view was due not only to the infrequency with which rulings of that court are appealed and to the capitulation of the Supreme Court. The Department of Justice has felt free to act on its own, as I will argue at length in Chapter 8. That latitude was apparent, for instance, when school board districts for Sumter County, Georgia, were redrawn after the 1980 census. The plan submitted to the Attorney General for preclearance indisputably met the retrogression test, in that the number of majority-black districts had risen. Yet the Justice Department lodged an objection, based on the availability of an alternative, presumably "better," plan.[40] Did the availability of such a plan suggest discriminatory intent on the part of the county, or was this a case of impermissible impact? The letter of objection did not say. And although no court has held that the failure to adopt an alternative plan is evidence of discriminatory effect, the Department of Justice, in its enforcement capacity, does not hesitate to fix such "flaws" in case law. Such initiatives are rarely challenged. A jurisdiction can ask that a Justice Department decision be reviewed internally, but the attorneys assigned to assessing the objection will be those who made the decision in the first place. The alternative is to start anew before the D.C. court—an expensive, lengthy, and often politically costly process.

Given the Court's prior commitment to providing proportional racial and ethnic representation in its annexation decisions, the retrogression test for electoral discrimination was off to an inauspicious start. The test was further weakened by *City of Rome, Georgia v. United States*, a 1980 Supreme Court decision.[41]

Rome had a black voting-age population of only 20.6 percent; its black registration figure was even lower. In 1966 the General Assembly of Georgia had amended the city charter, reducing the number of wards from nine to three but providing for three numbered posts within each ward. The assembly instituted both a majority-vote requirement and staggered terms. Only in November 1974 were these amendments, as well as sixty annexations made over the course of a decade, submitted for preclearance. At that time the Attorney General objected to thirteen of the annexations and every change in the city charter. Rome sued in the D.C. court but lost. Finding a pattern of racial bloc voting, the court ruled that the adoption of a majority-vote requirement, numbered posts, and staggered terms was discriminatory in effect. Prior to the change, said the court, only a plurality of votes was required to win; thus, if whites split their vote and blacks engaged in single-shot voting, a black candidate could gain a city council seat. The revised scheme forced head-to-head contests in runoff elections between blacks and whites, and was thus retrogressive in impact. By increasing the number of votes it took to win, the new system also increased the degree of white support required for black success.[42]

The city took its case to the Supreme Court, where it lost again. The opinion, written by Justice Marshall for a majority of six, added nothing to what the lower court had already said. In the Supreme Court's view, the majority-vote requirement had "significantly decreased" a black candidate's chance to win. Moreover, although nine out of the thirteen annexed areas to which the Justice Department had objected were unpopulated, and the annexations had thus resulted in a drop of only 1 percent in the black population, the city, nevertheless, "bore the burden of proving its electoral system 'fairly reflect[ed] the strength of the Negro community as it exist[ed] after the annexation.' "[43]

Writing in dissent, Justice Rehnquist (joined by Justice Stewart, the author of the *Beer* decision) complained that the lower court had found facts that were "conspicuously absent from the Court's opinion."[44] Blacks had freely registered in Rome in the previous seventeen years. No other barriers stopped blacks from voting or running for office. In fact, white officials were reported to have encouraged blacks to seek elected posts in Rome, and evidence suggested that they had made efforts to upgrade black neighborhoods and otherwise to respond to the needs and interests of the black community. Although only whites had been elected to political office, a black candidate, running for the board of education in 1970, had received close to 40 percent of the white vote.[45] (The low black turnout kept him from winning.) A black had been appointed to fill a vacancy in an elective post, and white candidates commonly pursued black support vigorously. Several commissioners, in fact, testified that they had spent a disproportionate amount of time campaigning in black neighborhoods because they "needed that vote to win." Indeed, the D.C. court had found that blacks often held the balance of power in Rome elections.[46]

The evidence of black political inclusion referred to by Rehnquist was incontrovertible, but irrelevant. He had confused the *White v. Regester* test for unconstitutionality with the standard contained in the Voting Rights Act. *Rome* made clear what *Beer* had not: that by 1980 it was assumed that only blacks could represent blacks, and that the point of the statute had become the promotion of black officeholding. If a black's chances of being elected were even slightly diminished as a result of a proposed electoral change, that change was deemed objectionable— unless, of course, there was no evidence of racial bloc voting, of a racially polarized electorate. But a finding of bloc voting was almost a certainty. No court had ever defined such voting, and, lacking a settled definition, courts had little basis on which to question its alleged presence.

To assume that only blacks could represent blacks was to sanction the conclusion to which the D.C. court and the Justice Department had already come: that blacks were entitled to maximum officeholding, to proportionate representation. The one followed logically from the other. The Court had not renounced its retrogression test, but it had stripped that test of its initial logic, thereby heightening the internal tension that already plagued the Voting Rights Act. The point of section 5 had been to stop racist jurisdictions from implementing new laws that had the effect of either nullifying or softening the impact of the central, enfranchising provisions of the act. But Rome was clearly no racist city cunningly attempting to disfranchise blacks; evidence of black political inclusion was abundant. And by implicitly embracing the standard of proportionate racial and ethnic representation, the Court was exacerbating the problem created by the juxtaposition of *Beer* and *Richmond.* The Court had pulled the act in conflicting directions, and the consequent tension broke the hold of *Beer.* That tension had allowed the district court and the Justice Department to choose a side—legitimately to embrace one position at the expense of the other. The decisions of that court and the administrative objections that have stressed entitlement to proportionate officeholding have thus been indirectly sanctioned by the Supreme Court.

The Voting Rights Act survives as a statute divided against itself. In a 1982 decision, *Port Arthur v. U.S.*, the Supreme Court took the annexation standard one step further, ruling that not even proportional representation satisfied the statutory requirement if further measures could be taken to promote black officeholding.[47] In 1978 Port Arthur, Texas, had enlarged its boundaries, and had subsequently traded its at-large election system for a plan providing for the election of eight councilmen and a mayor. Six of the councilmen were to be elected by districts and two city-wide. The method of election, in other words, had been altered to promote the election of black city councilmen; inevitably some of the districts would be majority-black and thus "safe" for black candidates. Indeed, following elections in 1981, the city, with a black voting-age population of 35 percent, had a council of four blacks and five whites; blacks were thus proportionately overrepresented. The Supreme Court nonetheless declared that the plan violated section 5. With respect to the two at-large council positions, it said, the majority-vote requirement that the city had retained was an impermissible impediment to the election of blacks.

The Court has not extended the principle announced in *Port Arthur* to nonannexation cases. The retrogression test has most recently been reaffirmed in *City of Lockhart, Texas v. United States* (1983).[48] Nonetheless, that standard has had little impact on the decisions of the district court. *Lockhart* overturned a district court ruling that made clear the lower court's persistent commitment to subverting the high Court's test. That persistent commitment was apparent, as well, in a case involving Sumter County, South Carolina. Its appointed county council had been replaced with one elected at large. Since the county was 44.1 percent black, any method of election—even one that was county-wide—would seem to have offered blacks a greater chance to elect candidates of their choice. But the district court found the plan retrogressive, on the ground that "a fairly drawn single-member election plan" would be preferable.[49] Needless to say, such a holding directly contradicted *Beer*, in which the Supreme Court had explicitly rejected arguments based on the superiority of alternative plans.

In the Sumter County case, the D.C. court circumvented *Beer* by redefining "retrogression." In decisions such as *City of Pleasant Grove v. U.S.* (1983), the lower court has solved the problem of a constricted definition of discriminatory effect by expanding the "intent" category.[50] In the 1970s Pleasant Grove, an all-white Alabama city, annexed two neighboring parcels of land, one vacant, the other occupied by a single white family. It is difficult to see how black voting rights had been abridged by the boundary change, since Pleasant Grove had no black voters to begin with. Nonetheless, the court found a violation of section 5, ruling that the city had failed to prove that, in annexing areas devoid of black population, it had not engaged in intentional vote discrimination. If circumstantial evidence of invidious purpose is defined with enough breadth, there will never be a need to rest an objection upon a finding of discriminatory impact. The retrogression test can thus simply be ignored.

That the Supreme Court could not sustain its own vision of section 5 accounts in part for the amendment of the preclearance provision in the hands of the D.C. court and the Justice Department. The Court touched base with the act only twice: in *Beer* and in *Lockhart*. Its previous annexation decisions and subsequent *Rome* ruling pulled the act in conflicting directions and broke the hold of the "retrogression" standard. But the problem was not just that the decisions were inadequately thought out and inconsistent; the Court also faced insurrection. Neither the D.C. judges nor, more important, the Department of Justice stayed in line. The Supreme Court was a central government without provincial control, a general barely in command of his troops. That the links between the Supreme Court and the Department of Justice were even more tenuous than those between the two courts is the subject to which I next turn.

# Detours around the Law

The Voting Rights Act mystifies even those who know it best. To begin with, as I suggested in Chapter 4, there is the baffling question of the relationship between the statute and the constitutional guarantees it purports to enforce. And the uncertainty of that relationship has been symptomatic of a broader problem. Although the preclearance provision had, by 1975, become the focus of enforcement, the standards used to judge electoral changes submitted for review have been unexplained and seemingly inexplicable.

Administrative review, it should be clear, substitutes for a full-scale trial. And, in theory, the legal standards used by the Department of Justice to interpret section 5 simply track those that the courts have developed. In practice, however, government attorneys and judges have more often diverged than converged in their approach to preclearance questions. More precisely, administrative decisions have diverged from those of the Supreme Court, to which the D.C. court has not faithfully adhered either. The Justice Department decisions appear to follow no principle. Yet appearance is deceptive; as this chapter will argue, the record is less mysterious than it looks. The Justice Department, it is true, has been creating detours around the law, but generally to a common and clear end.

The previous chapter emphasized the impact of Supreme Court and district court decisions—the damage done by the contradictions contained in the former and the revisionism of the latter. Yet the judicial record, I have noted, is also remarkably thin. Only one redistricting case, for instance—*Beer*—has reached the high Court.[1] Both action and inaction opened the door to administrative innovation.

In 1965 it was not expected that the administrative route to preclearance would be the normal one; that route was provided to permit the expeditious handling of submissions that seemed clear-cut. Yet from the early 1970s, when section 5 acquired real force, litigation was the exception. In 1972, when *Petersburg* was the only Voting Rights Act case to have come before the D.C. court, 942 voting changes were submitted to the Attorney General. The number has steadily and dramatically risen. In 1980 it was 7,340; in 1983, 12,416. For the period August 1965 to June 1984, the total was 77,227.[2] Some submissions involve obviously acceptable proposals—an increase in the number of registration hours, for instance. But a plan to open an additional registration site—in a police station, for example—will not be automatically approved. And suggested changes frequently involve districting and other immensely complex questions, the resolution of which is the responsibility of a small cadre of attorneys and paralegals in the voting section of the Civil Rights Division of the Department of Justice.

Litigation is the exception for two reasons: time and money. Administrative action is faster and cheaper. The Richmond city council was frozen for seven years while the case wended its way through the courts; few jurisdictions are willing or able to pay such a political price. Nor can they afford the financial drain. When the city of Rome, Georgia, went to court, the bill came to approximately $230,000.[3] This was not a particularly high figure for such a case, and although the state of Georgia can afford substantial legal fees, a small city cannot. An impoverished rural county is hard-pressed to pay its everyday bills, much less extraordinary legal ones. Jurisdictions often find themselves in court, of course, but suits filed in the D.C. court are significantly more expensive to pursue than those brought before the local bench. There are costs for food, housing, travel, and Washington attorneys. And more likely than not, the money will be wasted. "Thus far . . . the reception received by those who have chosen judicial preclearance has been less than friendly," one attorney wrote in 1984.[4] The statistics make the point: of the sixteen reported section 5 decisions, only two have been decided in favor of the city, county, or state hoping to alter its electoral procedure.

The administrative preclearance process was spelled out in 1971 in a document entitled "Procedures for the Administration of Section 5 of the Voting Rights Act of 1965."[5] It reviewed such matters as the type of electoral changes covered by section 5, the address to which a submission should be sent, the required contents of that submission, the right of private individuals to comment on the proposed change, and the speed with which the Department of Justice was expected to act. Jurisdictions and other interested parties were informed that all changes affecting voting, even ones that appeared minor, indirect, or of benefit to blacks, had to be submitted. In addition, the guidelines stated that the burden of proof was on the jurisdiction; that a submission to the Attorney General did not affect the right of the jurisdiction to bring suit in the D.C. court; that the change must be enacted but not implemented prior to submission for approval; and that submissions were expected to include relevant material of a demographic, geographic, or historical nature. Furthermore, any individual or group could forward information to the Attorney General concerning the proposed electoral change, and such individuals or groups could request that their identity be kept confidential, although the Department would maintain a registry of interested individuals and groups. The Attorney General was to act on a submission within 60 days, unless further information from the jurisdiction was required, in which case the clock would be started anew. Finally, after an objection, a jurisdiction could request reconsideration in light of new information.

For all their seeming comprehensiveness, however, the guidelines were mute on vital aspects of the preclearance process. Although the Attorney General has final responsibility for any decision made by the Department of Justice, in fact the final word on section 5 submissions usually rests with the assistant attorney general for civil rights. Moreover, the decisive work is often done by employees without legal training or, in some cases, even a college degree. "After a period of training by Voting Section attorneys, the research analysts . . . assumed principal responsibility for examination of voting changes," one scholarly study has reported.[6] The submitted material is reviewed, phone contacts are made, but "just about never" (in the words of a staff attorney) is a staff member sent to the local jurisdiction to view the situation up close.[7] Since the burden of proof in these submissions is on the jurisdiction, the fact that review is conducted from afar makes a favorable decision even more unlikely. Only on-site appraisal is likely to raise doubts about the evident working assumption that southern jurisdictions are racist and that the evidence they submit must be regarded with suspicion. Only up close do complexities become apparent. The Supreme Court has stressed the importance of an "intensely local appraisal" in Fourteenth

Amendment voting rights cases; the Court's point is no less relevant when it comes to the preclearance process.[8]

If the Justice Department almost never goes south (or elsewhere), the South sometimes comes to it. State or local spokesmen will travel to Washington to engage in a process of negotiation with the Department—no hint of which is provided in the guidelines. And, in the course of such negotiations, federal attorneys, charged with the task of barring discriminatory electoral schemes, can slip into quite a different role— that of actually drawing district lines or otherwise arranging election systems. Conflicting claims normally resolved by the political process are thus left to the discretion of the Department of Justice. In the previously mentioned case of Sumter County, Georgia, a staff attorney took the unusual step of making a local visit. Before departing, he drew up an alternative plan. As he reported in a subsequent departmental memo, "I allowed Mr. _____ to keep the map which I had marked with the understanding that it not be publicized as a Department of Justice proposal so as to avoid any public misperception that the Department was wedded to a particular plan. Mr. _____ agreed."[9] But even if more than one plan was theoretically acceptable, only one had been presented, and it could hardly be said that the county was under no pressure to adopt it.

The process of negotiation may actually begin prior to enactment of the voting change. In theory, advisory opinions cannot be offered with respect to proposed revisions in electoral procedure, since they would constitute a form of coercion inconsistent with both democratic processes and the aim of the act. Selecting electoral arrangements goes to the heart of democratic politics, and the statute hardly sought to eliminate all local discretion in the matter; it was simply intended to prevent an abridgment or denial of the right to vote. Nonetheless, such advisory opinions are freely offered. As a staff attorney has described the process, local jurisdictions "want to know what we are going to look for. They're going to revise their city charter and the city attorney will call me up to ask . . . We'll do what we can for them . . . We try to make things go smoothly for them so they can hold elections."[10] In a letter to a spokesman for Eufaula, Alabama, James P. Turner, acting assistant attorney general for civil rights, stated: "The Attorney General is precluded from reviewing the merits of any proposed changes affecting voting which are submitted prior to final enactment or which are not yet capable of being officially administered. 28 C.F.R. 51.7. However, Department officials have reviewed proposed changes on an informal basis and would be willing to give Barbour County the benefit of our views concerning any of its proposed plans."[11] The asserted distinction is thus between formal and informal review—although the guidelines would seem to prohibit both.

Most conspicuously missing from the guidelines was any mention of the criteria to be used in judging submissions—the question on which jurisdictions most needed guidance. Localities were informed only that these standards would not differ from those employed by the D.C. court. The point has been reiterated time and again by the Justice Department. "In the conduct of our preclearance function under section 5 of the Voting Rights Act, we traditionally have considered ourselves to be a surrogate of the district court, seeking to make the kind of decision we believe the court would make if the matter were before it," an objection letter to Port Arthur, Texas, stated.[12] To jurisdictions seeking to revise their methods of voting within the law, that information has been next to useless. "Courts, covered jurisdictions, interested citizens, and even the Department of Justice lack guidance in determining how a particular covered change should be decided under section 5," Hiroshi Motomura noted in a 1983 article reviewing voting section policy. "Objection letters," he went on, "do not cite other objection letters or make any apparent effort to create an independent body of section 5 law based on precedent."[13] "The preclearance process transpires in the absence of specified decision criteria that are well known in advance to those who have the obligation to comply with Section 5," another study concluded.[14]

"In light of the limited number of section 5 cases, the Attorney General can only 'guess' what the court would do with any particular case," one scholar has explained.[15] But the paucity of decisions has been only part of the problem, as I argued in the previous chapter. The D.C. court is, to some extent, a law unto itself; as for the Supreme Court, mixed signals have sanctioned, if not encouraged, judicial and administrative license. As a consequence, a jurisdiction in the process of altering its electoral arrangements must operate in the dark, unsure of the legality of the various options it is considering. Consider redistricting, for instance. Prior to 1980 South Carolina had no black state senators. When the state drew a new map for its senatorial seats, it had no way of ascertaining, on the basis of judicial and administrative precedent, whether nine majority-black districts would meet the requirements of the law, or whether the creation of a tenth would be necessary. (A nine-district plan would provide more protection for incumbents than one that gave blacks a good shot at a tenth seat.) Redistricting is a politically complex and laborious process, and a plan that is rejected has been a waste of extensive political effort. More important, when the Justice Department interposes an objection, for all intents and purposes it assumes a legislative function normally assigned to the state. Assuming such power is certainly legitimate when a state has been testing its power to circumvent the law. But the imposition of such federal control in the face of good-faith efforts to comply with federal standards raises serious questions involving federalism.

Provisional new guidelines were published by the Department of Justice in 1985, and for the first time an effort was made to suggest criteria for section 5 decisions. As the political scientist Timothy O'Rourke aptly remarked, they read like a criminal statute that states: "Among the things you may be arrested for are . . . "[16] In other words, the proposed guidelines provide no guidance. But they do make clear the pathways that the Department of Justice has charted around the law.

The image of the Attorney General as surrogate for the D.C. court is both uninformative and misleading. The court has been remarkably consistent in its commitment to maximizing minority officeholding, yet it has not quite cast its judicial robes aside. But the voting section has the aura of a law office; its files suggest attorneys at work constructing a case for clients.

This is not a recent development; the picture has not changed with different administrations. In July 1974, the last month of the Nixon presidency, Charleston, South Carolina, submitted for preclearance twenty-five annexations stretching over a ten-year period. Their cumulative result was to decrease the black population from 47 to 45 percent. In 1960 the city had been a majority-black one, but an annexation that year had brought the percentage down; that annexation, having occurred before the passage of the Voting Rights Act, was not eligible for review. At the time the submission was made, although candidates were required to reside in separate sections of the city, they ran city-wide and needed a majority vote to win.

The Attorney General objected to the annexation of areas with significant population—those seven which together added 3,554 whites and only 98 blacks to the city. Voting in Charleston was racially polarized, the Justice Department concluded, and the 2 percent drop in black population had affected the outcome of elections in 1971. Moreover, the Department had received allegations—not proved or disproved—that the annexations were racially motivated.[17]

On the latter question, that of a racist intent, the Department was understandably noncommittal. Attorneys and paralegals within the voting section had made a valiant effort to construct a case for racial motivation. But they appeared to have only two unimpressive bits of evidence, neither of which would stand up in any court. The first was a phone call on August 27, 1974, from a Charleston civil rights attorney, who said he had overheard a white woman state that everyone knew that the annexations had been made to add white voters to the city rolls. The second was an undated phone conversation in which the caller charged that the city had never made an effort to annex black areas— that blacks, in fact, had been warned that residence in the city would mean higher taxes. It was "common knowledge" that the city had altered its boundaries in order to keep Charleston from going black.[18]

The city was in fact becoming steadily more black, and in a speculative memo addressed to the voting section head, a research analyst suggested that whites "might well have a significant interest in annexing to keep this from happening." Yet, as the memo itself readily acknowledged, the city could argue that its tax base was shrinking as a result of a steady decline in population. Moreover, that memo, as well as an earlier one, noted that annexations required petitions signed by a majority of the freeholders in the area and eventual approval by the voters. These conditions had not been met in black areas outside the city, which had consistently elected to stay out.[19]

When the process of review began, an attorney assigned to the case was chafing at the bit in his eagerness to demonstrate racist intent; the head of the voting section restrained him. An earlier memo by this attorney betrays an eagerness for quick conviction and a disdain for thorough and careful investigation. The memo asserted that the annexations were to "benefit the town and the white property owners." The city had "unequivocally told blacks they [would not] be annexed." Blacks, however, wanted "to participate in the town's government" in order to "get their area improved." The city had responded by offering to "annex a small area that include[d] the most vocal black leaders, but

the leaders rejected this as tokenism." "The effect is clear and purpose is well indicated," the memo concluded. "If you concur, I'll draft a
letter."[20]

Nothing in the file substantiated these assertions. And, as we have
seen, a more sustained inquiry produced contrary evidence. In reply,
Gerald Jones, head of the voting section, wrote: "I agree that this is a
situation which something should be done about but one basic problem I
have is, How does this annexation have a racially discriminatory effect
(or dilutive effect) on the black vote? Let's discuss. I'd also like to know
something about how the council is elected, what [are] the methods of
annexation in South Carolina . . . and what exactly are the efforts which
the blacks claim they have been making over the last 3 years to become
annexed."[21]

Jones had concluded that this was "a situation which something should
be done about" and then requested evidence. His staff offered the following reply: The city, it said, had not sustained its burden of proving
that the annexation did not prevent blacks from electing representatives
of their choice.[22] The candidates preferred by the blacks would have
won except for the votes of persons in the annexed areas. There were
three implicit contentions contained in this assertion: that the racial
makeup of the city would have been different had there been no post-
1964 annexations; that elections were extremely close, heightening the
significance of even a small drop in the percentage of blacks; and that the
preferred candidates of blacks were losing.

Each of these contentions was questionable. Although the annexations
probably did somewhat alter the racial balance in the city, the actual
situation was less clear-cut than that depicted in the departmental
memos. The purported 2 percent drop in black population due to annexations from 1964 to 1974 was computed on the basis of the 1960 and
1970 censuses. But was the black population in 1964 (four years after
the census) still 47 percent? It is possible that black migration out of the
city had already cut the black population by two points by the time the
first annexation took place. A communication from civil rights attorney
Armand Derfner argued that the black residents in the territory incorporated by annexation number 13 were former residents of the city who
had moved out.[23] He thus opposed including these residents in the list of
additions to the city population. This argument suggests another: although some blacks moved into the subsequently annexed territory,
others moved into neighboring parts of the county. There were, after

all, several black residential areas adjacent to the city, and early voting section memos had accused the city of refusing to annex them. The assumption that annexations were solely responsible for the demographic shift of 2 percent was thus questionable.

Furthermore, was the drop itself significant? Were elections so close and so racially polarized that even a small shift in racial balance could actually change their outcome? It is true that the 1971 mayoral contest, on which the Justice Department rested its case, was extremely close. But one contest does not make a case, and the files contained no close analysis of voting patterns to substantiate these claims.

Finally, had the city council candidates preferred by blacks also lost? In the 1971 election (again, the only race referred to in the departmental files) three blacks had won seats, but a voting section memo contended that they were the "wrong" blacks, unsupported by their own community.[24] Again, the evidence is hearsay—two random phone calls. Although the Department gets in touch with and listens to interested parties, these individuals are not always knowledgeable. Those who dial the phone are not "experts" but self-selected citizens eager to deliver a particular message, the accuracy of which is not verified. And the list of contacts—of minority or white "spokesmen"—maintained by the voting section for each jurisdiction often bewilders those who find themselves on it. Such reliance on questionable authorities is one more price the Department pays for so rarely making local visits.

The departmental memos actually went beyond the assertion that unrepresentative blacks had been elected and argued that no black could gain office except by inclusion on a mayoral slate, a situation discriminatory in itself. The Democratic Party slated only those blacks who had worked a long time in the community and were well known; yet ordinary blacks, it was argued, should be able to run "and not have to depend on being . . . extra special."[25] One memo stated, "If a fairly drawn single-member district plan were used, blacks would finally be able to achieve real representation in city government and representation in proportion to their strength in the population."[26] By reducing the black population by 2 percent, the annexations were thus said to perpetuate an electoral process in which only "extra special" blacks could gain office. It was not that blacks per se were losing, but that "average" blacks were not chosen to run.

With these questionable arguments, the Department had built a case for objecting to the at-large voting that gave the annexations their supposed discriminatory impact. The evidence relied upon was far from solid—a phone call purporting to have overheard a conversation between unidentified citizens, for example. The attorney assigned to the submission was ready to object with an argument certainly unworthy of a surrogate court; additional perfunctory research revealed serious factual flaws in the case constructed. Yet the pressure was clearly on to find a means of condemning the at-large voting; it was "a situation which something should be done about," the head of the voting section had concluded, even before a shred of credible evidence had emerged. An alternative argument was soon offered and accepted, although its validity rested on several unsubstantiated allegations. Moreover, federal attorneys and paralegals, who stuck to their Washington desks, assumed they could legitimately distinguish between "real" and "unreal" blacks—between those who held office as true black representatives and those who, in effect, were impostors, having the right color skin but the wrong color politics.

From the perspective of the Department of Justice, it appears, all at-large voting in covered jurisdictions is a situation "which something should be done about." Even in the South, however, judicious procedure should require that racist political exclusion be proved on a case-by-case basis. Southern cities and counties are not interchangeable; knowing one does not mean that you know them all. Those in the voting section who reviewed the Charleston submission appeared to know nothing of that city's recent and distinctive history; indeed, it was not even a subject of interest.

By 1974 Charleston, like New Orleans, was not a stereotypical southern racist city. To begin with, it had the advantage of being located in South Carolina; as Bass and DeVries were to write two years later, "In no state did the political role of blacks change so completely, so quickly, or with fewer jagged edges."[27] In part, the emerging importance of blacks was a response to the early onset of two-party politics; by 1964, when Senator Strom Thurmond switched parties and Goldwater swept the state, the Republican Party had become a formidable force. But there appears to have been, as well, an unusual commitment to law and orderly change, stemming perhaps from an aristocratic respect for civility. South Carolina leaders, one observer has written, "were concerned lest they be lumped with what they considered to be the vulgarities and crudities of Mississippi and Alabama."[28] Certainly the course of action taken by a series of South Carolina governors contrasted strikingly with the policies of Ross Barnet and George Wallace. In 1963 Wallace vowed "segregation today, segregation tomorrow, segregation forever," and six months later he literally stood in the schoolhouse door to prevent the integration of the University of Alabama. That same year incoming South Carolina governor Donald Russell held an inaugural barbecue that was attended by both blacks and whites; in his final address, outgoing governor Ernest Hollings urged the state to "make clear its commitment to a government of law, not men."[29]

By 1968 the county of Charleston had elected its first black commissioner, at-large, and in 1970 the city sent Herbert Fielding, its first black delegate, to the state legislature. Two years later Fielding led the ticket, even though the district was two-thirds white. Looking back, he would later comment: "When the transition [to an integrated society] came, during the '60s . . . there was no doggone problem." In fact, "a whole lot of those same people who were resisting like hell, when it finally came about, they were happy as a pig in a puddle of mud." Fielding chose to return to Charleston after World War II, convinced that integration would work better in the South than in the North.[30] For other blacks, as well, the experience of Charleston nurtured optimism. One of the city's leading black politicians today, William Saunders, was a follower of Stokely Carmichael in the 1960s; by 1982 he could say, "To me, the South is the place that is going to make a change in black life."[31]

Charleston's small size (as a peninsula city) and high degree of residential integration seems to have fostered an unusual degree of community between whites and blacks. "Charleston is a little bit different," Fielding said, "and it goes back a long way; it goes back because of the fact that blacks and whites never really lived apart."[32] He may have exaggerated, but the city's antebellum living pattern—whites in the main house, blacks (then slaves) in back—gave way to easy residential mixing. In *Porgy and Bess*—set in Charleston in the 1920s—Porgy lived in a tenement amidst upper-class whites. Franklin Frazier, in his study of the black bourgeoisie, cites Charleston as the prime example of a city in which blacks were widely scattered.[33]

Contact between the races in Charleston took a variety of forms. Local residents, interviewed in 1982, depicted a life that in significant ways was shared. "There are a lot of things they cared about together," one lifelong resident remarked. "And I think they cared about the town."[34] A sense of community and a tolerance of diversity seem to have gone hand-in-hand. Gedney Howe, the guiding light of Charleston politics from the 1950s to the 1980s, openly and successfully orchestrated black campaigns, yet he was never ostracized from white society. "I think there is just an inborn tolerance for eccentricities of any kind," Howe's widow said of Charleston. "You know, somebody said that a civilization can be judged by the way it treats its eccentrics, and . . . Charleston has so many eccentrics . . . Of course, it's a seaport town, and that makes a difference too. It doesn't have the straight-laced approach that an up-country, all Presbyterian village would have."[35]

Howe himself held public office only briefly, but black politicians agreed that he was the "mastermind" behind their success. Herbert Fielding described him as a "kingmaker . . . a master maneuverer, and a master politician . . . White on the outside . . . no color on the inside."[36] Others said that nothing really important had happened in Democratic circles after 1944 that Howe did not guide. "I guess his philosophy on politics was an embracing one, that you . . . get as many people under your umbrella as you can," the city attorney said. "Gedney really early saw that the needs of the black community could only be met within a strong Democratic Party and vice versa." In Charleston, he added, there developed "a real sense of kinship between the black and white political leadership in the Democratic Party."[37] The culmination of Howe's work can be said to have come with the election, in 1975, of Mayor Joe Riley, nicknamed "LBJ" or "Little Black Joe" in recognition of his sensitivity to black needs.

This is not a definitive analysis of Charleston history and politics, and perhaps I have accented the positive, omitting the darker side. The city was hardly free of racism. And a great deal of black discontent, for instance, was registered in a survey of the political climate done on behalf of a mayoral candidate one year after the Justice Department decision (although Riley was subsequently said to have dispelled it).[38] But the Justice Department memos had a "get-the-racist-bastards" tone inappropriate to their subject. Perhaps the work of people like Howe was nothing but white paternalism, but many felt otherwise. And even paternalism cannot control black power, once it is unleashed. In any case, my quarrel is not with the Department's decision, which may have been right, but with its methods. The radical shift in power allowed by the Voting Rights Act, the extraordinary usurpation of traditional local prerogatives by federal authorities, was acceptable on only one condition—that the Department of Justice truly function as a surrogate court. The task of attorneys hired by a client is to concoct a case; the role of the voting section of the Civil Rights Division should be different. *Petersburg*, by sanctioning the institution of ward voting on the basis of perfunctory inquiries into the question of political exclusion, allowed the Justice Department to dismantle with ease long-standing at-large systems and thereby to blur the distinction between traditional rules and recent changes that was initially so integral to the act. The case of Charleston showed just how perfunctory—how devoid of judiciousness—the Department's inquiry could be.

The Department of Justice has failed in its role as surrogate court in a second sense: it objects to districting plans and other electoral changes on grounds that violate legal precedent, responsibly read. Submissions involving annexations inspire few attempts to stretch the law. The Supreme Court, it could be said, already did the job. The decisions in *Petersburg* and *Richmond* allowed the Department to insist that jurisdictions abandon their at-large voting systems and institute racially "fair" single-member districts whenever an annexation caused a shift in racial balance. In Statesboro, Georgia, the Department filed an objection after a boundary change caused a drop of 0.9 percent in the black population; in Newellton, Louisiana, an objection was filed after the addition of seventy-two whites made blacks a voting minority.[39] In fact, an objectionable annexation may have no immediate effect; the absorption of uninhabited land thought likely to be occupied by whites at some future point will suffice to condemn an at-large system. But only with respect to annexations does administrative enforcement so closely follow case law. On questions of redistricting and other changes affecting voting, the Supreme Court, on the one hand, and the D.C. court and the Department of Justice, on the other, have been at odds. In fact, from the outset, the Supreme Court's retrogression test had few friends and many enemies. The civil rights groups and their allies—off the bench and on—called it a major defeat.

That defeat was, in fact, short-lived. By 1980 the Justice Department all but ignored *Beer*. Lower courts cannot close their eyes to a Supreme Court decision, but the voting section has done just that. In 1983 the high Court reaffirmed its ruling in the New Orleans case, yet, for all intents and purposes, that decision has been wiped from the books.[40] The New Orleans plan approved by the Supreme Court in *Beer* would not now pass administrative review; what the high Court precleared, the Justice Department will not.

The Justice Department clearly violates the rules of precedent, yet not entirely without encouragement, I have argued. Given the annexation decisions, with their guarantee of ward voting "fairly reflecting" the minority population, the retrogression test was off to a weak start. The distinction between annexations and other changes made, at best, imperfect sense. In *Beer* the Court had argued that a section 5 review posed a narrow question: Was the method of election being altered to reduce the impact of the new black vote? Yet not only *Richmond* but *Rome*, too, had promised something more: the promotion of black officeholding. The Court stuck by *Beer*, but its decision was buffeted by winds the Court itself had generated.

If the Supreme Court had inadvertently led the way, the Justice Department charged ahead with startling boldness. The process of enforcement has, in effect, amended the act. The Republican administration of Ronald Reagan has pressed as diligently in this direction as its predecessors. Indeed, it is hard to imagine a Civil Rights Division more responsive to the demands of minority and civil rights spokesmen with respect to districting than that headed by William Bradford Reynolds, the assistant attorney general for civil rights—at least prior to 1986, when policy did somewhat alter. The judicial restraint often preached by conservatives appears not to extend to quasi-judicial administrative action, at least not in the sphere of minority voting rights. In the final chapter I will speculate on why this should be so.

*Beer* thus still stands, while the Justice Department has veered around it. Briefs and letters signed by Reynolds fall into two categories: those that maintain a pretense of adhering to the law, and those that do not even bother to put up a front. A pretense is maintained, for instance, when an existing districting plan is labeled an inappropriate benchmark against which to measure retrogression—when lines in place at some earlier date are said to be the true point of comparison. Measuring a newly proposed plan against a long-discarded one only makes sense, of course, if that earlier plan appears more advantageous to blacks than that which has been most recently in use. The argument has to be that the current plan had been erroneously precleared, that blacks had been better off at some earlier date. These tough conditions were met, in the view of the Justice Department, in the case of *South Carolina v. United States*.

Senate redistricting was the issue. South Carolina, trusting the D.C. court more than the Department of Justice, decided to litigate. The state senate has 46 seats. By a plan enacted in late 1983, all members were elected from single-member districts, nine of them majority-black. That plan would seem to have been a radical improvement over the previous one, which provided for multicounty, multimember districts, all of which were majority-white, and under which only one black had been elected. However, the Department of Justice, representing the United States as defendant in the case, argued that the previous plan was not the proper point of comparison. In 1964 South Carolina senators had been elected on the basis of one per county; that scheme had succumbed to the one person, one vote standard, since counties were obviously not equal in population. But at that time, when few of the state's blacks could vote, there had been fifteen (malapportioned) majority-black counties—equivalent, the Department said, to single-member districts. And it would appear inconsistent with the intent of Congress to preclear a plan that left blacks worse off than they had been at the time when the statute was passed. The system with fifteen majority-black districts was thus selected as the benchmark, and the proposed provision of nine was deemed "retrogressive."[41]

The argument was deeply flawed. A county-unit system of representation is not the same thing as single-member districts, and it is misleading to label it as such. And in the years between 1964 and 1983, six South Carolina districting schemes had been precleared; in reaching back to 1964 the Justice Department ignored that history, dismissing plans that were lawfully in effect. Equally important, any plan that met the one person, one vote standard would result in fewer than fifteen majority-black districts: the number fifteen depended on malapportionment, which was prohibited by law. In addition, if severely malapportioned plans were in general an improper benchmark, as the district court had declared, then that principle applied in this case as well.[42]

In fact, the Justice Department itself has often argued that since existing districting plans have inevitably become malapportioned with the passage of time, any newly drawn plan should be compared to a hypothetical, properly apportioned, racially fair alternative. A plan that is not "fairly drawn" is thus "retrogressive." "Fairly drawn" plans are those that give blacks "safe" seats in proportion to the black population—to the degree possible. As the voting section staff explained to Reynolds in a 1981 memo on county council districts for Barbour County, Alabama, calculating what was "fair" was simple. "Since blacks constitute 40.5 percent of the voting age population, they would be entitled to 2.8 districts, that is two viable districts plus a third district in which their interests must be taken into account even though they cannot control the election."[43] The voting section itself drew up the right plan, demonstrating that, in fact, "a seven-member plan could be drawn which afforded blacks an opportunity to elect three of the seven members (42%) which is roughly equal to the black percentage of the county's population (44%)."[44] Such calculations are a routine part of the preclearance process. Thus, the file on Sumter County, Georgia, contains the following comment from Reynolds: "I agree that an objection is required. The submitted plan provides for but two black-majority districts out of the 7 proposed. In view of the fact that the black population of Sumter County commands 43.4% of the total population, and a fairly drawn plan can be—and indeed was—drawn giving blacks three majority districts, the submission cannot survive Section 5 scrutiny without full explanation from the County."[45]

"Viable" or "electable," by voting section standards, means districts that are not simply majority-black, but have a black concentration of 65 percent. Thus when Reynolds, as a novice, questioned his staff as to why the plan submitted by Barbour County did not meet the test of proportionality, the answer was that only one out of seven districts was, in fact, "viable."[46] That 65 percent is a rule of thumb is acknowledged in both the Department's internal memos and its communications with localities. For instance, a staff attorney, writing up notes on a meeting with a representative of the Independent School District of Nacogdoches, Texas, recalled informing the representative that "65% + minority districts were rule of thumb." "Minority contacts," he went on, had "confirmed" the Department's view that districts less heavily black were not likely to elect a black.[47] Frequently, however, those "contacts" are themselves potential candidates, pleased to obtain the protection from white competition that such heavily black districts provide; safe minority districts reduce the work and expense of a campaign.

In the Barbour County plan, one out of seven districts was "viable" only if the calculation was based on voting-age population (raw population figures for blacks are almost never used). Alternatively, as the voting section staff pointed out, it could rest on either black registration or black turnout levels. The test was the concentration required to "result in a majority of black voters at the polls."[48] The role of the Department was not to provide an opportunity to create that majority by means of registration drives and other organizational tactics, but to take the current level of electoral participation as given and to build a district-ing plan around it. Giving blacks the "opportunity to elect candidates of their choice" (another frequently used phrase) required districts that compensated for low black turnout.

Retrogression is a comparative, before-and-after test. But to ask whether a districting plan is "fairly drawn" is to measure discriminatory effect by some absolute standard of racial fairness. In doing so, the Justice Department implicitly ignores the Supreme Court's quite differ-ent focus on relative status—backsliding or slippage. Often the Depart-ment objects to plans that do not "fairly reflect" the minority population. Reynolds thus refused to approve proposed plans for North Carolina's senate and congressional districts, the South Carolina senate, the New York city council, and the board of supervisors in Adams County, Mis-sissippi, among others, for not "fairly reflect[ing] black voting strength." But even though the Department brief in the South Carolina case ar-gued that a "plan which does not fairly reflect black voting strength . . . constitute[s] a 'retrogressive' plan," clearly the assertion robbed retrogression of its obvious and legal meaning.[49] In a brief submitted in the same case, the NAACP offered its own inventive definition of retro-gression. "No efforts," it said, "were made by the State to develop or maximize the voting strength of minorities. Therefore Act 257 [the enacted plan in question] is retrogressive with respect to the effective exercise of the right to vote for candidates for members of the Senate who are the choice of the Black community."[50] The Justice Department itself vetoed a districting plan proposed by Sumter County, Georgia, because "alternative plans" would result in "more effective black major-ity districts."[51]

The Supreme Court's test for discriminatory effect is often simply openly ignored. All pretense of adherence to the retrogression standard is dropped when districting plans are said, for instance, to either "need-lessly pack" or "needlessly fragment" black population concentrations. Needless "packing" tainted congressional districts in Texas and those for the Virginia House of Delegates. But a commissioner precinct plan for Uvalde County, Texas, "unnecessarily fragment[ed]" the Mexican-American community, and thus had the "inevitable effect" of diluting minority voting strength. Fragmentation was likewise the problem with Texas state legislative districts in two counties.[52] No amount of argu-ment can persuade the Justice Department that it is legitimate to divide black voters between districts in order to protect a white liberal incumbent who has served the black community well, and who perhaps has seniority on legislative committees that are important to blacks. And the voting section invariably assumes that rural blacks have more in common with urban blacks than with rural whites. Race is the line that counts; communities of interest are defined by color. Assumption Parish, Louisiana, submitted a districting plan whose lines followed the natural contours of the local bayou. A local contact informed the Department that "people from either side of the bayou [did] not have much in common," and the director of the section 5 unit recommended that the Department approve the plan because any alternative would necessitate "odd shaped districts"—districts that grouped people by race but paid no heed to the communities of interest that contiguity created. But the Department spurned his advice and lodged an objection.[53] The voting section, it appears, has two concerns (although the latter was inapplicable to Assumption Parish). The fragmentation of black electoral strength is the primary one. But staff members have also argued that blacks residing in a "compact and residentially segregated . . . community" that has been divided by a districting plan will have difficulty "in knowing which district is theirs."[54] Evidently neighboring whites assigned to different districts can figure out where to vote, while blacks cannot. Such statements would seem to cross the important line between protection and paternalism.

Discriminatory effect is one question; purpose is another. Yet one searches through voting section memos in vain for a clear discussion of what constitutes evidence of discriminatory intent. Files contain such illuminating statements as: "While it is not possible to conclude that the change was made with the proscribed racial purpose, the totality of the facts indicate that race may have been a purpose."[55] Such murky messages provide little guidance to jurisdictions attempting to avoid accusations of unlawful purpose.

In fact, such accusations may indeed be unavoidable, since the Justice Department appears to make no real distinction between action that is purposefully discriminatory and that which has a forbidden effect. For example, when the South Carolina senate plan fragmented black residential concentrations, this was in itself considered evidence of discriminatory impact, but that fragmentation was also seen as evidence of prohibited purpose. "The State," the Department said, "seeks a judgment 'on the issue of effect under Section 5,' a judgment that in our view is broader than the issue of whether Act 257 is retrogressive. Relevant to the Section 5 issue of the racially discriminatory 'effect' of Act 257 is the issue of the potential effect of a plan intentionally drawn to minimize black voting strength or one that has a discriminatory 'result' in violation of Section 2."[56] The reasoning here is impenetrable. Given that proof of discriminatory intent alone is sufficient to condemn a plan, why must the court decide whether that intent has had an actual effect?

Likewise, when the plan submitted by Barbour County was found to be not "fairly drawn" and thus to have had an impermissible impact, the county, having failed to adopt an alternative plan, was also judged guilty of discriminatory intent. In the case of Sumter County, a staff member had proposed a proper scheme which the county then rejected; that rejection, in itself, was evidence that the preferred plan was discriminatory in both purpose and effect.[57] Letters from the Justice Department routinely object to submitted plans on grounds of both purpose and effect, and a jurisdiction has no way of knowing what sort of evidence contributed to which finding.[58]

Is there action that is discriminatory in effect but not intentionally so? Are purpose and effect one and the same thing? Ironically—given the militant opposition of the civil rights groups to any purpose test in the 1982 congressional hearings—both minority spokesmen and the Justice Department seem to assume as much. And intent, in the view of organizations such as the NAACP, is remarkably easy to prove. The NAACP's brief in the South Carolina case implies that any jurisdiction that fails to implement redistricting suggestions made by that organization stands guilty of deliberately obstructing black voting rights.[59] Can any minority organization (not just the NAACP) with a plan of its own thus veto that of the state? Has discriminatory intent been proved once such an alternative plan is presented? If so, the carefully constructed detours around *Beer* are superfluous, since the effects test is barely needed as a means by which to condemn proposed redistricting schemes.

Both the D.C. court (in its decision in *Pleasant Grove*) and the Department of Justice have moved perilously close to this position, frequently suggesting that jurisdictions refusing to implement an alternative, more racially "fair" plan have engaged in deliberate discrimination. And with recourse to that option, *Beer* can be safely ignored. Sumter County might complain that section 5 demands only a relative test for discriminatory impact—that slippage or "retrogression," not statistical parity, is the proper question. But the Department of Justice can simply counter by shifting the ground of its objection to that of racially tainted intent.

Which of the available arguments will be made under what circumstances? A legal standard, one assumes, is a method of judging particular facts; in reviewing redistricting submissions, the voting section lets the facts dictate the appropriate standard. The unstated but determining question is almost invariably: by what method (or methods) of reasoning will black officeholding be maximized? The belief in maximum protection was precisely, of course, the point on which the views of the Justice Department and the D.C. court diverged from those of the Supreme Court in *Beer*; the revised standard represents a victory for those whom the high Court had overruled. *Beer* definitively ruled out requiring any jurisdiction to create black seats in proportion to black population; the decision has been quietly, covertly overturned.

In importing the "fairly reflects" annexation standard into the redistricting context, the Justice Department refers to the D.C. court's decision in *Mississippi v. United States*.[60] Yet that 1979 ruling reads quite differently from the way the voting section suggests. The "plaintiff's burden," the court said, ". . . is to demonstrate that the reapportionment plan . . . [does] not lead to retrogression . . . or that the proposed change fairly reflects the strength of the black voting power as it exists."[61] In other words, if there is backsliding, the plan must at least "fairly reflect" black voting strength. A new districting plan, based on the 1980 census, may contain fewer safe black districts than the one it replaces if, say, black outmigration has reduced the black population, or growing residential dispersion has made majority-black districts more difficult to draw. A discarded plan may contain ten black districts and a new one only eight, but the law demands not a remedy for a reduction that is unavoidable, but only a scheme that "fairly reflects" the altered demographic picture. In the Mississippi case, the district court approved the plan because it did not find the scheme retrogressive; it did not require the state to meet a proportionality test as well. The Department of Justice implies that the lower court overturned *Beer*; a true reading of the Mississippi case suggests otherwise.

Objection letters involving redistricting plans often cite *Mississippi*; sometimes they cite *Richmond* (despite its clear inapplicability); sometimes they refer to cases remote from the matter at hand. In one "Legal Analysis and Recommendation," for instance, the director of the section 5 unit drew upon *Gomillion v. Lightfoot* in arguing for an objection to districts that fragmented black residential concentrations.[62] Yet the sole question posed by that case was whether a city could alter its external boundary to rid itself of black voters.

Since 1980, the Justice Department in reviewing districting plans has frequently cited *Wilkes County v. United States*, a 1978 decision of the D.C. district court.[63] For example, when Barbour County, Alabama, submitted new county council districts for preclearance in 1981, the Department informed the locality that "since the prior plan is unconstitutionally malapportioned . . . our standard of comparison . . . is 'options for properly apportioned single-member district plans.' *Wilkes County* . . ."[64] Likewise, a 1983 letter to Sumter County, Georgia, states: "In the context of the circumstances that exist in Sumter County, the burden on the school district is to establish that the proposed redistricting was not adopted with a racially discriminatory purpose and that it would not have that effect when compared 'with options for properly apportioned single-member district plans,' . . . *Wilkes County* . . ."[65]

Although the *Wilkes County* decision is somewhat ambiguous, the Justice Department has bent it all out of shape. Wilkes County had switched from single-member districts to at-large voting. Blacks could hardly be considered less likely to get elected under the new system, since none at all had been elected before. But the court ruled this comparison improper. Drawn prior to *Reynolds v. Sims*, the abandoned districts were malapportioned as only pre-1964 districts were likely to be. The appropriate comparison was thus between the new at-large voting and the variety of "options" for single-member districts that could be drawn to meet the one person, one vote requirement. The court's concern was unstated, but clear: to ask the normal retrogression question would be to reward with easier preclearance a jurisdiction that had severely malapportioned districts by virtue of unconstitutional inaction. But these were very special circumstances; *Wilkes County* was not a case in which properly apportioned districts had suffered normal malapportionment in the course of a decade. Doubts about the previous plan as a benchmark arose only because that plan was not "previous" in the customary sense; it was not a legitimate plan against which slippage could legitimately be measured.

The facts in both Barbour and Sumter counties resembled those in Wilkes County, in that the submitted plan was preceded by one of doubtful legality. But *Wilkes County* did not require that the jurisdiction devise a districting scheme that maximized black officeholding, as the Justice Department insisted. The decision noted only that *any* equal-

population plan—any districting plan that was not malapportioned—
was likely to result in one safe black district, and it required that any
proposed plan be assessed with that in mind. The plan that Barbour
County submitted was one "properly apportioned" option, and, as such,
legitimate.

The decision did contain one ambiguous sentence. The court said:
"Although a comparison of the at-large plan with the malapportioned
single-member district plan demonstrates that the effect of the voting
change has been to diminish black voting strength . . . the discriminatory
effect is even more apparent where the at-large plan is compared with
possibly fairly-drawn single-member district plans."[66] In the context,
"fairly drawn" clearly seems to refer to districts that meet the equal-
population standard. The Justice Department nonetheless reads "fairly
drawn" to mean racially "fair," and, as a result, objects to plans if it can
be shown that alternative lines would increase the number of safe black
seats. Early in his term as assistant attorney general, Reynolds did
express puzzlement at the use being made of *Wilkes County*. In his 1981
memo on Barbour County, he asked, "What is the basis for a finding of
'retrogression' in this case?" In other words, what happened to *Beer*? It
was the right question—the central question—but he immediately dismissed it, letting the voting section off the hook: "Plainly, reliance on the
immediately preceding election system is no help (both because it was
an unlawful scheme and because it demonstrated no 'retrogression').
Alternatively, we can presumably look to a 'fairly drawn plan' for purposes of comparison."[67]

The Department of Justice has slipped with remarkable ease from a
judicially sanctioned perspective to one that the Supreme Court has
explicitly rejected, and it has done so by couching novel arguments in
conventional terms. Briefs and letters of objection are littered with
citations—but inappropriate ones, I am suggesting. In fact, the use of
citations in Justice Department documents has become a form of art. By
pasting together phrases from decisions, lifted out of context and distorted, the department invents law; it creates a legal collage out of
known but altered elements.

The routes around the law that Reynolds has sanctioned, I have argued, have precisely that end to which the civil rights groups are committed: a maximum number of minority officeholders—which usually
means a maximum number of safe minority districts. Sometimes the
Department will settle for less. Reynolds, for instance, approved a congressional district for New Orleans that was only 44.5 percent black

when a higher percentage could have been attained. The plan was not retrogressive and the white incumbent was likely to win, whatever the racial composition.[68] Another submission involved a racing commission in Greene County, Alabama, control of which had been switched from the county's legislative delegation (predominantly black) to the governor. Reynolds initially objected to the proposal but later changed his mind on the ground that the matter lay beyond the scope of the Voting Rights Act.[69]

In the case of Barbour County, the plan that was ultimately precleared fell one black district short of the maximum potential. But the alternative plan, it was explained, "would place the strongest county leader in the rural majority black district." That county leader was white, and the voting section concluded that, as long as he chose to run, "black voters would not have a chance of electing anyone else. He is wealthy, politically astute, and has given the black community some support. In the county's proposed plan no incumbents reside in the majority black districts . . . therefore under this plan black voters would have a very good chance . . . of choosing candidates of their choice."[70]

This argument suggests that majority-black districts in which strong white incumbents reside are not "viable." It is pointless to give blacks control of a district if they are not likely to return a "candidate of their choice"—such a candidate being, by definition, black. By implication, if blacks vote for a white incumbent, they are succumbing to the coercion of incumbency or being dupes of paternalism.

Dougherty County, Georgia, submitted what local authorities assumed to be a legally safe plan, since the districts conformed almost precisely to those that had been precleared just four years earlier. However, the voting section staff concluded that "a reapportionment plan could have been drawn that would have provided for three majority black districts" rather than the proposed two. Reynolds was not opposed to an objection: the black population in the county had sharply risen in the intervening years, and the new plan had failed to reflect that demographic change. In fact, in the face of a county-wide increase in the black population, in those districts that had previously been heavily black, that population had actually dropped. The plan was thus retrogressive under *Beer*. But, Reynolds wrote, "I am not persuaded that the County needs to submit a redistricting plan having three majority-black districts, and I think we should make that point clear in our letter."[71] In other words, two would do; that was what the old plan had provided, and that was what was demanded of the new. Out of the blue, a voting section memo had relied on *Beer*, using the retrogression test as the Court had instructed. It was, one might say, a lapse in Justice Department policy.

There is a troubling use of the law in Department of Justice enforcement, I have argued. A troubling use of numbers, as well, runs through both judicial and administrative rulings. The changing, expanding use of statistics runs like a leitmotif through the history of the Voting Rights Act; that story can be read between the lines in preceding chapters. It was precisely the point of the original act, it will be recalled, to substitute a statistical rule of thumb for the extended and complex judicial process by which Fifteenth Amendment questions were traditionally decided. But the 50 percent turnout mark that triggered coverage worked only with the 1964 figures. Those who wrote the legislation knew which states had been systematically, persistently infringing black voting rights, and they designed a test to achieve the desired results. Yet, as I suggested in Chapter 2, once established, these carefully selected numerical criteria took on a life of their own. The registration and turnout figures for 1968 were added to the statistical "trigger," and the act was instantly and substantially changed. The statute and the statistical test that it contains have had, in fact, a symbiotic relationship. A change in the method by which electoral discrimination was measured—the additional use of the 1968 figures—helped to reshape the meaning of disfranchisement, and the revised definition both further changed the method of assessing voting rights violations and stimulated additional amendments to the act.

The use of statistical information has thus governed the shape of the statute itself. Statistical data have also played a vital role in the enforcement of section 5, as well as in section 2 litigation. Two statistical assertions, it may be recalled, were integral to the case against Charleston: first, that the annexation reduced the black population by 2 percent, and second, that white bloc voting kept candidates preferred by blacks from gaining office. In subsequent years, the revised section 5 standard—that which rejected *Beer* in favor of such decisions as *Wilkes County, Mississippi*, and *Richmond*—further increased the importance of statistical data. In comparing a proposed plan to one that is racially "fair," the Justice Department must calculate both how many majority-black districts can be drawn and how many black candidates those districts are likely to return. And these calculations demand, in turn, information on minority population numbers (raw population data and voting-age figures) and on residential and voting patterns—where blacks live, the level of minority registration and turnout, and the degree of racial bloc voting. Yet such data, on which the outcome of a section 5 review will often depend, are usually of questionable worth. Jurisdictions seldom record registration by race; both registration and turnout can only be crudely estimated; there is no consensus among experts on how to measure racial bloc voting; and even the raw population figures are sometimes open to doubt. Equally important, the seeming objectivity of numbers works to conceal subjective judgment; allegedly simple statistical questions obscure complex normative issues.

It is the normative importance of the statistical calculations, in fact, that makes them so important. At the heart of a disagreement over the impact of a redistricting plan, for example, is frequently a dispute over how to count minority voters, how to measure racial bloc voting, how to determine the level of minority voter turnout, and where to draw the line between the percentage of minority residents in a district that will ensure the election of a minority candidate and that which will "waste" minority votes by excessively concentrating them. And often a proposed voting change will only be accepted if the state or political subdivision (county or city) can persuade the Attorney General that the rules by which such statistical questions have been resolved by spokesmen for minority voters are wrong.

The negotiations between the Justice Department and New York City in 1981 and 1982 over the city's councilmanic lines offer an excellent example of the role that statistical considerations play in the resolution of districting questions, and thus, indirectly, in the distribution of power among racial and ethnic groups in covered jurisdictions.[72] The New York city council is large, containing 45 members in all, 2 elected at large from each of five boroughs (counties) and 35 from single-member districts. Prior to redistricting in 1981 the council was slightly smaller, including only 43 members. But in the previous decade the city's population had declined by about 10 percent, and the redistricting commission, meeting after the 1980 census, had expanded the size of the council to protect incumbents, especially those who were black and Hispanic. Not only had the city as a whole lost population in the decade, but districts that were once considered safe for minority councilmen had become more heavily white as a consequence of gentrification. One solution was a contraction of the districts' boundaries, which could be accomplished only by increasing the total number of electoral districts, and this was precisely what was done. The council was expanded, in great part to preserve its minority membership. At the same time, district lines were redrawn to comply with the constitutional prohibition against population disparities.

When the plan was submitted to the Justice Department for preclearance, it was challenged not by incumbent minority councilmen (who liked the plan), but by civil rights groups.[73] Of course, a plan that left blacks and Hispanics worse off—that is, with fewer districts in which minority voters were in the majority—would fail the retrogression test. But under New York's old plan, there had been eight minority councilmen, and those eight were almost certain of retaining their seats under the new system. The council, however, was now slightly larger, and thus the minority share would drop from 18.6 to 17.8 percent even though the minority population in the city had actually grown. Nevertheless, the city contended, the plan was not "retrogressive." In fact, it suggested, the new lines were actually an improvement. Civil rights groups were both counting minority residents incorrectly, and demanding an excessive concentration of minority voters to make minority districts "safe." By New York City's calculation, its plan contained fifteen such districts, nine of which had a minority concentration of more than 65 percent.[74]

With census findings in hand, counting minority residents in the new districts would seem straightforward. But a serious dispute arose between civil rights groups and the city over how to measure the minority population. The 1980 census had asked respondents if they were "of Spanish/Hispanic origin or descent" and then, in a separate question, what their race was. Some Hispanics identified themselves as white, others as black, and still others as "other." The question was how many there were in each category. In the summer and fall of 1981, when the city was submitting its plan to the Justice Department, the responses to the two questions had not yet been broken down, leaving it unclear how many safe minority districts had been created. The number of Hispanics in each district could be reliably ascertained; so too could the number of persons who identified themselves as nonwhite. But the two figures could not simply be added together to obtain the minority total, because an undetermined number of Hispanics reported themselves as nonwhites. To the extent to which such people were double-counted, the minority total would be inflated. Civil rights organizations charged that a high proportion of Hispanics identified themselves as nonwhite, and that the city's estimates of the total minority population in various districts were thus too high.[75]

To deal with this problem, New York City relied on national figures supplied by the Census Bureau, which showed that 55.6 percent of all Hispanics considered themselves white, 40 percent as "other," and the rest as black, American Indian, Eskimo, Aleut, or Pacific Islander. In coming up with the fifteen minority districts, the city had relied on the 55.6 percent figure, the only one available at the time.[76] As it turned out, the estimate was somewhat off for New York. A census tabulation made available on the eve of the Justice Department's objection to the plan put the proportion of New York Hispanics who identified themselves as white at 39.9 percent. Using this figure reduced the minority total in the fifteen districts significantly, though not dramatically. In any case, neither the city nor the minority spokesmen could agree on how significant these new numbers were, since they disagreed on the minority concentration required to create equal electoral opportunity.

Obtaining an accurate count of the Hispanic population has also been a problem outside of New York, especially before the 1980 census with its question about Hispanic ancestry. "There is no statistical information available concerning Mexican-American population, candidates, voters, etc.," a February 1980 letter from Nacogdoches County, Texas, informed the Justice Department. "The census bureau has heretofore counted persons here as part of the white population. This is particularly appropriate since the Spanish-surname members of the Nacogdoches community have for more than a century and a half been an integral part of it. There is no Spanish-speaking population and those with hispanic names are no more proficient in that language than the general population."[77] The letter thus argued not only that counting Mexican-Americans was difficult, but that Hispanics, in any case, constituted part of the "white" population. The assertion that Mexican-Americans in Texas saw themselves as culturally indistinguishable from whites seems dubious, but minority categories are, in fact, often fluid. In a section 2 case involving Norfolk, Virginia, civil rights groups counted Asian-Americans, Native Americans, and others (totaling 4 percent of the city population) as white.[78]

In New York, there was considerable disagreement over how to categorize those classified as "other." New York had substantial numbers of Chinese, Japanese, Koreans, South Asians, and American Indians. The size of these groups was not in dispute, but their classification was: were these voters "white" or "minority"? The New York Civil Liberties Union placed them in the former category, the city in the latter. "One can draw no conclusions about the way 'non-Hispanic others' will vote," the NYCLU argued. "It, therefore, follows that the inclusion of 'non-Hispanic others' in calculating the total minority population within each district is unjustified and deceptive."[79] As the city pointed out, however, "The law is clear that the 'other' racial and language minority groups residing in New York are . . . classified as non-white for the purposes of the Voting Rights Act." Asian-Americans and American Indians were among the minority groups specifically named in the statute as entitled to protection, and if these groups did not vote predictably, neither did blacks and Hispanics. A black will not "necessarily vote for a Hispanic, or for a member of his own race," attorneys for the city wrote the Department of Justice.[80]

It is not the sheer size of the minority population but the number who are registered or who vote that usually determines both the count of "minority" districts and the weight given a jurisdiction's claim of equal electoral opportunity. Some states record the race of those who register, but they are the exception. Registration and turnout figures are usually, at best, rough estimates. Even the data base may be a matter of contention. Norfolk, Virginia, for instance, is a city with a major naval base, and naval personnel (77 percent white) were included in the census, could vote in municipal elections, and were counted for the purpose of state legislative redistricting.[81] Yet in gauging relative participation rates, civil rights groups omitted consideration of that group, arguing that it did not constitute an "active electorate." Black and white registration and turnout estimates were obviously affected; in fact, had the military personnel been included, the city argued, black participation rates would have been shown to be substantially higher than those of whites—a finding that would have seriously weakened the minority plaintiffs' case.[82] In states that do classify registrants by race, better figures are available, but even then questions can arise. In South Carolina, for instance, voters are racially identified, but only by precinct. When a new plan splits old precincts, the number of minority voters assigned to new districts must be estimated. And in the South Carolina senate redistricting case, the opposing sides arrived at very different estimates.

In the case of New York, however, both sides skirted these complex methodological issues. A "minority" district, the city assumed, was simply one in which more than half the residents were nonwhite; that was the premise on which its count of fifteen rested. In such districts, the city argued, minority candidates could win. The prime example was a district which, with a minority population of 53.6 percent (according to the 1970 census), had elected a black to the city council in 1977.[83] However, civil rights groups countered that by 1977 blacks and Hispanics in that district far outnumbered whites. In any case, a fight on that front was particularly hopeless; the 54 percent figure was 11 points below the Justice Department standard. In 1981 a Department spokesman denied any interest in getting into a "numbers game."[84] But ten years earlier, following a challenge to the New York State legislative lines, the Department's suggested goal for minority districts had been 65 percent, and that figure was known to be the one to which the voting section was committed.[85] Using that standard, civil rights groups counted minority districts and arrived at a total much smaller than that of the city.

*UJO v. Carey*

Of course the number of minority districts a city can draw depends not only on the number of "minority" voters and the required level of minority concentration, but on where those voters reside. The black and Hispanic population in a municipality can double, but its electoral weight will depend on how that population is distributed. The charge of retrogression assumed that New York could draw more minority districts; the city argued that although the minority population had grown, the number of potential minority districts had not. "Pervasive integration on a scale never experienced before has taken place over the decade since the prior census," a memo stated.[86] As a result, the city claimed, no additional minority districts could be created. The civil rights groups disagreed. "New York City is no more integrated in 1981 than it was in 1970," the Civil Liberties Union reported.[87] The same maps could thus tell very different stories.

There was, finally, the difficult issue of racial and ethnic bloc voting—of who votes for whom. Were whites in New York engaged in bloc voting against minority candidates? There was no iron law, the city argued, that blacks could only win in safe black districts; black voters were not necessarily unequal participants in the electoral process in every district in which they were a numerical minority.[88] The question of racial polarization is central to any voting rights dispute, but there is no consensus on how to measure it. Statistical methods can only estimate the percentage of a racial or ethnic group that voted for a particular candidate. Direct information as to how individuals have cast their ballots is rarely available, and techniques that use census data to analyze election returns at the precinct level only permit inferences about individual voter behavior. Turnout by race may be inaccurately gauged on the basis of voting-age population data. Calculations must assume that voting patterns evident in some precincts will hold for all precincts—that black and white voters residing in different demographic and socioeconomic contexts will nevertheless behave the same at the polls. Moreover, mathematical calculations may inadequately reveal *why* voters cast their ballots as they did. As one federal judge has put it, "A healthy dose of common sense and intuitive assessment remain powerful components to this factual inquiry. For example, a token candidacy of a minority unknown outside his minority voting area may attract little non-minority support and produce a high statistical correspondence of race to loss." Yet someone truly familiar with politics in the locality "may know that race played little role at all."[89] Black candidates, like white ones, lose elections for a variety of reasons, including insufficient support from black constituents, the power of incumbency, inadequate name recognition, age, experience, reputation, and political orientation. In Norfolk, Virginia, for instance, the incumbency rate was higher than 79 percent in elections from 1968 to 1984; in four of the nine elections, every incumbent who sought reelection won.[90] Those figures are not unusual.

Statistics often constitute the language of argumentation both in the section 5 submission process and in section 2 cases. But if statistical questions frame the debate, they also hide its substance. Behind the statistical facade lie fundamental, deeply divisive judgments. For instance, racial bloc voting may seem to be a technical question: how can we best estimate who has voted for whom? But complex questions of social science methodology are, in fact, secondary; the central issue is what to do with the results, how to interpret the findings.

In the South Carolina senate redistricting case, an expert witness for the Department of Justice argued that elections were polarized "when the black community and the white community voted differently." In his view, the test for bloc voting had been met when 50.1 percent of whites gave their support to a white candidate whom the majority of blacks opposed.[91] Since blacks are predominantly Democratic, every election won by a Republican would thus be "racially polarized." In a North

Carolina state redistricting case, the court found polarization in one multimember district despite the fact that two black candidates had received more than 40 percent of the white vote and had won. The majority of whites, the court observed, voted for unsuccessful whites.[92] *Gingles*  Was the election in that multimember district in fact infected with racism, such that blacks and whites stood on unequal electoral footing? To those who see American society as fundamentally racist, 40 percent white crossover voting is *only* 40 percent. Moreover, blacks remain politically dependent on whites when blacks need white support to win. To those who take a more sanguine view, a *full* 40 percent of the white electorate in that district backed two black candidates and ensured their victory.

In the case of New York, the issue was much the same: not the extent of white solidarity, but whether that solidarity was a sign of racial hostility. Despite the city's protestations, the two sides did not fundamentally disagree about the likely election of a white in a district more than half white. The question was the meaning of that likely result. Disputes over the extent of racial bloc voting and the record of minority electoral success disguise the real question: how much weight should one give to the fact that whites tend to vote for whites, blacks for blacks, in designing an electoral system?

To those who believe that American society is deeply racially divided, and that only blacks can represent black citizens, the exceptions to the general rule of ethnic and racial solidarity are insignificant. The risk of leaving minorities without a voice in the political system is too high to permit less racially conscious line-drawing. But to those impressed with the dangers of classifying citizens by color and of promoting racial separation, the record of sporadic minority success in majority-white districts appears full of promise. And different perspectives mean a different ordering of priorities. For instance, the New York Civil Liberties Union characterized concern about the reelection of incumbents as a "selfish, inappropriate consideration."[93] But city spokesmen, less impressed with the urgency of blacks and Hispanics holding office roughly in proportion to the minority population, stressed the continuity in government that the return of incumbents promoted.[94]

Where the line is drawn between the excessive concentration and the undue dispersal of minority voters within and between districts ultimately depends on the weight given to minority officeholding. To the civil rights groups in New York, the risk of "wasting" minority votes by creating districts with a 65 or 75 percent minority concentration appeared more acceptable than losing seats. The city began with a different premise—that the number of black officeholders could rise, and yet real black power decrease. From this perspective, black interests are served to the degree that black *or* white elected officials who are responsive to the black community hold office. To assume that concentrating the black and Hispanic population necessarily benefits those voters, an attorney for the city suggested, "fails to recognize that minority access to the political process can also be enhanced by placing minority voters in largely white constituencies. That way, the minorities will have a political foothold in more than one district. Otherwise, the pure white districts are free to ignore the interests of minorities with impunity."[95]

Both the city and the civil rights groups laboriously pored over census figures in an effort to determine the number of "minority" districts, but they came to that required exercise with different priorities. It was not just that the city found racial and ethnic solidarity less solid than alleged and less significant, or that it saw the promise of minority influence as often more important than that of guaranteed control. The city doubted the justice of the 65 percent rule, based as it was on the principle that blacks and Hispanics were entitled to compensation when minority leaders failed to get out the vote. And it believed the term "minority" itself was deceptive. The tendency of civil rights groups was to blur the difference between blacks and Hispanics, to see the great divide in American society as between whites, on the one hand, and minorities, on the other. Blacks and Hispanics were assumed to have more in common with one another than either had with whites. Districts were thus labeled either "minority" or "white." Yet almost 40 percent of New York's Hispanics (Puerto Ricans, for the most part) classified themselves as white on the census questionnaire, whereas almost none checked "black." The city wondered why civil rights advocates looking at a "minority" section of the Bronx assumed a community of interest, a natural political unit. Why were minority citizens considered "fungible"?[96]

Equally questionable was the notion that all blacks (or all Hispanics) had the same interests. That they gave the same answer to the census taker did not demonstrate group cohesion on political matters. Figures on the racial and ethnic composition of the population, the city contended, did not mark the boundaries of distinct political interest groups.

Despite all the serious objections raised by the city, the Justice Department was unmoved. Siding with the civil rights groups, it found New York City's plan retrogressive, the voting racially and ethnically divided, and the number of minority districts too few.[97]

This chapter has concentrated on the record of enforcement under the Reagan administration; however, as the example of Charleston suggests, the pattern prior to 1980 was much the same. Inventive new detours around the law will likely be the legacy of Reagan's assistant attorney general for civil rights, but no predecessor kept to the main road. In a rare scholarly effort to decode the record of the Department of Justice, Hiroshi Motomura argued in a 1983 article in the *North Carolina Law Review* that the Department's obvious indifference to the retrogression standard has a legitimate foundation in the *Beer* decision.[98] *Beer* required that the Justice Department or the D.C. court, in reviewing an electoral change submitted for preclearance, study both the impact of the new scheme and its constitutionality. Thus, newly proposed methods of election in covered jurisdictions could not be approved if they were retrogressive—their effect being to leave minority voters politically weaker than before—or if they violated the Fourteenth or Fifteenth Amendment.

Motomura's view is a misreading of *Beer*, in my opinion; the Supreme Court had approved a districting plan for New Orleans that would not meet subsequently developed Justice Department standards that were, in theory, based on *Beer*. Those standards could not, in fact, be justified by that decision. In effect, the voting section has thrown out the retrogression test that was at the heart of the Supreme Court's ruling. But Motomura was correct in one crucial respect: in reviewing voting changes, the practice of the Justice Department has been to ask the question once relevant only to a Fourteenth Amendment case and, since 1982, pertinent only to a section 2 inquiry. The decisive consideration has become whether the submitted proposal is one that gives minority voters "fair and effective" representation, an equal opportunity to elect candidates of their choice. The question of retrogression, of backsliding, has given way to that of racial fairness.

But if the voting section has taken to trying, in effect, constitutional or section 2 cases, it measures electoral discrimination by a standard rejected by the Supreme Court in its constitutional decisions, as well as by Congress in amending the statute in 1982. The test developed in *Whitcomb* and *White* (and imported into section 2) was that of equal access.

The lower courts had been instructed to focus not on minority office-holding, but on the electoral environment—the setting in which the voting took place. Proportional racial and ethnic representation had been ruled out as a right. Yet, as the Justice Department came to interpret the preclearance provision, an absence of proportionality became the test of discriminatory effect. The voting section has thus lifted the focus on minority officeholding in section 5 case law—a focus appropriate in answering the backsliding question—and used it in responding to quite a different inquiry: that of equal electoral opportunity. The result, as Katharine Butler has put it, has been to turn a provision designed as a "shield" into a "sword."[99] Section 5 has become a means of forcing jurisdictions to "correct" their electoral laws—to shape up and meet the proper standards of democratic representation as the voting section envisions them.

Enforcement policy, it is true, is not always uniform. But the exceptions to the use of the standard of proportionality for measuring the acceptability of a submitted plan are as troubling as the simple counting of minorities likely to gain office. Justice Department decisions that deviate from the preponderant pattern generally show no greater conformity to the Supreme Court's standard than those that follow the pattern. The decisions appear, in fact, to be governed by no discernible principle. Improvised arguments that may or may not reappear are relied upon. In a document submitted to the D.C. court, South Carolina complained that "the State . . . has been significantly hampered in its preparation for trial because of the uncertainty surrounding the standard."[100] Districting is a politically charged issue, and minor changes in a map may have major political repercussions. In covered jurisdictions, those entrusted with the redistricting task are both pressured by politics and uncertain as to what the law will permit. Every incumbent wants a secure seat, yet the law does not permit white security to be purchased at the expense of black opportunity. In South Carolina, black districts had to come out of territory previously "held" by whites. But how many were required? Where did politics end and the law begin? As a legislative committee attempted delicately to balance competing interests and to heed both state and federal guidelines, it had no way of anticipating how the Justice Department was likely to interpret the statute. The Department might, for instance, view any effort to protect white incumbents from black voters as discriminatory; that was the position of the NAACP.[101] Or it might compromise, arguing (as it had in the case of

Barbour County) that blacks gained little from majority-black districts that were home to white incumbents popular with black voters.

Envisioned as an emergency provision, section 5 fundamentally alters traditional federal-state relations. And federal intrusion on constitutionally sanctioned local prerogatives is all the greater when the legal boundaries are not clear and decisions are made on the basis of seeming administrative whim. The alternative to administrative subjectivity, however, is not simply principles that are more clearly defined and yet avoid the implication of a right to proportionate ethnic and racial officeholding. The administrative process is inadequate to the task imposed by the broadening of the preclearance inquiry, which resulted in blurring the line between equal access and discriminatory "effect" (or "result"). The retrogression standard, on the other hand, was both in keeping with the design of the act and appropriate to administrative preclearance.

# NINE

# The Meaning of Electoral Equality

The proposed amendment of section 2, Senator Orrin Hatch had warned in 1982, would bring about "an incalculable transformation in the purposes and objectives of the Voting Rights Act."[1] Could the Voting Rights Act really be further transformed? The preclearance provision had already become an instrument for affirmative action, a means to promote minority officeholding roughly in proportion to the population. Districting plans and other changes in electoral procedure submitted for federal approval were routinely screened for their racial "fairness" by standards sanctioned by neither case law nor statutory history.

But the coercive power of the preclearance provision continued to apply only to covered jurisdictions. The reach of section 5 was thus limited. Moreover, only methods of voting instituted after November 1964 were subject to Justice Department review. At-large voting introduced before 1964 in South Carolina or in Boston, whatever the date of its inception, was thus invulnerable to attack. Of course minority voters could turn to the Constitution and seek relief by filing suit in a federal district court, but constitutional suits were hard to win—especially after the 1980 *Mobile* decision.

Proponents of the section 2 amendment argued that such suits had always been difficult to win and thus had rarely been filed. In contrast to the preclearance process, the burden of proof in constitutional cases was on the minority plaintiffs, who could not avoid a full-scale trial—often in a southern court. Hatch's fears were thus unfounded, advocates of the 1982 amendment claimed. The revision of section 2 would alter the act, but only to restore the limited power that minority voters had enjoyed before *Mobile*. The change would simply allow the former trickle of laborious litigation to resume, although under statutory rather than constitutional auspices.

The trickle has turned out to be a flood, and minority plaintiffs almost always prevail. These suits are not hard to win; they are exceedingly hard to lose. Plaintiffs, in fact, usually prevail even before the trial has begun, since jurisdictions faced with politically costly and financially draining litigation are generally quick to settle out of court. And the rate of success cannot be explained by the vulnerability of the targets selected. Methods of voting—particularly at-large elections—have been challenged in places with strong records of minority electoral participation, places with small minority populations, and places where minorities have had considerable electoral success. Plaintiffs must prove actual discrimination in a section 2 suit, whereas suspected wrongdoing is sufficient to trigger a section 5 objection. Yet redistricting plans approved by the Justice Department have been successfully attacked under section 2. The more difficult standard of section 2 has proved easier to meet.

The 1982 revision of the statute has thus redefined the rights of minority voters. Black and Hispanic voters have acquired unprecedented power to insist on methods of voting that will facilitate minority officeholding, and the act has become a national instrument for instituting "racially fair" electoral arrangements. In the four years since the amendment was passed, plaintiffs have gone to court not only across the South but also in such northern localities as Chicago, Los Angeles, and Mount Vernon, New York. As a consequence, at-large voting is close to disappearing as an acceptable means of selecting city and county officials, and multimember districts for state legislatures have become an endangered species. New districting plans that do not provide for a maximum number of safe minority seats rarely survive a section 2 challenge. The responsiveness of the political system to minority demands is often not even tested before plaintiffs take legal action. As one such plaintiff explained: "Our attorneys didn't want us to come before the [county] commission and plead our case for single-member districts. They said it would be easier to go to court."[2] Section 2 litigation has thus become a quick and easy means of "improving" electoral procedures— one that circumvents uncertain and time-consuming political channels and yields almost guaranteed results.

What happened, it might be asked, to the Dole "compromise"? By the terms of that compromise, a discriminatory electoral result was explicitly defined as a situation in which minority citizens had "less opportunity than other members of the electorate to participate in the political process and to elect representatives of their choice." Minority voters were not guaranteed their "fair share" of public offices. The new section 2 language was lifted directly from *Whitcomb* and *White*. And, reflecting Congress's commitment to the standard those decisions contained, the new provision included a clear rejection of proportionality as the proper standard for measuring the presence of discrimination.

The wording of the amended provision, it now seems, was a compromise of little long-term significance. The legal standard set forth in *Whitcomb* and *White* was soon abandoned in the process of statutory interpretation. Perhaps that development was inevitable. As I argued in Chapter 6, the language of section 2 did little more than paper over ongoing differences between opponents in the 1982 debate; neither side was fully committed to the ultimate settlement. The battle thus persisted in the legal briefs submitted by plaintiffs and defendants in subsequent cases, and the courts became partisans in a continuing conflict.

Yet in important respects the Supreme Court had already settled the outcome of that conflict—a fact obscured in the unabated fray. As noted earlier, the constitutional cases revived by the statutory revision—most notably *White v. Regester*—had provided the courts with inadequate guidance. By failing to define democratic representation, the Court had neglected to identify inadequate electoral opportunity. But the question had not been left wide open. The Supreme Court had unequivocally rejected the views of Judge Kerner in *Chavis v. Whitcomb*, to which the civil rights groups remained committed. Disproportionately low minority officeholding and evidence of black residential clustering did not alone suffice to make a case, it held. In both *Whitcomb* and *White* the Court stressed the importance of assessing the electoral environment—the setting in which voting took place. It thus instructed trial court judges to distinguish the failure of minority voters to elect candidates of their choice for reasons of race from normal electoral defeat—that to which every group, however defined, was vulnerable.

Not only the statute but the 1982 Senate Judiciary Committee Report reaffirmed the emphasis on electoral context. The heart of the report's elucidation of section 2 is a list of "factors" to which courts are instructed to refer in judging the merits of a vote dilution suit. They are as follows:[3]

1. The extent of any history of discrimination . . . that touched the right of members of the minority group to register, to vote, or otherwise to participate in the democratic process.

2. The extent to which voting . . . is racially polarized.

3. The extent to which the state or political subdivision has used unusually large election districts, a majority vote requirement, anti–single shot provisions, or other voting practices or procedures that might enhance the opportunity for discrimination against the minority group.

4. If there is a candidate slating process, whether members of the minority group have been denied access to that process.

5. The extent to which members of the minority group . . . bear the effects of discrimination in such areas as education, employment, and health, which hinder their ability to participate effectively in the political process.

6. Whether political campaigns have been characterized by overt or subtle racial appeals.

7. The extent to which members of the minority group have been elected to public office in the jurisdiction.

The report goes on to list "additional factors" that might have "probative value":

1. Whether there is a significant lack of responsiveness on the part of elected officials to the particularized needs of the members of the minority group.

2. Whether the policy underlying the state or political subdivision's use of such voting qualification, prerequisite to voting, or standard, practice or procedure is tenuous.

The list is clearly intended to help courts identify those situations in which either a history of discrimination or ongoing racism has left black and Hispanic voters at a distinctive disadvantage in the electoral process. The level of minority officeholding is one criterion by which minority electoral exclusion is to be measured—but only one. And although only *minority* officeholding is mentioned, the language of the statute—guaranteeing minority voters an equal opportunity to elect "representatives" of their choice—unambiguously rejects the notion that only blacks can represent blacks. "Representatives of their choice" plainly suggests a definition of representation broader than would have been conveyed had the phrase read "*minority* representatives of their choice."

Not only the list of factors but other language in the Senate Judiciary Committee Report makes the intention to focus on past and present racism clear. That language rejects the standard of minority officehold-ing as the measure of electoral discrimination. A South Carolina district court decision was cited as a faithful application of the already familiar results test.[4] The plaintiffs had prevailed in that decision because black candidates, the court found, tended to lose elections "not on their merits but solely because of their race."[5] A report issued by Senator Hatch's subcommittee expressed concern that precisely that distinction would be lost—that section 2 would encourage courts to assume that racial groups were natural political units and that race determined political preference.[6] Not so, retorted the full committee's own report. In "*most*" jurisdictions, as the subcommittee had suggested, white voters give substantial support to black candidates. But "unfortunately," the report noted, ". . . there still are some communities . . . where racial politics do dominate the electoral process." And in such communities "a particular election method can deny minority voters equal opportunities to partici-pate meaningfully in elections."[7]

The aim in amending section 2 was thus clearly stated: to enable minority voters to shape electoral systems so as to minimize the impact of racism in those exceptional communities in which it still held sway. The failure of the courts to adhere to this standard has been due only in part to continuing pressure from civil rights attorneys to adopt a different view. A more fundamental problem has plagued judicial attempts to resolve these cases: although the statutory language explicitly ruled out entitlement to proportional representation, the Senate report directed courts to judge when black ballots had "full value."[8] And that order virtually invited a definition that gave those ballots maximum weight, defined as officeholding; anything less suggested a compromised right. It was a conflict that defied easy resolution, and, for this reason too, the battle that was settled neither by the courts in the constitutional deci-sions nor by Congress was carried forward in the section 2 cases.

Where have the courts gone off track, and how might they stay on course? How much guidance is really provided by the Senate report's list of "typical factors" suggesting electoral discrimination? The discussion that follows reorders the items appearing in that report—or more precisely it imposes order on a disorderly list. The factors have been arranged chronologically, to follow the course of the electoral process itself. The list can be seen as an attempt to identify roadblocks along the path to equal electoral participation—to specify the points at which past and present racism acts as a barrier to equality. And as we proceed along that path from start to finish, we will see the full range of possible obstacles to minority political participation.

Registration starts the electoral process, and minority citizens plainly lack an equal opportunity "to elect representatives of their choice" if they cannot register. Literacy and understanding tests have been permanently banned, but even without them, the Senate criteria suggest that a history of discrimination and continuing economic inequality may serve to screen potential registrants and voters on the basis of race by depressing minority participation rates. Clearly, though, in jurisdictions where black registration and turnout rates are as high as those of whites, such inequalities are not keeping blacks from the polls.

However obvious this point would seem, plaintiffs' attorneys and the courts often dispute it. By 1980 blacks in Norfolk, Virginia, were registering and voting at a higher rate than whites—a by no means uncommon phenomenon. Nevertheless, in a suit challenging Norfolk's at-large system, plaintiffs' attorneys argued that proof of relatively higher black participation rates did not preclude a finding that socioeconomic disparities between blacks and whites impeded minority electoral participation.[9] In a Lubbock City, Texas, case the district court pointed to past discrimination in areas such as education and employment as evidence of electoral inequality, despite undisputed evidence that minority registration was as high as that of whites.[10] Black registration surpasses white in the entire state of Louisiana, yet in a decision involving congressional districting in New Orleans Parish, the court declared itself "persuaded that the deleterious repercussions of historical discrimination persist in hindering the political access of minorities."[11]

Such statements clearly miss the intended point. In no community is the socioeconomic status of blacks and whites equal, and no southern jurisdiction can claim a history free of racial discrimination. But differences in income and history do not always result in differences in levels of political participation. Were such disparities, in and of themselves, evidence of electoral exclusion, minority plaintiffs would have a head start in every section 2 case. In fact, the Senate report directs courts to take note of previously segregated schools and unequal employment opportunities only in places where whites turn out to vote and blacks do not. "The courts have recognized that disproportionate educational, employment, income level and living conditions arising from past discrimination tend to depress minority political participation," a footnote explains. [12] The concern is thus depressed minority participation (resulting from past and present inequality) and its effect on the level of electoral opportunity in places where the method of voting rewards high turnout.

In jurisdictions with at-large voting, multimember districts, or districting plans that fragment minority residential concentrations, black political influence heavily depends on black turnout. For instance, in a majority-white municipality with city-wide voting, blacks can be an important swing vote—but only if they get to the polls. Districting plans with safe minority wards do nothing to enhance the influence of those individual voters who do not vote, but they do promote minority officeholding. And to the extent that minority officeholders best represent the interests of voting and nonvoting blacks, ward elections compensate for low minority participation. No such compensation is called for, however, when black participation patterns are no different from those of whites. To argue for a "racially fair" districting plan by simply pointing to a Jim Crow past or to continuing income disparities, without any evidence of depressed minority political activity, is implicitly to assert that safe minority districts are a right, since blacks are entitled to representation and only blacks can speak for blacks.

Elections involve not only voters but also candidates, of course, and the starting point for candidates is the process of selection. Today there remain almost no jurisdictions in which the preferred candidates of minority voters experience white harassment. With respect to candidate selection, the Senate report's sole concern is slating. The term is defined in neither case law nor the legislative history, but perhaps the clearest example of the phenomenon can be found in the system prevailing in Dallas in the years 1955 to 1975. Elections were largely controlled by a white-dominated group, the Citizens' Charter Association (CCA), a subsidiary of the Citizens' Council, once described as "a collection of dollars represented by men." [13] Membership was restricted to the chief executive officers of major corporations—men who could act unilaterally to commit company funds to civic endeavors.

Though politics was not its chief preoccupation, the Citizens' Council, working through the CCA, selected candidates and did its best to see that they won. The aim was the protection of municipal government from politicians; rule by the business elite was thought to ensure a hospitable environment for economic growth. The candidates slated by the CCA were usually white and conservative, and they were expected to serve no more than two terms. Longer tenure might produce professional politicians, with an agenda of their own.

But in Dallas, as elsewhere, it is difficult to keep politics out of the political system indefinitely, and in time, outsiders began to gather electoral strength. As *Fortune* put it in 1964: "The political goal of the business leadership is to get the right kind of people elected with as little commotion as possible. Sometimes this means embracing dissidents who have developed independent political support, rather than bucking them."[14] Such pressures, before long, led the CCA to slate two blacks and one Mexican-American. Still, the size of the municipality and the funds required to run a successful city-wide campaign made it very difficult for independent candidates to win. Between 1959 and 1975 (when a successful constitutional challenge overturned the at-large system), the CCA had had an 82 percent batting average.[15] No member of a minority group had ever won without the organization's endorsement. Blacks and Hispanics thus had a few representatives, but only those approved by a white-run organization.

Was this system clearly discriminatory? Minority community leaders had considerable input in the selection of candidates. For instance, George Allen, the first black to serve on the city council, was chosen at a meeting of the Dallas Negro Chamber of Commerce; the thirty-six blacks who attended the gathering represented organizations ranging from SNCC to a black medical association. The recommendation was accepted by the CCA.[16] Moreover, once on the council Allen never acted as a simple tool of the business elite—at least by his own description. "I'm expected to champion the cause of the black community," he explained. "The other council members expect me to do it. My constituents in the black community expect me to do it and I do it."[17]

Perhaps Allen underestimated the degree of control his white benefactors ultimately exercised, yet once the CCA became solicitous of the minority vote, the process of slating indisputably assured minority seats on the city council. Like an ethnically balanced party ticket, the

Dallas system gave minorities a place in city government they might otherwise have lacked. Indeed, the influence of blacks and Mexican-Americans in Dallas politics, though limited, may still have been greater than that of whites opposed to the business elite. The bitterness of white outsiders was evident in a 1979 letter sent to the Justice Department. "In Dallas, the political power structure resembles a country club," the head of an East Dallas community organization wrote. "Certain people are politely, yet regularly, refused admission . . . One has to observe only a single council meeting to see the paternalistic, condescending manner in which Dallas' 'leadership' regards Dallas' citizens."[18] Those whites who were handpicked to run for the city council were certainly not "representative"; there was nothing democratic about the way in which any CCA candidate was selected. The process of slating certainly discriminates, but it severely restricts the grassroots influence of voters on both sides of the color line.

Whatever the merits of such arguments, however, they now have no legal relevance. Dallas-style slating has been judicially condemned as clearly discriminatory. But Dallas was a uniquely blatant case. Political parties elsewhere routinely slate candidates, but, being democratically structured, they permit black and Hispanic entry into the leadership ranks. The question has thus become: How open must political coalitions be in order to qualify as nondiscriminatory?

Attorneys and judges in section 2 cases have labeled as slating a wide variety of informal tickets and endorsement mechanisms. Plaintiffs in the Norfolk, Virginia, case argued that "candidates often do ally themselves with other candidates thereby forming informal [slates] or tickets."[19] In 1982 the Democratic Committee in Norfolk ran two blacks along with two whites—hardly a discriminatory slate. In fact, the strongest candidate endorsement organization was the black-run Concerned Citizens. In a case involving Austin, Texas, plaintiffs cast the Austin Progressive Coalition (APC) in a conspiratorial light, but in fact the coalition had endorsed minority candidates, and minority groups had participated in the endorsement process. Moreover, a plethora of endorsement groups existed in the city, with no one of them controlling the electoral outcome. "There is nothing in the evidence," the judge concluded, "to establish that the value or effect of an endorsement by the APC is any greater than that of the NAACP or the Mexican-American Democrats, or that the support of any of these groups is pursued with any greater vigor than any other endorsement."[20]

"Slating," Judge Nowlin wrote in the Austin decision, "involves the creation of a package or slate of candidates, preceding filing, by an organization with sufficient strength to make the election merely a stamp of approval on the candidates already preordained."[21] He might have added that slating also requires a special setting. In a sparsely populated rural county or small town, where running for office is inexpensive, independent candidacies are easily mounted and thus the power of a slating group can be readily challenged. In any locale a few candidates may occasionally collaborate, but such collaboration does not necessarily deny minority voters equal access to the electoral process. And only groups that *deny* access meet the Senate report's unambiguously worded test.

Slating can be defined both too generously and too narrowly. It can also take covert forms not recognized by either the Senate report or the courts. In Burke County, Georgia, for instance, candidates for the county commission were selected to run at-large through a process of consultation within a closed white network. The clearly marked path to public office was open to neither blacks nor their rare white spokesmen. This is how a county commissioner (in response to an attorney's questions) described the system:

Q. What caused you to run?

A. Well, I had some friends and neighbors [who] asked me to run and I talked to some more . . .

Q. How did this occur . . . did people just call you up . . . ?

A. Oh, I'd meet them on the street or in the road.

Q. There wasn't any kind of formal meeting . . . ?

A. Oh no, no.

Q. Just a few people who just wanted you to run for office, that kind of thing?

A. Right.[22]

In the tightly knit society of Burke County, with its exceedingly low black registration and turnout rates, no candidate could win unless he or she had emerged from this friends-and-neighbors selection process. Victory depended on the strength of the particular network from which the candidate was chosen, and black networks lacked the resources of white ones. Black political organizations had formed, but none could rival the long-established alliances that whites had built on the basis of social and business ties.

Thus prior to 1982 when the at-large system succumbed to a constitutional challenge, candidates in Burke County were, in effect, slated. The only viable candidates were chosen by a process in which blacks played no part. The system was markedly different from those in Norfolk and Austin, where a few candidates occasionally cooperated or competing candidates sought the endorsement of competing groups—never exclusively white. Thus a phenomenon that courts and plaintiffs have called slating fails to meet the test, while one that is never recognized as such qualifies. In fact, one witness at the Burke County trial claimed that local blacks would have welcomed allegedly discriminatory slates or "tickets."[23] It was precisely the discreet informality of the process that permitted black exclusion; a ticket formally arrived at could never have been all-white. For instance, in Hollendale and Indianola, Mississippi, where slating has dominated politics, blacks have gained office as a result.[24]

Minority candidates on the campaign trail may confront other obstacles not on the path of whites: for instance, the predictable endorsement of white candidates by the local newspaper, or limited access to white churches and to business and civic organizations such as the Rotary Club. The Senate report, however, lists only one such roadblock: "overt or subtle racial appeals." The reference, of course, is to such appeals on the part of whites in majority-white jurisdictions; the message from blacks to vote black is never considered a forbidden racial appeal. Courts cannot change the tenor of campaigns, but they can limit the impact of racism by insisting that city-wide voting be replaced by a districting plan that contains some safe minority seats.

What is a "subtle" racial appeal? Subtlety in campaigns risks political ineffectiveness; only overt appeals are reliably heard. The phrase would seem to invite courts to condemn messages the voters do not get—to condemn indiscriminately all discussions of issues connected to race. Plaintiffs in the Norfolk case sought to persuade the judge that news accounts of the 1982 city council campaigns mentioning both the candidates' race and their references to busing were invidious appeals for white solidarity. But the court held that the candidates had been racially identified not by whites but by blacks, who were alleging black underrepresentation, and furthermore that busing was a legitimate topic for public debate.[25] Comments on an issue with a racial dimension do not necessarily constitute racial appeals—that is, calculated efforts to deny black candidates white support.

Of course not all campaign references to busing and other racially related issues fall within the bounds of acceptable political discourse. Nor are all racial appeals subtle. North Carolina Republican Senator Jesse Helms certainly played upon racist sentiments in his 1984 fight for reelection against Democratic Governor James B. Hunt. Helms's opposition to a national Martin Luther King holiday, his advertisements in rural newspapers picturing Hunt with Jesse Jackson in the governor's mansion, and his references to the need to counter "their vote" or the "bloc vote" all sent clear messages to whites inclined to listen.[26] But such obvious signals are rare. More common is questionable action at the sidelines of a campaign. A Jackson, Mississippi, constitutional case raised the issue of racist tactics in a campaign to defeat a proposed change in the structure of city government.[27] Jackson was governed by a commission elected at-large, but in 1977 the city held a referendum on a proposal for single-member districts and a council-mayor form of government. Although the mayor and other prominent whites backed the change, the proposal was defeated by a margin of 12 percent. In a subsequent suit plaintiffs attributed the result to a fear of blacks in public office whipped up in the course of the campaign.

The evidence did suggest some effort to play on racial fears. The White Citizens Council newspaper declared that a mayor-council plan "assures certain elements which vote in a bloc that they will have representation on governing bodies."[28] A witness for the plaintiffs cited door-to-door canvassers who asked such questions as: "What are you trying to do, get niggers elected to the government?"[29] Minority spokesmen also charged that newspaper advertisements, articles, and editorials mobilized opposition to the proposed change by using such code words as "black representation," "black gains," "federal courts," "federal intervention," and "neighborhood government."[30]

The White Citizens Council was not identified as an important organization in Jackson, however. The number of racist canvassers may well have been small, their efforts geographically limited, their impact negligible. The use of those particular code words was more telling, yet not decisive. The referendum was defeated, but 51 percent of the voters may have opposed single-member districts on grounds unrelated to race. In fact, the district court identified eleven other reasons why voters chose to retain the commission government and at-large elections; the list included confusion and uncertainty, a belief that cities with councils were generally financially troubled, concern that the new mayoral position would be too powerful, and a belief that the part-time, poorly paid councilman's job would be left to the rich.[31]

Evidence that political campaigns—whether on behalf of candidates or of propositions on the ballot—have been "characterized by overt or subtle racial appeals" is certainly pertinent to the question of equal electoral opportunity in a jurisdiction. But that evidence must involve more than one campaign. The Senate report refers explicitly to "campaigns" in the plural. In addition, the appeal in question must be truly racial. When an "expert" for the plaintiffs in North Carolina litigation cited as examples of racial slurs slogans such as "Eddie Knox will serve all the people of Charlotte" and "Knox can unify this city," he certainly seemed to be reaching too far.[32] And even though the Senate report does not mention the need to demonstrate that racial appeals had a significant influence on election results, this surely is a key question. The American political scene is filled with fringe candidates peddling lines to which no one listens, and in many communities racists operate on the fringe. Minority voters have a legitimate claim to safe single-member districts—safe enclaves—in communities where intense racism genuinely denies them an opportunity to elect candidates of their choice. But where racial appeals have had no discernible impact, blacks and Hispanics require no protection from them.

Overt or subtle racial appeals may constitute important evidence that "racial politics . . . dominate[s] the electoral process." Equal access is likewise denied where there is scarcely any campaigning at all—a point that the Senate report, civil rights spokesmen, and judges all seem to miss. Consider again the situation in Burke County, Georgia, where prior to 1982 elections were conducted (and public decisions made) in what amounted to a political vacuum. Often only one candidate sought a county commission seat. And even when seats were contested, no disagreement on basic policy questions was apparent. Indeed, such questions were seldom raised. Asked what issues he discussed in his 1968 campaign, county commissioner James Flynt Buxton replied, "There were no issues involved."[33] Another commissioner was asked, "What was it that the voters were deciding on . . . between you and this other candidate, what kind of factors were apparent to the voters?" His answer: "I don't know." "Did you campaign?" "Very little."[34] Running for office required no funds and seldom involved any formal meetings or speeches. Buxton recalled one occasion on which he attended a barbecue and spoke for five minutes on the need to reduce county expenditures. Fiscal responsibility, attendance at church, and commitment to the family: these were the qualifications for office, and every candidate met the test. Nor was Burke County unique. "There is very little outright campaigning . . . People know each other, know what they stand for," a Mexican-American explained in Ozona, Texas. Asked what the political issues were in Georgetown, South Carolina, a local minister replied, "Gosh, I don't know . . . We're not like a big city." "For a long time . . . there just wasn't that much politics," a county judge in Crocket County, Texas, noted.[35]

The Burke County pattern is familiar to students of rural and small-town politics. Slating along the Dallas model is a political abnormality; racist appeals in effective campaigns are a sign of political pathology. Yet in most settings there is nothing amiss if issues scarcely distinguish one candidate from another, if campaign organizations are family affairs, and if campaigning consists mainly of phone calls among friends and neighbors. But, for reasons that I will explore at greater length, southern rural counties such as Burke are special in that "not that much politics" will stack the deck against black candidates. And in those counties in which legislative seats appear largely reserved for whites, black voters lack an equal opportunity to elect candidates of their choice.

The end of a campaign comes on election day. The Senate report directs courts to look at who has won, who has lost, and how blacks, Hispanics, and whites have cast their ballots. A crude count of minorities in office does not indicate whether black and Hispanic voters have had the "opportunity . . . to elect representatives of their choice," nor whether they have actually succeeded in doing so. Section 2, referring only to "representatives of their choice," does not equate minority representation with the election of blacks or Hispanics to office; it clearly allows for the possibility that such representatives could be whites elected with strong minority support. Moreover, a tally of those in office (whether white or black) only marks the starting point for the inquiry into opportunity. Voting patterns must be analyzed to determine not only the level of support for competing candidates, but the reasons *why* voters have cast their ballots as they have. A candidate preferred by black voters may have been defeated in spite of adequate opportunity for black voters to organize for common ends. Success is not the measure of opportunity, and opportunity is the section 2 question.

Some contend that the level of opportunity may be gauged simply by looking at who has voted for whom. That whites and blacks prefer different candidates is seen as decisive evidence of electoral exclusion. Thus, in *Thornburg v. Gingles* (1986), the only section 2 case to reach the Supreme Court to date, Justice Brennan argued: "It is the difference between the choices made by blacks and whites—not the reasons for that difference—that results in blacks having less opportunity than whites to elect their preferred representatives . . . Only the correlation between race of voter and selection of certain candidates, not the causes of the correlation, matters."[36]

Justice Brennan's view was that of only a minority on the Court,[37] and it is an odd definition of opportunity. Black voters clearly lack an equal chance to elect representatives of their choice when whatever candidate they choose—simply by virtue of having been their choice—can almost never garner enough white votes to win, and when the usual rules of politics that permit shifting coalitions in response to changing issues do not seem to apply to them. In such circumstances, their race has left them politically isolated—without potential allies in electoral contests. But unless black voters in a majority-white jurisdiction are entitled to representation, the absence of white support for black candidates does not per se constitute a denial of electoral opportunity. And such a right to representation was explicitly rejected both by the Supreme Court in the constitutional decisions resurrected by section 2 and by Congress in amending the act.

Justice Brennan distorts the meaning of electoral opportunity while simultaneously showing excessive faith in statistical analyses of voting patterns. It is no easy matter to establish the correlations that he relied on, nor to arrive at a consensus on how to read them. Estimates of racially polarized voting have acquired linchpin status in voting rights disputes, yet serious methodological and conceptual problems surround these estimates. As Jacobs and O'Rourke have persuasively argued, "Definitive measures of racially polarized voting have remained elusive in both case law and political science literature." The Senate report, they point out, offers no clear definition of bloc voting, no statistical benchmarks to identify it, and no statement as to the role of such voting within the "totality of circumstances" that courts are asked to judge. "Indeed," they say, " 'polarized voting' does not even rate an explanatory footnote, unlike many of the enumerated elements."[38] Moreover, from one judicial decision to the next there has been little consensus on methodology. Some courts have relied on homogeneous precinct analysis, others on ecological regression; some have found polarization if a majority of whites vote differently from the way a majority of blacks do, while others have used quite a different threshold.

As the previous chapter pointed out, expert witnesses cannot definitively answer the question of who has voted for whom, much less why. Data on voter registration by race are only sometimes available. Although it is generally possible to obtain the total turnout in a precinct for a particular election, calculating the racial breakdown of that turnout can be hazardous; usually it must rely on voting-age census data, which may not bear a close relation to relative black and white registration and turnout rates. In addition, statistical techniques assume that black and white voters behave more or less similarly across all precincts, whatever their socioeconomic and racial composition. Such methodological problems (touched upon only briefly here) are further compounded in the case of multicandidate races in which every contestant runs for every open seat.

Even more troubling than these methodological issues is a basic conceptual one: How large must the racial differences in voting behavior be to constitute "polarization"? Expert witnesses for the defendants and plaintiffs in a given case may agree on how black and white voters have cast their ballots, but differ sharply as to what that pattern means. If 90 percent of black voters but only 45 percent of those who are white support a minority candidate, does that constitute polarization? As the dictionary defines it, polarization means groups "at opposite extremes of opinion"; yet some argue that *any* difference, however slight, in black and white preferences is evidence of racial bloc voting. In fact, the district court in *Gingles* accepted the "separate elections" test, which identifies an election as polarized when the results would have been different depending on whether it had been held among only white voters or only black voters.[39] Thus an election in a community that is half black and half white is seen as racially polarized when 50.1 percent of the blacks and 49.8 percent of the whites voted for the winner, even though only 0.3 percent of whites disagreed with their black neighbors and the candidate favored by a majority of the blacks was elected. Applying this amazing standard makes it possible to condemn a particular method of election even though it has permitted considerable electoral success for minority candidates. Brennan's opinion in *Gingles*, in fact, explicitly states that "the success of a minority candidate in a particular election does not necessarily prove that the district did not experience polarized voting in that election."[40] A multimember district in which the majority of whites voted differently from the majority of blacks is thus suspect even if blacks are winning in proportion to their numbers.

Of course the disparity between white and black preferences is usually greater than 0.3 percent; overlaps of more than 99 percent are rare. But how large a disparity amounts to polarization, a situation in which white hostility to black electoral aspirations is sufficiently plain to suggest the need for an electoral arrangement that protects black candidates from white competition? Clearly there is no indisputable threshold above which voting patterns can be described as polarized—no one point at which unequal access becomes obvious. Glaring racial differences are more suspect than modest ones, but, except at the extremes (95 percent of whites either never voting for strong black candidates or predictably doing so), numbers are only suggestive, never conclusive.

Most important, such calculations barely begin to answer the questions posed by the statute and the Senate report with respect to election day itself. As a majority on the Supreme Court has agreed, no court can determine whether "racial politics do dominate the electoral process" by looking solely, as Justice Brennan recommends, at "the correlation between race of voter and selection of certain candidates." Nor will a more sophisticated multivariate analysis—rejected by Brennan—yield conclusive results. As Judge Leon Higginbotham astutely observed in one section 2 case, "Math models [will not] always furnish an answer . . . Detailed findings are required to support any conclusion of polarized voting. These findings must make plain that they are supported by more than the inevitable by-product of a losing candidacy in a predominantly white voting population. Failure to do so presents an unacceptable risk of requiring proportional representation, contrary to congressional will."[41] *Jones v. Lubbock.*

Of what might those "detailed findings" consist? This is the question addressed by the remainder of this chapter.

The Senate report identifies minority electoral performance as just one of the "factors" that plaintiffs "could show" in establishing a case against a particular method of election. Yet plaintiffs literally have no case if the proportion of elected blacks and Hispanics corresponds to minority population strength, except in cases where that electoral success can be explained away. "Underrepresentation" measured by the number of minorities in office is thus the occasion of these suits—their starting point.[42] Plaintiffs go to court to argue that the disproportionately low number of minorities holding office is symptomatic of unequal electoral opportunity, hoping to force the jurisdiction to restructure its method of election to increase those numbers. Other pivotal issues emerge only in the course of trial; plaintiffs' attorneys will not weaken their clients' case by initially conceding that whites in office may represent blacks or that the level of electoral opportunity may have been greater than the record of minority candidate success suggests. These are points that defendants must make and courts must weigh.

While plaintiffs and defendants can always be expected to differ over the great issues of representation and opportunity, one would expect them to agree at least on the record of black and Hispanic electoral success. But that is not the case. Take *Thornburg v. Gingles*, involving redistricting for the North Carolina legislature. The state argued that blacks had had considerable success within the House and Senate districts in question. Although the districts at issue on appeal were majority-white and multimember, black victories in both primary and general-election races since 1978 had been impressive.[43] In 1982 blacks had won in all but one of the challenged districts, and even before that year, blacks had gained seats in proportion to the black population or close to it in three of the five contested districts.[44] The record looked very different to the plaintiffs, however, who argued that these victories did not count. They contended that black voters had had to vote exclusively for blacks in order to elect blacks, forfeiting their right to cast ballots for a full slate of candidates. In some contests blacks were incumbents; and since incumbency is indisputably an advantage, they dismissed white support for these candidates as no true test of white hostility to black contestants in general. Likewise, a race in which a black candidate ran unopposed was seen as no measure of white receptivity to black officeholding, since whites had no choice but to support the black. The plaintiffs acknowledged that whites had supported black contestants in 1982 but argued that the initiation of litigation had given black candidates a one-time advantage by galvanizing unusual white support, inspired by the hope of forestalling single-member districting. The number of blacks in office was thus depicted as no indicator of authentic black electoral success. The district court accepted that argument;[45] so did the Supreme Court, which on appeal affirmed the trial court's findings.[46]

Leaving aside the question of the authenticity of these black and Hispanic victories, minority officeholding can be disproportionately low for a variety of reasons: insufficient minority support for minority candidates; insufficient white support; few (or no) minority candidates; or some combination of these factors. Needed black support for black candidates is lacking when minority voters either throw their support to white contenders or simply fail to show up at the polls in sufficient numbers. Given a choice, black and Hispanic voters will usually vote overwhelmingly for a minority candidate over a white one. A high degree of political cohesion, especially among blacks, is the rule. But there have been exceptions. East Chicago, Indiana, is almost 45 percent Hispanic and 30 percent black. But, in a mayoral election in 1983, the Hispanic candidate came in a distant third; the white incumbent took not only the white vote but every Hispanic ward and a majority of the black vote (though a black lawyer was also in the race).[47] In city-wide elections in Norfolk, Virginia, in 1974, 1978, and 1980, white candidates received a majority of black votes.[48] When the majority of blacks and Hispanics vote for a white candidate over a strong black contender, clearly minorities have had an equal "opportunity . . . to elect representatives of their choice"—their choice being white. That is, they have defined the pool of potential "representatives" as including both whites and minorities, and have elected representation by a white.

In general, however, when whites defeat a black candidate with black help, that support comes from only a minority of blacks. And in that case, the question of equality becomes more complicated. Even a small minority of blacks who vote for a white over a black can make a difference in an election. As Lawrence Hanks comments in a study of three Georgia rural counties, the election of blacks requires that "leaders . . . break down anything divisive in the black community. Black class antagonism must be replaced with a sense of 'group consciousness' which lays the foundation for racial bloc voting."[49] A civil rights attorney made the same point to the political scientist Paul Stekler. "We got to get blacks to vote black to win," he observed. "It's ironic, but we got to be as racist as the white folks or we lose."[50] Asked why a black candidate needing only 20 percent of the white vote could not win in Mobile, Alabama, a local politician replied: "No black candidate is going to get the entire black

*Swain*

vote. His white opponent will cut into his support."[51] In Selma, Alabama, a city in which a majority of the registered voters are black, the black mayoral candidate (Frederick D. Reese) lost in 1984 when a minority of black voters failed to "vote black." The incumbent white mayor picked up 18 to 20 percent of the black vote, an achievement he attributed to his appointment of blacks to public jobs and his effort to improve black neighborhoods.[52] A black attorney, analyzing the outcome, suggested that "Reese's biggest mistake was in seeking white votes rather than galvanizing the black community on a racial basis."[53] In 1984 Lindy Boggs won reelection from Louisiana's majority-black Second Congressional District with approximately 35 percent of the black vote.[54] In New York Democratic primaries in September 1984, white incumbents overwhelmed black challengers in three predominantly black districts.[55] And in Los Angeles a white was elected to the city council over a period of eighteen years from a district that, by the time he resigned in 1985, had become 75 percent Hispanic.[56]

When a white candidate siphons off a significant number of black votes (whether that bloc is a minority faction within the black community or represents the majority view), the white candidate either has managed to attract minority support or has benefited from weak black opposition. For instance, Representative Lindy Boggs, who had held her seat since 1973, was simply an unbeatable incumbent. Los Angeles city councilman Art Snyder had learned to speak Spanish and was known for his skill in obtaining city funds for his Hispanic district. The three whites who beat black challengers in New York City in 1984 were described, by one reporter, as incumbents who "exemplified the promise of neighborhood integration" and had "longtime neighborhood roots that transcended racial ties."[57] These are cases of genuine biracial politics. Section 2 guarantees minority voters an opportunity to elect the representatives of their choice, but it does not promise that the law will step in where blacks are not a unified group, where a minority within the minority is providing the swing vote that elects a white. Andrew Young was elected to Congress from the Fifth District in Atlanta when that district was 62 percent white. Young was succeeded by Wyche Fowler, a white, who beat a black contestant after the district had become majority-black. "Being black doesn't make you automatically right," explained one middle-aged black woman who had voted for Fowler.[58] For such a voter, politics transcends the question of race.

That is not the case, however, when blacks support whites out of long-standing deference to established white leaders. White candidates can be unbeatable for reasons that suggest continuing electoral inequality between whites and blacks. Before Burke County, Georgia, adopted single-member districts, a local black explained, blacks used to vote for the "big farmer because they felt he was 'the man' and they couldn't do without him." Others in Burke made the same point: "Blacks felt responsible to white landowners who took care of them when they were sick or in trouble with the law," one resident remarked.[59] "Black people feel kind of obligated to the white man as a leader . . . because this is the way they've been taught all their life," a black candidate in Humphreys County, Mississippi, explains in the documentary film "Hands That Picked Cotton."[60]

The film reveals another aspect of black voting patterns. "They don't vote for the black necessarily," a disc jockey in Belzoni remarked. "I guess psychologically it's because everybody is in such a small area and everybody knows everybody. They think that somebody might get that much further advanced than they are." He added: "You have to be a better candidate than your white counterpart in order to convince the black vote to vote for you in large numbers."[61] Rosellen Brown fictionalizes the point in her novel *Civil Wars*. The heroine visits the black mayor of a Mississippi town who had failed in her first bid for office and who blamed her defeat on black resentment over the purchase of a new house. "If I'd still a been in the shack . . . those folks wouldn't have Judased me like they done," she remarks. "They ain't seeing no one get too far out in front . . . I don't know but what they don't really deep down inside think they don't *deserve* no chance to get out of the mud. See, even my own peoples got me down for a uppity nigger."[62] Interviewed in Burke County in 1986, a black county employee remarked: "Blacks don't want to put a black in authority; they don't want a black to get ahead."[63]

Of course, some black candidates simply appear less qualified. Others who are qualified may fail to launch an effective campaign. The line dividing weak and strong candidates (or campaigns) is not always clear. Poor candidates, it can be said, are candidates who lose, and poor campaigns those that fail; only hindsight allows a sure judgment. But it is hard to take seriously the black candidate in Fort Lauderdale who admitted to having spent less than $100 on his race and to having taken out no advertisements. Another black candidate in the same city limited her campaigning to one street. Neither had been active in civic affairs. Still another black candidate alienated union members by using bumper stickers that failed to include a union "bug" on them.[64] Some losing minority campaigns are, by objective standards, simply badly run.

The important question is why? Candidates without credentials who run poor campaigns are hardly unusual. Yet in certain contexts they do signal inequality in electoral access between whites and blacks. At the time a suit was brought in Jefferson County, Alabama, which is one-third black and has at-large elections, no serious black candidate had ever run for the county commission. The fact that most blacks voted for whites was due not only to the paucity of minority candidates but also to the quality of those who ran. "We won't support a black just for the sake of getting a black in office," one black leader explained. If the candidate is mediocre, there is that "second thought in the people's heads, if they get in, are they going to know what to do?"[65] At the same time, the county seat, Birmingham, was governed by a black mayor; why was Jefferson County different? There were no strong candidates, in the view of that same leader, because "the name of the game in politics is to win. You don't run to lose." Just being a candidate "is nothing to write home to Mama about." Blacks could win in Birmingham, that is, but not out in the county—with the possible exception of one black legislator, it was said.

In Mobile, Alabama, a black candidate ran for the city council in 1981 (before the city went to single-member districts) against white incumbents. The whites got the black vote. "Taylor Hodge was one of the first people I met in the city when I came seventeen years ago . . . yet when he asked me for my political support, I couldn't give it to him," a black businessman remarked in a 1982 interview. "He was too old, and without sufficient support in the community."[66] Why had no serious black candidate come forward? As in Jefferson County, blacks claimed that none could win. Whites said the "right" black had not tried. But to the one black leader who many thought could have run a successful city-wide campaign, Mobile city government did not seem particularly enticing, for he had already held a cabinet position at the state level.[67] Had blacks in Mobile adequately tested white receptivity to black electoral aspirations? Do plaintiffs in a section 2 suit against a city with a history similar to Mobile's need to show that indisputably highly qualified black candidates have run, with good support from black voters? The whites who won in Mobile did not appear so obviously "highly qualified."

Even in southern rural settings where whites who seek local office are likely to hold traditional racial attitudes, blacks will not vote for just any black candidate, Paul Stekler reports in his study of Mississippi Delta counties. It was not a lack of interest in local office that kept potentially strong black candidates away. Blacks as well as whites seek in elected officials such "middle-class" traits as education, social status, and experience in community leadership.[68] And in many of those economically depressed Delta counties, it was the white candidates more frequently than the black who had the requisite skills and background. Those who might have qualified had fled—in search of greater opportunity elsewhere.[69] Moreover, getting blacks to "vote black" requires more than a good candidate. Strong black organizations—which characterize some rural communities but by no means all—help both to raise black political consciousness and to bring out the vote.[70]

In Jefferson County, Mobile, and the Delta counties that Stekler studied, when a decisive fraction of the black electorate spurned black candidates who had neither the credentials nor the organizational support of their white opponents, were electoral opportunities equal? Clearly these settings did not resemble Louisiana's Second Congressional District, in which 35 percent of black voters chose Lindy Boggs over Israel M. Augustine, Jr., a former state appeals court judge who had the endorsement of the major black political organizations. At the same time, important differences in political climate also separated Jefferson County from Mobile, and Mobile from rural Mississippi. Equal electoral opportunity, the issue in section 2 cases, is never either totally present or totally absent. The jurisdictions scrutinized by the courts in section 2 suits will inevitably be characterized by a range of opportunities, with no one point clearly dividing localities with equal electoral access from those that lack it.

Minority voters may give white candidates their needed edge not by voting directly for those who are white, but by dividing their vote among competing minority candidates.[71] In Brooklyn, New York, in districts approximately three-quarters minority, two white state senators were renominated as the Democratic candidates in 1982 when their black and Hispanic opponents divided the minority vote.[72] In that same election, a Hispanic incumbent lost in a three-way race when his brother-in-law split the Hispanic vote with him.[73] Stekler reports that in Bolivar County, Mississippi, which was 62 percent black in 1980, constant feuding among the black mayors of several small majority-black towns created black factions that helped ensure white victories.[74]

Whites also gain office when blacks fail to show up at the polls, when the votes are there but are not cast. Twenty years after the passage of the Voting Rights Act low levels of black political participation remain a problem, especially in the rural South—hence the number of majority-black counties still controlled by whites. Not only first-time black candidates but also black incumbents are affected. For example, in predominantly black Peach County, Georgia, only 57 percent of voting-age blacks were registered in 1980; two years later low black turnout defeated a black mayor running for reelection.[75] As noted earlier, the Senate report suggests that low participation rates together with both socioeconomic disparities between blacks and whites and a history of discrimination constitute evidence of unequal electoral access. However, the report provides no guidance as to how much weight to assign to these factors. The answer surely depends on how low black turnout is relative to white, how steadily blacks appear to be catching up, and on the apparent source of the problem. The last question is of course the hardest to answer, and the answers the hardest to assess. But in the black-belt counties of the South, the picture is much clearer than in a dynamic metropolis. "Politics is an acquired skill," Stekler notes.[76] An acquired taste as well, he might have added. "People don't understand politics—registration and turning out," explained a black in Burke County. "For blacks, those actions are not like going to church."[77] "People *pray* for better jobs, better roads, water to their house . . . They don't realize the Lord gave them the privilege to vote," a black candidate in rural Mississippi noted in "Hands That Picked Cotton." In addition, elderly blacks remain reluctant to register at the county courthouse—historically the symbol of injustice—and many are ashamed to expose their illiteracy. In such settings, low levels of black political participation are symptomatic of historical and ongoing inequality between whites and blacks—the political toll that racism continues to take.

Just as minority voters may help elect whites, often it takes both black and white support to carry black candidates into office. In jurisdictions where blacks are a minority, black candidates will obviously lose if they gain no white support.

With increasing frequency that support has been forthcoming. Significant white support for minority candidates is no longer headline news. When Dutch Morial was elected mayor of New Orleans, his margin of victory was provided by about 15 percent of New Orleans whites.[78] Also in 1982, Katie Hall won Indiana's First Congressional District (75 percent white) and Alan D. Wheat carried Missouri's Fifth Congressional District (80 percent white).[79] In the 1983 Chicago mayoral race, Harold Washington's edge came from 18 percent of the white vote.[80] That same year, Wilson Goode and Harvey Gantt swept into the mayor's office in Philadelphia and in Charlotte, North Carolina—Goode with an estimated 27 percent and Gantt with 39 percent of the white vote.[81] Less than 20 percent of Los Angeles's population is black, yet Mayor Tom Bradley was elected to an unprecedented fourth term in 1985 with almost 68 percent of the vote.[82] In 1985 black mayors were elected in several cities with populations less than one-third minority, including Pasco, Washington; Battle Creek, Michigan; Peekskill, New York; South Boston, Virginia; and Gainesville, Georgia.[83] Although neither the district court nor the Supreme Court in *Gingles* found white crossover voting impressive in the challenged legislative districts in North Carolina, white support for blacks was in fact high—commonly above 30 percent in the primaries and above 40 percent in the general election.[84]

If the phenomenon of whites voting for blacks is not headline news, it is not quite politics as usual either. Thus a central question with respect to minority electoral opportunities is the record of white support for minority candidates and what explains that record. Whites, of course, may cast their ballots for white candidates for reasons other than racial hostility. Although Justice Brennan in *Gingles* refers to whites "refusing" to vote for blacks, not all such choices amount to refusals. White voters may reject a black candidate for precisely the same reasons that whites may reject a white and blacks a black: on the merits, or inadequate appeal. In fact, although Justice Brennan rejected as illegitimate any inquiry into voter motivation, even a cursory scan of voting patterns in the North Carolina districts challenged in *Gingles* would suggest that whites cared about matters other than race.[85]

In *Whitcomb*, it will be recalled, the Supreme Court found that party, not race, was the deciding factor; blacks were Democrats in that heavily Republican Indiana county. In a trial on at-large voting in Fort Lauderdale, Florida, a black candidate conceded that he may have lost because he was a Democrat in a strongly Republican community.[86] In nonpartisan local elections, too, whites can find themselves ideologically to the right of the minority candidate. "People have a tendency to think blacks spend all the money, raise taxes, blow it on social programs," one white in Burke County explained. "We are much more tight-fisted about dollars than the black leadership," another reported.[87] Such conservative white perceptions do not necessarily square with reality; the blacks eventually elected from single-member districts in Burke County showed no inclination to milk the taxpayers or to squander county money. A Mexican-American who held office in Ozona, Texas, described whites as "worried that we were going to turn the county upside down." Yet "I'm no radical," he said; "just an official representing the people electing me."[88]

Of course some minority leaders do stand well to the left of mainstream white opinion, and to an extent their views reflect differences between black and white voters. Joseph Lowery, president of the Southern Christian Leadership Conference, has contended that "blacks are less provincial than whites because they are in touch with and understand the struggles of other oppressed people around the world." In addition, he said, they are "more sensitive to the needs of the poor."[89] In Boston, black mayoral and congressional candidate Mel King professed more confidence in Fidel Castro than in Ronald Reagan and embraced a black separatist movement to create an independent black city within the metropolis.[90] Plainly some whites may "refuse" to vote for particular black candidates not because they are nonwhite but because they are politically unacceptable.

Not all ideological differences are alike, however. White loyalty to the GOP in Marion County, Indiana, was quite different from whites voting for whites in Burke County, Georgia. The white voters in Burke County were undoubtedly in part making a judgment about differences in priorities between the white and black communities. But other factors were at work. Where there is minimal campaigning and almost no issues other than fiscal responsibility, race and incumbency assume special importance. In rural counties, as Stekler points out, the voters personally know all the candidates. He asks: "Whom would one vote for in a typical county supervisor race? The probable answer, given some degree of public satisfaction or plain association with the job, would be to vote for the incumbent. In 1965, all incumbents in the South were white. All the local official role models, as such, were white. In lieu of an incumbent, you would probably vote for the person you knew the best or the person who you thought would do the best job. For whites, that choice would be exclusively among white candidates given the lack of social relationships with even middle class blacks."[91]

As Stekler suggests, incumbents are hard to beat. And in the rural settings he describes, that circumstance can contribute to overall black exclusion. But the power of incumbency is part and parcel of normal electoral politics, and the tendency of whites to vote for a white incumbent against a black challenger does not necessarily signal racism. For instance, in Norfolk, Virginia—a city where black-supported candidates, both black and white, have had considerable success—incumbents were reelected more than 79 percent of the time from 1968 through 1984. In four out of the nine elections, every incumbent (black *and* white) who sought reelection won.[92] The Norfolk pattern is not unusual; voters tend to reelect those who hold office, whatever their race. In a study of blacks and Hispanics in California politics, Browning, Marshall, and Tabb found that minority incumbents won approximately 80 percent of the time—the same rate as for white incumbents.[93] In Tunica County, Mississippi, where the voting-age population is 70 percent black, a black won the post of circuit clerk as a result of a split in the white vote among several white opponents and the absence of a runoff requirement. In subsequent elections the black, as an incumbent, was able to beat single white opponents in both the Democratic primary and the general election.[94]

In majority-black jurisdictions, whites often continue to win as incumbents but are replaced by blacks as soon as they retire. Without the advantage of incumbency, even well-positioned whites are defeated. In Holmes County, Mississippi, for instance, a white incumbent representing a county supervisor district that was 80 percent black had been supported by most local blacks. He had a black foreman, and upon his retirement in 1983, supported that foreman's campaign to succeed him. The ensuing victory gave blacks a majority on the county board. In Humphreys County, Mississippi, a black won a seat on the board of supervisors following the retirement of a white who had held office for thirty-two years and was one of the largest landowners in the area. His opponents had been the incumbent's white foreman and the white mayor of a local town.[95]

Stekler suggests that the drawing power of white incumbents has special meaning in rural settings with little or no record of black electoral success and low levels of black political participation. So too does the tendency of whites (when no incumbent is running) to support the person whom they know best or think will do the best job. Whites tend to know whites best. And the process of gaining visibility may lessen, rather than enhance, black prospects. The way to become a viable black candidate in Jefferson County, whites suggested, was to appear at county commission meetings, come before the state legislature, and develop a rapport with the media. Yet, as a white commissioner pointed out, blacks who took that course were quickly labeled "black spokesmen," which served to alienate them from white voters.[96] Those viewed as likely to do the "best job"—the question of social proximity aside— would also usually be white. The majority of whites wanted commissioners who were fiscally responsible; business acumen was thus considered a prime qualification for office; and most large landowners and prominent businessmen were white.

Other political and social inequalities may indicate limits on black electoral opportunities. In Randolph County, Georgia, a visitor to the courthouse in 1986 would not have found a single black employee. Some poll watchers in the county were black, but none of them were managers. No black had been sent to a training course on election procedure offered by the state. The county argued that qualified blacks could not be located, but it had made no effort to qualify any.[97] Likewise, Mobile, Alabama, defending its record in court, claimed that although it was prepared to appoint blacks to a city board when they requested it, few made the request. Yet the city had taken no initiative to invite applications; the city commissioners (all white) simply recruited friends.[98] The process was not strictly racist, but it lacked racial sensitivity. In the Burke County case, the district court found a segregated laundromat within a few blocks of the county courthouse and, in the courthouse itself, rest-room doors with "colored" and "white" signs inadequately concealed by faded paint.[99] In the view of the court, these significd persistent racism, pertinent to the question of electoral equality.

Racism or racial insensitivity can take other forms. In New Orleans, a black candidate was endorsed by one of the city's two major newspapers as early as 1969; in Mobile, by contrast, the only daily newspaper at the time consistently whipped up racial animosity. And according to witnesses at the two trials on at-large voting in the city, civic activities were generally racially segregated. For instance, blacks and whites in Mobile held separate Mardi Gras celebrations, and black candidates had little contact with white audiences through church or other groups. The private and political life of white Mobile residents, one witness claimed, were of a piece. "White support [for black candidates] is as apparent in an election as white shopping in a black business," he said.[100] Not surprisingly, white witnesses at the Mobile trial drew a different picture, and it was the unenviable task of the trial judge to weigh such claims and counterclaims.

The willingness of Mobile whites to elect a black to the governing commission could partly be gauged by their record with respect to other elected offices. The county had one black commissioner, elected from a majority-white district; he had been opposed by another black as well as a white, and well-known black leaders had campaigned against him. Furthermore, white conservatives had backed a black running for the state legislature against a more liberal white. Likewise, in Jefferson County, Alabama, although no black had served on the county commission, two blacks had been elected at-large to other posts. A black had also garnered a majority of the county's vote in his successful campaign for election to the Alabama Supreme Court. Blacks who qualify for one office will not necessarily (in the view of whites) qualify for another, however. In Mobile, for instance, the office of mayor rotated among the three commissioners. Since whites did not want a black mayor, they resisted the election of a black commissioner.[101] Blacks in Jefferson County argued that only a minority spokesman with a track record of officeholding could gain a seat on the county commission, but that demonstrated competence in one office did not necessarily suggest qualification for another. "All that we've done is to retain positions [to which blacks were initially appointed]," one advocate of single-member districts in the county explained. Try to transfer experience in one position to electability in another, and "that gray area of doubt about black competence would reappear."[102]

It is indisputable that white doubts about black competence—in short, racism—continue to deny blacks in some jurisdictions an equal opportunity to elect the representatives of their choice. In such communities, considerations of race dominate the electoral process; minority candidates face obstacles on the path to election that whites do not—obstacles clearly related to past and present racism. Public office is, in effect, largely reserved for whites. And where this is true section 2 has clearly been violated.

It is easy to count minority faces in office, but it is not so easy to decipher the meaning of that number. A majority of the Supreme Court has agreed that the question of why voters have cast their ballots as they have is pertinent, yet statistical analysis can only tell part of that story. Not only must courts weigh evidence that may touch upon almost every aspect of public and quasi-public life in the jurisdiction, they must also define a number of basic terms: the "touch" of historical discrimination, "effective" participation, slating, racial appeals, and polarized elections. The definitional question is raised as well by one of the criteria not yet discussed: "responsiveness" to the "particularized needs" of the minority group. What happens after the polls close? The issue was relegated to secondary status by the Senate report, and, indeed, electoral opportunities are exceedingly hard to judge on the basis of postelection records. The link between the two assumes that only those elected whites who feel free to ignore black votes will be indifferent to black demands, and that if whites can win without black support, black electoral opportunities are unequal to white. In fact, however, only extreme indifference to black demands is easily identified; there is no consensus on the definition of indifference. And, more important, the test has serious logical flaws.

How much responsiveness is "responsive"? What constitutes an adequate performance in attempting to meet the "particularized needs" of the minority group? Blacks in Burke County charged that the county acted to meet black needs only when pressured, and even then on a minimal level. They also complained that contracts for work such as road construction usually went to white firms. The county responded that all qualified firms in the immediate area were white. How did the authorities define a qualified construction firm? Was quality linked to color—or at least to a track record, which only whites had? A county's boards (the Hospital Authority and the Economic and Industrial Committee, for instance) may be predominantly white, yet the county may argue that "most of the time [it is] searching for someone to serve rather than eliminating people."[103] And that may be the case. There is often a shortage of candidates for both elected and appointed positions in small towns and rural counties. In the case of Burke County, however, the general racial environment made such claims suspect.

"The Mexican-American revolution is about paving the damn streets and getting better schools," a Southwest Hispanic activist has remarked.[104] And certainly in towns where the paving happens to end just where Mexican-American houses begin, local authorities have not been adequately "responsive." Is the picture equally clear when the white sector of a town has sidewalks paid for by homeowners and the Hispanics want the taxpayers to pick up the tab in their neighborhood? Sidewalk assessments are standard practice in many American communities; does the disparity between white and Mexican-American income against a background of employment discrimination suggest that the practice is discriminatory?

One might measure the performance of white officials in meeting minority needs against that which one would expect from blacks or Mexican-Americans, were they to gain political control. The sidewalk question would then have a clear answer. But such an approach would yield limited results. In small cities, towns, and rural areas, few issues considered by the governing council or commission are "racial." Most votes are unanimous, whether blacks serve or not. Georgetown, South Carolina, is a typical small town as far as political life is concerned. Asked about tension between whites and blacks on the city council, a black member replied, "No issues have divided the council along racial lines except that of single-member districts. Most of our work involves technical matters." The city administrator could only come up with drainage as an issue on which the city council voted along racial lines. Even in Charleston, political observers in 1981 spoke of few clear black issues. When warring factions on big city councils do debate hot issues, minority representatives do not necessarily take "minority" positions; cleavages are not always racial. In addition, fiscal and other constraints on local government vary from place to place, and the precise demands made by the minority community may be more or less easy to meet.[105]

In their study of California cities, Browning, Marshall, and Tabb argue that, despite differing economic constraints and political styles, policy becomes more responsive to certain minority demands when blacks and Hispanics are part of the dominant coalition on a city council—in other words, when minorities and white liberals make up the majority.[106] Although such findings suggest that blacks and Hispanics should get to the polls on election day, they are irrelevant to the question of inadequate responsiveness as evidence of minority electoral exclusion. If there is a direct correlation between the election of blacks and liberal whites, on the one hand, and responsiveness, on the other, the absence of such responsiveness only tells the courts who governs, and that information can be had more directly. The message of Browning, Marshall, and Tabb is that white conservative control does not bode well for affirmative action and similar programs. But section 2 gives neither minority voters nor their white political allies a right to control a majority of seats on a governing body, and if conservative city councils are not as responsive as liberal ones to black demands, that does not necessarily signify the absence of equal electoral opportunities. A lack of responsiveness to the "particularized needs" of a minority group does not suggest that no candidate has sought minority votes, but only that those candidates who did, lost. And electoral defeat is not conclusive evidence of inadequate opportunity.

A majority-vote requirement, a prohibition on single-shot voting, and other such potentially discriminatory procedural rules listed in the Senate report pose no definitional problems. They are, in fact, the one cluster of "objective" factors on a list allegedly composed entirely of nonsubjective items.[107] In the 1984 presidential race Jesse Jackson campaigned strongly against runoff elections in Democratic primaries. Do such elections impermissibly deny minority voters an equal electoral opportunity? The impact of the requirement depends, in part, on the electoral context—whether elections are at-large or from districts; whether there is, as well, a full-slate rule; and whether candidates run for separate "posts." More important, its effect depends on the number of candidates running and on voter response, and both that number and voter behavior may change with an alteration in procedures. In a single-member district in which blacks are in the minority (the circumstances that were the focus of Jackson's concern), a black candidate who leads the first primary with 40 percent of the vote may lose in the subsequent runoff. But without the runoff, there might not have been that 40 percent support to begin with. As Harold Stanley notes, without a majority-vote rule the field of candidates is likely to shrink; certainly where the white community is determined to keep blacks out of office, preelection bargaining to settle on one white candidate is likely to occur if the first election is the decisive one.[108] In fact, if one assumes that such preelection bargaining will not occur, then black candidates may actually be in trouble without a second election. In Yazoo County, Mississippi, for instance, four blacks and one white ran for a county supervisor seat in a beat (district) that was 75 percent black; the black vote was thus splintered, and the white might have won without a subsequent runoff.[109]

Even if the number of candidates remains large, voters will cast their ballots differently depending on how many chances they expect to have to register their choice. As Katharine Butler has put it: "The majority [vote] requirement allows a voter to vote 'for' his candidate, without much thought about the opponents. The voter may realize that his first choice is a long shot, but will support the candidate anyway, knowing he will get another chance to affect the 'real' election. If the first election is the only election, the same voter may select his second or even third choice . . . hoping to . . . defeat a candidate he hopes will not be elected."[110] This strategy may fail, of course, but if the candidate a voter dislikes is a black Democrat, in the general election the voter can usually cross party lines and vote for a white Republican. A change in procedure that appears good for blacks may thus benefit Republicans.

Where whites are determined to stop the election of a black, plurality rules will not help. On the other hand, where whites are not thus determined, a majority-vote rule may aid a black or a white moderate. In the primary, moderate white votes may be distributed among several candidates. But if the choice in the second round is between a conservative white and a moderate—black or white—a biracial coalition may form to defeat the conservative.[111] Without a majority-vote requirement, that biracial coalition would perhaps have formed for the first and only election. This is not to assert the superiority of a majority-vote requirement over plurality elections, but only to indicate the uncertain value and unpredictable effect of either. Moreover, majority-vote rules and anti–single shot provisions (both explicitly referred to in the Senate report) are not offensive to democratic government. They do increase the number of votes that a candidate who is the choice of any minority must receive to win, be it gays, fundamentalists, or blacks. Such rules thus favor the majority, pushing the political system toward the center, but they are not inherently antidemocratic or discriminatory. They violate section 2 of the Voting Rights Act only when they operate in an environment in which considerations of race dominate the electoral process.

"Small towns, rural counties, are just different from large cities," the narrator in "Hands That Picked Cotton" explains. And, in fact, the phenomenon of legislative seats largely reserved for whites is mainly confined to the rural and small-town black-belt South. In that setting the task of organizing blacks poses a multitude of problems: the drain of middle-class resources and talent, the generally low visibility of politics, cultural patterns in the black community working against mobilization, a lack of trust among various black factions (its impact being greater in places where everyone knows everyone else), and continuing problems of economic intimidation in places where every voter knows who is hiring farm workers, approving bank loans, running the store, and where few of these powerful people are black. Urban areas, in contrast, generally provide a propitious environment for black political mobilization. Residentially clustered, the black population is accessible to door-to-door canvassing and other traditional get-out-the-vote techniques; skilled campaign workers are in plentiful supply; black candidates are likely to benefit from divisions within the white community; and politics is important to civic life. In some cities such as New Orleans, black political organizations have become stronger than white ones.

I have argued that the proper test for electoral exclusion is the presence of legislative seats largely *reserved* for whites—not legislative seats *occupied disproportionately* by whites. Disproportionately low officeholding by minorities does not necessarily mean that considerations of race are controlling electoral outcomes, or that the legacy of past discrimination is distorting the entire political process. Whites, I have argued, often represent blacks. Blacks have put whites in office in New York City, Selma, Baltimore, New Orleans, and other majority-black districts and cities, and in minority-black districts and jurisdictions, whites have received a majority of black votes. Yet the North Carolina district court's opinion in *Gingles* makes no reference to black support for white candidates. Indeed, no attempt was made to explore the question of whether some elected whites were the choice of minority as well as white voters.

In the Norfolk case, however, the issue was central. Elections in Norfolk were at large; blacks were a minority; a black endorsement group (Concerned Citizens) had frequently backed white candidates over blacks; and those whites had garnered a majority of the black vote. Thus, in a 1974 contest for three city council seats, the Concerned Citizens endorsed two whites and one black; three other blacks ran. In homogeneous black precincts the two endorsed whites received more than 55 percent of the vote, while one of the unendorsed blacks got only 36 percent. In 1980 Concerned Citizens endorsed one white and one black, while another black ran unendorsed. The white candidate garnered 73 percent of the black vote, the unendorsed black only 35 percent.[112]

Not only can whites represent blacks, but black voters who have had an equal "opportunity . . . to participate in the political process" can find themselves without representation—either black or white. The absence of representation alone does not establish a voting rights violation; the candidates who are the choice of blacks may simply have gone down to defeat for reasons unrelated to race. Blacks may be active and equal participants in the Democratic Party in a county that is predominantly

Republican; black candidates may be regularly slated, black voters energetically courted by whites on the ticket. This was the finding in *Whitcomb* that led the Supreme Court to conclude that the claim of electoral discrimination in that case was a "mere euphemism for political defeat." And *Whitcomb*, it will be recalled, was one of the Fourteenth Amendment decisions ratified by the amendment of section 2.

No voters are guaranteed representation. The only difference between whites and blacks is that whites, given their history, are generally assumed to have adequate electoral opportunity. But whites who continually vote for losing candidates are without representation in the section 2 sense; the candidates of their choice have not been elected. The Supreme Court, in a 1977 decision involving blacks, Hispanics, and Hasidic Jews in Brooklyn, New York, implied that Hasidim were well represented by whites in other districts—a bewildering contention given the radical distinctiveness of Hasidic culture.[113] In *Gingles*, Katharine Butler has pointed out, both courts seemed to assume that whites were overrepresented because a disproportionate share of elected officials were white. Yet, as she explained, "nothing in the record of the trial court demonstrated that white voters who supported losing white candidates were . . . more represented by the candidates elected than were blacks who supported losing black candidates."[114] Particular groups of whites often feel politically excluded—in the early 1980s, the well-to-do in Mobile and working-class whites in New Orleans, for instance.[115]

Only rarely will courts lend a sympathetic ear to whites claiming political exclusion.[116] Blacks without representation are entitled to a remedy when evidence suggests an electoral process tainted by racism—its lingering effects from the past or its ongoing presence. Because there are no group rights but only individual ones, no clear distinction exists between a "minority" representative and a "white" one. An elected white may gain office with a minority of white votes and a black with a minority of black votes. In the former case blacks would have provided the swing vote, in the latter, whites. Blacks would be no less "represented" because whites picked the black winner—unless of course the process was racist.

The September 1986 race for the Democratic nomination for Congress from Georgia's Fifth Congressional District boiled down to two black candidates, Julian Bond and John Lewis. Lewis got only about 40 percent of the black vote but 80 percent of the white one; in a district that is 40 percent white, those white votes provided his margin of victory. "One [black] radio newsman said that white voters think I'm an 'uppity nigger,' " Bond is reported to have said.[117] In fact, no evidence of racism surfaced.

Perhaps some would argue that blacks in the Georgia congressional race had been denied an equal opportunity to elect the representatives of their choice. Kenny Johnson of the Southern Regional Council has complained that in Greene County, Alabama, where "blacks have been a powerful political voice for years," whites are "becoming a very powerful swing vote" and are thus acquiring *"undue* influence."[118] Such reasoning only takes one step further the contention of an expert witness in the Norfolk case. "Minorities in the city of Norfolk are unable to elect candidates of their choice in that blacks have never elected any candidate without some white support," he testified. Since blacks were a minority in the city, their candidates could not win without white support; the need for such support denied black voters the opportunity to elect the candidates of their choice.[119] This implies that blacks are entitled to choose their representatives without white input, and where blacks are a majority, whites (it would seem) should stay home on election day. Such arguments logically extend the commitment to group rights that the Supreme Court came close to making in *Gingles,* but such a commitment is not sustained by the language of section 2, its legislative history, or the constitutional decisions upon which the amendment rested.

I have tried here to suggest a way of thinking about the issues raised by section 2 litigation. They do not lend themselves to resolution by too great a preoccupation with the Senate checklist. I argued in Chapter 4 that, with the *Zimmer* factors to guide them, the constitutional decisions assumed "an orderliness and rationality that disguised their subjectivity." But the subjectivity derived from the arbitrariness of the listed factors themselves, which, in turn, resulted from an effort to measure an undefined phenomenon. What is justice in the electoral sphere? these cases asked. What is the normal relation between racial and ethnic groups in the political sphere? When are the "opportunities and occasions of power" properly shared? The inadequacy of the courts' decisions reflected the magnitude of the task before them.

The Senate's list is no improvement over the one provided by *Zimmer.* It obfuscates rather than clarifies; simplifies what cannot be simplified; makes orderly a process that is inherently disorderly. In section 2 suits, no less than in those which rested on the Fourteenth

Amendment, the assessment of conflicting claims demands not only a sense of what to look for, but the freedom to explore beyond the designated paths. Every county, every city, is different, and mapping out the terrain is a complex task. An eye for the subtle nuance that distinguishes one place from another is essential.

The Supreme Court in *Gingles* acknowledged the importance of trial court findings—of those "intensely local appraisals" that only the district court can engage in. This was, in fact, the clearest message in the Court's opinion.[120] But while only the trial court can appraise the subtle nuances in the racial atmosphere of a particular jurisdiction, that appraisal will always entail considerable subjectivity. And that inescapable element of subjectivity in section 2 decisions suggests the wisdom of judicial restraint in upholding plaintiffs' claims. As of 1986, however, such restraint has been in short supply. "No objective observer of the political process in the South can argue that it is less open to minorities today," Katharine Butler has noted, ". . . yet in the past plaintiffs never enjoyed the degree of success evidenced by recent decisions."[121]

Such unprecedented success would be appropriate, of course, if past legal standards had been found wanting. It is clear, however, that in amending section 2 Congress did not expect substantial deviation from what the Senate Judiciary Committee report described as an "extensive, reliable, and reassuring track record." The "results" test, as the report depicted it, was nothing "radically new" or "untested"; it was "well-known to federal judges" and not "easy."[122] It was easier, of course, than an intent test (defined as demanding evidence of a "smoking gun"), but the decision in *Mobile*, requiring proof of discriminatory intent, had virtually halted vote dilution suits, advocates of the amendment claimed. "We are acting to restore the opportunity for further progress," the report stated.[123] The intent was to restore normal traffic—to repair a light stuck on red.

What Congress envisioned is not what happened. In the first four years in the life of the amended provision, the success rate of plaintiffs in section 2 cases exceeded 90 percent. Civil rights spokesmen have long maintained that at-large voting is inherently discriminatory, and such voting is the most frequent target in section 2 suits. "In Norfolk," plaintiffs' attorney Frank Parker has argued, "black voting strength in at-large voting clearly is diluted when whites constitute over 60 percent of the population and over 64 percent of the registered voters citywide, but, if Norfolk were divided into single-member districts or wards, blacks would have voting majorities and be able to elect candidates of their choice in three wards."[124] In short, at-large voting impermissibly dilutes black voting strength. In every city with a significant minority population, at least one minority single-member district can be drawn, and, by Parker's reasoning, blacks have a right to such districts whenever it is possible to create them. That is, minority voters are entitled to control electoral outcomes—to elect whom they want—where methods of voting can be altered to permit such control. Precisely that commitment, however, had been ruled out by the Dole compromise; the statute had guaranteed no "fair share," only a "fair shake"—a chance to play the electoral game by fair rules. Yet Parker and others continue to press their view, and with overwhelming success.

Indeed, the plaintiffs' victories in court only hint at the magnitude of that success. An uncounted but unquestionably large number of suits are settled out of court by jurisdictions reluctant to commit scarce funds to an almost hopeless cause or to take a stand that might be interpreted as "anti-black."[125] Thus in October 1985 the city of Opelika, Alabama, took "measures to abandon its at-large electoral process in an effort to hedge off lawsuits by blacks," a local newspaper reported. "Other counties and cities throughout the state have already taken measures to abandon their at-large election methods when faced with similar lawsuits," it noted.[126] One such city was Tuscaloosa, which, having decided not to contest a challenge to its city-wide elections, had asked the Alabama legislature to institute single-member districts.[127] In 1985 hardly a week went by in which the Department of Justice did not receive at least one section 5 submission requesting approval of a change from at-large elections to ward voting; in all more than seventy submissions were received.[128] And that number includes only changes in the covered states and counties—not in Maryland or in much of Florida, for instance. These alterations, it can be assumed, came about not from any sudden affection for single-member districts but from a wave of threatened litigation.

By 1985 the campaign to eradicate at-large systems had gathered a relentless momentum. "Area-wide election systems—also known as at-large systems—are falling like dominoes," an Alabama newspaper reported in 1986. It noted that Escambia and Crenshaw counties had already reached out-of-court agreements with the Alabama Democratic Conference (ADC), a black political caucus. Officials in Henry County, worried that blacks would drag the county into an expensive court dispute, had drawn up a single-member district plan. "In other areas," the article stated, "incumbents and redistricting opponents are throwing in the towel because of the high legal cost of contesting the change." An ADC field director estimated that "by 1988 at least 50 [counties] will be divided into districts. By that time, we may have a legislative umbrella bill to bring in the rest who still have at-large systems."[129]

In 1982 Congress passed no judgment on the general merits of at-large systems, majority-vote rules, anti–single shot provisions, or districting plans that divide not only Republican and Democratic, rural and urban, and other such potential voting blocs, but also blacks and Hispanics. It had assumed that a variety of electoral rules were compatible with democratic government and that these procedures, in widespread use, had their advantages and disadvantages—for minority voters as well as white. Lawmakers had been persuaded, however, that in some jurisdictions the lingering effects of past discrimination and ongoing racism still had a significant effect on the opportunity of minority voters to elect the representatives of their choice, and in amending the statute, they acted to enhance the power of minority voters to institute electoral methods that minimized the impact of such racism. In "*most* communities," the Senate Judiciary Committee informed members of Congress, minority candidates "received substantial support from white voters." The concern was solely with those jurisdictions in which "racial politics play[ed] an excessive role," dominating the electoral process.[130] Elsewhere, section 2 would confer no special status upon black and Hispanic voters. The act guaranteed no group rights, no "racially fair" apportionment of legislative seats nationwide. In stressing an entitlement only to equal electoral access, the statute unequivocally rejected the principle that minority voters were entitled to representation and that only blacks could represent blacks.

Those in the civil rights community who fought hard for the 1982 amendments are justly elated by the results. Not only at-large systems, but also multimember and single-member districting plans that fragment black and Hispanic residential concentrations are "falling like dominoes." Perhaps their demise is nothing to mourn. But it has occurred not as a consequence of considered legislative judgment that such electoral procedures violate fundamental rights or entail unacceptable costs as a consequence of their disparate racial impact; rather, this change has resulted primarily from threatened legal action by attorneys whose arguments have been given credibility by confused courts—courts that have neglected the statute's focus on fair process and come close to embracing the principle of group rights to proportionate officeholding. Advocates of the statutory revision had calmed congressional fears by insisting that they wished only a restoration of former rights—those that the Constitution had guaranteed before the *Mobile* decision. Today they openly and justly celebrate a new era in minority voting rights.

# Conclusion

The reapportionment decisions promised more than they delivered, I argued early in this book. "The right of suffrage," the Supreme Court had said, "can be denied by a debasement or dilution of the weight of a citizen's vote just as effectively as by wholly prohibiting the free exercise of the franchise."[1] But when were votes debased or diluted? "Each and every citizen has an inalienable right to full and effective participation . . . an equally effective voice."[2] It was a promise bound to whet the appetite. The right to which the Court referred—one person, one vote—was (as Justice Harlan noted) a stripped-down, vulnerable version of the American system of representation. Solely concerned with the right of the individual, autonomous voter to cast a ballot of equal weight, the Court had ignored the fact that citizens are politically "effective" only as members of groups. Full and effective participation, an equally effective voice: the promised equality was not one that individuals, as individuals, could attain.

It was not only the logic of those decisions that raised the question of group rights, but also their timing. The entrance of the Supreme Court into the political thicket coincided with the revolution in civil rights. The nation's growing commitment to racial equality and the Court's commitment to ballots that "count" came together to provide, in subsequent years, the increasing protection afforded blacks and Hispanics. But the unfinished business of the reapportionment cases remains unfinished; the courts, Congress, attorneys, and scholars are still fumbling to define the vote at "full value without dilution or discount."[3]

The question is unresolved, but the record is now cluttered with unsatisfactory, often inconsistent, judicial and administrative decisions, and, from Congress and the press, careless rhetoric. In theory, no group is entitled by law to proportional representation on a legislative body. Yet both lower courts and the Department of Justice—encouraged by mixed signals from the Supreme Court—rest decisions involving minority voting rights on that unacknowledged standard. A maximum number of safe minority districts—or close to it—has become the rule in an electoral landscape from which at-large voting is being systematically cleared. Moreover, if newspapers and news magazines are any gauge, the view that proportionality is "fair" has been widely accepted. Even the Republican-dominated Senate Judiciary Committee, in its 1982 report, came close to equating "direct, overt impediments to the right to vote" with "more sophisticated devices that dilute minority voting strength"—that is, with districting plans and other arrangements that provide minorities with less than a maximum number of black or Hispanic districts.[4]

This is controversial policy that has somehow stirred no controversy. It is scarcely an exaggeration to say that affirmative action in the electoral sphere has only adherents. The opposition to busing and to affirmative action goals and timetables is loud and clear; protest against racial gerrymandering to increase minority officeholding is too muted to be heard. Who is there to protest? Black and white parents care where their child goes to school, but few voters pay attention to the rules by which their county governing board (or even their congressman) is elected.

Low voter interest combines with high interest on the part of civil rights groups and minority politicians, who have made attitudes toward minority voting rights a litmus test of sensitivity to questions of racial justice. Civil rights issues have an almost protected status in Congress, and voting rights issues have been especially sacrosanct. The stringent provisions of the Voting Rights Act especially affect the South, yet in 1982 more than 90 percent of white southern Democrats in the House voted to strengthen the statute. In the Senate, every southern Democrat and eighteen out of twenty-two Republicans supported the amendments. State and local officials have been equally reluctant to speak out on voting rights issues. South Carolina might fight a specific suit involving state redistricting, but its congressional representatives will not even debate legislation that threatens to condemn all districting plans that do not promote proportional minority officeholding. In jurisdictions where blacks and Hispanics are concentrated, few candidates will simply write off that vote. A tarnished image on civil rights jeopardizes the support of not only minority voters but also whites who see themselves as sympathetic to minority concerns and equate such sympathy with uncritical support for policies advocated by civil rights groups.[5]

Democrats (both white and minority) frequently owe their election to black and Hispanic support. Republicans, too, have courted the black vote, among them New Jersey Governor Thomas Kean and Senators Alfonse D'Amato (New York), Arlen Specter (Pennsylvania), and Thad Cochran (Mississippi).[6] Republicans have an additional reason for overlooking racial gerrymandering that benefits black candidates: what is good for black candidates is often good for Republicans. As blacks are drained from white districts, the latter become fertile ground for conservative candidates. In Jefferson County, Alabama, an out-of-court settlement in 1985 replaced an at-large system—under which only whites had been elected—with five single-member districts. Two safe black districts were created, leaving three that were almost completely white, and the Republicans benefited from the change. Unless unopposed, Democrats could not win in districts that contained few blacks, and in 1986 two Democratic incumbents lost.[7]

The Jefferson County story was not unique. As a consequence of a compromise reached by South Carolina and the Department of Justice (joined by the NAACP), the state increased the proportion of black voters in two senatorial districts. In the 1984 election, in four districts from which blacks had been drained, conservative Republicans replaced incumbent liberal Democrats.[8] In *Gingles*, the North Carolina case, state Republican leaders openly acknowledged the "happy coincidence" between the interests of blacks and Republicans. Indeed, they had much to celebrate. Following the district court decision, the North Carolina general assembly created thirty-one single-member districts out of eight that had been multimember. In 1984 the new districting helped Republicans double their share of state legislative seats. Ironically, it was the Democrats—usually quick to charge the Republicans with lax civil rights administration—who were unhappy. Safe black districts, they said, isolate black voters and deprive liberal white Democrats of crucial black support.[9]

There is one more reason that may help explain why the civil rights view on electoral questions has rarely been challenged. In the ongoing war against racial inequality, victory on most fronts appears elusive. Such problems as black unemployment, teenage pregnancy, and inferior inner-city schools all seem intractable. By contrast, the commitment to maximizing minority officeholding yields concrete results. When minority plaintiffs won their suit in Mobile, Alabama, and single-member districts replaced at-large voting, blacks were elected to the city's previously all-white governing body. That outcome was a virtual certainty. Voting rights is a moral crusade with a guarantee of something to show at the end.

Public policy on voting rights has slipped across important lines. Distrust of the South was appropriate in 1965, but the "emergency" provisions have now been extended beyond the year 2000, with little prospect that any jurisdiction will be able to bail out. In 1969 the Supreme Court recognized that the impact of the black vote could be deliberately reduced by a municipal annexation, the adoption of at-large voting, and other changes in the method of election. Now jurisdictions must abandon long-standing at-large methods of voting if an annexation prompted by economic considerations reduces the minority population (even by less than 1 percent), and in interpreting the amended section 2, courts often come close to condemning such voting as discriminatory per se. However legitimate is the concern that legislative seats not remain reserved for whites, judicial and administrative decisions too frequently suggest that only blacks can represent blacks, and that, for political purposes, race is a citizen's most important characteristic. We have crossed, as well, the line separating the appropriate use of Justice Department personnel, on the one hand, and reliance on the administrative process to sort out complicated issues of electoral equality that merit a full-scale trial, on the other. Finally, our sensitivity to the special significance of black officeholding in the South, where blacks were disfranchised before 1965, has shaded into a belief in the entitlement of black and Hispanic candidates everywhere to extraordinary protection from white competition.

In the preceding chapters I have tried to describe how and why these changes came about. It is a story of amendment through inadvertence, of minor tinkering with large consequences; of change precipitating change; of a skilled civil rights lobby working in a hospitable environment and blessed with both an opposition prone to self-inflicted wounds and extraordinary access to the chairman of a House subcommittee; of the slapdash, inattentive habits of Congress; of contradictory Supreme Court decisions; of a D.C. district court with a revisionist vision of the act, consistently asserting the right of racial and ethnic minorities to proportional representation; of the frequent application of a standard close to proportionality in the interpretation of section 2 as well; and of Department of Justice attorneys who invent law as they enforce it.

We have arrived at a point at which we need not stay. We need an alternative destination—a new consensus on the purpose of the act. Or, more precisely, on the multiple purposes of the act. Different provisions serve different ends, and power should be allocated accordingly.

My views on preclearance should be clear. Section 5 was intended to protect against purposeful discrimination and, beyond that, only against backsliding—attempts to undermine the effectiveness of the enfranchisement that other statutory provisions provided. That core notion need not be abandoned. Preclearance should still address only two questions: Does the proposed change manifest hostility to blacks and Hispanics as participants in the political process? If not, will the change nevertheless leave minority groups with fewer actual or potential legislative seats than they previously had? Has mandatory redistricting, for instance, been used as an occasion to lessen the impact of the black vote? Has an annexation significantly reduced the weight of Hispanic ballots? Minority officeholding is the measure of impact and weight, but only for section 5 purposes. The preclearance provision was founded on the assumption that, faced with the new and unwelcome prospect of blacks going to the polls, white racists in states that had denied basic Fifteenth Amendment rights might try to prevent blacks from actually gaining legislative seats. The provision provided a means to stop such action. Section 2, on the other hand, asks courts to address a much more complex issue: that of equal electoral opportunity. That question of electoral process cannot be answered by the standard of actual or potential result—the number of minorities actually in office or likely to gain seats.

Backsliding is a question appropriate to the administrative process; that of equal electoral opportunity is not. Adjudicating competing claims about racial fairness requires, as the Supreme Court has noted, an "intensely local appraisal"—the specific, detailed knowledge that only a court can obtain. Voting section procedures are no substitute for a trial. In fact, there is no surrogate for a court; the institution is sui generis.[10] In the internal memos that pass for argument within the Justice Department, no one speaks for the jurisdiction. A city undertaking an annexation will submit required material, but it may have no opportunity to challenge the evidence (perhaps hearsay) that minority or other contacts, often arbitrarily selected, provide. The forum is not judicious and the opinions are not judicial. A letter of objection seldom reveals the basis of decision; stock phrases substitute for close analysis.

In addition, to allow a process of federal administrative review to settle the broad and subtle question of equal electoral opportunity is to permit excessive intrusion upon constitutionally sanctioned local prerogatives. Section 5, by all accounts, is a drastic provision. The decision to alter the location of a polling place or to draw a district line along a natural boundary (such as a Louisiana bayou) is now subject to federal veto if discrimination is even suspected. The burden is on the jurisdiction to prove the racial neutrality of its action beyond any doubt. In other words, section 5 entails a radical shift in federal-state relations, originally sanctioned on an emergency basis and assumed to be of limited scope. That limited scope is critical to its continuing validity. A switch to single-member districts in Port Arthur, Texas, produced a city council with a disproportionately *large* number of minority councilmen; nevertheless, the plan was condemned because of the retention of a majority-vote requirement, on the ground that in some future election that requirement might contribute to a black candidate's defeat.[11] Yet the point of preclearance was not to ensure optimal electoral arrangements for minority candidates, but to stop an already suspect jurisdiction from taking steps to minimize the impact of the enfranchisement guaranteed by other provisions in the act. By dictating the rules of election procedure, a section 5 objection overrides decisions arrived at democratically. To do so, as in *Port Arthur*, on the basis of suspected continuing inequality—with that suspicion, in turn, resting on some unarticulated theory involving good government and racial justice—would seem to strain the bounds of constitutionality. Certainly the intrusiveness of such power strains the bounds of wisdom.

The previous chapter spelled out my views on section 2. The provision promises "political processes . . . equally open to participation" without regard to race, color, or language minority status. The breadth of the promise is actually somewhat misleading. Income and educational disparities alone may tip the balance of power in electoral contests to the side of whites. The effort to compensate for every potential source of inequality, however, can only lead to a covert system of reserved seats such as those India provides for its "scheduled castes." Congress settled, it might be said, for imperfect equality, lest inequality in a different form result.

The Senate Judiciary Committee and a key civil rights witness should be taken at their word. The Senate report distinguished between communities in which minority candidates receive substantial support from white voters and those in which "racial politics . . . dominate the electoral process." The former, the report stated, was the category into which "most communities" fell; by implication, the use of section 2 would be rare.[12] Armand Derfner, a distinguished civil rights attorney, stated at the 1982 hearings that there was no "precisely correct racial mix" in single-member districts. And with respect to an at-large system, the question before a court would not be whether, under an alternative system, minority voters would "get more or less." The issue would be "some versus nothing." Are city-wide elections providing blacks and Hispanics with "nothing"? Is the situation "frozen," or do minority voters have "some influence"? Claims of dilution rest, Derfner said, on "evidence that voters of a racial minority are isolated within a political system . . . 'shut out,' i.e. denied access . . . [without] the opportunity to participate in the electoral process." In labeling situations of "nothing" his sole concern, he implicitly acknowledged that protection against only partial exclusion implies a right to electoral arrangements that ensure maximum proportionality.[13]

Derfner offered no definition of total electoral exclusion except to say that the test had been met when a group had "really been unfairly throttled."[14] "Unfairly throttled" by racism, the Senate report made clear. Norman Dorsen, a professor of law at New York University, had tried to suggest that the new results test would "take the racism issue out of the criteria." "Well, Professor, that is what discrimination is all about, proving whether people are acting wrongfully because of or on account of race," Senator Hatch had replied.[15] Can there be any doubt that Hatch was right? Thomas C. McCain, the black chairman of the Democratic Party in Edgefield County, South Carolina, denied any intention to "indicate that persons in Edgefield County are racists." He explained that blacks had "just . . . not gotten the opportunity to participate."[16] It was a non sequitur. Exclusion on the basis of race can only be the consequence of racism; a county free of racists is a county open to blacks.

There is no doubt that where "racial politics . . . dominates the electoral process" and public office is largely reserved for whites, the method of voting should be restructured to promote minority officeholding. Safe black or Hispanic single-member districts hold white racism in check, limiting its influence. And where whites—and often blacks—regard skin color as a qualification for office (in part because no experience suggests otherwise), the election of blacks helps to break both white and black patterns of behavior. In the documentary film "Hands That Picked Cotton," a white store owner in a county supervisor race in Mississippi explains that he chose to run because he didn't want the job to get in the hands of the "wrong person," someone who couldn't manage money.[17] In such a setting, the lesson that blacks are not necessarily the wrong people, that money can be safe in black hands, is one that only experience can teach.

Pulling blacks into the political process where they have been excluded serves ends other than holding racists in check and heightening confidence in black political competence. Whether on a city council, on a county commission, or in the state legislature, blacks inhibit the expression of prejudice, act as spokesmen for black interests, dispense patronage, and often facilitate the discussion of topics (such as black crime) that whites are reluctant to raise. That is, governing bodies function differently when they are racially mixed, particularly where blacks are new to politics and where racially insensitive language and discrimination in the provision of services are long-established political habits.[18]

In fact, roads in white and black neighborhoods may be of comparable quality, and a public health facility used by blacks adequately funded, yet neither perceived as such. Blacks in office alter both reality and perception. Few would disagree that, in a heavily black southern city with a long history of police brutality, black confidence in the police force demands that it be integrated. The point applies in politics as well: where blacks have been long disfranchised and remain excluded from office, black confidence in government is in the public interest. Tom McCain, the first black since Reconstruction to run for office in Edgefield County, South Carolina, put the point this way: "There's an inherent value in officeholding that goes far beyond picking up the garbage. A race of people excluded from public office will always be second class. I know it, and the people who keep Edgefield County government all white know it."[19] Shared political power is integral to both respect and self-respect. A black politician in Jefferson County, Alabama, when questioned whether a white on the county commission who was sensitive to black needs would not adequately "represent" blacks, replied: "Having a white . . . who is supported by blacks wouldn't have cured that yearning for someone who is black."[20] It was the same point: the desire for citizenship without qualification, for respect and self-respect—the symbolic importance of blacks in positions of power in a county in which blacks still appear excluded from county office.

It might be said that blacks in *every* jurisdiction benefit from having their own in office. However, that is an argument not for federal intervention but for black political organization. "The extension of trust or 'friendship' beyond the family and of citizenship beyond race, ethnicity, and religion, is a significant political achievement," Michael Walzer has written. "I think," he adds, "we will want . . . to limit the ways in which group membership counts as a qualification for office, much as we limit the ways in which blood relationship counts, and for similar reasons."[21] In amending section 2, Congress unequivocally and wisely rejected the notion of group entitlement to even one legislative seat. Group membership counts as a qualification for office only where blacks and other minority citizens can prove themselves distinctively excluded from the electoral process. A maximum number of majority-black single-member districts is thus a remedy, not a right. That Norfolk, Virginia, could have guaranteed blacks more seats on the city council by substituting a ward plan for city-wide voting, as proposed by plaintiffs in a suit, did not impose an obligation upon the city to do so. The number of blacks likely to gain election under the ward plan did not set a standard against which the existing arrangement should have been measured. Only when black voters are "isolated" within the political system—only when the electoral process is distorted by racism—do they become entitled to single-member districts drawn to protect black candidates from white competition.[22] And, at that point, all counterarguments fade in importance. In defending its at-large method of voting, Jefferson County, Alabama, argued that its commission form of government was not only traditional but cost-effective, smooth-running, and efficient.[23] Yet Congress plainly valued minority officeholding in situations of exclusion above such considerations of good government.

I have argued that the Senate report and the testimony of Armand Derfner, a key civil rights witness at the 1982 hearings, properly focused the section 2 inquiry. Nevertheless, an implied trust in the political process left substantially to its own devices is not shared by most spokesmen for the civil rights organizations. They see America as too racially divided to sustain a political life that transcends color. They believe that minority representation means minority officeholding, that whites cannot represent blacks, and that blacks elected with white support have questionable credentials. In "Hands That Picked Cotton," a defeated black candidate says of his victorious black opponent: "He got all the white votes . . . Doc is not classified as black to me. You black when black folks elect you. White folks don't vote for black folks."

This is too bleak a picture, too hard a line, and it confuses the issues. The "two societies" argument rests on the fact of severe and continuing economic and other problems in the black community to which whites appear largely indifferent. But the appalling level of black teenage pregnancy is not an argument for creating a maximum number of 65 percent black districts. Racially mixed dinner parties may still be rare, but a mix of blacks, browns, and whites in politics is not. "To start and stop analyses on the assumption that race is all that matters," Harold Stanley has written, "distorts rather than delivers an understanding of southern politics."[24] The same can be said about northern politics. Not all whites are racists (whether in Boston or in Selma, Alabama), and whites vote for whites for reasons other than skin color. Personalities and issues divide the black community as well as the white. Most blacks who vote for whites are neither intimidated nor misguided. Furthermore, when blacks and Hispanics fail to vote, factors other than racist electoral obstacles are often at work. And when blacks and Hispanics do vote, they do not necessarily vote together; a black candidate cannot count on Hispanic support, or vice versa. Nonwhite groups, that is, are not interchangeable; categorizing citizens as either white or nonwhite distorts reality.

Charles Hamilton has argued that affirmative action goals and time-tables resulted from experience showing the inadequacy of good intentions.[25] But reliance on good intentions in the political sphere is by and large unnecessary. As a black scholar in Mississippi has remarked, "Racists . . . know how to count. No matter what you think of their past, many white politicians count the black vote."[26] Political necessity drove Dixiecrat politicians such as Strom Thurmond and George Wallace to seek black support, and the same pressures operate at every level of government in most jurisdictions with significant black populations. "I vote the same way a black would," a three-term white Democrat from a largely black New York district told a reporter.[27] These votes were political, not charitable. In Ernest J. Gaines's novel *A Gathering of Old*

*Men*, a lynch mob forms to take care of a black who has murdered a white. But the expected leader backs out, persuaded by two sons whose futures have come to rest with blacks as well as whites. "Those days are gone . . . The world has changed, Papa," one son says.[28] Especially in the South, "the world has changed"; in politics the conditions of success have permanently altered. There remain places, I have made clear, where only federal intervention will break the firm hold of whites on elected office. But black and Hispanic political exclusion in a "frozen" setting is now the exception, not the rule.

If a community of citizens is an unattainable ideal, and if blacks and Hispanics are represented only by one of their own, then aggressive federal action to restructure methods of voting to promote minority officeholding is appropriate. But if the logic of politics works for inclusion (once basic enfranchisement has been assured), then a lighter touch, a more hesitant intervention, is possible.

Why not err on the side of safety, though? Why risk the underprotection of historically oppressed groups? Because there is a dark side to affirmative action in the electoral sphere, as in others. I do not have in mind, needless to say, the defeat of whites who could win at-large, or in a differently constituted district, or with the benefit of a majority-vote requirement. Whites denied medical school admission as a consequence of minority preference have been arguably denied a right; those disadvantaged by a change in the electoral rules cannot make that claim. There are no "objective" criteria for elected office—no equivalent of the Medical College Aptitude Test. A white denied a seat on a city council cannot claim entitlement on the ground of "merit." In addition, safe black and Hispanic districts carry no stigma with respect to minority self-esteem. If it is true, as often contended, that whites and blacks alike suspect the ability of blacks promoted by affirmative action on a job, no comparable stigma attaches to election from a safe black district. Qualification for office is not measured by meritocratic standards in the customary sense.

At various points in this book I have touched upon the potential costs attached to maximizing minority officeholding. Perhaps most important is the danger that categorizing individuals for political purposes along lines of race and sanctioning group membership as a qualification for office may inhibit political integration. As James Blumstein argued at the 1982 Senate hearings, such categorization amounts to a racial "piece-of-the-action approach," perhaps freezing rather than thawing the previous system of racial politics.[29] The heightened sense of group membership works against that of common citizenship. And as Donald Horowitz pointed out at those same hearings, ethnic boundaries, by diminishing the sense of common citizenship, may "ultimately smother democratic choice and threaten democratic institutions."[30]

In V. S. Naipaul's splendid novel *The Suffrage of Elvira*, the following exchange takes place:

> "Lorkhoor going about telling people that they mustn't think about race and religion now. He say it ain't have nothing wrong if Hindu people vote for a Negro like Preacher."
>
> "This Lorkhoor want a good cut-arse," Baksh said.
>
> Chittaranjan agreed. "That sort of talk dangerous at election time. Lorkhoor ain't know what he saying."[31]

In fact, as Naipaul makes clear, Lorkhoor knew precisely what he was saying, and the game he was playing was one that his opponents were forced to engage in as well. Only the candidate who successfully reached across religious and ethnic lines could hope to win in that small multiethnic election district in Trinidad. Democratic politics (only four years old) was thus working to ameliorate interethnic conflict.[32]

The pressure for such interracial, interethnic coalitions lessens with the existence of single-member districts drawn to maximize minority officeholding. Political necessity brings groups together. The majority-white county, city, or district in which whites vote as a solid bloc against any minority candidate is now unusual. Especially in districts or localities with a substantial minority population, divisions among white voters send white candidates scurrying for those important black votes. The process not only enhances political integration but also may serve to heighten minority electoral influence. "For thirty years, the minority vote was the deciding vote in the [at-large] Anniston [Alabama] elections," a black former city councilman noted. "Now it has gerrymandered itself into a corner where it can't wield any power at all," he continued.[33] In city-wide elections, or in cities in which no districts are safe for either blacks or whites, blacks are often the swing vote in every election contest. A ward plan may sacrifice influence for guaranteed seats.

Candidates who have joined hands in a victorious biracial coalition will tend to stick together on a governing body, since the next election is never far off. But when whites on a city council or other legislative body owe nothing to black support, blacks in the minority may find themselves consistently outvoted and thus isolated. "I am bitterly opposed to any effort to resegregate me . . . ," a black judge in Norfolk, Virginia, testified at a voting rights trial. "How does it help the black community to limit itself to two predominantly black wards and be of no consequence in the remainder of the community? Political power is not merely symbolic."[34]

To emphasize the dark side of current affirmative action policy is too pessimistic a note on which to conclude. As President Lyndon Johnson stated in 1965, the Voting Rights Act flowed from a "clear and simple wrong."[35] At that time no one imagined that the statute would so quickly and effectively right that wrong. Eighteen years later, giving a sermon in Boston, Andrew Young recalled his fear when driving through Georgia in the early 1960s. "It was the worst place in the world," he said. "If someone had told me then that I would be a congressman in Georgia, an ambassador to the United Nations, and a mayor of Atlanta, what I would have replied cannot be said in a church."[36] Particularly in the South, the Voting Rights Act has radically altered politics. "Southern politics today is like the sprawling shopping mall that rises on a former tobacco field," one observer has noted. "The old lay of the land is still there, but the transformation has left it barely recognizable."[37] The 1965 act was the source of that transformation.

Public policy on voting rights has slipped across important lines. Yet, had the line been drawn at simple enfranchisement, it would have been unjustly placed. By 1969 it had become apparent that access to the polling booth would not everywhere prevent racism from distorting the electoral process, and seventeen years later that continues to be the case. Political power, as Judge Jordan pointed out in Norfolk, is not "merely symbolic." But, in Mobile, symbolic change was probably a necessary first step on the road to electoral equality. In Texas in 1981 some blacks voiced doubts about the wisdom of trading two Democratic congressional seats for one that would be black and one that would probably become Republican.[38] In another setting, however, the importance of a black in office would clearly outweigh the desirability of having an additional representative sympathetic to black concerns. Minority voting rights is a problem with no simple answers. And that is what makes the issue—central to the question of democratic representation—so compelling.

Appendix
Notes
Glossary
Indexes

---

# The Voting Rights Act

The following text reproduces verbatim sections 2 through 5 of the Voting Rights Act. Two versions of section 2 are included for comparison: the original 1965 version and the amended 1982 version. Also included is part of section 14, which defines the terms used in the act.

VOTING RIGHTS ACT OF 1965
(as amended through 1982)

AN ACT To enforce the fifteenth amendment to the Constitution
of the United States, and for other purposes.

*Be it enacted by the Senate and House of Representatives of the United States of America in Congress assembled,* That this Act shall be known as the "Voting Rights Act of 1965".

## TITLE 1   VOTING RIGHTS

SEC. 2 [1965]   No voting qualification or prerequisite to voting, or standard, practice, or procedure shall be imposed or applied by any State or political subdivision to deny or abridge the right of any citizen of the United States to vote on account of race or color. [Amended in 1975 to cover language minority groups.]

SEC. 2. [1982]   (a) No voting qualification or prerequisite to voting or standard, practice, or procedure shall be imposed or applied by any State or political subdivision in a manner which results in a denial or abridgement of the right of any citizen of the United States to vote on account of race or color, or in contravention of the guarantees set forth in section 4(f)(2), as provided in subsection (b).

(b) A violation of subsection (a) is established if, based on the totality of circumstances, it is shown that the political processes leading to nomination or election in the State or political subdivision are not equally open to participation by members of a class of citizens protected by subsection (a) in that its members have less opportunity than other members of the electorate to participate in the political process and to elect representatives of their choice. The extent to which members of a protected class have been elected to office in the State or political subdivision is one circumstance which may be considered: *Provided*, That nothing in this section establishes a right to have members of a protected class elected in numbers equal to their proportion in the population.

SEC. 3.    (a) Whenever the Attorney General or an aggrieved person institutes a proceeding under any statute to enforce the voting guarantees of the fourteenth or fifteenth amendment in any State or political subdivision the court shall authorize the appointment of Federal examiners by the Director of the Office of Personnel Management in accordance with section 6 to serve for such period of time for such political subdivisions as the court shall determine is appropriate to enforce the voting guarantees of the fourteenth or fifteenth amendment (1) as part of any interlocutory order if the court determines that the appointment of such examiners is necessary to enforce such voting guarantees or (2) as part of any final judgment if the court finds that violations of the fourteenth or fifteenth amendment justifying equitable relief have occurred in such State or subdivision: *Provided*, That the court need not authorize the appointment of examiners if any incidents of denial or abridgement of the right to vote on account of race or color, or in contravention of the guarantees set forth in section 4(f)(2) (1) have been few in number and have been promptly and effectively corrected by State or local action, (2) the continuing effect of such incidents has been eliminated, and (3) there is no reasonable probability of their recurrence in the future.

(b) If in a proceeding instituted by the Attorney General or an aggrieved person under any statute to enforce the voting guarantees of the fourteenth or fifteenth amendment in any State or political subdivision the court finds that a test or device has been used for the purpose or with the effect of denying or abridging the right of any citizen of the United States to vote on account of race or color, or in contravention of the guarantees set forth in section 4(f)(2), it shall suspend the use of tests and devices in such State or political subdivisions as the court shall determine is appropriate and for such period as it deems necessary.

(c) If in any proceeding instituted by the Attorney General or an aggrieved person under any statute to enforce the voting guarantees of the fourteenth or fifteenth amendment in any State or political subdivision the court finds that violations of the fourteenth or fifteenth amendment justifying equitable relief have occurred within the territory of such State or political subdivision, the court, in addition to such relief as it may grant, shall retain jurisdiction for such period as it may deem appropriate and during such period no voting qualification or prerequisite to voting, or standard, practice, or procedure with respect to voting different from that in force or effect at the time the proceeding was commenced shall be enforced unless and until the court finds that such qualification, prerequisite, standard, practice, or procedure does not have the purpose and will not have the effect of denying or abridging the right to vote on account of race or color, or in contravention of the guarantees set forth in section 4(f)(2): *Provided*, That such qualification, prerequisite, standard, practice, or procedure may be enforced if the qualification, prerequisite, standard, practice, or procedure has been submitted by the chief legal officer or other appropriate official of such

State or subdivision to the Attorney General and the Attorney General has not interposed an objection within sixty days after such submission, except that neither the court's finding nor the Attorney General's failure to object shall bar a subsequent action to enjoin enforcement of such qualification, prerequisite, standard, practice, or procedure.

*[Note: The following provision, section 4(a), is in effect only until August 5, 1984:]*

SEC. 4.   (a)  To assure that the right of citizens of the United States to vote is not denied or abridged on account of race or color, no citizen shall be denied the right to vote in any Federal, State, or local election because of his failure to comply with any test or device in any State with respect to which the determinations have been made under the first two sentences of subsection (b) or in any political subdivision with respect to which such determinations have been made as a separate unit, unless the United States District Court for the District of Columbia in an action for a declaratory judgment brought by such State or subdivision against the United States has determined that no such test or device has been used during the nineteen years preceding the filing of the action for the purpose or with the effect of denying or abridging the right to vote on account of race or color: *Provided,* That no such declaratory judgment shall issue with respect to any plaintiff for a period of nineteen years after the entry of a final judgment of any court of the United States, other than the denial of a declaratory judgment under this section, whether entered prior to or after the enactment of this Act, determining that denials or abridgements of the right to vote on account of race or color through the use of such tests or devices have occurred anywhere in the territory of such plaintiff. No citizen shall be denied the right to vote in any Federal, State, or local election because of his failure to comply with any test or device in any State with respect to which the determinations have been made under the third sentence of subsection (b) of this section or in any political subdivision with respect to which such determinations have been made as a separate unit, unless the United States District Court for the District of Columbia in an action for a declaratory judgment brought by such State or subdivision against the United States has determined that no such test or device has been used during the ten years preceding the filing of the action for the purpose or with the effect of denying or abridging the right to vote on account of race or color, or in contravention of the guarantees set forth in section 4(f)(2): *Provided,* That no such declaratory judgment shall issue with respect to any plaintiff for a period of ten years after the entry of a final judgment of any court of the United States, other than the denial of a declaratory judgment under this section, whether entered prior to or after the enactment of this paragraph, determining that denials or abridgements of the right to vote on account of race or color, or in contravention of the guarantees set forth in section 4(f)(2) through the use of tests or devices have occurred anywhere in the territory of such plaintiff.

An action pursuant to this subsection shall be heard and determined by a court of three judges in accordance with the provisions of section 2284 of title 28 of the United States Code and any appeal shall lie to the Supreme Court. The court shall retain jurisdiction of any action pursuant to this subsection for five years after judgment and shall reopen the action upon motion of the Attorney General alleging that a test or device has been used for the purpose or with the effect of denying or abridging the right to vote on account of race or color, or in contravention of the guarantees set forth in section 4(f)(2).

If the Attorney General determines that he has no reason to believe that any such test or device has been used during the nineteen years preceding the filing of an action under the first sentence of this subsection for the purpose or with the effect of denying or abridging the right to vote on account of race or color, he shall consent to the entry of such judgment.

If the Attorney General determines that he has no reason to believe that any such test or device has been used during the ten years preceding the filing of an action under the second sentence of this subsection for the purpose or with the effect of denying or abridging the right to vote on account of race or color, or in contravention of the guarantees set forth in section 4(f)(2) he shall consent to the entry of such judgment.

*[Note: The following provision, section 4(a), is effective on and after August 5, 1984:]*

SEC. 4.    (a)(1) To assure that the right of citizens of the United States to vote is not denied or abridged on account of race or color, no citizen shall be denied the right to vote in any Federal, State, or local election because of his failure to comply with any test or device in any State with respect to which the determinations have been made under the first two sentences of subsection (b) or in any political subdivision of such State (as such subdivision existed on the date such determinations were made with respect to such State), though such determinations were not made with respect to such subdivision as a separate unit, or in any political subdivision with respect to which such determinations have been made as a separate unit, unless the United States District Court for the District of Columbia issues a declaratory judgment under this section. No citizen shall be denied the right to vote in any Federal, State, or local election because of his failure to comply with any test or device in any State with respect to which the determinations have been made under the third sentence of subsection (b) of this section or in any political subdivision of such State (as such subdivision existed on the date such determinations were made with respect to such State), though such determinations were not made with respect to such subdivision as a separate unit, or in any political subdivision with respect to which such determinations have been made as a separate unit, unless the United States District Court for the District of Columbia issues a declaratory judgment under this section. A declaratory judgment under this section shall issue only if such court determines that during the ten years preceding the filing of the action, and during the pendency of such action—

(A) no such test or device has been used within such State or political subdivision for the purpose or with the effect of denying or abridging the right to vote on account of race or color or (in the case of a State or subdivision seeking a declaratory judgment under the second sentence of this subsection) in contravention of the guarantees of subsection (f)(2);

(B) no final judgment of any court of the United States, other than the denial of declaratory judgment under this section, has determined that denials or abridgements of the right to vote on account of race or color have occurred anywhere in the territory of such State or political subdivision or (in the case of a State or subdivision seeking a declaratory judgment under the second sentence of this subsection) that denials or abridgements of the right to vote in contravention of the guarantees of subsection (f)(2) have occurred anywhere in the territory of such State or subdivision and no consent decree, settlement, or agreement has been entered into resulting in any abandonment of a voting practice challenged on such grounds; and no declaratory judgment under this section shall be entered during the pendency of an action commenced before the filing of an action under this section and alleging such denials or abridgements of the right to vote;

(C) no Federal examiners under this Act have been assigned to such State or political subdivision;

(D) such State or political subdivision and all governmental units within its territory have complied with section 5 of this Act, including compliance with the requirement that no change covered by section 5 has been enforced without preclearance under section 5, and have repealed all changes covered by section 5 to which the Attorney General has successfully objected or as to which the United States District Court for the District of Columbia has denied a declaratory judgment;

(E) the Attorney General has not interposed any objection (that has not been overturned by a final judgment of a court) and no declaratory judgment has been denied under section 5, with respect to any submission by or on behalf of the plaintiff or any governmental unit within its territory under section 5, and no such submissions or declaratory judgment actions are pending; and

(F) such State or political subdivision and all governmental units within its territory—

(i) have eliminated voting procedures and methods of election which inhibit or dilute equal access to the electoral process;

(ii) have engaged in constructive efforts to eliminate intimidation and harassment of persons exercising rights protected under this Act; and

(iii) have engaged in other constructive efforts, such as expanded opportunity for convenient registration and voting for every person of voting age and the appointment of minority persons as election officials throughout the jurisdiction and at all stages of the election and registration process.

(2) To assist the court in determining whether to issue a declaratory judgment under this subsection, the plaintiff shall present evidence of minority participation, including evidence of the levels of minority group registration and voting, changes in such levels over time, and disparities between minority-group and non-minority-group participation.

(3) No declaratory judgment shall issue under this subsection with respect to such State or political subdivision if such plaintiff and governmental units within its territory have, during the period beginning ten years before the date the judgment is issued, engaged in violations of any provision of the Constitution or laws of the United States or any State or political subdivision with respect to discrimination in voting on account of race or color or (in the case of a State or subdivision seeking a

declaratory judgment under the second sentence of this subsection) in contravention of the guarantees of subsection (f)(2) unless the plaintiff establishes that any such violations were trivial, were promptly corrected, and were not repeated.

(4) The State or political subdivision bringing such action shall publicize the intended commencement and any proposed settlement of such action in the media serving such State or political subdivision and in appropriate United States post offices. Any aggrieved party may as of right intervene at any stage in such action.

(5) An action pursuant to this subsection shall be heard and determined by a court of three judges in accordance with the provisions of section 2284 of title 28 of the United States Code and any appeal shall lie to the Supreme Court. The court shall retain jurisdiction of any action pursuant to this subsection for ten years after judgment and shall reopen the action upon motion of the Attorney General or any aggrieved person alleging that conduct has occurred which, had that conduct occurred during the ten-year periods referred to in this subsection, would have precluded the issuance of a declaratory judgment under this subsection. The court, upon such reopening, shall vacate the declaratory judgment issued under this section if, after the issuance of such declaratory judgment, a final judgment against the State or subdivision with respect to which such declaratory judgment was issued, or against any governmental unit within that State or subdivision, determines that denials or abridgements of the right to vote on account of race or color have occurred anywhere in the territory of such State or political subdivision or (in the case of a State or subdivision which sought a declaratory judgment under the second sentence of this subsection) that denials or abridgements of the right to vote in contravention of the guarantees of subsection (f)(2) have occurred anywhere in the territory of such State or subdivision, or if, after the issuance of such declaratory judgment, a consent decree, settlement, or agreement has been entered into resulting in any abandonment of a voting practice challenged on such grounds.

(6) If, after two years from the date of the filing of a declaratory judgment under this subsection, no date has been set for a hearing in such action, and that delay has not been the result of an avoidable delay on the part of counsel for any party, the chief judge of the United States District Court for the District of Columbia may request the Judicial Council for the Circuit of the District of Columbia to provide the necessary judicial resources to expedite any action filed under this section. If such resources are unavailable within the circuit, the chief judge shall file a certificate of necessity in accordance with section 292(d) of title 28 of the United States Code.

(7) The Congress shall reconsider the provisions of this section at the end of the fifteen-year period following the effective date of the amendments made by the Voting Rights Act Amendments of 1982.

(8) The provisions of this section shall expire at the end of the twenty-five-year period following the effective date of the amendments made by the Voting Rights Act Amendments of 1982.

(9) Nothing in this section shall prohibit the Attorney General from consenting to an entry of judgment if based upon a showing of objective and compelling evidence by the plaintiff, and upon investigation, he is satisfied that the State or political subdivision has complied with the requirements of section 4(a)(1). Any aggrieved party may as of right intervene at any stage in such action.

(b) The provisions of subsection (a) shall apply in any State or in any political subdivision of a State which (1) the Attorney General determines maintained on November 1, 1964, any test or device, and with respect to which (2) the Director of the Census determines that less than 50 per centum of the persons of voting age residing therein were registered on November 1, 1964, or that less than 50 per centum of such persons voted in the presidential election of November 1964. On and after August 6, 1970, in addition to any State or political subdivision of a State determined to be subject to subsection (a) pursuant to the previous sentence, the provisions of subsection (a) shall apply in any State or any political subdivision of a State which (i) the Attorney General determines maintained on November 1, 1968, any test or device, and with respect to which (ii) the Director of the Census determines that less than 50 per centum of the persons of voting age residing therein were registered on November 1, 1968, or that less than 50 per centum of such persons voted in the presidential election of November 1968. On and after August 6, 1975, in addition to any State or political subdivision of a State determined to be subject to subsection (a) pursuant to the previous two sentences, the provisions of subsection (a) shall apply in any State or any political subdivision of a State which (i) the Attorney General determines maintained on November 1, 1972, any test or device, and with respect to which (ii) the Director of the Census determines that less than 50 per centum of the citizens of voting age were registered on November 1, 1972, or that less than 50 per centum of such persons voted in the presidential election of November 1972.

A determination or certification of the Attorney General or of the Director of the Census under this section or under section 6 or section 13 shall not be reviewable in any court and shall be effective upon publication in the Federal Register.

(c) The phrase "test or device" shall mean any requirement that a person as a prerequisite for voting or registration for voting (1) demonstrate the ability to read, write, understand, or interpret any matter, (2) demonstrate any educational achievement or his knowledge of any particular subject, (3) possess good moral character, or (4) prove his qualifications by the voucher of registered voters or members of any other class.

(d) For purposes of this section no State or political subdivision shall be determined to have engaged in the use of tests or devices for the purpose or with the effect of denying or abridging the right to vote on account of race or color, or in contravention of the guarantees set forth in section 4(f)(2) if (1) incidents of such use have been few in number and have been promptly and effectively corrected by State or local action, (2) the continuing effect of such incidents has been eliminated, and (3) there is no reasonable probability of their recurrence in the future.

(e)(1) Congress hereby declares that to secure the rights under the fourteenth amendment of persons educated in American-flag schools in which the predominant classroom language was other than English, it is necessary to prohibit the States from conditioning the right to vote of such persons on ability to read, write, understand, or interpret any matter in the English language.

(2) No person who demonstrates that he has successfully completed the sixth primary grade in a public school in, or a private school accredited by, any State or territory, the District of Columbia, or the Commonwealth of Puerto Rico in which the

predominant classroom language was other than English, shall be denied the right to vote in any Federal, State, or local election because of his inability to read, write, understand, or interpret any matter in the English language, except that in States in which State law provides that a different level of education is presumptive of literacy, he shall demonstrate that he has successfully completed an equivalent level of education in a public school in, or a private school accredited by, any State or territory, the District of Columbia, or the Commonwealth of Puerto Rico in which the predominant classroom language was other than English.

(f)(1) The Congress finds that voting discrimination against citizens of language minorities is pervasive and national in scope. Such minority citizens are from environments in which the dominant language is other than English. In addition they have been denied equal educational opportunities by State and local governments, resulting in severe disabilities and continuing illiteracy in the English language. The Congress further finds that, where State and local officials conduct elections only in English, language minority citizens are excluded from participating in the electoral process. In many areas of the country, this exclusion is aggravated by acts of physical, economic, and political intimidation. The Congress declares that, in order to enforce the guarantees of the fourteenth and fifteenth amendments to the United States Constitution, it is necessary to eliminate such discrimination by prohibiting English-only elections, and by prescribing other remedial devices.

(2) No voting qualification or prerequisite to voting, or standard, practice, or procedure shall be imposed or applied by any State or political subdivision to deny or abridge the right of any citizen of the United States to vote because he is a member of a language minority group.

(3) In addition to the meaning given the term under section 4(c), the term "test or device" shall also mean any practice or requirement by which any State or political subdivision provided any registration or voting notices, forms, instructions, assistance, or other materials or information relating to the electoral process, including ballots, only in the English language, where the Director of the Census determines that more than five per centum of the citizens of voting age residing in such State or political subdivision are members of a single language minority. With respect to section 4(b), the term "test or device", as defined in this subsection, shall be employed only in making the determinations under the third sentence of that subsection.

(4) Whenever any State or political subdivision subject to the prohibitions of the second sentence of section 4(a) provides any registration or voting notices, forms, instructions, assistance, or other materials or information relating to the electoral process, including ballots, it shall provide them in the language of the applicable language minority group as well as in the English language: *Provided,* That where the language of the applicable minority group is oral or unwritten or in the case of Alaskan Natives and American Indians, if the predominant language is historically unwritten, the State or political subdivision is only required to furnish oral instructions, assistance, or other information relating to registration and voting.

SEC. 5. Whenever a State or political subdivision with respect to which the prohibitions set forth in section 4(a) based upon determinations made under the first sentence of section 4(b) are in effect shall enact or seek to administer any voting qualification or prerequisite to voting, or standard, practice, or procedure with respect to voting different from that in force or effect on November 1, 1964, or whenever a State or political subdivision with respect to which the prohibitions set forth in section 4(a) based upon determinations made under the second sentence of section 4(b) are in effect shall enact or seek to administer any voting qualification or prerequisite to voting, or standard, practice, or procedure with respect to voting different from that in force or effect on November 1, 1968, or whenever a State or political subdivision with respect to which the prohibitions set forth in section 4(a) based upon determinations made under the third sentence of section 4(b) are in effect shall enact or seek to administer any voting qualification or prerequisite to voting, or standard, practice, or procedure with respect to voting different from that in force or effect on November 1, 1972, such State or subdivision may institute an action in the United States District Court for the District of Columbia for a declaratory judgment that such qualification, prerequisite, standard, practice, or procedure does not have the purpose and will not have the effect of denying or abridging the right to vote on account of race or color, or in contravention of the guarantees set forth in section 4(f)(2), and unless and until the court enters such judgment no person shall be denied the right to vote for failure to comply with such qualification, prerequisite, standard, practice, or procedure: *Provided*, That such qualification, prerequisite, standard, practice, or procedure may be enforced without such proceeding if the qualification, prerequisite, standard, practice, or procedure has been submitted by the chief legal officer or other appropriate official of such State or subdivision to the Attorney General and the Attorney General has not interposed an objection within sixty days after such submission, or upon good cause shown, to facilitate an expedited approval within sixty days after such submission, the Attorney General has affirmatively indicated that such objection will not be made. Neither an affirmative indication by the Attorney General that no objection will be made, nor the Attorney General's failure to object, nor a declaratory judgment entered under this section shall bar a subsequent action to enjoin enforcement of such qualification, prerequisite, standard, practice, or procedure. In the event the Attorney General affirmatively indicates that no objection will be made within the sixty-day period following receipt of a submission, the Attorney General may reserve the right to reexamine the submission if additional information comes to his attention during the remainder of the sixty-day period which would otherwise require objection in accordance with this section. Any action under this section shall be heard and determined by a court of three judges in accordance with the provisions of section 2284 of title 28 of the United States Code and any appeal shall lie to the Supreme Court.

SEC. 14. (a) All cases of criminal contempt arising under the provisions of this Act shall be governed by section 151 of the Civil Rights Act of 1957 (42 U.S.C. 1995).

(b) No court other than the District Court for the District of Columbia or a court of appeals in any proceeding under section 9 shall have jurisdiction to issue any declaratory judgment pursuant to section 4 or section 5 or any restraining order or temporary or permanent injunction against the execution or enforcement of any provision of this Act or any action of any Federal officer or employee pursuant hereto.

(c)(1) The terms "vote" or "voting" shall include all action necessary to make a vote effective in any primary, special, or general election, including, but not limited to, registration, listing pursuant to this Act, or other action required by law prerequisite to voting, casting a ballot, and having such a ballot counted properly and included in the appropriate totals of votes cast with respect to candidates for public or party office and propositions for which votes are received in an election.

(2) The term "political subdivision" shall mean any county or parish, except that where registration for voting is not conducted under the supervision of a county or parish, the term shall include any other subdivision of a State which conducts registration for voting.

(3) The term "language minorities" or "language minority group" means persons who are American Indian, Asian American, Alaskan Natives or of Spanish heritage.

# Notes

## Introduction

1. Marshall Frady's comment was made in the course of a talk given at the Nieman Foundation, Harvard University, November 3, 1981. Frady actually does tell the story of Johnny Ford in *Southerners: A Journalist's Odyssey* (New York: New American Library, 1980), pp. 261–278.

2. U.S. Commission on Civil Rights, *The Voting Rights Act: Ten Years After* (Washington, D.C., January 1975), table 3, p. 43. U.S. Department of Commerce, *Statistical Abstract of the United States, 1970* (Washington, D.C., 1970), p. 369. It should be noted that estimates of black registration and turnout prior to the passage of the Voting Rights Act vary widely. Figures are drawn from unofficial estimates by county personnel, the Department of Justice, the Voter Education Project, and other unofficial sources. Only Louisiana kept official data on registration by race in 1965. Pre-act progress was greatest in the large cities, least in rural areas, particularly those with a high percentage of blacks.

3. Steven F. Lawson, *Black Ballots: Voting Rights in the South, 1944–1969* (New York: Columbia University Press, 1976), p. 330.

4. United States Commission on Civil Rights, *Political Participation* (Washington, D.C., May 1968), Appendix VII, p. 223.

5. For the pre-act estimate, see U.S. Commission on Civil Rights, *Political Participation*, p.15. For figures for later years see U.S. Commission on Civil Rights, *The Voting Rights Act: Ten Years After*, pp. 48–52; U.S. Commission on Civil Rights, *The Voting Rights Act: Unfulfilled Goals* (Washington, D.C., September 1981), pp. 11–21. My 1980 figure is from *Black Elected Officials: A National Roster* (Washington, D.C.: Joint Center for Political Studies, 1980). My figure, it is important to note, is for the covered states of the South only—the states covered in 1965 by the special provisions of the Voting Rights Act. They are: Alabama, Georgia, Louisiana, Mississippi, North Carolina, South Carolina, and Virginia. North Carolina was not covered in its entirety, but for the sake of simplicity I have treated it as such. The raw numbers alone do not tell the story, of course. More than 1,800

black dog-catchers and county sheriffs would not signify impressive gains; black mayors, state representatives, and congressmen do.

6. The advertisement was the work of the Get Out To Vote Committee in Mobile, Alabama, and the election was on August 4, 1981.

7. The quotation on Senator Hollings is taken from a confidential interview. On Senator Thurmond's history, see Jack Bass and Walter De Vries, *The Transformation of Southern Politics: Social Change and Political Consequence since 1945* (New York: New American Library, 1977), pp. 253, 271–272; *Wall Street Journal*, 2 October 1978, pp. 1, 4.

8. Robert Clark was the candidate.

9. The decision was *Allen v. State Board of Elections*, 393 U.S. 544 (1969), discussed at length in Chapter 1.

10. Michael Walzer, *Spheres of Justice: A Defense of Pluralism and Equality* (New York: Basic Books, 1983), p. 15

11. *Colegrove v. Green*, 328 U.S. 549, 556 (1946).


## 1. The First Five Years

1. Carl M. Brauer, *John F. Kennedy and the Second Reconstruction* (New York: Columbia University Press, 1977), pp. 118–119.

2. John Doar and Dorothy Landsberg, "The Performance of the FBI in Investigating Violations of Federal Law Protecting the Right to Vote—1960 to 1967" (photocopy, copyright 1971), pp. 17–17a, quoted in Brauer, *John F. Kennedy*, p. 118.

3. Arthur M. Schlesinger, Jr., *Robert Kennedy and His Times* (Boston: Houghton Mifflin, 1978), p. 301.

4. Brauer, *John F. Kennedy*, p. 119.

5. U.S. Commission on Civil Rights, *Voting* (Washington, D.C., 1961), pp. 104–112, 252–307.

6. Schlesinger, *Robert Kennedy*, p. 209.

7. Ibid., p. 301.

8. Clayborne Carson, *In Struggle: SNCC and the Black Awakening of the 1960s* (Cambridge, Mass.: Harvard University Press, 1981), p. 154.

9. The conviction that the pressure from the Kennedy administration to concentrate on voting rights constituted an attempt to "kill the Movement . . . by rechanneling its energies" is discussed in Schlesinger, *Robert Kennedy*, pp. 301–302; Brauer, *John F. Kennedy*, p. 114; Carson, *In Struggle*, p. 39; Harris Wofford, *Of Kennedys and Kings; Making Sense of the Sixties* (New York: Farrar, Straus, Giroux, 1980), pp. 158–159.

10. The June 1961 meeting is described by a number of historians. See, for instance, Schlesinger, *Robert Kennedy*, pp. 301–302; Brauer, *John F. Kennedy*, p. 116; Carson, *In Struggle*, p. 39.

11. Carson, *In Struggle*, pp. 47–50.

12. V. O. Key, *Southern Politics in State and Nation* (New York: Alfred A. Knopf, 1950), p. 649.

13. Lecture by Maynard Jackson, February 25, 1983, Harvard University. It was the second lecture in a series of five on "Black Ballots and Southern Politics."

14. "In Southern Voting, It's Still 'White Only,' " *Atlanta Constitution*, 7 December 1980, reprinted in Hearings before the Subcommittee on Civil and Constitutional Rights of the Committee on the Judiciary, U.S. House of Representatives, 97th Congress, 1st session on Extension of the Voting Rights Act, May-July 1981, p. 280.

15. *The Shameful Blight: The Survival of Racial Discrimination in Voting in the South*, a report of the Washington Research Project (November 1972), p. 2.

16. Ibid.

17. *South Carolina v. Katzenbach*, 383 U.S. 301, 315 (1966).

18. Hearings before the Subcommittee on Civil and Constitutional Rights of the Committee on the Judiciary, U.S. House of Representatives, 94th Congress, 1st session on H.R. 939, 2148, and 3501, Extension of the Voting Rights Act, February-March 1975 (hereafter cited as 1975 House hearings), statement by J. Stanley Pottinger, assistant attorney general for civil rights, p. 167.

19. Key, *Southern Politics*, p. 576.

20. Bernard Taper, *Gomillion versus Lightfoot: The Tuskegee Gerrymander Case* (New York: McGraw-Hill, 1962), p. 68.

21. 1975 House hearings, statement of Peter Rodino, p. 6.

22. *Lassiter v. Northampton County Board of Elections*, 360 U.S. 45 (1959).

23. 1975 House hearings, p. 321.

24. Steven F. Lawson, *Black Ballots: Voting Rights in the South, 1944–1969* (New York: Columbia University Press, 1976), pp. 329–330.

25. U.S. Commission on Civil Rights, *The Voting Rights Act: Ten Years After* (Washington, D.C., 1975), p. 43.

26. Hearings before Subcommittee No. 5 of the Committee on the Judiciary, U.S. House of Representatives, 89th Congress, 1st session on H.R. 6400 and other proposals to enforce the Fifteenth Amendment to the Constitution of the United States, March-April 1965 (hereafter cited as 1965 House hearings), p. 17.

27. Ibid., p. 21.

28. *South Carolina v. Katzenbach*, 383 U.S. 301, 308–309 (1966).

29. 383 U.S. at 358.

30. Report of the Committee on the Judiciary, Report No. 439 ("The Voting Rights Act of 1965"), U.S. House of Representatives, 89th Congress, 1st session (hereafter cited as 1965 House report), Republican views, p. 45.

31. *Wall Street Journal*, 22 March 1965, quoted in 1965 House report, views of William M. Tuck, p. 74.

32. 1965 House report, p. 74.

33. Hearings before the Committee on the Judiciary, U.S. Senate, 89th Congress, 1st session on S. 1564 to enforce the Fifteenth Amendment to the Constitution of the United States, March-April 1965, p. 43.

34. 1965 House report, p. 74.

35. 1965 House hearings, p. 60.

36. Ibid., p. 379.

37. Ibid., p. 411.

38. Ibid., p. 456.

39. 1965 House report, p. 26.

40. 1965 House hearings, p. 399.

41. *Allen v. State Board of Elections*, 393 U.S. 544 (1969).

42. *Sellers v. Trussell*, 253 F. Supp. 915 (M.D. Ala., 1966).

43. Thus in 1966 no covered jurisdictions except South Carolina and Georgia submitted changes for preclearance, and while South Carolina submitted 25, Georgia submitted only one. In 1967 South Carolina submitted 52 changes for review, and it was the only state to submit any. It 1968 it was joined by Georgia. Department of Justice tabulations, reprinted, among other places, in the 1975 House hearings, pp. 182–185. The tables provided indicate the number and type of objections by year, as well.

44. 393 U.S. at 565.

45. 393 U.S. at 564.

46. 393 U.S. at 568. Justice Warren was quoting Attorney General Nicholas Katzenbach in the 1965 House hearings, p. 65.

47. 393 U.S. at 569.

48. U.S. Commission on Civil Rights, *Political Participation: A Study of the Participation by Negroes in the Elections and Political Processes in 10 Southern States since Passage of the Voting Rights Act of 1965* (Washington, D.C., May 1968), pp. 22–23.

49. 393 U.S. at 584 (opinion of Justice Harlan).

50. 393 U.S. at 584.

51. 393 U.S. at 589.

52. 393 U.S. at 584.

53. 393 U.S. at 585.

54. That the burden of proof was on the jurisdiction had not actually been written into the act, but has been inferred from the legislative history. The question, however, was not fully settled until 1971, at the time when the first guidelines for enforcing the preclearance provision were proposed. The Nixon administration wanted to object to changes in electoral method only when they clearly had a discriminatory purpose or effect. The U.S. Commission on Civil Rights was adamant in its opposition to the Department of Justice on this issue, and liberals in Congress organized to pressure the administration to adopt the Commission's view. See Steven F. Lawson, *In Pursuit of Power: Southern Blacks and Electoral Politics, 1965–1982* (New York: Columbia University Press, 1985), pp. 168–172. The logic had been explained in 1969 by Representative McCulloch, the ranking minority member of the House Judiciary Committee. "As in tort law," he said, "when circumstances give rise to an inference that there has been misconduct, the party that has access to the facts is called upon to rebut the inference and show that its conduct was proper." (115 Cong. Rec. 38486, Dec. 11, 1969.) Senator Fong, four months later, made basically the same point. "Those who know the law or procedure best and what motivated its passage," he noted, "must come forward and explain it." (116 Cong. Rec. 6154, March 5, 1970.) In *South Carolina v. Katzenbach*, the Supreme Court had sanctioned placing "the burden of proof on the areas seeking relief." (383 U.S. at

335.) After 1971 the matter was closed. Thus in 1975 the assistant attorney general for civil rights testified that "some of the Attorney General's objections under Section 5 are based primarily on the submitting authorities' failure to carry [their] burden [of proof]." (1975 House hearings, p. 171.) That objections were frequently to changes of uncertain impact was thus readily acknowledged.

55. 395 U.S. 285 (1969).
56. *Gaston County v. United States*, 288 F. Supp. 678 (1968).
57. 288 F. Supp. at 693 (Judge Gasch, concurring).
58. 395 U.S. at 296.
59. Lawson, *In Pursuit of Power*, p. 194.

## 2. Inadvertent Gains

1. *New York Times*, 15 March 1970, sec. IV, p. 2 (John W. Finney, "The Senate Holds Firm on Voting Rights in the South").

2. *New York Times*, 11 June 1969, p. 18. Nixon's southern strategy is described in Steven F. Lawson, *In Pursuit of Power: Southern Blacks and Electoral Politics, 1965–1982* (New York: Columbia University Press, 1985), pp. 121–124.

3. *New York Times*, 14 December 1969, sec. IV, p. 2. The statement was made by Abner Mikva (D-Ill.).

4. *New York Times*, 2 July 1969, p. 20. McCulloch's disagreement with the White House, it should be noted, could not have come as a surprise to the administration; he had been a steadfast supporter of civil rights legislation.

5. *New York Times*, 28 June 1969, p. 12; also 27 June 1969, p. 16 (column by Max Frankel).

6. *New York Times*, 12 December 1969, p. 1. Clarence Mitchell called it a "cataclysmic defeat."

7. There were two additional amendments, though not relevant here: the 18-year-old vote (later struck down as unconstitutional and revived as a constitutional amendment), and abolition of residency requirements for voting for President and Vice-President.

8. The jurisdictions newly covered as a consequence of the 1970 amendments were the following: four districts in Alaska, eight counties in Arizona, two counties in California, three counties in Connecticut, one county in Idaho, ten towns in New Hampshire, three counties in New York, eighteen towns in Maine, nine towns in Massachusetts, and one county in Wyoming.

9. Statement by the Attorney General before the House Judiciary Subcommittee on Civil and Constitutional Rights, July 1, 1969, reported in the *New York Times*, 2 July 1969, p. 20.

10. *New York Times*, 2 July 1969, p. 20.

11. *New York Times*, 2 July 1969, p. 26. The *Times* is quoting from the Attorney General's testimony before House Subcommittee No. 5.

12. Hearings before Subcommittee No. 5 of the Committee on the Judiciary, U.S. House of Representatives, 91st Congress, 1st session, on H.R. 4249, H.R.

5538, and Similar Proposals to Extend the Voting Rights Act of 1965 with Respect to the Discriminatory Use of Tests and Devices, May-July 1969 (hereafter cited as 1969 House hearings), p. 243.

13. *New York Times*, 20 June 1969, p. 23.

14. *New York Times*, 12 July 1969, p. 13.

15. *New York Times*, editorial, 28 June 1969, p. 20.

16. *New York Times*, editorial, 14 March 1970, p. 30. Lawson, *In Pursuit of Power*, p. 134, argues that the liberals were simply concerned that a flat ban on literacy tests might lead to a congressional fray that would result in an expiration of the special provisions by default. Moreover, they were suspicious of any proposal emanating from the White House. My own view, as the text makes clear, is that civil rights spokesmen at the time viewed such a ban as an emergency measure, inappropriate in the North. There were dissenting voices within the liberal community, it should be noted; the U.S. Commission on Civil Rights was not opposed to the nationwide ban.

17. *New York Times*, 11 March 1970, p. 21.

18. *New York Times*, editorial, 12 March 1970, p. 40. For further details on liberal opposition to the use of the 1968 turnout figures, see Lawson, *In Pursuit of Power*, pp. 150–151.

19. It can be argued that, in fact, there were two extraneous provisions. Puerto Ricans educated in American-flag schools in which the predominant classroom language was other than English could not be barred from voting by a literacy test in English. In addition, the Attorney General and the Secretary of Defense were ordered to study the question of vote discrimination involving citizens serving in the armed forces. The statute, however, is unusually long and complex, and these minor provisions do not, in my view, suggest the inaccuracy of my basic point.

20. *Torres v. Sachs*, 381 F. Supp. 309 (S.D. N.Y. 1984). It should be noted that a certain number of counties that could have bailed out did not, simply because of inertia. There were New Hampshire counties, for instance, in which voter turnout had fallen below the 50-percent mark in 1968, but which had no significant minority populations on the basis of which they could have been kept under coverage had they sued to bail out.

21. Hearings before the Subcommittee on Constitutional Rights of the Committee on the Judiciary, U.S. Senate, 91st Congress, 1st and 2nd sessions, on S. 818, S. 2456, S. 2507, and Title IV of S. 2029, Bills to Amend the Voting Rights Act of 1965 (July 1969 and February 1970), p. 2.

## 3. The Mexican-American Connection

1. Hearings before the Subcommittee on Civil and Constitutional Rights of the Committee on the Judiciary, U.S. House of Representatives, 94th Congress, 1st session, on H.R. 939, H.R. 2148, H.R. 3247, and H.R. 3501, Extension of the Voting Rights Act, February-March 1975 (hereafter cited as 1975 House hearings), statement of Arthur S. Flemming, p. 26.

2. Hearings before the Subcommittee on Constitutional Rights of the Commit-

tee on the Judiciary, U.S. Senate, 94th Congress, 1st session, on S. 407, S. 903, S. 1297, S. 1409, and S. 1443, Extension of the Voting Rights Act, April-May 1975 (hereafter cited as 1975 Senate hearings), p. 131.

3. 1975 House hearings, p. 32. These were figures supplied by the Voter Education Project and initially published in U.S. Commission on Civil Rights, *The Voting Rights Act: Ten Years After* (Washington, D.C., 1975), p. 53.

4. 1975 House hearings, p. 169.

5. U.S. Department of Justice, Office of the Attorney General, "Procedures for the Administration of Section 5 of the Voting Rights Act of 1965," 28 CFR part 51 (1971).

6. See *Perkins v. Matthews*, 400 U.S. 379 (1970), holding annexations to be changes in "voting" procedure requiring preclearance in covered jurisdictions.

7. "Number of Changes Submitted under Section 5 and Reviewed by Department of Justice, by Type and Year, 1965–September 30, 1981," Attachments to the statement of William Bradford Reynolds, assistant attorney general for civil rights, Attachment C-2, Hearings before the Subcommittee on the Constitution on the Voting Rights Act, U.S. Senate, 97th Congress, 2nd session on S. 53, S. 1761, S. 1975, S. 1992, and H.R. 3112, Bills to Amend the Voting Rights Act of 1965, January-March 1982, p. 1744.

8. 1975 Senate hearings, p. 38.

9. Ibid., p. 162.

10. 1975 House hearings, pp. 23, 26.

11. Thus Senator Birch Bayh said, "The right to vote is fine. It reaches its full value when it is expressed in such a way that people actually are in the seat of power" (1975 Senate hearings, p. 41). Arthur Flemming referred to the process of "full enfranchisement" (ibid., p. 74). Howard A. Glickstein testified that the "Voting Rights Act was a giant step forward toward the goal of full enfranchisement," but that "we have not yet reached it" (ibid., p. 219). Representative Edward Roybal of California defined the issue in 1975 as "the right of a people to cast a meaningful and effective vote" (ibid., p. 256). Mark White, secretary of state for Texas, assured the committee that "we believe, as you do, that the right to an effective vote should be afforded to every citizen in the Nation" (ibid., p. 271). The list could obviously be extended and the examples multiplied, but the point should be clear.

12. 1975 Senate hearings, p. 45.

13. 1975 Senate hearings, p. 3.

14. Report No. 94-196, "Voting Rights Act Extension," Committee on the Judiciary, U.S. House of Representatives, 94th Congress, 1st session, May 8, 1975 (hereafter cited as House Judiciary Committee report), p. 7.

15. 1975 House hearings, testimony of Armand Derfner, p. 635. Emphasis added.

16. The literature on electoral structures and minority representation is extensive. A good place to begin is with Albert K. Karnig and Susan Welch, *Black Representation and Urban Policy* (Chicago: University of Chicago Press, 1980).

17. Steven F. Lawson, *In Pursuit of Power: Southern Blacks and Electoral Politics, 1965–1982* (New York: Columbia University Press, 1985), p. 227. See, as well, the reference in the 1975 Senate hearings by Clarence Mitchell (director of the

Washington bureau of the NAACP) to early 1974 as the time when the problem of renewal began to be addressed. "We started working on renewal last spring—maybe as early as January, 1974," he was quoted as saying in the *Washington Post* (March 10, 1975). 1975 Senate hearings, pp. 48, 188.

18. This account is based in substantial part on confidential interviews with members of the civil rights groups who participated in the negotiations at the time. Quoted participants who are not identified preferred to remain anonymous.

19. Confidential interview, May 1981.

20. Ibid.

21. 1975 Senate hearings, pp. 698, 700. The memorandum was reprinted in the hearings as one of several exhibits submitted by J. Stanley Pottinger, assistant attorney general for civil rights. The 1921 figures were used because they were the ones supplied by the *Encyclopaedia Britannica* (1971 edition, vol. 15, p. 329), on which the Justice Department analysis relied.

22. The solution was lifted from the decision in *Torres v. Sachs*, 381 F. Supp. 309 (S.D. N.Y. 1974), which reinstated coverage over the three New York counties that had successfully bailed out in April 1972. English-only ballots were a literacy test, the court had held. In fact, there was nothing in the legislative history prior to 1975 to justify this holding. At the 1975 hearings, however, witnesses frequently equated literacy tests and ballots in English. See, for example, the memorandum submitted by David Tatel et al., 1975 Senate hearings, p. 779: "The effect of an English-only election on a Spanish-speaking voter is the same as a literacy test." Such witnesses neglected to point out that literacy tests, per se, were not prohibited—that it was only their fraudulent use in the hands of southern racists determined to keep the voter rolls white that made them suspect. By analogy, the English-only ballot was not discriminatory per se; it would become so only if it were being used intentionally to keep Hispanics away from the polls.

23. 1975 Senate hearings, p. 237.

24. Ibid., p. 536.

25. File, Charleston, South Carolina, Department of Justice, voting section.

26. In fact, as early as 1971–1972, in the seven states covered by the Voting Rights Act there were 8,767,138 whites and 2,142,925 blacks registered. U.S. Commission on Civil Rights, *The Voting Rights Act: Ten Years After* (Washington, D.C., January 1975), table 7, p. 53.

27. Confidential interview, May 1981. Fannie Lou Hamer was the youngest of a black Mississippi sharecropper's twenty children, and had been kicked off a plantation where she worked after trying to register to vote. She had been severely beaten in a police station after seeking service at a bus-station lunch counter, an experience that she described, with great eloquence, at the 1964 Democratic Party Convention in Atlantic City, to which she came as a delegate of the Mississippi Freedom Democratic Party, formed by civil rights groups in response to the exclusion of blacks from the regular Democratic organization in Mississippi. Her testimony, carried live over national television, stirred the party and the nation.

28. 1975 Senate hearings, p. 762.

29. Ibid., p. 764 (emphasis added).

30. Confidential interview, May 1981.

31. 1975 Senate hearings, p. 60.

32. U.S. Commission on Civil Rights, Staff Memorandum, "Expansion of the Coverage of the Voting Rights Act," June 5, 1975, p. 47.

33. 1975 House hearings, p. 294.

34. 1975 Senate hearings, pp. 543–544. Emphasis added.

35. Clifton McCleskey and Bruce Merrill, "Mexican American Political Behavior in Texas," *Social Science Quarterly*, 53 (March 1973), 785–798; O. Douglas Weeks, "The Texas-Mexican and the Politics of South Texas," *American Political Science Review*, 24 (August 1930), 606–627.

36. The list of charges with respect to electoral discrimination against Mexican-Americans has been compiled from the testimony of witnesses who appeared at the congressional hearings.

37. Confidential interview, May 1981.

38. Likewise, in the eleven cities with a Mexican-American voting-age population of over 58 percent, more than half the city council seats were occupied by Mexican-Americans, even though Mexican-American registration was disproportionately low in relation to population. In one of the counties named as a trouble spot, 75 percent of the commissioners were Hispanic, which precisely reflected the Mexican-American population strength. I base these calculations on tables contained in the June 1975 U.S. Commission on Civil Rights Staff Memorandum, pp. 10–11, 13–14.

39. 1975 Senate hearings, pp. 218, 295–296, 305, 308, 312, 314, 326–328, 330, 354.

40. House Judiciary Committee Report, p. 30.

41. Report No. 94-295, Voting Rights Act Extension, Committee on the Judiciary, U.S. Senate, 94th Congress, 1st session (July 22, 1975), p. 24.

42. House Judiciary Committee Report, p. 18.

43. House Judiciary Committee Report, p. 19. "These structures effectively *deny* Mexican-American and black voters in Texas political access," the report said. Emphasis added.

44. See *City of Petersburg v. U.S.*, 354 F. Supp. 1021 (D.D.C. 1972), aff'd, 410 U.S. 962 (1973) and *City of Richmond v. U.S.*, 422 U.S. 358 (1975).

45. Subsequent to 1982, the ground upon which suits challenging long-standing methods of voting rested became the amended section 2, rather than the Fourteenth and Fifteenth Amendments. See Chapters 5 and 6.

46. McCleskey and Merrill, "Mexican American Political Behavior," p. 786, n. 5, relying on an unpublished study by Jose Angel Gutierrez.

47. 1975 Senate hearings, prepared statement of George Korbel, pp. 467, 477.

48. Harry P. Pachon, "Political Mobilization in the Mexican-American Community," in *Mexican-Americans in Comparative Perspective*, ed. Walker Connor (Washington, D.C.: The Urban Institute Press, 1985), p. 247.

49. Leo Grebler, Joan W. Moore, and Ralph Guzman, *The Mexican-American People* (Glencoe, Ill.: The Free Press, 1970), p. 569.

50. Pachon, "Political Mobilization," p. 251. See also Harry P. Pachon and Joan W. Moore, "Mexican-Americans," *The Annals of the American Academy of Political and Social Science*, 454 (March 1981), 112–113. "Color differences," Pachon and

Moore note, "do not hurt Mexican-Americans as much as black Americans. As a result, Mexican-Americans have experienced a situation in which acceptable Chicanos, on a selective basis, 'have escaped from the barrio and assimilated into Anglo middle-class communities, attended Anglo schools and shared in the dominant culture' " (p. 112, quoting Alphonso Pinkey, "Prejudice toward Mexican and Negro Americans: A Comparison," in *Mexican Americans in the United States: A Reader*, ed. John Burma, Cambridge, Mass.: Schenkman, 1970).

51. On the point that whites are generally more receptive to Mexican-Americans than to blacks, see George Antunes and Charles M. Gaitz, "Ethnicity and Participation: A Study of Mexican-Americans, Blacks, and Whites," *American Journal of Sociology*, 80 (March 1975), 1205–1206. Antunes and Gaitz found, for instance, that only 8.4 percent of whites were willing to admit blacks into their family through marriage, while 41.6 were willing to admit Mexican-Americans. 53.1 percent of whites would admit blacks to a club to which they belonged, while the figure for Mexican-Americans was 79.8 "Blacks," they conclude, are "more socially distant from whites than are Mexican-Americans" (p.1206)—much more socially distant, they might have more accurately said, on the basis of their own findings.

On the question of greater residential dispersion, see Albert K. Karnig and Susan Welch, "Sex and Ethnic Differences in Municipal Representation," *Social Science Quarterly*, 60 (September 1979), 470. Karnig and Welch are relying on the work of Delbert Taebel, "Minority Representation on City Councils," *Social Science Quarterly*, 59 (June 1978), 142–152. See also Pachon, "Political Mobilization," p. 250.

52. Donald L. Horowitz, "Conflict and Accommodation: Mexican-Americans in the Cosmopolis," in Walker Connor, ed., *Mexican-Americans*, pp. 69–70. See also James E. Long, "Productivity, Employment Discrimination, and the Relative Economic Status of Spanish Origin Males," *Social Science Quarterly*, 58 (December 1977), 362. Long argues that Mexican-Americans and blacks differ in their economic status relative to that of whites. But, as the title suggests, Long's point refers only to males. He goes on to state that "the low earnings of Mexican American males were mainly due to their low productivity rather than employment discrimination" (p. 367). Although he makes no comparison between Mexican-Americans and blacks in this respect, it seems doubtful that he would attribute black economic status to "low productivity" to the same degree.

53. 1975 Senate hearings, p. 964, "Memorandum of Law, Re. Discrimination against Chicano Voters in Legislative Reapportionment," prepared by MALDEF.

## 4. Travels in a Political Thicket

1. *Colegrove v. Green*, 328 U.S. 549, 556 (1946).
2. *Baker v. Carr*, 369 U.S. 186, 300 (1962), dissenting opinion.
3. *Reynolds v. Sims*, 377 U.S. 533 (1964).
4. 377 U.S. at 562.
5. 377 U.S. at 623–624. Emphasis added.
6. 377 U.S. at 555.
7. 377 U.S. at 565.

8. 379 U.S. 433 (1965).

9. 379 U.S. at 439.

10. 384 U.S. 73 (1966).

11. *Report of the National Advisory Commission on Civil Disorders* (Washington, D.C.: Government Printing Office, 1968).

12. Ibid., pp. 1–11. The quotation is from p. 1.

13. *Chavis v. Whitcomb*, 305 F. Supp. 1364 (1969).

14. 305 F. Supp. at 1386.

15. *Whitcomb v. Chavis*, 403 U.S. 124, 150; 150 n. 30; 151–152 (1971).

16. 403 U.S. at 153.

17. 403 U.S. at 149.

18. The revision referred to is the amendment of section 2 of the act; the suit was *Ketchum v. Byrne*, 740 F.2d 1398 (7th Cir. 1984), in which the issue was city councilmanic districting in Chicago.

19. *White v. Regester*, 412 U.S. 755 (1973).

20. 412 U.S. at 766–767.

21. 412 U.S. at 768.

22. James Blacksher and Larry Menefee, "At-Large Elections and One Person, One Vote: The Search for the Meaning of Racial Vote Dilution," in *Minority Vote Dilution*, ed. Chandler Davidson (Washington, D.C.: Howard University Press, 1984), p. 215.

23. 412 U.S. at 766. Emphasis added.

24. Michael Walzer, *Spheres of Justice: A Defense of Pluralism and Equality* (New York: Basic Books, 1983), p. 310.

25. *Zimmer v. McKeithen*, 485 F.2d 1297 (1973).

26. 485 F.2d at 1305.

27. See, for instance, *Turner v. McKeithen*, 490 F.2d 191 (1973); *Moore v. LeFlove Board of Elections Commissioners*, 502 F.2d 621 (1974); *Wallace v. House*, 377 F. Supp. 1192 (W.D. La. 1974), aff'd 515 F.2d 619 (5th Cir. 1975), vacated and remanded 425 U.S. 947 (1976); *Hendrix v. Joseph*, 559 F.2d 1265 (5th Cir. 1976); *Nevett v. Sides*, 533 F.2d 1361 (5th Cir. 1977); *David v. Garrison*, 533 F.2d 923 (5th Cir. 1977). An excellent summary of Court of Appeals decisions in vote dilution cases prior to 1978 is contained in the appendix to the prepared statement of Frank R. Parker submitted to the Hearings before the Subcommittee on the Constitution of the Committee on the Judiciary, U.S. Senate, 97th Congress, 2nd session on S. 53, S. 1761, S. 1975, S. 1992, and H.R. 3112, Bills to Amend the Voting Rights Act of 1965, January–March 1982 (hereafter cited as 1982 Senate Hearings), vol. 1, pp. 1216–1226.

28. James F. Blumstein, "Defining and Proving Race Discrimination: Perspectives on the Purpose vs. Results Approach from the Voting Rights Act," *Virginia Law Review*, 69 (May 1983), 645. Blumstein's point was actually made in reference to the "results" test that was written into the Voting Rights Act in the amendments of 1982, but that test was asserted to be nothing more than a return to the legal standard contained in *White* and *Zimmer*. Hence Blumstein was referring indirectly to those two cases.

29. Timothy G. O'Rourke, "The Legal Status of Local At-Large Elections: Ra-

cial Discrimination and the Remedy of 'Affirmative Representation,' " 1982 Senate hearings vol. 2, Appendix, p. 478.

30. "We cannot endorse the view," the court said, "that the success of black candidates necessarily forecloses the possibility of dilution of the black vote. Such success might, on occasion, be the work of politicians who, apprehending that the support of a black candidate would be politically expedient, campaign to insure his election. Or such success might be attributable to political support motivated by different considerations—namely that election of a black candidate will thwart successful challenges to electoral schemes on dilution grounds." 485 F.2d at 1307.

31. Testimony of Benjamin L. Hooks, executive director of the National Association for the Advancement of Colored People, 1982 Senate hearings, vol. 1, p. 253.

32. Thus Article 1, Section 2 provides: "The House of Representatives shall be composed of members chosen every second year by the people of the several states, and the electors in each state shall have the qualifications requisite for the electors of the most numerous branch of the state legislature." The Fifteenth Amendment (1870) prohibits denial or abridgment of the right to vote on account of race, the Nineteenth (1920) on account of sex, and the Twenty-sixth (1971) on account of age for citizens eighteen or older.

33. Prepared Statement of James F. Blumstein, 1982 Senate hearings, vol. 1, p. 1358.

34. *City of Mobile v. Bolden,* 446 U.S. 55 (1980).

35. *Rogers v. Lodge,* 458 U.S. 613 (1982).

36. 412 U.S. at 769.

37. 412 U.S. at 769.

## 5. The Politics of Passage in the House

1. Hearings before the Subcommittee on Civil and Constitutional Rights of the Committee on the Judiciary, U.S. House of Representatives, 97th Congress, 1st session on Extension of the Voting Rights Act, May–July 1981 (hereafter cited as 1981 House hearings), p. 65.

2. *Time,* 11 May 1981. The comment followed a discussion of the options the administration was rumored to have under consideration. "Any attempt to undo the civil rights achieved under the act would be socially destructive and morally unjustified," the article concluded. Although the editorializing was indirect, buried in a news story, the message was clear: a return to 1964, if not 1877, was, indeed, possible.

3. Laughlin McDonald, "Voting Rights on the Chopping Block," *Southern Exposure* (Spring 1981), reprinted in the 1981 House hearings, p. 2640.

4. *Washington v. Davis,* 426 U.S. 229, 240 (1976).

5. The report of the House Judiciary Committee itself adopted the smoking gun image. "Efforts to find a 'smoking gun' to establish racial discriminatory purpose or intent are not only futile, but irrelevant to the consideration whether discrimination has resulted from such election practices." Report No. 97-227, Voting Rights Act Extension, Committee on the Judiciary, U.S. House of Representatives, 97th Con-

gress, 1st session, September 15, 1981 (hereafter cited as 1981 House Judiciary Committee report), p. 29.

6. *Village of Arlington Heights v. Metropolitan Development Corp.*, 429 U.S. 252, 266 (1977).

7. See, for instance, the "Voting Rights Act Fact Sheet" published by the Joint Center for Political Studies and widely circulated to members of the press and members of lobbying organizations (undated). The Joint Center called the amendment a clarification in its magazine, *Focus*, as well (May 1981). The literature of the Leadership Conference on Civil Rights regularly described the change as simply a clarification. "Congress must now decide whether to clarify Section 2 in order to maintain its original plan to reach discriminatory results," a January 1982 memo stated. (Memorandum to Participating Organizations from Ralph G. Neas, January 26, 1982, p. 3.) Numerous witnesses at the House hearings made the point. See, for example, the testimony of Jesse Jackson, 1981 House hearings, p. 171 ("I am here to urge that you . . . correct a misinterpretation of the act resulting from the recent Supreme Court decision in *City of Mobile v. Bolden*.") The 1981 House Judiciary Committee report stated that "the purpose of the amendment to section 2 is to restate Congress' earlier intent that violations of the Voting Rights Act, including Section 2, could be established by showing the discriminatory effect of the challenged practice" (p. 29).

8. Henry J. Hyde, "Why I Changed My Mind on the Voting Rights Act," *Washington Post*, 26 July 1981, p. D7.

9. 1981 House hearings, p. 2.

10. Ibid., p. 2.

11. Ibid., p. 8.

12. Ibid., p. 173.

13. Ibid., p. 482.

14. Ibid., p. 2.

15. Ibid., p. 927.

16. Ibid., p. 29; see also p. 483.

17. Ibid., p. 2.

18. Ibid., p. 388.

19. Julian Bond, statement at a meeting on foundation funding in support of the effort to lobby for passage of the House bill, New World Foundation, New York City, June 23, 1981.

20. 1981 House hearings, p. 386.

21. Joint Center, "Voting Rights Act Fact Sheet," undated.

22. Reginald Stuart, *New York Times Magazine*, 27 September 1981, p. 101. Others made virtually the same point. Thus Jesse Jackson warned of "forces in this land who want to turn back the clock—to weaken or destroy this legislation as a first step toward the redisfranchisement of black and Hispanic people" (1981 House hearings, p. 173), and Don Edwards argued that "without preclearance you have . . . an invitation to completely disfranchise the black population like it was before 1965" (ibid., p. 1590). A Mississippi state representative depicted the modification of section 5 as "closely akin to removing the troops in the 1870s" (ibid., p. 550), and another Mississippi witness said: "I have read my history and I know that the Hayes-

Tilden compromise of 1877 is about to reoccur," (ibid., p. 1672). Jack Greenberg of the NAACP Legal Defense and Education Fund warned that *"Expiration* of the Voting Rights Act in 1982 would bring . . . increases in voter registration to a halt" (memo from the NAACP submitted to an American Bar Association Symposium on voting rights, Washington, D.C., April 9–10, 1981; emphasis added). Greenberg, director and general counsel of the fund, suggested that literacy tests would return if Congress failed to pass the House bill—although the ban on such tests was permanent, of course.

23. 1981 House hearings, pp. 92, 1672.

24. Ibid., pp. 4, 173, 203, 1760.

25. *Focus*, May 1981, p. 3.

26. Michael Pertschuk, *Giant Killers* (New York: W. W. Norton, 1986), pp. 155–156.

27. Telephone conversation, August 1981.

28. Pertschuk, *Giant Killers*, p. 159.

29. 1981 House hearings, pp. 2101–2103 (Wilber Colum) and p. 214 (Harold Washington).

30. The complaints about registration hours, the limited number of counties using deputy registrars or black polling officials, and the use of "white establishments" as polling places were made by Dr. Joe Reed, chairman of the Alabama Democratic Conference (1981 House hearings, p. 1526). Reed also argued that white polling officials were in violation of the law in stopping blacks from choosing the person they wished to assist them in voting (ibid., p. 1584). Sheriff Prince Arnold (Wilcox County, Alabama) complained about the use of a white family's house as a polling place; the family kept blacks from voting, he charged. He also testified that whites attempted to keep blacks from voting by a variety of other means (ibid., p. 1579). The charge with respect to the absence of voting booths was made by Maggie Bozeman of Aliceville, Alabama (ibid., pp. 1569 and 1586). Other charges by Bozeman were resistance to black registration drives on the part of white officials, the harassment of blacks who requested absentee ballots, and an "outdated" use of paper ballots (ibid., pp. 1565–1566). W. C. Patton, retired national director of the NAACP Voter Education Project, told of efforts to discourage blacks from registering during a voter reidentification period (ibid., p. 1572).

31. 1981 House hearings, p. 1584.

32. Ibid., p. 486.

33. The charge was made by Dr. Joe Reed (ibid., p. 1526).

34. The paper ballot protest was lodged by Maggie Bozeman (ibid., p. 1566). The complaint against voting machines was contained in the testimony of Hon. Eddie Hardaway, district judge, Sumter County, Alabama (ibid., p. 825).

35. The charge that police were photographing those who assisted voters was made by Maggie Bozeman (ibid., p. 1585).

36. David H. Hunter, "Section 5 of Voting Rights Act of 1965: Problems and Possibilities," paper presented at the 1980 annual meeting of the American Political Science Association, Washington, D.C., August 28–31, 1980, p. 18.

37. 1981 House hearings, p. 174.

38. Ibid., p. 479.

39. Mark-up session, Committee on the Judiciary, U.S. House of Representatives, July 30, 1981, unofficial transcript.

40. Ibid.

41. 1981 House hearings, p. 927.

42. Donald L. Horowitz, "Conflict and Accommodation: Mexican-Americans in the Cosmopolis," in *Mexican-Americans in Comparative Perspective,* ed. Walker Connor (Washington, D.C.: The Urban Institute Press, 1985), p. 64.

43. 1981 House hearings, p. 13.

44. Ibid., p. 1521.

45. *South Carolina v. Katzenbach*, 383 U.S. 301, 360; 358; 360.

46. Interview with Representative Hyde, October 1983.

47. *Boston Sunday Globe*, 4 October 1981, p. A3.

48. Hyde's bill, H.R. 3948, was introduced on June 17, 1981. For a summary see the 1981 House hearings, pp. 1816–1817.

49. Pertschuk, *Giant Killers*, p. 160.

50. Ibid., p. 158.

51. Exchange between Edwards and Henry, 1981 House hearings, p. 485.

52. Pertschuk, *Giant Killers* p. 160.

53. *New York Times Magazine*, 27 September 1981, p. 105.

54. The suggestion was made by James M. Nabrit at the New World Foundation meeting, New York City, June 23, 1981.

55. Rolando Rios (Director of Litigation, Southwest Voter Registration Education Project), "The Voting Rights Act: Its Effect in Texas," document accompanying the testimony of William C. Velasquez, Executive Director, SVREP, 1981 House hearings, p. 39.

56. Testimony of Laughlin McDonald, 1981 House hearings, p. 591.

57. Ibid., p. 462.

58. Judge Minor Wisdom, quoted in the prepared statement of Frank Parker, ibid., p. 511.

59. President's Commission for a National Agenda for the Eighties, Report of the Panel on Government and the Advancement of Social Justice, Health, Welfare, Education, and Civil Rights (Washington, D.C., Government Printing office, 1980), p. 15.

60. 1981 House hearings, p. 489.

61. Ibid., p. 866.

62. Ibid., p. 550.

63. Ibid., p. 11.

64. An account of the evolution of the bill is contained in Thomas M. Boyd and Stephen J. Markman, *Washington and Lee Law Review*, 40 (Fall 1983), 1347–1428.

65. 1981 House Judiciary Committee report, "Dissenting views of Hon. M. Caldwell Butler," p. 68.

66. Not the bill itself but the explanatory House Report refers to at-large voting and the like—hence the small element of uncertainty. 1981 House Judiciary Committee report, pp. 42–43.

67. Timothy O'Rourke, "The New Bailout and Section 5 of the Voting Rights Act," paper prepared for delivery at the 1983 annual meeting of the American Political Science Association, Chicago, September 1–4, 1983, p. 18.

68. 127 Congressional Record H 6939 (October 5, 1981).

69. See the "Supplemental Views of Hon. Henry Hyde and Hon. Dan Lungren," 1981 House Judiciary Committee report, p. 57; "Dissenting Views of Hon. M. Caldwell Butler," ibid., p. 67.

70. 1981 House Judiciary Committee report, p. 57.

71. Ibid., p. 54.

72. Interview, October 1983.

73. Unofficial transcript.

74. Barton Gellman, "The New Old Movement," *The New Republic,* 6 September 1982, pp. 12–13.

75. 1981 House Judiciary Committee report, p. 56.

76. Ibid., p. 62.

77. Mark-up session, unofficial transcript.

78. Ibid.

79. 1981 House hearings, p. 1816.

80. The spokesman was Laura Murphy, quoted in the *New York Times,* 6 October 1981, p. A26.

81. An interim date for reconsideration has been set: 1997. But the political pressures are such that the likelihood that the special provisions will, in fact, be allowed to expire at that time is exceedingly small. Minority politicians will continue to want the extra protection that section 5 provides against white competition, and whites with minority constituents or national political aspirations will not take a stance labeled "anti–civil rights."

82. The Edwards statement is from the 1981 House hearings, p. 925 (emphasis added). The nationwide figure for black elected officials in 1982 comes from the *Statistical Abstract of the United States: 1986* (Washington, D.C.: Government Printing Office, 1985). The figure for the covered states of the South alone (including North Carolina but not Texas) was 1,930 in 1982. *Black Elected Officials: A National Roster* (Washington, D.C., Joint Center for Political Studies, 1982).

83. Roger H. Davidson, "Subcommittee Government: New Channels for Policy Making," in *The New Congress,* ed. Thomas E. Mann and Norman J. Ornstein (Washington, D.C.: The American Enterprise Institute for Public Policy Research, 1981), p. 13.

84. On the hiring practices of committee chairmen see Michael J. Malbin, *Unelected Representatives: Congressional Staff and the Future of Representative Government* (New York: Basic Books, 1980), p. 20.

85. Arthur Maass, *Congress and the Common Good* (New York: Basic Books, 1983), p. 67.

86. The figure was often repeated. See, for example, *New York Times,* 6 October 1981 and 1 November 1981; *Focus,* the publication of the Joint Center for Political Studies, February 1982, p. 4. The Joint Center's estimates are reported in the testimony of Armand Derfner at the 1982 Senate hearings (Hearings before the Subcommittee on the Constitution of the Committee on the Judiciary, U.S. Senate,

97th Congress, 2nd session on S. 53 and Other Bills to Amend the Voting Rights Act of 1965, January-March 1982), p. 832. Derfner provides a table with state-by-state estimates as to the number of counties that would be eligible for bailout. In a memorandum submitted as part of his testimony, he states: "It is estimated that one-fourth of covered counties—more than 200—may be eligible to bail-out when the new procedure goes into effect in 1984" (p. 833).

87. The following analysis of the inherent flaws in the calculation essentially summarizes that contained in O'Rourke, "The New Bailout."

88. Letter from Representative Don Edwards to all members of the House ("Dear Colleague: . . . ), September 30, 1981.

89. The exception was the amendment offered by Representative Millicent Fenwick of New Jersey, which restricted assistance to blind or otherwise disabled voters; the amendment was altered by the Senate to permit assistance by any person of the voter's choice, "other than the voter's employer or agent of that employer or officer or agent of the voter's union" (sec. 208).

90. Pertschuk, *Giant Killers*, p. 153.


## 6. Liberal Power in a Conservative Senate

1. Thomas M. Boyd and Stephen J. Markman, "The 1982 Amendments to the Voting Rights Act: A Legislative History," *Washington and Lee Law Review*, 40 (Fall 1983), 1384.

2. Jane Frank-Harman, "The Fate of America's Minority Rights May Rest on a Single Bill," *Los Angeles Times*, 31 May 1981, sec. IV, p. 3.

3. Reported to me by Thomas Boyd, minority counsel on the House Subcommittee on Civil and Constitutional Rights. Telephone conversation, January 15, 1982.

4. *New York Times*, 7 October 1981, p. B10.

5. Boyd, among others, made this argument. Telephone conversation, January 15, 1982.

6. Diane Pinderhughes, "Interest Groups and the Extension of the Voting Rights Act in 1982," paper delivered at the annual meeting of the American Political Science Association, Chicago, Sept. 1–4, 1983.

7. Hearings before the Subcommittee on the Constitution of the Committee on the Judiciary, U.S Senate, 97th Congress, 2nd session on S. 53, S. 1761, S. 1975, S. 1992, and H.R. 3112, Bills to Amend the Voting Rights Act of 1965, January-March 1982 (hereafter cited as 1982 Senate hearings, with all references to volume 1 unless otherwise specified), p. 1.

8. See, for instance, the description by lobbyist and litigator Armand Derfner contained in "Vote Dilution and the Voting Rights Act Amendments of 1982," in *Minority Vote Dilution*, ed. Chandler Davidson (Washington, D.C.: Howard University Press, 1984), p. 151. "Civil rights strategists meeting in late 1980 had three goals," Derfner writes. "To overturn *Mobile*" is the second goal he names.

9. 1982 Senate hearings, p. 2.

10. Ibid., p. 1.

11. Statement of William French Smith, ibid., pp. 71, 70. For the civil rights

view, see, for example, the statement of Jesse Jackson (Hearings before the Subcommittee on Civil and Constitutional Rights of the Committee on the Judiciary, U.S. House of Representatives, 97th Congress, 1st session on Extension of the Voting Rights Act, May-July 1981 [hereafter cited as 1981 House hearings], p. 171) and that of the president of the League of Women Voters (ibid., p. 197). The point was, in fact, made repeatedly by civil rights spokesmen.

12. 1982 Senate hearings, p. 271.

13. Ibid., p. 282.

14. Ibid., p. 219. Emphasis added.

15. Ibid., p. 245.

16. Ibid., p. 219.

17. *New York Times*, 7 October 1981, p. B7.

18. *Time*, 11 May 1981, p. 24.

19. *National Journal*, 1 August 1981, p. 1364.

20. Michael Pertschuk, *Giant Killers* (New York: W. W. Norton, 1986), p. 148.

21. *The New Republic*, 6 September 1982, pp. 12 and 10.

22. Pinderhughes, "Interest Groups," p. 19.

23. Ibid., p. 25.

24. Benjamin L. Hooks and Ralph G. Neas to William French Smith, February 9, 1982, reprinted in the 1982 Senate hearings, p. 1089.

25. Richard J. Margolis, "Voting Rights: The Obvious Takes a Little Longer," *Foundation News: The Journal of Philanthropy*, 24 (May-June 1982), p. 32.

26. Ibid., p. 29.

27. Hooks and Neas to William French Smith, 1982 Senate hearings, p. 1090.

28. *Congressional Quarterly*, 26 June 1982, p. 2.

29. Barton Gellman, "The New Old Movement," *The New Republic*, 6 September 1982, p. 12.

30. Pinderhughes, "Interest Groups," p. 11.

31. Gellman, "The New Old Movement," p. 12.

32. *Congressional Quarterly*, 39 (1981), p. 1111, as cited in Boyd and Markman, "The 1982 Amendments," p. 1387, n. 207.

33. *Congressional Quarterly*, 26 June 1982, p. 2.

34. Interview, April 1982.

35. *Human Events*, 15 May 1982, p. 3.

36. Boyd and Markman, "The 1982 Amendments," p. 1388. Markman wrote the section on the Senate; hence the reference to him as the author of the quoted statement.

37. Letter, President Ronald Reagan to Attorney General William French Smith, June 15, 1981.

38. *Washington Post*, 30 June 1981, p. A7.

39. *Washington Post*, 13 June 1981, p. A8.

40. The information on 1970 and 1975 comes from David Hunter and other staff who worked on the amendments of those years. Thomas Boyd supplied the information on White House support for Hyde in 1981. Telephone conversations, May–July 1981.

41. Boyd and Markman, "The 1982 Amendments," p. 1369.

42. The Dowdy victory and its political impact are discussed, among other places, in the *National Journal*, 1 August 1981, p. 1366.

43. *Report to the President from the Attorney General of the United States Concerning Amending the Voting Rights Act*, October 2, 1981.

44. *Washington Post*, 7 November 1981, p. A1; Boyd and Markman, "The 1982 Amendments," p. 1386.

45. *Washington Post*, 7 November 1981, p. 1.

46. *Boston Globe*, 11 November 1981, p. 26; Vernon E. Jordan, Jr., "Diluting Minority Voting Rights," *New York Times*, 16 November 1981, p. 23.

47. Interview, October 1983.

48. *New York Times*, 10 January 1982, pp. 1 and 15.

49. *New York Times*, 12 January 1982, p. 15.

50. Confidential telephone conversation, March 1982.

51. Confidential interview, April 1982.

52. *Human Events*, 15 May 1982, p. 4.

53. Letter, Anthony Lewis to Barry Gross, February 22, 1982.

54. Interview, October 1983.

55. 1982 Senate hearings, p. 79.

56. Ibid., p. 1406.

57. *New York Times*, 5 October 1981, p. 20.

58. *New York Times*, 10 May 1981, p. 20. The editorial called the House bill the target of "weakening amendments," with a clear implication that any amendment to the proposed amendment of section 2 would weaken the existing statute. The editorial fails to mention that the new section 2 in fact would greatly strengthen the act.

59. The initial *Washington Post* editorial supporting the *Mobile* decision had appeared on 28 April 1980, p. A16. For the argument that discriminatory intent was impossible to prove, see, for instance, the *Post*'s editorial ("Voting Rights: Be Strong"), 26 January 1982, p. A18.

60. *Boston Globe*, 1 July 1981, p. 15.

61. Thus, for instance, *Time*, 11 May 1981, p. 25, refers to Pickens County, Alabama, as an example of a majority-black jurisdiction with no black elected officials. The article quotes black spokesmen as linking future officeholding in such jurisdictions to an extension of the act, a view that *Time* clearly endorses. There is no hint that, in fact, in such majority-black counties, the election of blacks depends on black turnout and the solidity of black support behind the black candidate. The right of blacks to register, vote, and organize would not have been affected, whatever form the 1982 amendments took. Yet such articles imply that support for Hatch amounts to support for continuing all-white government, even where blacks are a majority—support, that is, for the oppression of blacks.

62. The *New York Times*, among others, simply dismissed out of hand the argument that the amended section 2 would more or less guarantee electoral arrangements that promoted proportionate racial and ethnic officeholding. See, for instance, 19 March 1982, p. A30: "By talking so anxiously about quotas at this point, the Administration unnecessarily inflames the debate over voting rights renewal."

63. *National Journal*, 1 August 1981, p. 1376.

64. 1982 Senate hearings, p. 199.

65. Ibid., p. 83.

66. Ibid., p. 268.

67. Ibid., p. 371; also p. 419.

68. Ibid., p. 1271.

69. 1981 House hearings, pp. 139, 852; Report of the Committee on the Judiciary, Senate Report No. 417, 97th Congress, 2nd session (hereafter cited as Senate Judiciary Committee Report), p. 26.

70. 1982 Senate hearings, pp. 1648–49.

71. Senate Judiciary Committee Report, p. 36.

72. 1982 Senate hearings, p. 1417.

73. Statement of Henry J. Kirksey, ibid., p. 665.

74. Ibid., p. 623.

75. Ibid., p. 1181.

76. Ibid., p. 1193.

77. Senate Judiciary Committee Report, p. 37.

78. 1982 Senate hearings, pp. 988–989.

79. Ibid., p. 373.

80. Ibid., p. 340.

81. Ibid., p. 1340.

82. Ibid., p. 1335.

83. Ibid., p. 1309. *Horowitz.*

84. Ibid., p. 644.

85. Ibid., p. 1358.

86. Ibid., p. 718.

87. Ibid., p. 1340.

88. Ibid., p. 1334.

89. Ibid., p. 1449.

90. Ibid., p. 1310.

91. Ibid., p. 1330.

92. Ibid., p. 1361.

93. Ibid., pp. 1327–28.

94. Ibid., p. 1311.

95. Report of the Subcommittee on the Constitution to the Committee on the Judiciary on the Voting Rights Act, 97th Congress, 2nd session reprinted in the Senate Judiciary Committee Report, p. 109 and n. 4.

96. Subcommittee Report, Senate Judiciary Committee Report, p. 110.

97. 1982 Senate hearings, p. 1661.

98. Ibid., p. 1644.

99. Ibid., p. 564.

100. Ibid., p. 449.

101. Ibid., p. 103.

102. Ibid., p. 548.

103. Ibid., p. 201.

104. Ibid., pp. 599, 601.

105. Ibid., p. 253.

106. Katharine I. Butler, "Constitutional and Statutory Challenges to Election Structures: Dilution and the Value of the Right to Vote," *Louisiana Law Review*, 42 (Spring 1982), 888.

107. Katharine I. Butler, "Reapportionment, the Courts, and the Voting Rights Act: A Resegregation of the Political Process?" *University of Colorado Law Review*, 56 (Fall 1984), 21.

108. *New York Times*, 16 November 1981, p. 23.

109. 1982 Senate hearings, p. 98.

110. "Minority Vote Dilution, An Overview," in Davidson, ed., *Minority Vote Dilution*, p. 12.

111. 1982 Senate hearings, pp. 252, 253.

112. Ibid., p. 84.

113. Ibid., p. 275.

114. Rauh, ibid., p. 979; Flemming, 1981 House hearings, p. 1170.

115. 1982 Senate hearings, p. 1295.

116. Ibid., p. 1273.

117. Ibid.

118. Ibid., p. 672.

119. Armand Derfner, "Section 2 and City of Mobile," paper delivered at the "Voting Rights Symposium" of the American Bar Association, Washington, D.C., April 9–10, 1981, p. 3. In the publications of the Joint Center for Political Studies in Washington, D.C., for which Derfner worked in 1981–1982, the South was generally depicted as unchanged. See, for instance, Kenneth H. Thompson, "The Voting Rights Act and Black Electoral Participation," a 1982 pamphlet issued by the Joint Center which states: "A visit to almost any southern town today reveals 'the same bleak testimonial to a still separated but unequal society,' " (p. 36).

120. Davidson, "Minority Vote Dilution," in Davidson, ed., *Minority Vote Dilution*, p. 12. Emphasis added.

121. Ibid., p. 14.

122. Frank R. Parker, "Racial Gerrymandering and Legislative Reapportionment," in Davidson, ed., *Minority Vote Dilution*, p. 86.

123. 1982 Senate hearings, p. 1247.

124. My imagery here is taken from Michael Walzer, *Spheres of Justice: A Defense of Pluralism and Equality* (New York: Basic Books, 1983), pp. 149–150.

125. 1982 Senate hearings, p. 1310.

126. Ibid., p. 230.

127. Ibid., p. 444.

128. Ibid., p. 846.

129. Ibid., p. 739.

130. Ibid., p. 473.

131. Ibid., p. 1662.

132. Ibid., p. 739.

133. Ibid., p. 442.

134. Ibid., p. 743.

135. Ibid., p. 237.

136. Ibid., p. 1336.

137. James F. Blumstein, "Defining and Proving Race Discrimination: Perspectives on the Purpose vs. Results Approach from the Voting Rights Act," *Virginia Law Review*, 69 (May 1983), 661.

138. Butler, "Reapportionment," p. 81.

139. Boyd and Markman, "The 1982 Amendments," p. 1414.

140. *Human Events*, 15 May 1982, p. 3.

141. The most important of these amendments altered section 203, which prior to 1982 mandated bilingual ballots and other election materials in jurisdictions in which more than 5 percent of the voting-age citizens were members of a single language minority and had an illiteracy rate above the national average. In 1982 the provision was amended to refer only to those jurisdictions in which, according to determinations made by the Director of the Census, 5 percent of the citizens both belong to a single language minority group and "do not speak or understand English adequately enough to participate in the electoral process." A new section (208) was also added to the act. It requires states to allow blind or disabled persons, or those unable to read or write, to be assisted in voting by anyone of their choice, except their employer, an agent of their employer, or an officer or agent of the voter's union. State restrictions as to who was eligible to assist voters were thus no longer valid.

## 7. Amendment by Enforcement

1. 354 F. Supp. 1021 (D.D.C. 1972), summarily aff'd, 410 U.S. 962 (1973).

2. 400 U.S. 379 (1971).

3. 354 F. Supp. at 1023.

4. 354 F. Supp. at 1025, 1028–29.

5. 354 F. Supp. at 1031.

6. 354 F. Supp. at 1026. Emphasis added.

7. File, submission of Charleston, South Carolina, voting section, Department of Justice.

8. 354 F. Supp. at 1029. Emphasis added.

9. Letter of objection to Statesboro, Georgia, December 10, 1979, cited in Hiroshi Motomura, "Preclearance under Section Five of the Voting Rights Act," *North Carolina Law Review*, 61 (January 1983), 222.

10. Letter of objection to Bamberg County, South Carolina, July 30, 1976, cited in Motomura, "Preclearance," p. 235.

11. 374 F. Supp. 363 (D.D.C. 1974).

12. 374 F. Supp. at 371. The city had submitted an earlier plan as well, which contained no majority-black districts. The one to which I refer is a second attempt to meet Justice Department standards.

13. 374 F. Supp. at 388.

14. 374 F. Supp. at 387.

15. 374 F. Supp. at 388.

16. 374 F. Supp. at 375.

17. 374 F. Supp. at 374.

18. 374 F. Supp. at 398.
19. Interview, Dr. Mack Spears, New Orleans, April 1981.
20. Confidential interviews, New Orleans, April 1981.
21. *City of Richmond, Virginia v. U.S.*, 376 F. Supp. 1344 (D.D.C. 1975).
22. 376 F. Supp. at 1349–50.
23. 376 F. Supp. at 1356.
24. 376 F. Supp. at 1354 n. 50.
25. 376 F. Supp. at 1353. Emphasis added.
26. 376 F. Supp. at 1353. Emphasis added.
27. *City of Richmond, Virginia v. U.S.*, 422 U.S. 358 (1975).
28. 422 U.S. at 371.
29. 422 U.S. at 373.
30. 422 U.S. at 374.
31. Ibid.
32. 422 U.S. at 378.
33. 422 U.S. at 375.
34. Ibid.
35. 422 U.S. at 383.
36. *Beer v. U.S.*, 425 U.S. 130 (1976).
37. 425 U.S. at 141.
38. Ibid.
39. 425 U.S. at 143–144. Justice White was arguing against the *Beer* standard. I have argued that *Beer* was correctly decided. By implication, I am suggesting that if annexation decisions were voting procedures for section 5 purposes, at least their treatment by the courts and the Justice Department should have been in line with *Beer*. Yet squaring the two types of decisions would have been no easy task. If a municipal boundary change brought a significant increase in relative white population, backsliding was unavoidable as long as the at-large system was retained. And if compensation for that backsliding was required, then single-member districts were the logical remedy. Furthermore, having identified ward voting as the appropriate remedy, it was almost inevitable that the Court would require districts in proportion to the minority population.
40. File, submission of Sumter County, Georgia, voting section, Department of Justice. Letter of objection, September 6, 1983.
41. 446 U.S. 156 (1980).
42. 472 F. Supp. 221, 242–249 (D.D.C. 1979).
43. *City of Rome, Georgia v. U.S.*, 446 U.S. 156, 187 (1980).
44. 446 U.S. at 208, Justice Rehnquist dissenting.
45. 446 U.S. at 184 n. 20. The decision provides raw numbers, not the percentage of votes received. The calculation of close to 40 percent (39 percent, to be precise) comes from Katharine I. Butler, "Constitutional and Statutory Challenges to Election Structures: Dilution and the Value of the Right to Vote," *Louisiana Law Review*, 42 (Spring 1982), 932 n. 309.
46. 446 U.S. at 208.
47. 459 U.S. 159 (1982).
48. *City of Lockhart v. United States*, 460 U.S. 125 (1983).

49. *County Council of Sumter County, South Carolina v. United States*, C.A. No. 82-0912 (D.D.C. May 25, 1984) (per curiam), p. 4.

50. 568 F. Supp. 1455 (D.D.C. 1983). In January 1987, after the text of this book went to press, the Supreme Court affirmed the lower court's decision. The case, while of minor importance, is troubling. Black voters are entitled to a remedy when an annexation alters the racial balance in a city and thus changes the impact of at-large voting on black electoral strength, *Petersburg* and *Richmond* had made clear. In *Pleasant Grove* the logic of those decisions appears to have been forgotten. The change in the municipal boundary had no impact on the racial balance within the city. As Justice Powell stated in dissent, "The city was composed solely of white voters before and after the annexation . . . The annexation therefore could not have had any effect whatsoever on minority voting rights, and the city could not have acted with a purpose to dilute the voting rights of black municipal voters." In other words, the city may have engaged in discriminatory action, but that action did not involve *electoral* rights—which are the sole concern of the Voting Rights Act.

## 8. Detours around the Law

1. *Beer v. United States*, 425 U.S. 130 (1976).

2. The Department of Justice keeps a regular count of the number of changes submitted. The figures for 1965 through 1981 are contained in the Hearings before the Subcommittee on the Constitution of the Committee on the Judiciary, U.S. Senate, 97th Congress, 2nd session on S. 53, S. 1761, S. 1975, S. 1992, and H.R. 3112, Bills to Amend the Voting Rights Act of 1965, January-March 1982, vol. 1, pp. 1742–1745. I obtained the 1983 figure and the total for the nineteen-year period from David Hunter, an attorney in the voting section of the Justice Department.

3. Douglas J. Mathis and L. Doyle Mathis, *The Voting Rights Act and Rome (Georgia) City Elections* (Athens, Ga.: Institute of Government, University of Georgia, 1981), p. 12.

4. Katharine Inglis Butler, "Reapportionment, the Courts, and the Voting Rights Act: A Resegregation of the Political Process?" *University of Colorado Law Review*, 56 (Fall 1984), 67.

5. Department of Justice, Office of the Attorney General, 28 CFR part 51.

6. Howard Ball, Dale Krane, and Thomas P. Lauth, *Compromised Compliance: Implementation of the 1965 Voting Rights Act* (Westport, Conn.: Greenwood Press, 1982), p. 79.

7. Ibid., p. 119.

8. *White v. Regester*, 412 U.S. 755, 769 (1973).

9. Abigail Thernstrom, "Memo on Submissions to the Department of Justice Involving Redistricting," U.S. Commission on Civil Rights (hereafter cited as Civil Rights Commission memo), 1985, p. 10. The staff attorney's visit was made on January 1, 1983.

10. Quoted in Ball, Krane, and Lauth, *Compromised Compliance*, p. 88.

11. Civil Rights Commission memo, pp. 9–10. The quotation is from a letter dated August 21, 1978.

12. Letter of objection to Port Arthur, Texas, March 12, 1982, as quoted in Hiroshi Motomura, "Preclearance under Section Five of the Voting Rights Act," *North Carolina Law Review*, 61 (January 1983), 191, n. 15. The regulations for section 5 also state that the "Attorney General shall make the same determinations that would be made by the Court in an action for declaratory judgement" (28 C.F.R. 51.39).

13. Motomura, "Preclearance," p. 192.

14. Ball, Krane, and Lauth, *Compromised Compliance*, p. 89.

15. Butler, "Reapportionment," p. 28 n. 123.

16. Timothy O'Rourke, telephone conversation, July 1, 1985.

17. Letter of objection, September 20, 1974.

18. Undated memo, Charleston file, Department of Justice. The memos and other material on which I rely in my discussion of Charleston were all contained in the public file when I examined it in 1981. In my account I have not identified Justice Department staff attorneys and paralegals or local Charleston contacts by name.

19. The two memos are dated September 16 and September 19. The former was written by a paralegal and the second by a staff attorney.

20. Undated staff attorney's memo.

21. Undated reply by Gerald W. Jones, chief, voting section.

22. Staff attorney to Jones, September 16, 1974.

23. Undated phone call, reported in a memo.

24. Staff attorney to Jones, September 16, 1974.

25. Phone call from local contact, August 29, 1974.

26. Paralegal to Jones, September 18, 1974.

27. Jack Bass and Walter DeVries, *The Transformation of Southern Politics: Social Change and Political Consequence since 1945* (New York: New American Library, 1977), pp. 249–250.

28. I. A. Newby, *Black Carolinians: A History of Blacks in South Carolina from 1948 to 1968* (Columbia, S.C.: University of South Carolina Press, 1973), p. 343. Newby goes on to say that "mob action and violence were viewed as unbecoming" in South Carolina. It is a point made by a number of observers. "There is still a lot of hardcore segregationist sentiment in South Carolina," John C. West, governor from 1970 to 1974, suggested. "But South Carolina people are basically law-abiding and won't tolerate violence" (Neal R. Peirce, *The Deep South States of America: People, Politics, and Power in the Seven Deep South States*, New York: W. W. Norton, 1974, p. 396). Charleston's best journalist argued that "the message in South Carolina, unlike Alabama, was that legislators were supposed to be gentlemen about integration, and in general they were . . . Because that's . . . the way it was supposed to be—dignified—that's generally the way things . . . happened" (interview, Barbara Williams, December 1981). And in the view of the Episcopal Bishop, a northerner, the value placed on law and order was the key to the astonishing degree of change since the early 1960s. "Now they bled and died over integration prior to the establishment of the civil rights law," he said. But "interestingly enough, once the law was passed, then as far as massive resistance was concerned, it was an accepted fact." The attitude was: "It's now the law, we think it's wrong, but if this is what the law is, then we'll obviously live with it and go on." The people of South

Carolina have a keen sense of history, the Bishop argued, and they thought: "We fought a battle and we lost; we fought the Civil War and we lost, and we had to go through Reconstruction . . . but we made it then, and we'll make it now. We lost [the] battle [over integration], but it's decided; now are we going to sit here and cry? There is no point in fussing about it, it's done; now let's get on with the business and see what we can do with it" (interview, Bishop Temple, December 1981).

29. Bass and DeVries, *Transformation*, p. 258.

30. Interview, Herbert Fielding, December 1981.

31. Interview, William Saunders, December 1981.

32. Fielding interview.

33. E. Franklin Frazier, *Black Bourgeoisie: the Rise of a New Middle Class in the United States* (New York: Collier, 1962), p. 237.

34. Interview, Marybelle Howe, December 1981. Howe linked the sense of a shared public life to that of a common private life. Her statement in full was as follows: "I guess," she said, "there was just plain physical closeness . . . In the peninsula city, everybody was in the same city and everybody knew it was the same city . . . They always had lived close, and this is one of the interesting things . . . People would be uptight over what the blacks were going to do when they started voting and this sort of thing. Well, you would go into a grocery store and there would be a black lady and a white lady picking out okra, and they never let things interfere with good manners on either side. Or really thoughtfulness. Because I mean they cared about okra. There are a lot of things they care about together. And I think they cared about the town." Robert Rosen, interviewed in December 1981, argued that the extensive and unusually open contact between the races had a long history. There was more openness about sexual liaisons between planters and black women in Charleston than elsewhere, he suggested. And even after the Civil War, there was great interdependence between black and white Charlestonians despite the turmoil. Black businesses (offering such services as tailoring, upholstering, and general repair work) served white clients, and black money in considerable sums was deposited in white banks.

35. Marybelle Howe interview. The reaction of Charleston to James L. Petigru was often given by those whom I interviewed as a prime example of the city's tolerance for eccentrics. Petigru opposed nullification and secession, but upon his death in 1863 the city closed down in mourning.

36. Fielding interview.

37. Interview, William B. Regan, December 1981. In the fifteen or twenty years before Howe's death, as Regan described it, everybody who ran for office went to see Howe. "He had a way of resolving problems and bringing the community together."

38. The findings of the survey were reported to me in interviews with Charleston politicians in December 1981.

39. Motomura, "Preclearance," pp. 222, 223.

40. *City of Lockhart v. United States*, 460 U.S. 125 (1983).

41. *South Carolina v. United States and The National Association for the Advancement of Colored People, Inc.,* Civil Action No. 83-3626, District Court for the District of Columbia.

42. *South Carolina v. U.S.*, Plaintiff's Response to Defendant's First Interrogatories, March 1, 1984, p. 49.

43. Civil Rights Commission Memo, p. 3.

44. Ibid., pp. 3–4.

45. Ibid., p. 4.

46. Ibid.

47. Ibid., p. 5.

48. Ibid.

49. *South Carolina v. U.S.*, Defendant's Response to Plaintiff's First Interrogatories, February 10, 1984, pp. 14 and 22.

50. *South Carolina v. U.S.*, NAACP-Defendant's Supplementary Response to Interrogatories, April 2, 1984, pp. 7–8.

51. Letter of objection to Sumter County, Georgia (William Bradford Reynolds to Henry L. Crisp), September 6, 1983.

52. Letter of objection to Texas (William Bradford Reynolds to David Dean, secretary of state), January 29, 1982; letter of objection to Virginia (Reynolds to Attorney General Gerald L. Bailes), March 12, 1982; letter of objection to Uvalde County (Reynolds to Jeffrey A. Davis, Esq.), February 18, 1982.

53. Civil Rights Commission memo, p. 12.

54. Ibid., p. 6. The staff, in its criticism of the districting plan submitted by the county in question, stated: "The County, to arrive at that percentage, drew boundaries which shape a district that is not compact, and which fragment the very visibly compact and residentially segregated black community in Eufaula. Such a district would not be desirable under any circumstances, given the difficulties that many voters living along these boundaries will face in knowing which district is theirs."

55. Civil Rights Commission memo, p. 14.

56. *South Carolina v. U.S.*, Memorandum for the United States in Opposition to South Carolina's Motion for Partial Summary Judgment, May 7, 1984, p. 9, n.**.

57. In the Barbour County case, the voting section had drawn a "fair" plan of its own (labeled "DOJ Plan No. 1"), but whether it became the standard against which other allegedly "fairly drawn" plans were compared is not clear. In any case, an October "Legal Analysis and Recommendation" refers to a newly submitted plan as an improvement over that to which the Department had objected in July. However, the plan still failed to meet the Justice Department standard. "It appears that the county, which, due to our July 21, 1981 letter, is on notice of its obligation to adopt a fairly-drawn plan, has done otherwise," a staff attorney wrote. "Thus . . . considering the notice which the county has and the configuration of District 3, it . . . appears that the county has deliberately drawn the plan to dilute black voting strength." Thus, once the county was told to draw a "fair" plan, its failure to adhere to the Department's particular definition of fairness left it open to the charge of purposeful discrimination. With respect to Sumter County, Gerald Jones, the chief of the voting section, says explicitly: "We took the unusual step of going down and helping them work out an acceptable solution which, apparently, they have rejected, along with other fairly drawn alternatives, for no racially neutral reason." That, in itself, was indicative of discriminatory purpose and effect. Civil Rights Commission memo, pp. 3 and 8. In the case of South Carolina, the United States argued that "as a result of

the fragmentation of the black communities, the State's proposed plan does not fairly reflect minority voting strength as it exists in South Carolina." In so fragmenting black communities, it suggested, the state violated its own reapportionment criteria. "The inconsistent application of reapportionment criteria leads to the conclusion that the State consciously minimized the number of minority districts in which black voters would have a reasonable opportunity to elect candidates of their choice." Defendant's Response to Plaintiff's First Interrogatories, February 10, 1984, pp. 4–6.

58. Letters of objection contain a standard sentence: "Under these circumstances we are unable to conclude, as we must under the Voting Rights Act, that the submitted plan does not have the purpose and will not have the effect of abridging the right to vote . . ."

59. NAACP-Defendant's Supplemental Response to Interrogatories, April 2, 1984, pp. 3–4: "The redistricting plan as drawn avoidably and deliberately denies Blacks the equal opportunity to elect a candidate of their choice . . . Moreover, the State . . . failed and or refused to implement suggestions for redistricting made by the NAACP Defendants, as well as other minority organizations."

60. 490 F. Supp. 569 (D.D.C. 1979).

61. 490 F. Supp. at 581.

62. Civil Rights Commission memo, p. 9.

63. 450 F. Supp. 1171 (D.D.C. 1978), aff'd 439 U.S. 999 (1978). The Supreme Court affirmed the lower court decision without an opinion. The oft-quoted phrase is thus that of the D.C. court.

64. Letter to T. W. Thagard, Jr., from James P. Turner, acting assistant attorney general, civil rights division, July 21, 1981.

65. Letter of objection to Sumter County, Georgia (Reynolds to Henry Crisp), September 6, 1983.

66. 450 F. Supp. at 1176 (1978).

67. Civil Rights Commission memo, p. 1.

68. *Major v. Treen*, 547 F. Supp. 325 (E.D. La. 1983), the decision in the section 2 suit brought subsequent to the action of the Attorney General on the section 5 question, contains the facts of the case.

69. The Greene County example was given to me by David Hunter, an attorney in the voting section. Telephone conversation, August 1985.

70. Civil Rights Commission memo, p. 7.

71. Ibid., p. 11.

72. I owe my knowledge of the New York City case to Lewis Liman, who graciously shared with me the material that he gathered in preparation for his senior honors thesis, written for the Committee on Degrees in Social Studies, Harvard College, 1983. The documents all come from the firm of Paul, Weiss, Rifkind, Wharton, and Garrison, retained by the city as counsel.

73. That incumbent minorities were satisfied with the plan was generally acknowledged. Congressman Charles B. Rangel (a black) and Kenneth B. Clark, a noted black social scientist, had both publicly urged Mayor Koch to sign the reapportionment bill. Memo entitled "Summary of 1981 Reapportionment: New York City Council" submitted by Fabian G. Palomino, Counsel, The Council of the City of New

York Redistricting Committee, undated. The lone voice of dissent appears to have been councilman Gilberto Gerena-Valentin, who stated that he "would not have voted for the plan if [he] had known for sure that more minority districts could have been created," and that he believed that the redistricting commission would have placed his residence outside his current district had he voiced public opposition. Affidavit, undated.

74. Letter from Paul, Weiss, Rifkind, et al. to William Bradford Reynolds, assistant attorney general for civil rights, September 21, 1981, p. 19. "We are satisfied that at least 15 such districts exist, that all of them exceed 53% minority population, that 9 of them exceed 75%, and that the number of minority districts on any standard has been increased from 9 to 15." Press release, undated. The city reiterates the point in many of its documents. The civil rights groups, on the other hand, predicted that whites would continue to win all ten at-large seats, and that from single-member districts the same number of blacks and Hispanics (eight) would be returned as before; that number, they said, would represent a proportionate drop in their officeholding, given the expansion of the council. "It is shocking and inexcusable," a spokesman for the Citizens Union argued, ". . . for minority representation to be reduced at the same time as the minority population has so substantially increased." Press release, Citizens Union of the City of New York, June 23, 1981.

75. The city argued, however, that if the New York City Hispanic population of 1,405,957 found by the 1980 Census were added to the remainder (7,071,030), the total city population would be 8,476,987, or close to 1.5 million more than it actually is. The figure for whites was thus inflated; many "whites" were, in fact, Hispanic, and were being double-counted. New York City Council Redistricting Commission, "Memorandum on Increase of Council Districts from Thirty-Three to Thirty-Five," June 3, 1981. "In 1970," the city's attorneys said, "over 86% of Puerto Ricans identified themselves as white." (Undated, unsigned memo in question and answer format). Again, the point is that a great many "whites" were actually Hispanic. In fact, the number of whites, the city charged, was inflated in two ways: not only was a certain proportion of the Hispanic population being counted as white, but groups normally identified as "minority" had been arbitrarily listed as white. Thus the Civil Liberties Union plan treated Chinese, Japanese, Koreans, South Asians, and American Indians as white. Letter, Edward N. Costikian (legal counsel to the New York City Council) to William Bradford Reynolds, October 19, 1981.

76. Memorandum to Hon. Thomas J. Cuite and Hon. Edward L. Sadowsky from Edward N. Costikian, September 16, 1981. "The Bureau of the Census," he said, "has informally advised that they know of no reason why the use of the national averages is inappropriate for the New York numbers."

77. Department of Justice, Section 5 files, submission from the Nacogdoches Independent School District (Texas).

78. *Collins v. City of Norfolk*, 605 F. Supp. 377 (E.D. Va. 1984), Defendant's Post-Trial Brief Containing Proposed Findings of Fact and Conclusions of Law, June 20, 1984, p. 58; Plaintiffs' Proposed Findings of Fact, point 41.

79. "Comment Submitted by the New York Civil Liberties Union in response to the September 21, 1981 submission by Paul, Weiss, Rifkind, Wharton & Garrison

Regarding the 1981 New York City Council Reapportionment Plan," October 15, 1981, pp. 19–20.

80. Letter, Edward N. Costikian to William Bradford Reynolds, October 19, 1981, pp. 2–4.

81. *Collins v. City of Norfolk*, Defendant's Post-Trial Brief, pp. 61–63.

82. Ibid., pp. 25 and 62.

83. The elected black councilman was Wendell Foster. The point is made in an undated memo written by Peter W. Schneider and addressed to Edward N. Costikian, as well as elsewhere.

84. The statement was made by James W. Turner, acting assistant attorney general for civil rights, and was reported in the *New York Times*, 17 September 1981, p. B4.

85. That figure made its first public appearance in *United Jewish Organization v. Carey*, 430 U.S. 144 (1977). Asked by New York to define an acceptably black district, the Department of Justice had mentioned 65 percent as the goal. That 65 percent districts are a "rule of thumb" is now frequently acknowledged by the Department, as I have previously suggested.

86. "Harlem decreased from 32% of the Black population in 1970 to 25% of the Black population in 1980," the city went on. "In contrast, other widespread areas in Manhattan outside of Harlem . . . showed significant increases in the Black populations." (Palomino memo, "Summary of 1981 Reapportionment.") "In this city in the last 10 years minority population has been dispersing itself into what were formally lily-white districts," an undated press release asserted. "Every district," it went on, "except three saw an increase in the minority population. The most startling change was in Queens County . . . In Queens, seven 1970 lily-white districts with an average 7.8% minority population had a 1980 average of 25.6% minority population."

87. "New York Civil Liberties Union Report on Opposition to the 1981 City Council Reapportionment Plan," submitted to the U.S. Department of Justice, July 1981, p. 7. Cesar A. Perales, president and general counsel of the Puerto Rican Legal Defense and Education Fund (PRLDEF), stated that "city representatives in claiming that additional minority seats could not be created, have attempted to deliberately mislead the Federal officials reviewing the proposed reapportionment plan. We can clearly show, that by drawing compact and contiguous districts in the Bronx, there would result three minority Council districts, and not the two established in the City's plan." PRLDEF press release, undated. The Citizens Union of New York asserted that "at least 2 additional minority districts (one in Brooklyn and one in the Bronx)" could be created. Letter addressed to James Turner, acting assistant attorney general for civil rights, June 22, 1981.

88. The city rested its case on the 1977 election of Wendell Foster, the black councilman who had been elected from a district that had a total minority population of approximately 54 percent (blacks and Puerto Ricans together). Letter from Paul, Weiss, Rifkind, et al. to William Bradford Reynolds, the assistant attorney general for civil rights, dated September 21, 1981. Likewise, in 1979 Judge Bruce Wright, a black, had received almost 60 percent of the vote in Manhattan, although the black population for that borough was less than 22 percent. And David Dinkins, running for Manhattan borough president, had received 48 percent of the vote, although the

Manhattan black population had dropped a dramatic 24 percent over the decade. (The reference to Dinkins is contained in an undated press release; the black population figures are contained in the Palomino memo, "Summary of 1981 Reapportionment.") There was, as well, no iron law that blacks were always elected from black districts, the city argued. In the 1977 Democratic mayoral primary, the sole black candidate, Percy Sutton, obtained only about 50 percent of the vote in election districts that were more than 90 percent black. "We do not know," Costikian wrote, "of any statistical basis for asserting that the election of a minority candidate in this city requires a minority population in excess of any number. Whatever voting patterns may exist elsewhere, it is clear that in New York minority members have repeatedly been elected from constituencies in which the minority was a true minority." Memo, Costikian to Cuite and Sadowsky, September 16, 1981.

89. Judge Higginbotham, concurring in *Jones v. Lubbock*, 730 F.2d 233, 234 (5th Cir. 1984).

90. *Collins v. City of Norfolk*, Defendant's Post-Trial Brief, p. 71.

91. *State of South Carolina v. U.S.*, Civil Action 83-2636, U.S. District Court for the District of Columbia, Deposition of Bernard Grofman, June 19, 1984, p. 43.

92. *Gingles v. Edmisten*, 590 F. Supp. 345, 000 (E.D.N.C. 1984).

93. "New York Civil Liberties Union Report," p. 10.

94. "Retention of existing councilmanic districts is necessary to preserve both continuity within the electorate, and the historic and traditional councilmanic districts. This continuity permits a district population to develop the political mechanisms and community groups which insure that their interests are adequately considered by their council representative." Section on incumbency in memo to Edward N. Costikian from Peter W. Schneider, written in preparation for a press conference; no date. The city firmly maintained, however, that the "claim (Citizens Union) that new district Councilmanic lines were drawn to protect white incumbents [was] *unfounded and unfair.*" Other considerations, including maximizing minority representation, came into play. Letter to James Turner from Fabian Palomino, July 22, 1981. (Other documents made this same point.) Maintaining, to the extent possible, existing district lines made sense on other grounds as well, the city argued. "The existing district lines had met the requirement of compactness, contiguity and convenience . . . [They] had the benefit of and withstood the test of time insofar as lines of communication, representation and providing such services and support as possible to communities, groups, organizations and individuals . . . Minimal alteration of existing lines would also place the least burden on the Boards of Election in the various counties of the City. Such boards have the responsibility of creating, describing and mapping new election districts . . . as well as establishing new polling places, notifying voters of changes in election districts, preparing registration lists, and transferring poll registration cards to new election districts. Further, most of these changes have to be completed prior to the first day for the circulation of designating petitions—June 16, 1981." Palomino memo. Lines that seemed well-established, legitimized over time, appeared racially gerrymandered, however, to the Puerto Rican Legal Defense and Education Fund. In fact, it accused the city of ignoring the requirements of compactness, contiguity, and convenience, and of destroying natural communities and boundaries. Press release, undated.

95. Memo by Edward Costikian addressed to Paul Hancock, U.S. Department of Justice, January 27, 1982.

96. Letter, Palomino to Turner, August 5, 1981. Palomino argued, in fact, that there were "distinctly identifiable minorities such as Hispanic" for whom "separate districts" had to be created. "They may not be homogenized with other minorities, as suggested by the CLU, merely to create additional minority districts," he wrote. "That would be as discriminatory as homogenizing them into white districts and denied separate representation" [sic]. See also letter of February 8, 1982, from Costikian to Paul Hancock: "It is simply inaccurate and misleading to describe the so-called 'minority concentration' outlined by the Citizens Union as a single, homogeneous 'community.' In fact, the rather large geographical area identified by the Citizens Union is characterized by diverse and rapidly changing types of residential and commercial development, and contains persons of widely varying national, ethnic and socioeconomic origin and status. To describe this area as a 'community' simply because a majority of its residents are either black or Hispanic is to rob the term of any useful meaning, and indeed to adopt a view of minority persons that smacks of racial stereotyping."

97. Letter from William Bradford Reynolds to Fabian Palomino, counsel, NYC Council Redistricting Commission, City Hall: "While the city is under no obligation to maximize minority voting strength, the District Court of the District of Columbia has required that the city demonstrate that the plan 'fairly reflects the strength of [minority] voting power as it exists.' " The letter cites *Mississippi v. United States*, the misuse of which has been discussed earlier.

98. Motomura, "Preclearance," pp. 196, 245, and passim.

99. Katharine I. Butler, "Comments Regarding the Proposed Revision of the Attorney General's Procedures for the Administration of Section 5 of the Voting Rights Act," submitted to Gerald W. Jones, chief, voting section, Civil Rights Division, Department of Justice, July 5, 1985.

100. *South Carolina v. U.S.*, Plaintiff's Reply to Memorandum for the United States in Opposition to South Carolina's Motion for Partial Summary Judgment, May 17, 1984, p. 22.

101. *South Carolina v. U.S.*, Defendants-NAACP Intervenors' Respondent to Plaintiff's Second Set of Interrogatories, April 19, 1984, p. 6. Interrogatory No. 7 reads: "With respect to the South Carolina Senate, do you contend that incumbency protection is equivalent to an intent to minimize black voting strength?" The answer of the NAACP is: "(a) Not necessarily, but the effect is the same. (b) A plan drawn for the State of South Carolina Senate wherein incumbency protection is evident, in and of itself would minimize black voting strength considering the fact that prior to the election of Dr. Newman during a special election, no Black in recent memory or during this century has been elected to serve in the South Carolina Senate." It could be argued that the NAACP had in mind a plan the sole purpose of which was to protect incumbents, a plan in which every incumbent was ensured a safe district. But it would then have been attacking a straw man. The state was not proposing such a plan; it had created nine majority-black districts, and what the NAACP wanted was simply a tenth, along with a change in black percentage in some of the nine. In any case, in the same document the NAACP made clear its position that any plan that

failed to maximize black voting strength—that is, that compromised that strength by giving some weight to considerations such as incumbency—should be viewed as discriminatory. "Within the context of the meaning to the NAACP and its members, 'fairly reflects black voting strength' means that a redistricting plan must contain elements that do not dilute the minority voting strength and in fact maximize the minority voting strength" (pp. 2–3).

## 9. The Meaning of Electoral Equality

1. Report of the Committee on the Judiciary on S. 1992 (Voting Rights Act Extension), U.S. Senate, 97th Congress, 2nd Session, Report No. 97-417 (hereafter cited as 1982 Senate report), additional views of Senator Orrin G. Hatch, p. 94.

2. *Opelika-Auburn News*, 1 October 1985, p. 1.

3. 1982 Senate report, pp. 28–29.

4. Ibid., p. 26. The decision was *McCain v. Lybrand*, which involved at-large voting in Edgefield County, South Carolina.

5. *McCain v. Lybrand*, D.S.C. No. 74-281 (April 17, 1980), reprinted in 1981 House hearings, p. 302, as cited in Paul W. Jacobs, II, and Timothy G. O'Rourke, "Racial Polarization in Vote Dilution Cases under Section 2 of the Voting Rights Act: The Impact of *Thornburg v. Gingles*," *Journal of Law and Politics*, III (Fall 1986), 350 n. 179.

6. The Report of the Subcommittee on the Constitution to the Senate Committee on the Judiciary, 97th Congress, 2nd Session (1982), reprinted in the 1982 Senate report, pp. 148–149.

7. 1982 Senate report, p. 33. Emphasis added.

8. Ibid., p. 19, quoting *Reynolds v. Sims* in explaining "the basic dilution principle."

9. *Collins v. Norfolk*, 768 F.2d 572 (4th Cir. 1985), Reply Brief for Appellants (December 5, 1984), p. 8.

10. *Jones v. City of Lubbock, Texas*, C.A. 5-76-34 (E.D. Tx. 1983), p. 8. The court dismissed the fact that minority registration was as high as white on the ground that this was attributable to special effort, a registration drive in the minority community. Past discrimination thus overrode evidence of present access, particularly when attaining that access required an effort directed at the black and Mexican-American communities.

11. *Major v. Treen*, 574 F. Supp. 325, 351 (E.D. La. 1983). In theory, of course, black registration rates could be lower relative to white in New Orleans, despite the state average; in fact that is not the case.

12. 1982 Senate report, p. 29, n. 114.

13. Warren Leslie, *Dallas Public and Private: Aspects of an American City* (New York: Grossman, 1964), p. 63.

14. Richard A. Smith, "How Business Failed Dallas," *Fortune*, 70 (July 1964), 214. On this point see also Carol Thometz, *The Decision-Makers: The Power Structure of Dallas* (Dallas, Tex.: Southern Methodist University Press, 1963), pp. 80–82.

15. *Lipscomb v. Wise*, 399 F. Supp. 782, 786 (N.D. Tex. 1975).

16. *Lipscomb v. Wise*, trial record, deposition of George Allen, January 4, 1974, pp. 24–25.

17. *Lipscomb v. Wise*, deposition of George Allen, p. 49.

18. Letter to Drew Days III, assistant attorney general for civil rights, from John H. Fullinwider, Bois d'Arc Patriots, October 24, 1979.

19. *Collins v. City of Norfolk, Virginia*, 605 F. Supp. 377 (E.D. Va. 1984), Plaintiffs' Memorandum in Support of Motion for Preliminary Injunction (April 5, 1984), p. 6.

20. *Overton v. City of Austin, Texas*, C.A. No. A-84-CA-189 (W.D. Tex. March 12, 1985), p. 18.

21. Ibid., pp. 16–17.

22. *Lodge v. Buxton*, C.A. No. 176-55 (S.D., Ga., October 26, 1978), trial record, deposition of Thomas Lovett, pp. 6–7.

23. *Lodge v. Buxton*, transcript of record, p. 404.

24. Paul Jeffrey Stekler, "Electing Blacks to Office in the South: Black Candidates, Bloc Voting and Racial Unity Twenty Years after the Voting Rights Act," paper delivered at the Conference on Voting Rights and the Democratic Process: Where Do We Stand Today? The Center for Legal Studies on Intergovernmental Relations, Tulane Law School, New Orleans, March 29, 1985, p. 19, n. 21. A shortened version of the paper was later printed in *The Urban Lawyer*, 17 (Summer 1985), 473–487.

25. 605 F. Supp. at 392.

26. My assessment of the Helms/Hunt race has relied heavily on Lee E. Goodman, "Helms-Hunt 1984: Racially Polarized Voting in North Carolina," student paper for a course on minority voting rights submitted to Professor Timothy G. O'Rourke at the University of Virginia, 1985.

27. *Kirksey v. City of Jackson, Miss.*, 506 F. Supp. 491 (1981); 663 F.2d 659 (5th Cir., 1981). The at-large voting was the issue in the case; the question of the referendum was raised in the context of debate on the intent behind the maintenance of the system.

28. *Kirksey v. City of Jackson*, Reply Brief for Appellants, p. 16.

29. Ibid., p. 17.

30. Ibid., p. 20.

31. 506 F. Supp. at 515.

32. *Thornburg v. Gingles*, 106 S.Ct. 2752 (1986), Appellant's Brief, p. 30. I am indebted to Katharine Butler for this point.

33. *Lodge v. Buxton*, deposition of James Flynt Buxton, p. 6.

34. *Lodge v. Buxton*, deposition of Ray De Laigle, p. 6.

35. The quotations from residents in the two Texas communities are from confidential interviews conducted by Bill McKibben, a research assistant, in April 1982. The quotation from the Georgetown minister comes from notes taken in the course of voting rights hearings conducted by the South Carolina State Advisory Committee to the U.S. Commission on Civil Rights, November 20, 1985.

36. *Thornburg v. Gingles*, 106 S.Ct. at 2773 (1986). Justice Brennan's argument has been made as well in articles and briefs by attorneys and expert witnesses

for plaintiffs in section 2 suits. See, for example, Richard L. Engstrom, "The Reincarnation of the Intent Standard: Federal Judges and At-Large Election Cases," *Howard Law Journal*, 28 (1985), 495–513. Engstrom's argument (reiterated in the Brennan opinion) is that any other view revives the intent test explicitly rejected by Congress in amending section 2. It does so by requiring an inquiry into the motivation of voters. Yet the concern of those who urged the amendment of section 2 was the seeming insistence in *Mobile* on examining the motivation of legislators who adopted or maintained a challenged electoral system. The argument was that, first, such motivation was difficult to establish, and second, it was irrelevant to the question of black electoral exclusion. No witness at the 1982 hearings suggested that courts should not consider whether the failure of white voters to support a black candidate might have a legitimate, nonracial basis.

Brennan dismisses the relevance of factors such as greater candidate visibility as a consequence of more advertising. It would be anomalous, he argues, to consider socioeconomic factors in establishing a section 2 violation, as the Senate report directs courts to do, and yet to allow the defendant to contend that such disparities and not racism explain voting patterns. But the two questions that Brennan merges are distinct. Socioeconomic differences between blacks and whites suggest unequal electoral opportunities when they are linked with low political participation, whether or not whites and blacks are engaged in bloc voting. The Senate report lists the factors separately, and they should be considered as distinct items. To turn most of the listed factors into subcategories under "racial polarization" is to confuse the whole issue.

37. He was joined on this point by Justices Marshall, Blackmun, and Stevens.

38. Jacobs and O'Rourke, "Racial Polarization," pp. 301 and 308. I have relied heavily on this thorough and thoughtful article in my discussion of racial bloc voting, both in this chapter and in Chapter 8. The Supreme Court's opinion in *Gingles*, moreover, only further muddied already murky waters. Brennan writes: "There is no simple doctrinal test for the existence of legally significant racial bloc voting" (106 S.Ct. at 2770). At the same time, however, Brennan elevates minority electoral success and bloc voting to the status of prime factors, with no support from the Senate report or the legislative history (ibid. at 2766 n. 15). Nor does case law support Brennan's decision. *White* hardly considered the factor of polarization, and *Zimmer* did not include it on its famous list. For a lucid explanation of statistical methodology—ecological regression, for instance—see Jacobs and O'Rourke, "Racial Polarization."

39. *Gingles v. Edmisten*, 590 F. Supp. 345, 368 (E.D.N.C. 1984).

40. 106 S.Ct. at 2770.

41. *Jones v. City of Lubbock*, 730 F.2d 233, 234 (5th Cir. 1984).

42. That disproportionately low minority officeholding must be the starting point of any suit was explicitly recognized by the Supreme Court in *Thornburg v. Gingles*. "It is obvious," Justice Brennan notes in a footnote, "that unless minority group members experience substantial difficulty electing representatives of their choice, they cannot prove that a challenged electoral mechanism impairs their ability 'to elect.' " By "representatives," Justice Brennan means minority officeholders, the footnote makes clear. In fact, it elevates the "extent to which minority group mem-

bers have been elected to public office" to one of the two most important factors on the Senate list, although the report explicitly states that all factors are to be considered equally important (106 S.Ct. at 2766 n. 15). *Gingles* also argued that plaintiffs literally have no case if the minority group is not "sufficiently large and geographically compact to constitute a majority in a single-member district." If minority voters challenge a multimember districting scheme and yet are without the potential to elect representatives in the absence of that scheme, they cannot claim to have been injured by its use (106 S.Ct. at 2766 n. 17). Nothing in the legislative history suggests that a minority group that does not qualify as a majority in a single-member district is not entitled to relief from a discriminatory electoral environment—one infused with racism. Remedies other than single-member districts are available. Moreover, the Court's rule creates a multitude of problems. For instance, suppose that in a city that elects at-large the minority group is very small, but doubling the size of the city council would permit very small single-member districts to be drawn. Under such circumstances, does the minority group qualify? Are blacks and Hispanics to be counted together in making up a qualifying minority group? Does a group that will constitute 51 percent of a district qualify, or does it have to meet the Justice Department standard of 65 percent—a standard built on the premise that a simple majority will not give the minority voters assured control of the district? I am indebted to Katharine Butler for spelling out some of these complexities.

43. Blacks had been nominated in fourteen out of twenty-one primary contests, and in three of the remaining seven, the black candidate had lacked support from a majority of blacks. In nine out of fourteen general elections in which black Democrats ran, the black had won. See the appendix to the Supreme Court's opinion, 106 S.Ct. at 2782–2783. In addition to this success in races involving House and Senate seats, in every district at issue on appeal blacks had been elected to city councils, school boards, judgeships, and other such local offices.

44. The fact of proportionate or nearly proportionate black officeholding in three out of five contested districts is acknowledged by Justice O'Connor in her concurring opinion (in which Justices Burger, Powell, and Rehnquist joined). Nevertheless, she did not find the district court's opinion on this score clearly erroneous, except with respect to House District 23, in which in each of six elections since 1970 one of the three who won was black. Her logic with respect to the other two districts is difficult to follow, and the concurrence reads like a dissent. 106 S.Ct. at 2794.

45. 590 F. Supp. at 367–369.

46. 106 S.Ct. at 2780. The Court held that "as a matter of law" the district court did not err "in refusing to treat the fact that some black candidates have succeeded as dispositive of appellees' §2 claim. Where multimember districting generally works to dilute the minority vote, it cannot be defended on the ground that it sporadically and serendipitously benefits minority voters" (ibid.). The Senate report had stated that "the election of a few minority candidates does not 'necessarily foreclose the possibility of dilution of the black vote,' " yet was the record of black success in North Carolina that of "a few minority candidates"? The Supreme Court sanctioned not only the effort of the district court to explain away every black electoral victory, but also its conclusion that black success was "too limited" (ibid. at 2782). By what measure? No standard was explicitly provided, although proportionality was clearly

the implicit one. A further question can be raised: if the reasons for black electoral victory were considered pertinent to a section 2 inquiry, did it not follow that the reasons for defeat were also relevant? Justice Brennan subscribed to the former view but not the latter. As Katharine Butler has pointed out to me, decisions such as *Gingles* suggest that a record of minority electoral success never counts *for* the jurisdiction, although its absence of course counts against it. The point applies equally to a history of discrimination, slating, and racial appeals: their presence is a mark against the defending state, county, or city; their absence is not a point in the jurisdiction's favor.

No suggestion was made in *Gingles* that black electoral success could be dismissed because whites voted for the "wrong" blacks, although that is a frequent argument. Whites, it is said, will only vote for an "extra-special" black or a black who is particularly acceptable to the white community. Though this may be true, and in some instances is relevant to the question of exclusion, in general the argument should be approached with considerable skepticism. Only "certain" whites can get elected in particular communities or states; hence the enormous effort devoted to acquiring the right "image."

47. *New York Times*, 9 August 1983, p. A15.

48. *Collins v. City of Norfolk*, 605 F. Supp. at 400. Defendant's Post-Trial Brief Containing Proposed Findings of Fact and Conclusions of Law (June 20, 1984), p. 46.

49. Lawrence Julius Hanks, "Black Political Empowerment in the Black Belt South: The Quest for Black Political Power in Three Black Belt Georgia Counties," doctoral dissertation, Harvard University, 1984, p. 281.

50. Stekler, "Electing Blacks to Office," p. 2.

51. Confidential interview, Mobile, Alabama, January 1982.

52. *New York Times*, 12 July 1984, p. B7; *Boston Globe*, 11 July 1984, p. 3.

53. *New York Times*, 15 July 1984, p. E3. The quotation is the reporter's rendition of the point made by the attorney.

54. *New York Times*, 28 September 1984, p. 23; 30 September 1984, p. 28; 1 October 1985, p. B11.

55. Representative Joseph P. Addabbo won two-to-one over the former chairman of the New York City Housing Authority in a Queens district that was almost 60 percent black. Brooklyn state senator Marty Markowitz came away with a 64 percent victory in a 74 percent black district over a protégé of a powerful black community organization. In the third race, white assembly member Rhoda Jacobs, who represented a 65 percent black district, took 65 percent of the vote against a black businessman endorsed by that same coalition organization. *New York Times*, 22 September 1984, p. 25.

56. *New York Times*, 27 November 1985, p. 1; 8 December 1985, p. 30; 12 December 1985, p. 20.

57. Jim Sleeper, "A Message from New York City's Black Voters," op-ed, *New York Times*, 22 September 1984.

58. *Boston Globe*, 31 August 1982, p. 14.

59. Interviews in Burke County, May 1986.

60. "Hands That Picked Cotton: Black Politics in Today's Rural South," documentary film made for WYES, New Orleans; first broadcast, February 1985.

61. Ibid.

62. Rosellen Brown, *Civil Wars* (New York: Penguin Books, 1985), p. 216.

63. Confidential interview, Burke County, Georgia, May 1986.

64. *McCord v. City of Fort Lauderdale*, 617 F. Supp. 1093, 1096 (S.D. Fla. 1985).

65. Confidential interview, Birmingham, Alabama, May 1985.

66. Confidential interview, Mobile, Alabama, January 1982.

67. That leader was Gary Cooper, and his qualms about running for the post of city commissioner were expressed in an interview, Mobile, Janaury 1982.

68. Stekler, "Electing Blacks to Office," p. 15.

69. Ibid., p. 12.

70. Ibid., passim. This is the central point in the article.

71. Although in contests that pit white candidates against black, a high degree of black unity can generally be expected, blacks are certainly no strangers to factionalism. Interviewed in the *New York Times* in 1982, Georgia state senator Julian Bond referred to blacks in Georgia's Fifth Congressional District as a "cohesive community," with the implication that all black residential concentrations were "cohesive." 3 May 1982, p. B11. In fact, in that heavily black district a bitter fight was waged in 1986 between two black congressional candidates (Bond himself and John Lewis), revealing deep divisions. The Jesse Jackson campaign for the Democratic nomination for president in 1984 prompted considerable infighting within the black community.

72. *New York Times*, 28 September 1982, p. B1.

73. Ibid.

74. Stekler, "Electing Blacks to Office," p. 8.

75. Hanks, "Black Political Empowerment," p. 263. The problem of low black turnout, it should be noted, is not confined to the rural South or even the South in general. As Steven Erie has pointed out, the electoral base of black politics has eroded in the North as well. Between 1964 and 1977, the voting rate for young urban blacks dropped from 56 percent to 29 percent, while the rate for unemployed blacks went from 62 percent to 37 percent. "Low turnout hurt big-city black politicians seeking to challenge white-controlled machine and reform regimes," Erie writes. *Rainbow's End: Irish-Americans and the Dilemmas of Urban Machine Politics* (Berkeley: University of California Press, forthcoming), chap. 7.

76. Stekler, "Electing Blacks to Office," p. 15.

77. Confidential interview, Burke County, Georgia, May 1986.

78. *New York Times*, 22 March 1982, p. A10.

79. *New York Times*, 14 October 1983, p. A31, op-ed, Martin Kilson, "If Jesse Jackson Runs."

80. *New York Times*, 14 April 1983, p. B15.

81. *New York Times*, 10 November 1983, p. D28.

82. *New York Times*, 10 February 1985, p. 24; 7 April 1985, p. E4; 11 April 1985, p. 16.

83. *New York Times*, 22 March 1985, p. 10.

84. Thus in House District 36 the two black candidates running in 1982 got 50 percent and 39 percent of the white vote respectively in the Democratic primary and

42 and 29 percent in the general election. In Senate District No. 22 in 1978 the black candidate received 47 percent of the white vote in the Democratic primary and 41 percent in the general election. In House District No. 39 in 1980 a black candidate got 40 percent of the white vote in the Democratic primary, 32 percent in the general election. In that same district a black candidate running in 1982 received 36 percent in the Democratic primary, 46 percent in the general election. In House District 23 in 1982 a black candidate received 37 percent of the white vote in the primary, 43 percent in the general election. In House District No. 21 a black candidate in 1980 received 31 percent of the white vote in the primary, 44 percent in the general election. In 1982 in that same district the black candidate received 39 percent of the white vote in the primary and 45 percent in the general election. 590 F. Supp. at 365–372.

85. As Katharine Butler has pointed out, within a single North Carolina district the support received by the black candidate differed widely. In House District 36 in elections separated by just two years, the range was from 22 percent in 1980 to 50 percent in 1982. And that 50 percent assumes that the same whites voted for both black candidates and thus is a minimum figure. In the 1982 election, one black candidate was the choice of more white votes than the other.

86. 617 F. Supp. at 1096.

87. Interview, Burke County, Georgia, May 1986. It should be noted that white voters may vote *for* a black candidate because the black is more conservative than his or her white opponent. This was the case in a Charleston city council race and also in a Mobile race for a state legislative seat. Interviews in Charleston and Mobile, December 1981 and January 1982.

88. Confidential interview (conducted by Bill McKibben), Ozona, Texas, April 1982.

89. *New York Times*, 15 July 1984, p. E3. The quotation is the reporter's version of what Lowery said. Poll data show blacks generally to the left of whites on a number of issues. Thus a 1986 poll revealed that 65 percent of blacks but only 24 percent of whites thought the government should guarantee jobs. Eighty-six percent of blacks but only 55 percent of whites said the government should spend more on social programs. Poll conducted by Gallup and the Joint Center for Political Studies, reported in the *Washington Post National Weekly Edition*, 27 October 1986, p. 37.

90. *Boston Globe*, 9 October 1986, p. 33.

91. Stekler, "Electing Blacks to Office," p. 10.

92. *Collins v. City of Norfolk*, Defendant's Post-Trial Brief, June 20, 1984, p. 71.

93. Rufus P. Browning, Dale Rogers Marshall, and David H. Tabb, *Protest Is Not Enough: The Struggle of Blacks and Hispanics for Equality in Urban Politics* (Berkeley: University of California Press, 1984), pp. 142–143.

94. Stekler, "Electing Blacks to Office," p. 11.

95. Ibid., pp. 12–13.

96. Interview, Jefferson County, Alabama, May 1985.

97. Report of David H. Hunter, telephone conversation, October 1986.

98. *Bolden v. City of Mobile*, C.A. No. 75-279 P (S.D. Ala. April 15, 1982), personal notes taken during the trial, May 1981.

99. *Rogers v. Lodge*, 458 U.S. 613, 632 n. 1 (1982).

100. *Bolden v. City of Mobile*, testimony of Paul Whiteurs, from personal trial notes.

101. Interviews, Douglas Wicks, Robert Edington, and Pat Edington, Mobile, Alabama, January 1982. The information on black electoral success in Jefferson County came from *Taylor v. The Jefferson County Commission*, C.A. No. CV-84-C-1730-S, Defendants' Additional Facts, p. 13.

102. Confidential interview, Jefferson County, May 1985.

103. Interviews, Burke County, May 1986.

104. Interview (conducted by Bill McKibben), San Antonio, April 1982.

105. The quotations from Georgetown, South Carolina, officials come from notes taken as an observer at voting rights hearings conducted by the South Carolina State Advisory Commission to the U.S. Commission on Civil Rights, November 20, 1985. I make my point with respect to Charleston on the basis of interviews conducted in December 1981. My contention with respect to racial cleavages and the behavior of minority representatives rests on evidence from interviews in many jurisdictions in the South. The point, however, has been made by many other scholars, including Browning, Marshall, and Tabb, who provide a good bibliography on the impact of black officeholding on the provision of local services.

That most of the work on a county commission, for instance, involves "technical matters" is evident from the agenda for the Burke County commissioners' meeting of May 13, 1986. The agenda in its entirety consisted of the following items: (1) Call to order and reading of minutes. (2) Receiving of guests. (3) Proposal to close county dirt road running through property of Emily A. Daniel and Leonard E. Herrington. (4) Receiving of bids on one (1) motor grader. (5) Receiving of bids on two (2) pick-up trucks. (6) Receiving of bids on two (2) dump bodies. (7) Receiving of bids on two (2) cabs and chassis to be used as dump trucks. (8) Request from Ben Story and Sidney Cox for tentative approval of road repairs in Deerwood Subdivision. (9) Proposal from Waynesboro Rotary Club concerning addition to Burke County Office Park. (10) Application from George F. Agerton, Jr. for a Class B Beer and Wine License. (11) Application from Margie W. Grant for a Class B Beer and Wine License. (12) Bids on remodeling work on Four Points Voting Precinct building. (13) Request from Johnny Lovett for approval of mobile home park. (14) Request from Mike Betts for approval of mobile home park. (15) Request from Ricky Flakes for approval of mobile home park. (16) Request for approval of addition to Lake Crystal Subdivision. (17) Confirmation of bids on 2.8 miles of resurfacing on Collins Road (PR40-1). (18) Confirmation of bids on transport of diesel received on April 24, 1986. (19) Reports and information.

106. Browning, Marshall, and Tabb, *Protest Is Not Enough*, especially chaps. 4 and 5.

107. "If the plaintiff proceeds under the 'results' test then the court would assess the impact of the challenged structure or practice on the basis of objective factors," the Senate report explains in introducing its list of "typical factors." 1982 Senate Report, p. 27.

108. Harold W. Stanley, "Race and the Runoff," paper delivered at the annual

meeting of the Southwestern Political Science Association, Houston, March 20–23, 1985.

109. Telephone conversation, David Hunter, October 1986. Assuming that only one black candidate would have run had there been no second election, the race would have been between a black and a white, as in the runoff. Different procedural rules would thus have had the same effect. The race was in 1986 in supervisor beat 5.

110. Katharine Inglis Butler, "The Majority Vote Requirement: The Case against Its Wholesale Elimination," *The Urban Lawyer*, 17 (September 1985), 448.

111. See Jack Bass, "Democrats: Here's a 40% Solution," *The Washington Post*, 22 April 1984, pp. D1–2.

112. *Collins v. Norfolk*, 605 F. Supp. 377, 400 (E.D. Va. 1984).

113. *United Jewish Organizations v. Carey*, 430 U.S. 144, 166 (1977). Justice White (for the Court) noted that the proposed districting plan, challenged on constitutional grounds by Hasidic petitioners, "left white majorities in approximately 70% of the assembly and senate districts in Kings County, which had a countywide population that was 65% white. Thus . . . whites would not be underrepresented relative to their share of the population." The latter, however, was not the question. Plaintiffs had argued that they, as an insular group, had been denied representation when their district had been divided in half in order to create one that was majority-nonwhite.

114. Butler and Thernstrom, *"Thornburg v. Gingles."*

115. Confidential interviews, Mobile and New Orleans, January 1982 and December 1981.

116. See *Davis v. Bandemer*, 106 S.Ct. 2797 (1986).

117. *Washington Post National Weekly Edition*, 15 September 1986, p. 16.

118. *Alabama Journal and Advertiser*, 9 March 1986, p. B1. (Alvin Benn, "Single-Member Districts Chance Face of Government in Alabama.") Emphasis added.

119. *Collins v. Norfolk*, transcript of trial proceedings, pp. 790–791. The witness was Kimball Brace. Plaintiffs' attorney Frank Parker made the same point. Trial transcript, pp. 15–16.

120. The important issues in these cases are factual, not legal, and trial court findings will be overturned only when the court's conclusions are clearly erroneous, every member of the Supreme Court seemed to agree. But while the Court criticized the district court's aggregation of data, its failure to engage in district-specific ("intensely local") appraisals, in fact it cited the lower court's aggregate statistics in arguing that legally significant polarized voting had been found. I am indebted, again, to Katharine Butler for this point.

121. Katharine Inglis Butler, "Reapportionment, the Courts, and the Voting Rights Act: A Resegregation of the Political Process?" *University of Colorado Law Review*, 56 (Fall 1984), 21.

122. 1982 Senate Report, pp. 31–32.

123. Ibid., p. 31.

124. 768 F.2d 572 (4th Circuit 1985), Reply Brief for Appellants, p. 9. Parker's opening statement in the Norfolk trial argued that, in amending section 2, Congress

"was aiming particularly at at-large election systems . . . These at-large election systems," he said, "tend to dilute minority voting strength . . . Congress made a decision in passing this statute that minorities are advantaged when there are districts which are black majority rather than having majorities spread out throughout an entire community." Transcript of Trial Proceedings, pp. 5–6.

125. Timothy O'Rourke estimated that in 1986 it cost a jurisdiction at least $250,000 to contest a suit, assuming an appeal by one party or the other following the trial court's judgment. Such sums are easily borne by a city such as Norfolk, Virginia, but not by a small town such as Warrenton, Virginia, with a population of less than 4,000.

126. *Opelika-Auburn News*, 1 October 1985, p. 1.

127. *Tuscaloosa News*, 20 July 1985, p. 1.

128. My count is from the periodic notices issued by the Department of Justice listing section 5 submissions.

129. *Alabama Journal and Advertiser*, 9 March 1986, p. B1.

130. 1982 *Senate Report*, p. 33.


## Conclusion

1. *Reynolds v. Sims*, 377 U.S. 533, 555 (1964).

2. Ibid. at 565.

3. Ibid. at 555, n. 29, quoting Justice Douglas dissenting in *South v. Peters*, 339 U.S. 276, 279.

4. Report of the Committee on the Judiciary on S. 1992 (Report No. 97-417: Voting Rights Act Extension), U.S. Senate, 97th Congress, 2nd session (hereafter cited as 1982 Senate report), p. 10. The 1984 Democratic Party platform did not embrace proportional representation outright but did describe the right "to have one's vote counted fully and fairly" as "the most important civil right of every American citizen." "Fully and fairly" refers, of course, to protection from vote dilution, which, if not carefully defined, amounts to a proportional representation entitlement. "A Democratic President and Administration," the platform states, "pledge to eliminate any and all discriminatory barriers to full voting rights, whether they be at-large requirements, second-primaries, gerrymandering, annexation, dual registration, dual voting or other practices." The statement borders on condemning all such electoral procedures as per se discriminatory. *Congressional Quarterly Weekly Report*, 42 (July 21, 1984), p. 1767.

5. The Democratic Party's dependence in the South on the black vote was recognized as early as the 1964 presidential contest. See Mark Stern, "The 1964 Presidential Election: Partisan Shifts and the Southern Black Vote," unpublished paper. Increasing GOP gains among southern whites in subsequent years have of course increased Democratic Party dependence on its black constituents. On southern congressional support for civil rights questions, see Charles S. Bullock III "Congressional Voting and the Mobilization of the Black Electorate in the South," *Journal of Politics*, 43 (August 1981), 662–682; Merle Black, "Racial Composition of Con-

gressional Districts and Support for Federal Voting Rights in the American South," *Social Science Quarterly*, 59 (December 1978), 435–450; Mark Stern, "Southern Congressional Civil Rights Voting and the New Southern Political Demography," *Southeastern Political Review*, 11 (Spring 1983), 69–90; Mark Stern, "Legislative Responsiveness and the New Southern Politics," in *The Voting Rights Act: Consequences and Implications*, ed. Lorn S. Foster (New York: Praeger), pp. 105–122.

6. On Governor Kean, see *New York Times*, 6 November 1985, p. 1. Kean was reported to have picked up approximately 60 percent of the black vote. On D'Amato and Specter, see *New York Times*, 19 October 1986, p. 34. On Cochran, see *New York Times*, 26 October 1984, p. 19. *The National Review* has argued that Senator Jesse Helms owed his 1984 victory to an eleven-percentage-point surge in black support in the closing days of the contest. Henry Klingeman, "I Just Called to Say I Love You," 7 November 1986, p. 28. Senator Strom Thurmond has regularly courted the black vote; see, for instance, *New York Times Magazine*, 27 November 1983, p. 38.

7. Telephone conversation with William D. Barnard, Birmingham, Alabama, November 1986. In the third "safe" white district, the Democratic incumbent ran unopposed. Barnard, a scholar of Alabama history and politics, argued that one of the Democrats who lost would unquestionably have won had voting remained county-wide.

8. My source on the partisan consequences of redistricting in South Carolina is Katharine Butler, telephone conversation, July 1985.

9. *Washington Post*, 30 June 1985, p. 23. "You want redistricting, with lines drawn so that some districts include at least 65 percent black?" one reporter quotes Republicans and "dwellers-in-the-suburbs" as saying. "Fine, we'll give you 90 [percent black districts]." Tom Bethel, *The American Spectator*, 15 (July 1982), 5. The political scientist Charles Bullock reports that the Joint Center for Political Studies, a black-run Washington research institute, has suggested that black legislators ally themselves with Republicans when devising legislative districting plans. Bullock examined partisan shifts in state legislatures as a consequence of redistricting subsequent to the 1980 census, and concluded that "overall the GOP did better in the preclearance states than elsewhere in the South or in the nation as a whole." In other words, in those states that either made or were forced to make a special effort to create majority-black districts in order to comply with section 5 requirements, not only black candidates but Republican ones fared better than elsewhere. Charles S. Bullock, III, "The Effects of Redistricting on Racial and Partisan Representation in Southern State Legislatures," unpublished paper.

This is not to say that Republican gains in southern state legislatures have only one explanation: the loss of potential support for Democratic candidates that results from creating safe black districts and removing Democratic voters from adjacent districts. White southerners began to drift away from the Democratic Party after its 1948 convention. In 1964 GOP presidential candidate Barry Goldwater showed the South to be fertile ground for Republican aspirations. See George B. Tindall, *The Disruption of the Solid South* (New York: W. W. Norton, 1972); Reg Murphy and Hal Gulliver, *Southern Strategy* (New York: Charles Scribner, 1971); Everett Carll

Ladd, Jr., and Charles D. Hadley, *Transformations of the American Party System: Political Coalitions from the New Deal to the 1970s* (New York: W. W. Norton, 1975).

Of course Republicans have had their eye on Congress as well. "The Voting Rights Act . . . has become the [Republican Party's] ally in its bid to take control of Congress," the *Washington Post* observed in 1981. "We didn't know it would turn out this way when they passed the Voting Rights Act, but it sure helps us now," a Texas Republican remarked (20 May 1981, p. 9). That same year a group of black Democrats and white Republicans in Georgia (labeled a "cynical coalition" by the liberal *Atlanta Constitution*) sought to raise the black concentration in the Fifth Congressional District from 57 percent to 69 percent. In defending the action, Julian Bond simply said, "On this issue we have a lot in common" (*New York Times*, 28 September 1981, p. 14).

Republicans early saw another benefit the Voting Rights Act might bring them. Attorney General Mitchell "is known to believe that Negro registration benefits Republicans because it drives the southern whites out of the Democratic Party," the *New York Times* reported in 1969 (14 December 1969, sec. IV, p. 2).

10. For this reason, only the discriminatory purpose and retrogression questions should be asked in the course of a preclearance review. The Justice Department, I argued in Chapter 8, has never in this respect adhered to the law; by creating detours around established and commonsense legal standards, it has assumed freewheeling power to object to districting plans and other electoral changes that do not seem "right." Nevertheless, those detours never became officially sanctioned routes and could thus be abandoned with ease. The situation dramatically changed, however, in January 1987—after the text of this book went to press. In its newly revised section 5 guidelines ("Procedures for the Administration of Section 5"), the Justice Department "incorporated" section 2 into section 5. Electoral changes submitted for federal review under section 5 will henceforth be judged by section 2 standards as well, it announced. In other words, an objection will be lodged if a method of election is intentionally discriminatory or has either a discriminatory effect or a forbidden result.

Detours around the law have become official policy. It will now be asked of every revised electoral procedure subject to a preclearance review: Does the proposed change deny minority voters an equal opportunity to elect candidates of their choice? Does the "totality of circumstances" suggest electoral inequality between minority and white citizens? Federal administrators, remote from the scene, will consequently play plaintiff, defendant, and judge all rolled into one, with no reliable way of gathering information on race and politics in the local jurisdictions remotely comparable to that which opposing attorneys present at a trial. As the Justice Department itself admits in its "comments" introducing the new guidelines, "Unlike court proceedings, administrative review . . . does not include the kind of hearing procedures that provide for the full presentation of evidence and rebuttal evidence by contesting parties and others interested in the proceedings. There is no formal record developed with finds of fact and conclusions of law." Without the minimum safeguards of a judicial proceeding, districting and other plans in covered jurisdictions will thus be judged by the vague and subjective standards contained in section 2.

Civil rights groups had for some time argued that every section 5 review should address the section 2, discriminatory "results," question. Reynolds briefly went along with their arguments, changed his mind in September 1986, but reversed his position four months later. Yet, apart from one footnote buried in the Senate Judiciary Committee report and unsupported by the text to which it is appended, nothing in the legislative record supports Reynolds' decision. During the debates of 1981–1982, civil rights spokesmen directly and indirectly assured members of Congress that the amendment of section 2 would not change section 5. (See, for instance, the Congressional Record of June 23, 1982, pp. H3844 and 3845, recording an exchange between Representatives Don Edwards and Elliott H. Levitas.) Moreover, no witness at the hearings questioned the adequacy of judicial power under the preclearance provision; that provision was not a topic of discussion. The change in section 5 thus rests on the assumption that Congress, without debate, acted to give dramatic new force to a provision, the limits of which were well understood.

Once again, the process of enforcement has substantially amended the act. What explains Reynolds' decision? The political power of the civil rights groups—discussed at length in Chapters 5 and 6. As in 1982, the administration had nothing to gain and everything to lose from opposition to the civil rights community—particularly since the press was bound to depict doubts about changing section 5 (without congressional authority) as hostile to civil rights. Press reporting, in fact, on Reynolds' decision may have reached a new low. The *New York Times*, for instance, stated that the new regulations permitted the Justice Department to reject electoral changes if they were "determined to have a discriminatory effect on black voting power, regardless of whether the local authorities intended such a bias" (6 January 1987). The power to reject changes on the basis of their discriminatory effect, of course, was never in question. "Result" was the issue, and effect and result, it should be clear, are two quite different questions.

11. *City of Port Arthur v. United States*, 459 U.S. 159 (1982).

12. 1982 Senate report, p. 33.

13. Hearings on the Voting Rights Act, Subcommittee on the Constitution of the Committee on the Judiciary, U.S. Senate, 97th Congress, 2nd session (hereafter cited as 1982 Senate hearings), testimony of Armand Derfner, pp. 803 and 810.

14. 1982 Senate hearings, p. 803.

15. Ibid., testimony of Professor Norman Dorsen, p. 963.

16. Ibid., testimony of Thomas C. McCain, p. 1138.

17. "Hands That Picked Cotton: Black Politics in Today's Rural South," a documentary film made for WYES, New Orleans. First broadcast, February 1985.

18. In making this point, I rely heavily on the interviews I conducted in such cities and counties as Mobile, Charleston, New Orleans, and Burke County (Georgia) in the years 1981 to 1986. Marshall, Browning, and Tabb, on the basis of interviews with blacks and Hispanics in California, make the same point. Rufus P. Browning, Dale Rogers Marshall, and David H. Tabb, *Protest Is Not Enough: The Struggle of Blacks and Hispanics for Equality in Urban Politics* (Berkeley: University of California Press, 1984), especially pp. 141–143. See also Leonard Cole, *Blacks in Power: A Comparative Study of Black and White Elected Officials* (Princeton, N.J.: Princeton University Press, 1976).

19. Quoted in American Civil Liberties Union, *Civil Liberties*, June 1981.

20. Interviews, Jefferson County, Alabama, May 1985.

21. Michael Walzer, *Spheres of Justice: A Defense of Pluralism and Equality* (New York: Basic Books, 1983), p. 148.

22. In Justice O'Connor's concurring opinion in *Thornburg v. Gingles*, there was marked confusion on this point. O'Connor argued that any test for dilution must be based on some notion of undiluted voting strength. She suggested three numerical measures, with the implication that these were disparate racial impact cases—cases about blacks having less than their "fair share." 106 S. Ct. 2752, 2786–2787 (1986).

23. Interview, Jefferson County, Alabama, May 1985.

24. Harold Stanley, "The 1984 Presidential Election in the South: Race and Realignment," in Robert P. Steed, Lawrence W. Moreland, and Tod A. Baker, *The 1984 Presidential Election in the South* (New York: Praeger, 1986), p. 316.

25. Charles Hamilton, "On Affirmative Action as Public Policy," in *Bakke, Weber, and Affirmative Action*, Working Papers, The Rockefeller Foundation (New York, 1979), pp. 177–202. This is the implicit point in Hamilton's argument as I read it.

26. John Quincy Adams, chairman of the political science department, Millsaps College, Jackson, Mississippi, quoted in "Black Political Power in Mississippi," Fall-Winter 1981–1982, NAACP/Mississippi (A Political Action Committee Report), p. 3.

27. U.S. Representative Fred Richmond, quoted in David J. Blum, "Black Politicians Fear They Can't Do Much To Help Their People; They Often Lack Influence, and When They Have It Conditions Thwart Them; Is It Better To Elect a White?" *Wall Street Journal*, 29 October 1980, reprinted in the 1982 Senate report, p. 1128.

28. Ernest J. Gaines, *A Gathering of Old Men* (New York: Alfred A. Knopf, 1984), p. 143.

29. 1982 Senate hearings, prepared statement of James F. Blumstein, p. 1361.

30. 1982 Senate hearings, statement of Donald L. Horowitz, p. 1310.

31. V. S. Naipaul, *The Suffrage of Elvira* (New York: Penguin Books, 1969), pp. 49–50.

32. On the general question of the use of electoral structures to ameliorate ethnic conflict, see Donald L. Horowitz, *Ethnic Groups in Conflict* (Berkeley: University of California Press, 1985), pp. 628–651.

33. *Alabama Journal and Advertiser*, 9 March 1986, p. B1.

34. Judge Joseph A. Jordan, a member of the city council from 1968 to 1977, vice-mayor from 1972 to 1977. Norfolk trial transcript, pp. 1524, 1527–1528.

35. Remarks upon signing the act, August 6, 1965, quoted in the 1982 Senate hearings, prepared statement of Benjamin L. Hooks, p. 270.

36. *Boston Globe*, 17 October 1983, p. 19.

37. *New York Times*, 15 July 1984, p. E25.

38. *New York Times*, 20 December 1981, p. 36.

# Glossary

*Anti–single shot (or full slate) rule:* A prohibition against single-shot or bullet voting. Each voter must mark his or her ballot for the same number of candidates as there are offices to be elected. Thus, if there are five places to be filled on a county or city council, voters must register their choices for all five places; ballots marked for four or fewer candidates will not be counted.

*At-large elections:* A method of voting in which the entire city, county, or school district is one electoral district. Thus all voters select all members of the governing body.

*Bailout:* A jurisdiction's removal from coverage under the special provisions of the Voting Rights Act through a successful lawsuit brought in the U.S. District Court for the District of Columbia. The 1982 amendments made counties, as well as states, eligible for bailout.

*Covered states or counties:* Jurisdictions to which the special (temporary) provisions of the Voting Rights Act apply, the most important of which is section 5. All covered jurisdictions must preclear all changes in the method of voting with either the Attorney General or the U.S. District Court for the District of Columbia, the only trial court authorized to hear section 5 suits.

*Full-slate rule:* See anti–single shot voting rule.

*Majority-vote rule:* A stipulation that a candidate must receive a majority of votes in the primary or general election in order to be nominated or elected. If no candidate receives a majority, a runoff election is held. Thus, in a large field of candidates, a contender who garners less than 50 percent of the vote cannot take office. In the absence of a majority-vote rule, candidates are nominated or elected by a plurality of the votes; that is, the candidate who receives the most votes is declared the nominee or winner.

*Multimember district:* A district from which more than one member of a legislative body is elected. For example, if the district elects three state legislators, then all voters residing in the district may cast their ballot for three candidates.

*Numbered post requirement or place rule:* A requirement that candidates running at large or in a multimember district file for a specific seat ("post" or "place"). Each office or place is thus separately elected, although by all the voters in the district or jurisdiction.

*Redistricting:* The redrawing of electoral district lines. To meet the one-person, one-vote standard (the equal population rule), jurisdictions must redraw the boundaries of their electoral districts after each decennial census.

*Residency rule:* A requirement that candidates in an at-large system or multimember district reside in a particular area or subdistrict in order to run for a particular seat. Candidates thus run as potential representatives of a particular neighborhood or locality, although voters in the entire jurisdiction or multimember district control the outcome of races.

*Retrogression:* The test for a discriminatory "effect," in violation of section 5 as the Supreme Court outlined it in *Beer v. United States.* A change in electoral method is retrogressive if it leaves minority voters worse off than they previously had been, by the measure of potential minority officeholding.

*Section 2:* In the original act, a restatement of the guarantees of the Fifteenth Amendment. In 1982 the section was amended to allow minority voters nationwide to challenge any method of election (whenever instituted) on the ground of discriminatory "result." The constitutional requirement (as laid out in *Bolden v. City of Mobile*) that minority plaintiffs prove discriminatory intent behind a challenged electoral procedure was thus circumvented. In the amended provision a method of election is said to have a discriminatory result when minority voters are found to have "less opportunity than other members of the electorate to participate in the political process and to elect representatives of their choice." The provision explicitly states, however, that it does not establish a right to minority officeholding in proportion to the minority population.

*Section 5:* The preclearance provision of the Voting Rights Act, which requires that all covered jurisdictions obtain approval for any change in a voting "standard, practice, or procedure." Thus, a covered county must submit all proposed annexations, districting changes, and shifts in the location of polling places, as well as the institution of rules such as a majority-vote requirement, to the Department of Justice or the U.S. District Court for the District of Columbia.

*Single-member districts:* Districts from which single members of a governing body are elected. Thus a city employing such districts might have a city council of five members, each of whom would run from a separate ward or district.

*Single-shot (or bullet) voting:* Voting for less than a full slate of candidates in an at-large system in order to aid a single favored candidate. For example, in a field of 13 candidates with 5 seats to be filled and 1 black candidate, if blacks bullet vote for the single black candidate, they deprive white contestants of potential votes and thus aid the black.

# Index of Voting Rights Cases

Lower court decisions are included with Supreme Court citations only when the former are relevant to my discussion.

# General Index